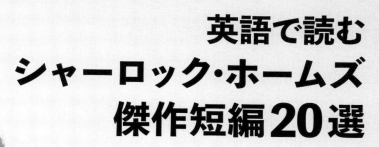

英語で読む
シャーロック・ホームズ
傑作短編**20**選

Sherlock Holmes
A Collection of 20 Short Stories

原著＝**コナン・ドイル**
Sir Arthur Conan Doyle

IBCパブリッシング

リライター
Diane Gruenstein, David Olivier, Ron Davidson, Anna Udagawa
•
ナレーター
Jack Merluzzi, Chris Koprowski, John Bell
•
カバー写真
iStock.com/cnx4004
•
本文イラスト
塩澤 文男

本書は、ラダーシリーズ「シャーロック・ホームズの冒険」「シャーロック・ホームズの思い出」「シャーロック・ホームズの帰還」「シャーロック・ホームズの事件簿」「シャーロック・ホームズ傑作短編集」を再構成したものです。

はじめに

　　　19世紀から20世紀初頭にかけてのイギリスを味わうなら、ホームズを読めばいい。世界の中心ともいえた活気あふれるロンドンで、馬車の御者に行き先をつげ、パイプとステッキをもって、ホームズとワトソンが乗り込む。そこは、伝統と世界のあちこちにあったイギリスの植民地から流れ込んできた人々が行き交う混沌とした街だ。世界各地で資産を蓄え、執事やメイドを抱えた豪邸をもつ英国紳士もいれば、スキャンダルを嗅ぎ回る新聞記者、警棒と口髭をトレードマークに半ズボンの非行少年を追いかける警察官、時にはあのマッチ売りの少女のような資本主義とのはざまで苦しむ人々など。ロンドンはそんな人々でいつもごった返していた。

　この短編集には、そんな昔の物語があふれています。ラダーシリーズは英語読本として、20年にわたって読者の皆様に愛されてきました。今回、日本人にも読みやすく、そして当時のイギリスのフレーバーを味わえるように編集したラダーシリーズから、ホームズの短編を一冊に収録しました。ホームズの短編は56点あるといわれています。そのうちの20編を厳選して、音声もダウンロードできるようにまとめたのがこの一冊です。

　英語でホームズを味わおうといっても原作であれば、それなりの難しい表現が含まれます。19世紀と現在では日常会話のフレーズそのものにも変化があります。それを読みやすく、かつ英語の勉強にもなるように配慮したのがラダーシリーズです。

　この一冊を読み終えたとき、あなたはきっと読了できた満足感と共に、英語にいつの間にか馴染んでいる自分に気づくはずです。就寝前に1編ずつ、あるいは週末に2編ずつ、ストーリーを楽しみ、時にはネット検索して、当時のロンドンの地図を見ながら読んでいくのはどうでしょう。知らず知らずのうちにイギリス

の文化や歴史に触れ、教養の中から新たなホームズの楽しみ方を発見できるかもしれません。

ところで、ホームズの活躍した時代は、イギリスの黄金期ともいわれたビクトリア王朝の時代です。19世紀、イギリスには蒸気機関車がお目見えし、鉄道網が整い、ロンドンではあらゆる階層の人々が集まっていました。コナン・ドイルは、ホームズを通してそうした人々の背景の光と影に触れることで、犯罪の推理を通して当時の世相を描き上げてきました。中でも注目したいのが、イギリスが世界に持っていた植民地との人々の活発な行き来です。インドやアフリカ各地、そして時には中国の大都市にあったイギリスの租界など、人々の活動の舞台はヨーロッパ各地からその先へと広がっていました。そのことが、推理小説のプロットをより複雑にし、我々を惹きつけます。この手法は、その後アガサ・クリスティなどにも引き継がれ、小説の題材にたびたび取り上げられました。人々はロンドンと繋がるそんなエキゾチックな世界へと目を向けてゆくのです。

短編集を楽しみながら、そんな19世紀へのタイムマシーンの旅を満喫していただければ幸いです。

IBC編集部

●**音声一括ダウンロード**●

本書の朗読音声(MP3形式)を下記URLとQRコードから無料でPCなどに一括ダウンロードすることができます。

https://ibcpub.co.jp/audio_dl/0768/

※ダウンロードしたファイルはZIP形式で圧縮されていますので、解凍ソフトが必要です。

※MP3ファイルを再生するには、iTunesやWindows Media Playerなどのアプリケーションが必要です。

※PCや端末、ソフトウェアの操作・再生方法については、編集部ではお答えできません。
　付属のマニュアルやインターネットの検索を利用するか、開発元にお問い合わせください。

■ラダーシリーズについて

　ラダーシリーズは、「はしご（ladder）」を使って一歩一歩上を目指すように、学習者の実力に合わせ、無理なくステップアップできるよう開発された英文リーダーのシリーズです。初心者から中級者までのレベルに分かれており、自分に合ったレベルから学習を始めることができます。

　ラダーシリーズの特長は、次のとおりです。

・中学校レベルから中級者レベルまで、5段階に使用する単語を限定して、やさしい英語で書き改められた本です。自分に合ったレベルからスタートできます。

・クラシックから現代文学、ノンフィクション、ビジネスと幅広いジャンルを扱っています。あなたの興味に合わせてタイトルを選べます。

・巻末のワードリストで、単語の意味を確認できます。レベル1、2では、文中の全ての単語が、レベル3以上は中学校レベル外の単語を掲載しています。

・カバーにヘッドフォンマークのついているタイトルは、オーディオ・サポートがあります。ウェブ上から購入／ダウンロードし、リスニング教材としても併用できます。

・弊社ラダーシリーズ特設サイトでは、毎月おすすめタイトルや検索急上昇タイトルを紹介しています。(https://ibcpub.co.jp/ladder/)

■ラダーシリーズを使った英語多読法

　ここでは、英語多読を効果的に行うためのコツをご紹介します。

・自分のレベルに合った本を選ぶ：効率的に英語力を向上させることができます。

・速く読む：スピードを重視し、スムーズな読解力を養います。

・訳さず英語のまま読む：直訳に頼らず、英語のまま理解する力を養います。

・辞書を使わずに読む：文脈から推測して理解する力を養います。

・巻末ワードリストで調べる：どうしてもわからない所は、無理せずに調べます。

・毎日少しずつ読む：英語多読は、続けることが大切です。

・発信する：読んだ内容を、英語で話したり書くことで発信力を高められます。

　ラダーシリーズを使った英語多読は、英語力を効率的に向上させるための最適な方法です。ぜひ、ラダーシリーズを使って、英語多読を始めてみてください。

Foreword
The Great Observer of Trivia

"My method is founded upon the observance of trifles."

Do you know the synonymous terms 'Holmesian' and 'Sherlockian'? That's what you can call yourself if you deeply enjoy and/or study the Sherlock Holmes mystery stories written by the Scottish writer Sir Arthur Conan Doyle (1859–1930). I have to admit I have been one since I was quite young. And I am not alone. So are millions of people worldwide, including Britain's King Charles III, who has described himself as "a lifelong devotee of the great detective".

How did my personal Sherlockian interest develop? Well, as I was growing up in Birmingham, England's equivalent of Osaka, like many children I enjoyed games and activities to improve observation skills, including noticing trivia. For example, I was an ardent trainspotter. That involved spotting not only train numbers but also names, as hundreds of major British locomotives bore interesting nameplates. They were based on a wide variety of themes, including famous schools (Eton, Rugby), history and legend (Excalibur, Hercules, Wolf Hall, Windsor Castle), famous people (William Shakespeare, Winston Churchill), the British Empire (Bombay, Hong Kong, Canada), living creatures (Bongo, Kingfisher, Salmon Trout), football teams (Arsenal, Liverpool), and royalty (Queen Elizabeth, King Henry VIII, the only 'King Class' engine I never spotted!)

On long family car trips, my sister and I would do our best to note down the name of every pub we passed, and in those days there were far more than there are today. I still have our notebooks, containing

序 文
偉大なトリビア観察者

「取るに足らないことを観察するのが僕のやり方の基本だ」

　Holmesian（ホームジアン）とSherlockian（シャーロキアン）という同義語を
ご存じですか？　スコットランド人作家、アーサー・コナン・ドイル（1859-1930）
が書いたシャーロック・ホームズの推理小説を愛読し、かつ研究している方、あ
るいはそのどちらかである方なら誰でもご自身をそう名乗ることができる。何を
隠そう、私自身かなり若い頃からそのひとりだ。そして私だけではない。そうい
う人は世界中に何百万といる。自らを「名探偵の終生のファン」と称するイギリ
ス国王のチャールズ三世も然り。

　個人的にどのようにシャーロキアンへの関心を深めていったのか？　というと、
イギリスの大阪に相当するバーミンガムで育つ中、私はトリビア（雑学的な事柄）
に注目するなど、多くの子供たちと同様に観察力を高めるゲームや活動を楽しん
でいた。その一例は、熱心なトレインスポッターだったこと。何百というイギリ
スの主要機関車には面白い銘板が付いているので、列車の番号だけでなく、名前
にも注目したのだ。銘板は多種多様なテーマで展開されていて、例えば、有名校
（イートン、ラグビー）、歴史や伝説（エクスカリバー、ヘラクレス、ウルフホー
ル、ウィンザー城）、有名人（ウィリアム・シェイクスピア、ウィンストン・チャ
ーチル）、大英帝国（ボンベイ、香港、カナダ）、生き物（ボンゴ、キングフィッ
シャー、サーモントラウト）、サッカーチーム（アーセナル、リバプール）、そし
て王族（エリザベス女王、キングクラスのエンジンで唯一発見できなかったヘン
リー8世）などがある。

　家族で遠出のドライブをするときなど、姉と私は通り過ぎるパブの名前をひと
つ残らず最善を尽くしてメモ書きしたものだ。で、当時、パブは今よりはるかに
多かった。その何百もの魅力的なパブの名前をアルファベット順に丁寧に整理し

hundreds of charming pub names carefully organized alphabetically, such as Drum and Monkey, Old Slipper Inn, Sacks of Potatoes, Unicorn Inn, Ye Olde Saracen's Head, and even Stuart Lodge (presumably named after the Scottish royal family, not me!) Of course, we tried to imagine what the story behind those fascinating names might be, but we were just travelers passing by and had no chance to ask. We could only strive to deduce the reason for their use ourselves.

And then, somewhere around that time, I came across the Great Observer and Deducer himself, the master of 'analytical reasoning', the pipe-smoking, violin-playing 'consulting detective' who introduced himself like this: "My name is Sherlock Holmes. It is my business to know what other people don't know." (*The Adventure of the Blue Carbuncle*, 1892) And I discovered this comment in another story: "You have not observed. And yet you have seen." (*A Scandal in Bohemia*, 1891) Ah, yes, he was indeed a superman who put close observations of tiny details to very practical use – namely, the solving of crimes. He gathered and observed the necessary facts and clues, and ignored all those which were of no use to him.

Well, once I'd discovered Holmes (pronounced the same as 'homes', with a silent 'l'), he became a great model detective who had so many exciting 'Adventures' and 'Cases'. I would enjoy trying to deduce, for example, what my school friends had had for breakfast by looking for stains on their neckties, or attempt to work out where they had been by checking the mud on their shoes. And on my way home, I would invent stories about complete strangers whom I quietly observed in the bus queue. Ah, what fun it was! Dear grumpy, brilliant, enigmatic Sherlock and his sidekick Dr. Watson have been with me ever since. I have even performed stage recitals of the Holmes stories and recorded audio books, and I regularly re-read the books for fun. And, as you

たノートは今でも持っている。例えば、ドラム＆モンキー、オールド・スリッパー・イン、サックス・オブ・ポテト、ユニコーン・イン、イエ・オールド・サラセンズ・ヘッド、さらにはステュウット・ロッジ（おそらくはスコットランドの王室にちなんだ名前だろう、私ではない！）。私たちがそれらの魅力的な名前の背景にどんな物語があるか想像を巡らせたのは言うまでもない。だが、ただの通りすがりの旅行者には人に尋ねる余裕もなく、自分たちでそのわけを推し量るしかなかった。

そして、その頃、私には、偉大な観察者にして推理者である人物との出会いがあった。「分析的思考」の達人であり、パイプをたしなみ、ヴァイオリン奏者の「探偵」であるその人は自分自身をこんな風に紹介した。「私の名前はシャーロック・ホームズ。人の知らないことを知るのが私の仕事だ」（『青いガーネット』1892年）。また私は別の物語でこんなコメントも見つけた。「あなたは見てはいるが、観察していない」（『ボヘミアの醜聞』1891年）。たしかに、彼は細かいところまで注意深く観察して、それを実際に用いて役立てる、つまり、犯罪解決に導く、まさにスーパーマンだった。必要な事実や手がかりをくまなく集めて調べ、無用なものはすべて無視した。

ホームズ（homesと同じ発音、lは発音しない）に出会ってからというもの、私にとって彼は、わくわくする数多くの「冒険」や「事件」を経験した名探偵のモデルになった。例えば、学友のネクタイのシミから彼らの朝食を推測したり、靴についた泥を調べて彼らがどこに行っていたかを探ってみる、など楽しんだものだ。また、帰り道、バス待ちの列でそっと観察した見ず知らずの人たちを題材に物語を作ったりすることもよくあった。ああ、何と楽しかったことか！　それ以来、無愛想で、聡明で、謎めいた、愛すべきシャーロックとその相棒のワトソンは、ずっと私の傍らにいる。ホームズの物語を舞台で朗読したり、オーディオブックの収録を行ったこともある。そして今は定期的に読み直して楽しんでいる。お察しのとおり、私はやはりトリビアが大好きなのだ。

can probably tell, I'm still very fond of trivia.

Now you may be wondering how the characters who seem so real to us came about in the first place. Well, Doyle originally trained to be a physician, and the persona of Holmes who has considerable skills in interpreting circumstances scientifically was based on Doyle's university teacher in Edinburgh, Dr. Joseph Bell, who observed minute details in his medical studies. He said of Doyle, "His education as a student of medicine taught him how to observe, and he is gifted with eyes, memory, and imagination." As for Dr. Watson, he was, at least in part, most likely a parody of Doyle himself, and, like the author, he was skilled with guns.

Why do the Sherlock Holmes stories remain so popular today, nearly 100 years since the final one was published? The attractive central characters and their actions are, of course, a main reason. But there is actually a vague nostalgic interest in what life was like back in late Victorian and Edwardian Britain, with the infamous London fog, gaslights, and horse carriages: no smartphones, no Internet, no TV, no DNA tests! There is also the fact that the stories are quintessentially British, which has helped to make them of interest around the world as well. That accounts for the statue of Holmes and Watson near the British Embassy in Moscow, erected in 2007.

Another reason is the huge number of stage plays, TV and radio dramas, and movies based on the Doyle stories, some of them very faithful to the originals, others largely imaginative. In fact, in 2012, Sherlock entered The Guinness Book of World Records as 'the most portrayed literary human character in film and TV'. Up to then, he had been played by over 75 actors in 254 appearances, considerably more than Shakespeare's character Hamlet.

　さて、ここまでリアルに感じられる人物がそもそもどのようにして生まれたのか、皆さんは不思議に思われるかもしれない。ドイルはもともと医師を目指していた。状況を科学的に解釈する並々ならぬ能力を持つホームズの人物像は、エジンバラの大学で学んだドイルの先生であり医学の研究で細かいところまで観察した医師のジョセフ・ベル教授がモデルになっている。教授はドイルについて、「医学生としての教育で観察の仕方を身につけ、観察眼と記憶力と想像力に恵まれている」と話している。ワトソンについては、少なくとも一部はドイル自身のパロディである可能性が高く、しかも作者と同じく、銃の扱いに長けていた。

　シャーロック・ホームズの物語は、最終作が発表されてから100年近く経った今日でも、なぜこれほどまでに人気があるのだろうか？　魅力的な中心人物とその活躍が大きな理由であることは言うまでもない。だが、かの悪名高きロンドンの霧、ガス灯、馬車などに見る、ヴィクトリア朝後期からエドワード朝にかけてのイギリスはどんな暮らしぶりだったのか、ということへの漠然としたノスタルジックな関心が現実にあるのも事実だ。すなわちスマートフォンも、インターネットも、テレビも、DNA鑑定もない時代への郷愁である！　また、物語は極めて英国的であるという事実もあり、そのため、世界でも注目されるようになった。そのことは、2007年にモスクワの英国大使館近くに建てられたホームズとワトソンの像が物語っている。

　もう一つの理由は、ドイルの物語に基づいた舞台劇、テレビドラマ、ラジオドラマ、映画などが無数にあること。原作に非常に忠実なものもあれば、かなり創作的なものもある。実際、2012年に、シャーロックは「映画やテレビで最も多く描かれた文学上の人物」としてギネスブックに登録されている。登録時点で75人あまりの俳優が254回演じており、その数はシェイクスピアのハムレットよりもはるかに多い。

Stage performances began as early as 1893, but they became a breakout hit in the USA in 1899 when Holmes was played by the American actor William Gillette, who would go on to perform the role 1,300 times over a period of 30 years. He introduced the now familiar curved pipe and also coined the phrase "Elementary, my dear fellow!". That later developed, in the first talking Holmes movie, into the phrase everyone now knows: "Elementary, my dear Watson!" The stage production moved to Britain in 1901, and the 14-year-old boy who played Billy, the young boy hired to do personal chores and run errands, was none other than Charlie Chaplin in his first major role.

The very first (silent) Holmes movie was made in 1900, and the (talking) movie series from 1939 starring Basil Rathbone was extremely popular. Then the 41-episode series from 1984 to 1994 produced by Granada TV in Britain, starring the actor Jeremy Brett, became a huge hit. It remains a great favorite of Holmesians and is regularly re-broadcast in many countries, including Japan.

Moving into the twenty-first century, there have been several dynamic Doyle adaptations to appeal to the younger generations. For example, the 2009 *Sherlock Holmes* movie directed by Guy Ritchie, starring Robert Downey Jr., Jude Law, and Mark Strong, and its 2011 sequel, feature Holmes' prodigious fighting skills, which were only hinted at by Doyle. They also show the return of arch-rival Moriarty and Irene Adler, '*the* woman' who outwitted Holmes in *A Scandal in Bohemia*. In the case of the BBC TV series titled *Sherlock* (2010–2017), written by two devoted Sherlockians and starring Benedict Cumberbatch and Martin Freeman, the stories were very effectively modernized. The characters make full use of texting, GPS, and the Internet, in the same way as Doyle's original characters used the latest technology available over a century ago.

　舞台での上演は早くも1893年には始まっていたが、ホームズをアメリカ人俳優のウィリアム・ジレットが演じた1899年に大ブレーク、ジレットはその後30年間にわたって1300回もホームズ役を演じることになった。彼は、今やおなじみの吸い口の大きく曲がったパイプを導入し、「君、初歩的なことさ」というフレーズも編み出した。これが後に、ホームズのトーキー版映画で、今では誰もが知る「初歩的なことだよ、ワトソン君」というフレーズに変化した。舞台は1901年にイギリスに渡り、雑用や使い走りのために雇われた少年、ビリーを演じた14歳の少年は、自身にとって初めての大役となった、他ならぬチャーリー・チャップリンだった。

　1900年にはホームズの一番最初のサイレント版映画が作られ、1939年からはベイジル・ラスボーン主演のトーキー版映画シリーズが大人気となった。その後、ジェレミー・ブレット主演で1984年から1994年にかけてイギリスのグラナダTVが制作した全41話のシリーズが大ヒットした。現在もホームズの熱烈なファンから絶大な支持を得ており、日本をはじめ多くの国々で定期的に再放送されている。

　21世紀に入り、若い世代にアピールするため、ドイル作品のダイナミックな翻案が行われている。例えば、2009年に公開されたガイ・リッチー監督、ロバート・ダウニー・Jr、ジュード・ロウ、マーク・ストロング主演の映画『シャーロック・ホームズ』と2011年の続編では、ドイルはほのめかしただけだったが、ホームズの並外れた戦闘術を取り上げている。また、宿敵モリアーティや、『ボヘミアの醜聞』でホームズを出し抜いた「あの女性」アイリーン・アドラーの再登場というシーンもある。ベネディクト・カンバーバッチとマーティン・フリーマンが主演し、2人の超シャーロキアンが脚本を手掛け、2010年から2017年までBBCで放送された『シャーロック』というテレビシリーズについて言えば、物語は非常に効果的に現代化されていて、登場人物たちはメールやGPS、インターネットを駆使する。ちょうどドイルが創作した人物たちが一世紀以上前に利用可能だった当時の最新技術を駆使したのと同じように。

Once you've become a confirmed Holmesian/Sherlockian, and I hope you will, there are many fun Holmes-related locations to visit. And the best place to start is Baker Street Tube Station in central London. Since 1999, there has been a 3-meter-tall statue of Holmes right in front of it. But he doesn't just stand there: it is, in fact, a 'talking statue' with a lighthearted message from the detective himself. At the bottom of the instructions on how to scan the QR code or visit a link to hear his voice, it says 'Be amazed'. I'm sure you will be! In the handbook to celebrate the statue's unveiling, then Prime Minister Tony Blair wrote, 'the Great Detective is a great British institution', which is certainly true.

Incidentally, the first two Holmes statues were both erected eleven years earlier, in 1988, to mark the centenary of the publication of the first Holmes story. One is in Meiringen, in Switzerland, the location of the Reichenbach Falls, the setting for *The Final Problem*. The other is in Karuizawa in Japan, at the place where the distinguished translator Ken Nobuhara did a lot of his work on the Doyle stories. There is also a bronze statue in Edinburgh, in Scotland, erected in 1991, outside Doyle's birthplace. You may notice that the statues all show Holmes wearing the 'deerstalker' hat that never in fact appeared in the original stories but has become a vital part of Holmes' iconic image. It was the idea of Sidney Paget, the artist who illustrated the stories when they were first published in *The Strand* magazine. He drew his own hat.

Going back to London, you can visit the Sherlock Holmes Museum, just up Baker Street from 221b, Sherlock's globally famous address which most people think never actually existed. However, a blue plaque on the wall declares that he lived there from 1881 to 1904, so maybe he really did! Also recommended is a visit to the

　間違いなく熱狂的なホームズファンになった暁には、ぜひそうなることを願っているが、訪れるべきホームズゆかりの楽しい場所がたくさんある。旅のスタートに最適な場所はロンドン中心部の地下鉄ベーカーストリート駅。1999年から、この駅の目の前に高さ3メートルのホームズ像が立っている。が、ただ立っているだけではない。実は、この像は「話す像」で、探偵本人からの軽妙なメッセージを聞くことができる。そしてホームズの声を聞くためのQRコードのスキャンの仕方やリンクの訪れ方の下方に、「びっくりしてください」とある。きっとびっくりするでしょう！　この像の除幕式を祝ったハンドブックに、当時のトニー・ブレア首相は、「名探偵は英国の名物的存在だ」と書いているが、いかにもそのとおり。

　ちなみに、最初の2体のホームズ像は、いずれも11年前の1988年に、ホームズ第1作の出版100周年を記念して建てられたものである。一つは、『最後の事件』の舞台となったライヘンバッハの滝のあるスイスのマイリンゲンにある。もうひとつは日本の軽井沢で、著名な翻訳者の延原謙がドイル作品を多くこなした場所である。また、スコットランドのエジンバラには、1991年にドイルの生家の外に建てられた銅像がある。これらの銅像はいずれも、ホームズが「鹿撃ち帽」をかぶっていることにお気づきになるかもしれない。この帽子は原作には登場しないが、ホームズの象徴的なイメージとして欠かせないものになっている。これは、作品が初めて『ストランド・マガジン』に掲載された当時の挿絵画家シドニー・パジェットのアイデアによるものだ。パジェットは自分自身の帽子を描いたのである。

　話をロンドンに戻すと、世界的に有名なシャーロックの住所221bからベーカー・ストリートを少し行ったところにあるシャーロック・ホームズ博物館を訪れることができる。この住所はたいていの人たちが実際に存在するとは思っていない。が、壁にはホームズが1881年から1904年まで住んでいたことを示すブルー・プラーク（青い銘板）が掲げられているので、もしかしたら本当に住んでいたの

ever-popular *The Sherlock Holmes* pub just round the corner from Trafalgar Square. It features lots of Holmes memorabilia, a detailed recreation of the 221b Baker Street flat, and delicious British food and drinks.

There are also flourishing societies of Holmes fans worldwide. The Sherlock Holmes Society of London is a major one, of course. Its members can even join in a Holmes-themed Xmas card design competition. Holmes was introduced to Japan in 1894 and the Japan Sherlock Holmes Club is probably the biggest in the world. Its website states that Holmes stories 'have had a profound influence on our culture. Sherlock Holmes provides an outstanding example of justice and fair play.'

But perhaps the most important reason of all for Sherlock's continuing popularity is that avid fans still read the stories, and this book is a great introduction to the Holmes 'canon'. It features twenty of the most thrilling Holmes adventures and cases for you to dive into and try to solve the mysteries along with Holmes and Watson. Some of them feature murders, other involve Holmes preventing murders from occurring. They all include the fine arts of observation and deduction. I hope you will enjoy them as much as I continue to do and that you will then feel eager to read all sixty of the original stories.

Happy reading and careful observation!

Stuart Varnam-Atkin
Holmesian/Sherlockian & Trivia Collector

かもしれない！　また、トラファルガー広場のすぐ近くにある、人気のパブ「シャーロック・ホームズ」もおすすめだ。ホームズ関連の品物がたくさんあり、ベーカー街221bのアパートが細かく再現されていて、おいしいイギリス料理と飲み物が楽しめる。

　世界にはまたホームズファンで盛況な会もある。言うまでもなくロンドン・シャーロック・ホームズ協会はその代表的なものだ。会員は、ホームズをテーマにしたクリスマスカードのデザインコンペに参加することもできる。ホームズが日本に紹介されたのは1894年、そして日本シャーロック・ホームズ・クラブはおそらく世界最大の団体だろう。そのホームページには、ホームズの物語は「我々の文化に多大な影響を与えた。シャーロック・ホームズは正義とフェアプレーの極めて優れた例である」と書かれている。

　しかし、シャーロックの衰えることのない人気のおそらく最も重要な理由は、熱心なファンが今でも物語を読み続けている、という事実だろう。そして本書はホームズの真作への入門書として最適である。ホームズの最もスリリングな冒険と事件の中から20作品を収めてあり、ホームズやワトソンとともに謎解きに挑むことができる。殺人事件を題材にしたものもあれば、ホームズが殺人事件の発生を未然に防ぐものもある。いずれも観察力と推理力が問われる作品だ。私がずっと読み続けているように皆さんも楽しんでいただけたら、そして60編の原作を全部、無性に読んでみたいと思っていただけたなら幸いだ。

　楽しく読んで注意深い観察を！

ステュウット　ヴァーナム-アットキン
ホームズの熱狂的ファンでトリビア収集家

（訳：とよざきようこ）

CONTENTS

01

A Scandal in Bohemia

ボヘミアの醜聞

読み始める前に

A Scandal in Bohemia ボヘミアの醜聞

56の短編のうち最初に発表された
1891年のストランド・マガジン初出
1892年発行の「シャーロック・ホームズの冒険」に収録

［主な登場人物］

Sherlock Holmes シャーロック・ホームズ 世界的に有名な私立探偵。優れた観察眼と推理力を有する。ロンドンのベーカー街221Bに下宿している。

Watson ジョン・H・ワトソン 医師。ホームズの相棒でこの物語の語り手。かつてベーカー街221Bでホームズと同居していた。

Wilhelm Gottsreich Sigismond von Ormstein ヴィルヘルム・ゴッツライヒ・ジギスモンド・フォン・オルムシュタイン ボヘミア国王。スカンディナヴィアの王女と婚約している。

Irene Adler アイリーン・アドラー オペラ歌手。かつてボヘミア国王と親しい間柄だった。

Godfrey Norton ゴドフリー・ノートン 弁護士。アイリーンと親密そうな間柄。

［あらすじ］

　ホームズのもとにボヘミアの国王が訪れるところから物語は始まる。国王は近々結婚することになっているが、かつての恋人であるアイリーン・アドラーが王と二人で写っている写真を持っていることから、その写真が公にされた時のスキャンダルを恐れてホームズに助けを求めてきたのだ。その写真を取り戻すため奔走するホームズだったが、聡明なアドラーはその策略を見抜き、ホームズを出し抜くことになる。

［総単語数］3,636語

A Scandal in Bohemia

To Sherlock Holmes, she is always *the* woman. I have seldom heard him call her anything else. In his eyes she represents the very best of all women. It was not that Holmes loved the late Irene Adler. He did not allow himself to feel any emotion, particularly love for a woman. He kept his mind cold and exact and very balanced. In my opinion Sherlock Holmes was the most perfect mind that the world has ever seen. But he never spoke of the softer feelings, except with sarcasm. He would not let himself feel a strong emotion; it would upset him too much. But there was one woman for him, and that woman was Irene Adler, someone remembered by perhaps nobody else.

Holmes and I had not met for a long time. I had married and now spent a lot of time with my wife in complete happiness. Our new home kept me busy. Holmes, by contrast, kept away from people as far as possible, living at our old apartment on Baker Street, reading his thousands of books and making plans with his fiery mind. As in the old days, he studied crime, trying to help solve mysteries which the police had given up trying to understand. From time to time, I heard about him helping the police to solve a mystery of this sort. The last time he had helped the ruling family of Holland solve one of these problems. But I only learned through the newspaper, and I shared this information with all the other thousands of readers of the British papers. It had been a long time since I had met my friend and talked with him.

One night, it was March 20, 1888, I was passing Baker Street on my way from a patient's home. How I missed my friend. I wondered what case he was working on now. As I looked in the window, I saw his tall body. I knew the way he was walking, holding his hands behind his back. I rang the bell, and he opened the door to let me into the rooms I had shared with him before my marriage.

He did not say anything, but he seemed glad to see me. With a kindly look, he waved me to an armchair. After I had sat down, he stood in front of the fire, and looked at me very carefully. Then he said, "I think you have gained seven and a half pounds since I last saw you."

"Seven," I answered.

"A little more, I think," Holmes continued. "And you did not tell me that you were going to work as a doctor again. Finally, it appears your servant girl is very careless."

"Holmes! How do you know all these things? If you had lived several hundred years ago, they would have burned you as a witch. It is true that I went for a long country walk and got caught in the rain last week, but I am wearing different clothes today. How can you say that my servant is careless?"

"Well," Holmes replied with a smile on his lips, "I see your shoe has been scraped carelessly. There are many cuts on it as though someone was trying to remove mud. As for your working again as a doctor, well, I smell strong chemicals on your hands and I see the bump under your hat of the stethoscope which you carry there."

I could only laugh when he explained how easy it was for him to understand my recent past. "When you give your reasons, the thing always appears so simple, I feel silly. I wonder how you see so many things. My eyes are just as good, but I can't see them until you explain them."

"The problem, Watson, is that you do not pay attention," Holmes kindly explained. "For example, you have seen the hall steps that lead to this room?"

"Of course I have."

"How many times?"

"Well, hundreds."

"Then, how many steps are there?"

"How many? I've never counted them."

"Quite so. You have not observed. And yet you have seen. That is just my point. Now, I know that there are seventeen steps because I have both seen and observed."

Holmes continued, "By the way, have a look at this letter I received today." It told Holmes that he would have a visitor at eight o'clock that night and that he must not miss his visitor. The note sounded very important.

The paper was very thick. Holmes told me to hold it up to the light and I saw the letters "Eg P Gt" but I did not know what they meant. Holmes continued, "'Gt' is a standard way of referring to business in German. 'P' of course stands for paper. The 'Eg,' well, looking at the map of Germany, I see the town Egria. So what do you make of that?"

I replied slowly, "That the paper is made in Germany."

"Quite. And the man who wrote it is German."

It was just eight o'clock and we heard horses coming down the street. I tried to leave, but Holmes pushed me gently into a chair and asked me to watch carefully.

The man who entered was very, very tall. He looked like Hercules and was wearing a dark blue coat with a red scarf at the neck. His boots were lined in thick brown fur and he carried a hat in his hand. We could not see his face because he was wearing a mask.

"Did you receive my note?" he asked with a heavy German accent.

"Please sit down," Holmes replied.

The man began to tell his story.

"You must not tell anyone about what I am about to say. I have a small problem, but if it is told to a newspaper, it could cause great embarrassment to one of the most important families in Europe."

Holmes and I both nodded our heads in understanding. Then Holmes sat down and after closing his eyes, said, "If you do not tell me the problem, though, I cannot help you."

At this the man jumped up and tore off his mask saying, "All right! I am the King. I will not hide it."

"Why, indeed?" Holmes asked. "As soon as you entered this room I knew that you were your Majesty, Wilhelm Gottsreich Sigismond von Ormstein, Grand Duke and the future king of Germany."

Hearing this, our visitor sat down and spoke quietly. "But I am not used to speaking to people directly. I came from Prague to talk to you because I cannot trust anyone else with this matter."

"Please tell me," Holmes said, again closing his eyes.

"Yes, the facts are very short. Five years ago I met an opera singer named Irene Adler from New Jersey while she was singing in Warsaw. I wrote her some letters expressing my feelings, and now I would like to have those letters back again."

"Why are you so worried about a few letters?" Holmes asked.

"It is the photograph of both of us which I sent her that I most want back."

"Oh, that was foolish," Holmes advised him.

"Yes," the prince replied, "it was. I was insane. And very young. I am thirty now. And I am about to be married to the second daughter of the King of Scandinavia. If she heard anything about this Adler affair, I would have no chance of marrying the woman of my dreams in Scandinavia."

"Are you sure she would try to ruin your chances of happiness with another woman?"

"Yes, she has promised to send the picture on the day of my formal engagement, which is next Monday."

"So, we have three days," said Holmes with a yawn. "Leave me your hotel number so that I can contact you. And what about money?"

"There is no limit. I would give you part of my country to save my name. For the moment, I'll give you three hundred pounds in gold and seven hundred in notes," he said, laying the money on the table.

Holmes got the address for Irene Adler and asked me to come back at three o'clock the following day to chat about the matter.

2

At three o'clock the next day, I was at his room, but he was nowhere to be seen. The maid told me that he had not returned since morning when he left around eight a.m. I decided to wait for him, no matter how long, and sat down. It was always such a pleasure to study his system of work. His reasoning was so fast. He had such quick and subtle methods of solving mysteries. He never failed, either.

About an hour had passed quietly when, suddenly, he came in, looking very tired. He disappeared into the bedroom for five minutes. When he came back in the sitting room, he looked fresh and relaxed. Then he sat down, laughing.

"You cannot imagine how I passed my morning."

"I suppose you were watching Miss Adler."

"Yes. But it was still a very unusual morning. I found her house. The sitting room has long windows almost to the floor. They can be easily opened by a child from outside. I walked around the house and examined it carefully. Nothing unusual. Down the road I found a mews and the horsekeepers. I helped them clean their horses, and they told me all about the people in the neighborhood. Most of their talk was very boring, but at least I could learn a lot about Miss Adler, too."

"What about her?" I asked.

"She has turned all the men's heads in the town. She is beautiful, lives quietly, sings at concerts, drives at five every day and returns for dinner at seven. She has only one male visitor—a lawyer named Mr. Godfrey Norton. He comes once, sometimes twice a day. He is very handsome and young.

"After I listened to the horsekeepers' talk, I walked around those streets for a while. Who was this Mr. Godfrey Norton? If she hired him to protect her from the king, maybe she had given him the photograph. But if he is her lover, then she wouldn't give him the photograph.

"As I was walking, a cab drove up to her house. A gentleman of the horsekeepers' description jumped out. He was in the house for about half an hour. I could see him talking and waving his arms. I couldn't see Miss Adler. Then he jumped into the cab and shouted, 'To the Church of St. Monica's.'

"I was trying to get a cab to follow him, when she came running out of the house and jumped into her cab. She was a lovely woman, with a face that a man might die for.

"'Hurry to the Church of St. Monica,' she called out to her driver.

"A cab passed at that moment and I jumped into it, calling out, 'The Church of St. Monica, as fast as you can go.'

"My cabby drove fast, faster than I had ever gone in my life, I think. But when we reached the church, the two other cabs were standing empty with steaming horses in front of the door. I walked into the back of the church quietly, as though I was just an ordinary sightseer. Suddenly, to my surprise, Godfrey Norton came running as hard as he could toward me.

" 'Thank God,' he cried. 'You'll do. Come! Come!'

" 'What then?' I asked.

" 'Come, man, come, only three minutes, or it won't be legal.'

"He almost carried me to the altar where I repeated things I was told to say so that the man and woman standing there became man and wife. Thinking about me being the only person invited to their wedding is what made me burst out laughing just now.

"The minister told them they had to have a friend with them at the wedding or he couldn't marry them. That is why Mr. Norton was so upset. The bride gave me a gold coin after the ceremony.

"I thought they would leave together from the church and that I would have a lot of trouble getting the photograph. But he drove away alone and she went back to her home. 'I shall drive out in the park at five as usual,' she said as she left him. I heard no more. I drove off to make my own plans."

"Which are?" I asked.

"To have dinner and explain the work that you will do with me."

"I shall be delighted," I replied.

"I was sure that I could rely on you, Watson. We must be at Miss Adler's home when she returns from her drive in the park. There will be a small problem, and I will be carried into her house. You must promise not to help me. Only do as I instruct you. Remain close to the front window."

"I see."

"Watch me."

"Yes."

"And when I raise my hand, throw into the room what I give you to throw, and call out 'Fire!' Do you understand?"

"Completely."

Then he gave me a brown roll from his pocket.

"This is not dangerous. When you throw it into the room, it will catch fire. When you call out 'Fire,' many people will come running. You will leave the house and walk down to the street corner where I will meet you after ten minutes. Everything clear?"

"Yes."

"Excellent."

Again he disappeared into his bedroom, and when he came out after a few minutes he was changed completely. Now he was a friendly and simple-minded minister, dressed in a black hat with big trousers, a white tie, kindly smile and look. It was not only his clothes that Holmes changed. It was his entire being. His very soul seemed to change with the new part he took. He would have been a great actor on the stage, or a great scientist in the laboratory.

We reached Miss Adler's home ten minutes before she was expected to return from the park. Lamps were being lit on the street and it was getting dark. But the street was not quiet. There was a group of men talking — they did not look respectable; a couple guards visiting with one of the girl servants and other well-dressed young men walking up and down the street.

"The photograph might be a problem for Miss Adler, too," Holmes said to me. "She probably does not want Mr. Norton to see it any more than the king wants his princess to see it. The question is, 'Where are we to find the photograph?'

"She probably doesn't carry it with her. Too large. It is either with her banker or her lawyer. But remember, the king said that she wrote that she would use the photograph in a few days. It must be where she can lay her hands on it quickly. It must be in her own house."

"But the King sent robbers into her house twice, and they could not find it."

"Pshaw! They did not know where to look."

"But how will you look?"

"I will not look."

"What will you do?"

"I will get her to show it to me."

"She won't do that."

"She will. Here she comes. Do exactly as I told you."

Miss Adler's guards rushed up to her carriage to open the door for her. But some of the strange men on the street also came to the door, hoping to receive a small gift of money by helping the beautiful woman from her seat. They began to fight over who would help her. Holmes rushed into the crowd of men to protect Miss Adler, but just as he reached her, he gave a cry and fell to the ground, blood running down his face. Seeing blood, the rough men ran away and the kinder ones helped the lady to her house and attended to the injured man. Before going in her house, Miss Adler looked back into the street.

"Is the poor man hurt badly?" she asked.

"He is dead," someone said.

"No, he is still alive, but there is not much time," called out another.

"He's breathing now," said another. "What a kind man. Those rough men would have stolen your purse if he hadn't come running over to protect you. Can we bring him into your house for a moment, ma'am?"

"Of course."

I do not know how Holmes felt to be lying in her home with such a plan. I felt more ashamed than any other time in my life to be working against a lady of such grace and kindliness. I had promised him, though, so I hardened my heart and took out the smoke-rocket from under my overcoat. Holmes sat up and gave me the signal. I tossed my rocket into the room with a cry of "Fire!" Immediately, a whole crowd of people came to the house, but I ran to the street corner as I had agreed, and ten minutes later my friend joined me. We walked in silence for a few minutes.

"You did very well, Doctor," he finally said.

"Did you get the picture?"

"No, but I know where it is."

"How did you do it?"

"It was very simple. I splashed some red paint on my face. She felt sorry for me and had me brought into her house. But when a woman thinks that her house is on fire, she runs to the thing she values most. The smoke and shouting worked perfectly. She ran straight to the photograph behind a sliding panel in the wall. When I cried out that it was a false alarm and no real danger, she put the photograph back in the panel and rushed from the room. I also escaped from the house."

"Now what do we do?" I asked.

"We must visit with the King tomorrow. We will wait for her in the sitting room. But when she enters, she may find that both we and the photograph have gone. His Majesty would be pleased to regain the picture with his own hands."

"What time will we go?"

"At eight in the morning. Her marriage may change her life and habits completely."

3

We were having toast and coffee early the next morning when the King of Bohemia rushed into the room.

"Have you got it?"

"Not yet."

"But you have hopes?"

"I have hopes."

"Then let's go."

"Irene Adler is married," Holmes said to the King.

"Married? To whom?"

"An English lawyer named Norton."

"But she could not love him."

"I hope she does."

"Why?"

"Because if she loves him, she does not love your Majesty. And if she does not love your Majesty, she will not interfere with your Majesty's plan."

"That is true. And yet — she would have made a wonderful queen. I wish she had been of my class..."

The king was silent until we reached Miss Adler's home, where an elderly woman was waiting at the door.

"Mr. Sherlock Homes, I believe?" said she.

"I am Mr. Holmes," answered my friend, looking at her in surprise.

"Indeed. Miss Adler told me you might come this morning. She left with her husband this morning for France."

"What? Do you mean that she is not in England?"

"And never coming back."

"We shall never get the photograph," cried the King.

"Let us look," said Holmes as he dashed into the house.

He tore open the panel and pulled out one photograph and one letter. It was a view of Miss Adler in an evening dress. The envelope of the letter was addressed to Mr. Sherlock Holmes. It read:

My dear Mr. Sherlock Holmes:

You are very clever. But after the fire I realized who you were. I had been warned about you several months ago. It was hard for me to be angry with a kind minister, as you seemed to be. But I also changed clothes and followed you to your door. Now that I know the King has asked you to help him, I talked to my husband and we decided it was best to leave England rather than deal with you.

Concerning the photograph, the King need not worry. I love and am loved by a better man than he. The king may do as he likes, and though he has been cruel to me, I will cause him no harm. I only keep the photograph so that he will not cause me trouble in future. The photograph he may keep if he likes. I remain, Mr. Holmes,

Yours most sincerely,
IRENE NORTON, *née* Adler.

Reading the letter, the King cried out, "Oh, what a woman! Wouldn't she have made an admirable queen?"

"She is indeed very clever," Holmes said. "I am sorry that I was not able to successfully get back your photograph."

"On the contrary," said the King, "she is a woman of honor and I now understand that the photograph is as safe as if I had thrown it into the fire."

"I am glad to hear your Majesty say so."

"And I would like to give you anything you ask. How about this emerald ring I am wearing?"

"Your Majesty has something I would value even more."

"Please name it."

"This photograph."

The King stared at Holmes in amazement.

"Irene's photograph? Certainly, if you wish."

"I thank your Majesty. There is no more to be done. I wish you a good-morning." Bowing, we returned to Holmes's rooms.

That was the only time I can remember that Holmes's plans were ruined by a woman. Since then, I have never heard him laugh about women. When he speaks of Irene Adler, it is always as *the* woman.

The Red-Headed League
赤毛組合

読み始める前に

The Red-Headed League 赤毛組合

56の短編のうち2番目に発表された
1891年の8月号のストランド・マガジン初出
1892年発行の「シャーロック・ホームズの冒険」に収録

［主な登場人物］

Sherlock Holmes　シャーロック・ホームズ　世界的に有名な私立探偵。優れた観察眼と推理力を有する。ロンドンのベーカー街221Bに下宿している。

Watson　ジョン・H・ワトソン　医師。ホームズの相棒でこの物語の語り手。かつてベーカー街221Bでホームズと同居していた。

Jabez Wilson　ジェイベズ・ウィルソン　質屋の店主。燃えるような赤い髪をしている。楽な仕事でお金をもらえる「赤毛組合」に加入。

Vincent Spaulding　ヴィンセント・スポルディング　質屋の店員。ウィルソンに「赤毛組合」の仕事を紹介する。

Duncan Ross　ダンカン・ロス　「赤毛組合」の組合員。ウィルソンを審査し、新たな組合員として認める。

policeman　警察官　スコットランド・ヤードに勤務。ホームズたちとジョン・クレイを捕まえに行く。

Merryweather　メリーウェザー　銀行の頭取。銀行の地下室にあるフランス金貨をクレイに狙われているという。

John Clay　ジョン・クレイ　イギリスでも指折りの犯罪者。若くて賢い。

［あらすじ］

　ロンドンの実業家ジェイベズ・ウィルソンが、ホームズと同僚のワトソンに奇妙な事情を持ちかけるところから物語は展開する。燃えるような赤毛を持つウィルソンは、「赤毛組合」という組織にひょんなことで加入することになった。だが、組合は何の前触れもなく突如、解散してしまう。ウィルソンは得ていた収入を失うことになり困り果てたのだ。この不思議な事態に興味を持ったホームズは、この事件の調査を引き受ける。ウィルソンの質屋で働くヴィンセント・スポルディングがよく地下室にこもっていることに気づいたホームズは、スポルディングがこの組合と何らかの関係を持つことに気づいた。

［総単語数］3,819語

The Red-Headed League

It was one day last fall. I called on my friend, Mr. Sherlock Holmes. He was deep in conversation with a stout, older man who had red hair. I thought I should leave and turned away, but Holmes took my arm and pulled me into the room, closing the door.

"You have come at a perfect time, my dear Watson," he said with a smile.

"You seem to be busy."

"And so I am."

"Then I can wait in the next room."

"Not at all. Mr. Wilson, please allow me to introduce my friend, Mr. Watson, who helps me in all my work. I think he will help me on your case, too."

The stout man stood up and bowed to me quickly with small eyes which seemed to have a questioning look.

"Please sit on the sofa," Holmes said to me as he sat in his usual chair. "I know that you are interested in my unusual cases, so different from the humdrum routine of everyday life, because you have written so many of them into stories."

"Your cases have always been of interest to me, it is true," I replied.

"You will recall just the other day, I told you that life itself has the most unusual situations, more daring than we can even imagine."

"And I doubted you."

"You did, Doctor, but I will give you so many facts that you will come around to seeing things my way soon. Now, Mr. Wilson here has come to visit me this morning and tell me a story. I have often told you, Watson, that the strangest things often happen with the smallest crimes. I have not heard his whole story yet, but it seems that it is the most unusual story I have ever been told.

"Mr. Wilson, please begin your story again. I ask you to do this not only for Mr. Watson, but also because it is such an unusual story, I would like to hear every word again from your lips. Usually, when I begin to study a case, I think of thousands of other cases like it, and I am guided in my decisions. But in this case, I cannot think of a single one which is similar. The facts are, as best I can tell, unique."

Then the heavy man pulled a piece of newspaper from his inside pocket. He spread the advertisement section on his knee. I looked at him carefully, trying to understand what kind of a man he was.

But I could understand very little. He seemed a very average laborer, overweight, proud, and slow. His clothes were old and unclean. The only unusual thing about him was his blazing red hair and the unhappy look on his face.

Sherlock Holmes was watching me. He smiled, "I can tell that Mr. Wilson has been a laborer, that he believes in God, that he has been to China and that recently he has done a lot of writing. Otherwise I can tell nothing about him."

Mr. Wilson was surprised to hear Holmes say all this.

"How do you know all that about me?"

"Well," Holmes began, "the muscles of your right hand are much more developed. So you have worked hard with it. The coat pin shows your religious interest. The lower five inches of your right sleeve is shiny because you have moved it along your writing paper as you sat at a desk writing, while the left elbow is thin where you rested it on the desk."

"What about China?"

"I see an inked mark on your hand which could only have been painted in China. That light pink color only comes out of China. I also see a Chinese coin on your watch chain. It was all very simple."

Mr. Wilson laughed loudly. "Well, at first I thought there was some magic, but I see it is very simple."

"I wonder if I should tell all my secrets, Watson. No one will be impressed with me any more if I tell everything. Can't you find the advertisement, Mr. Wilson?"

"Yes, I have got it here," he said marking it with his finger. "Please read it for yourself."

Holmes took the paper and began to read:

"Opening for one red-headed man. Must be healthy and strong, over twenty-one years old. Easy work. Pay: four pounds a week. Apply in person on Monday, at eleven o'clock, to Duncan Ross, at the office of the League, 7 Pope's Court, Fleet Street."

"What does it mean?" I asked.

Holmes laughed with pleasure. "It is unusual, isn't it? And now, Mr. Wilson, tell us the effect that this advertisement had on your life. Note the date of the paper, Watson."

"It is *The Morning Chronicle* of April 27, 1890. Just two months ago."

"Very good. Now, Mr. Wilson?"

"Well, I have a small pawnshop in London, but I do not earn much money there. I used to have two helpers, but now I can have only one. Even he comes for only half pay to learn the business."

"His name?"

"Vincent Spaulding. I know he could earn more somewhere else, but if he wants to work for me, I will not say anything."

"Yes, you are lucky to get someone to work for you at less than the normal pay. I think he may be as unusual as the advertisement you have read us."

"Oh, he is all right, but he has his problems. He is always taking pictures. Then he runs downstairs to develop them. But generally he works hard."

"He is working for you now?"

"Yes, he and a girl of fourteen live with me. She cooks and keeps the place clean. I have no other family alive. We live very quiet lives. It was that advertisement that changed everything. Spaulding brought it to me saying, 'I wish I had red hair, Mr. Wilson.'

"'Why?' I asked.

"'This job at the League of the Red-headed Men—it is such easy work and so well-paid. They always need more men than they can find.'

"You see, Mr. Holmes, I am a stay-at-home man. My business came to me, and I often spend weeks in my home and office without even going outside. But Spaulding kept telling me about this job. So I asked him, 'What kind of a job is it?'

"'It is very easy and you can continue working as you are now. But you will be paid a couple hundred pounds a year extra.'

"Then I began to be interested, because the money would be useful.

"'Tell me about it,' I said.

"'The League was founded by an American millionaire who felt sympathy for other red-headed men. He left all his money to a club which has the power to give money to any red-headed man.'

"'But there must be thousands of men asking for the money.'

"'No, not so many, because your hair must be blazing, not light red, or dark red. I am sure that you would get some of their money if you went to the Fleet Street office next Monday, Sir.'

"I decided to try for the position. I asked Spaulding to lock up the house and shop and come with me. He was happy to have a day off work.

"Well, on the following Monday at eleven o'clock, every man who had even a little red in his hair had marched into London from north, south, east and west and come to the office of the League. There was every color of red: strawberry, lemon, orange, brick, Irish-setter, liver, clay. But no one had that flaming color that Spaulding talked about and was mentioned in the advertisement. When I saw all those men, I wanted to go home immediately, but Spaulding wouldn't let me. He pulled me through the crowd and into the office. We had to push through hundreds of bodies."

"Such an interesting story," Holmes commented. "Please continue."

"There was one man behind a desk. Every red-headed man who came up to him, he asked a question and then sent him away. It seemed to be very difficult to get this job. However, when Spaulding and I entered, he closed the door behind us so we could talk privately.

"'This is Mr. Jabez Wilson,' said my assistant. 'He is willing to fill your position.'

"'And he is well-qualified for the job,' the man behind the desk added. He stood staring for a long time at my hair until I felt embarrassed. Then suddenly he jumped forward and shook my hand, congratulating me on my success.

"'Now, please excuse me. I must check on your hair,' he said. Then he began to pull on my hair very hard. I yelled with pain and he stopped, saying, 'I see that it is real hair. There are tears in your eyes.'

"Then he went to the open window and shouted down to the crowd that the vacancy was filled. There was a groan of disappointment from below as everyone began to move away from the building.

"'My name is Duncan Ross. I am glad to meet you. Do you have a family, Mr. Wilson?'

"I answered that I did not.

"'Dear me!' he said quietly, 'that is very serious indeed! I am sorry to hear you say that. This money was given to our organization so that more red-headed sons might be born.'

"I was afraid that I did not have the job, then he said: 'However, your hair is so unusually red, that we will allow you to join us anyway. When can you begin your new duties?'

"'It is a little difficult,' I said, 'for I have a business already. What are these hours?'

"'Ten to two.'

"'I will take care of your pawnshop,' Spaulding broke in.

"Now, a pawnshop is busy mostly on Thursday and Friday evenings, just before payday, Mr. Holmes, so I thought that I would be able to work midday at the office with Mr. Ross. And I knew that my assistant was a good man and could take care of our office.

"'That would suit me,' I replied. 'And the work?'

"'Is purely nominal.'

"'What do you call purely nominal?'

"'Well, you have to be in the office, or at least in the building, the whole time. If you leave, you lose your position forever.'

"'Only four hours a day, though. That is not a problem.'

"'No excuse will be allowed.'

"'And the work?'

"'To copy the Encyclopedia Britannica. You must bring your own paper and pen. But we will give you a desk and chair. Can you start tomorrow?'

"'Certainly.'

"'Then, goodbye, Mr. Wilson, and congratulations. You have won a very important position for yourself.'

"I was very pleased with my new job. But I thought about it later after coming home and I began to feel bad about it. I thought it must be some trick. Who would pay someone so much money for doing such easy work? In the morning, however, I bought a bottle of ink and some paper and went over to Mr. Ross's office.

"The table was ready for me. Mr. Duncan came into my room from time to time. At two o'clock, he said good-bye and was pleased that I had copied so many pages.

"This continued for a long time. Every Saturday, the manager gave me four gold coins and every morning I came in at ten and every afternoon I left at two.

"Eight weeks passed like this and then suddenly the whole business came to an end."

"To an end?"

"Yes, sir. It was just this morning. I went to my work as usual, but the door was shut and locked, with this note on it":

THE RED-HEADED LEAGUE

IS

DISSOLVED.

October 9, 1890

Sherlock Holmes and I both read the note over and then broke out laughing.

"I do not think it is funny," our man said. "I can go somewhere else if you are just going to laugh."

"No, please don't go," said Holmes. "It is just so unusual. Tell us, what did you do when you found this note?"

"I went down to the ground floor and asked the landlord what had happened to the Red-headed League. He said that he had never heard of any such body. Then I asked him who Mr. Duncan Ross was.

"'Oh, he was a lawyer. He was using the room upstairs until his new office was ready. At 17 King Edward Street, near St. Paul's.'

"I went to that address, Mr. Holmes, but it was a different company and I could not find Mr. Ross."

"What did you do then?"

"I asked my assistant to help me, but he did not know what else to do, so I have come to you for help."

"I am happy to look into your case. I think it may be more serious than you expect."

"More serious? Why, I have lost four pound a week."

"I do not think you can complain against the League. You have earned thirty pounds and learned some of the Encyclopedia. But we will try to clear up things. How long had you known your assistant before he found this ad?"

"About a month."

"How did he come?"

"In answer to an advertisement."

"Why did you pick him?"

"Because he came at half-wages."

"Are his ears pierced for earrings?"

"Yes."

"Is he still with you?"

"Oh, yes, I have just come from the pawnshop."

"Are you satisfied with his work in your absence?"

"Yes, there is not much to do during the day."

"That will be all for now, Mr. Wilson. Today is Saturday. On Monday I will give you my opinion on the subject."

"Well, Watson," said Holmes when our visitor had left us, "what do you think?"

"I cannot understand it at all," I told him.

"Yes, all very strange. I must think quickly," he said, curling up in a chair and closing his eyes.

I thought he was falling asleep and I was, too. Then he jumped up, "There is a German concert this afternoon. Can you leave your patients, Doctor?"

"Oh, yes, I am never busy on Saturday."

"Then, let us take lunch on the way. Come along."

We took the subway to Aldergate and then a short walk to the small building that Mr. Wilson had told us about that morning. We saw a brown board with JABEZ WILSON in white letters. Holmes walked up and down the street, studying the buildings. Then he walked up the street to the pawnshop and knocked at the door. A young man opened the door and asked us to come in.

"Thank you. I would just like to ask the way to the Strand from here."

"Third right, fourth left," said the assistant, closing the door.

"Smart man," Holmes said. "Fourth-smartest man in London."

"I am sure that he is important in our mystery. You wanted to see him, didn't you?" I asked.

"Not him, the knees of his trousers."

"What did you see?"

"My dear doctor, this is the time for observation, not for talk. We are spies in an enemy's country."

We turned the corner from the pawnshop, and we were on one of the most expensive streets in London. It was hard to believe they were so close.

"Just a minute," said Holmes. "I am trying to learn all the buildings in this neighborhood."

After a few moments, he said, "And now, Doctor, we have done our work. Let us have a sandwich and some coffee, and then off to musicland where all is sweetness and harmony."

Holmes completely enjoyed music. He would listen at home, waving his long arms in the air. This poetic mood was so different from the mood of Holmes when he worked on difficult cases and mysteries. Later that day, as we sat listening to the music at St. James's I thought that the people he was hunting were soon going to be very sorry.

After the concert, Holmes suggested that I go home. "But I will need your help tonight."

"At what time?"

"Ten will be early enough."

"I will see you at Baker Street at ten."

"Very well, but Doctor, there may be some danger, so put your gun in your pocket."

I could not begin to understand what our business was that night. Where were we going, and what were we going to do? I couldn't understand anything although I had seen and heard every piece of evidence that Holmes had.

When I reached his rooms later that night, he was talking loudly with two men. One I recognized as a policeman.

"Ha! Our party is complete. Watson, let me introduce our guest from Scotland Yard. He is going to join us tonight."

I looked at the Mr. Merryweather whom Holmes introduced. He looked disagreeable and then said, "I am very sorry to be here tonight. I want you to know this is the first Saturday night in twenty-seven years that I have not played a game of rubber with my friends."

"I think you will find the game tonight more exciting," Holmes assured him. "We are looking for the most important head of crime in England."

"John Clay," the policeman said. "He is young but very clever and has been educated at Eton and Oxford. I've been looking for him for years but have never seen him yet. I hope you are right about tonight, Holmes."

"You two go in the first cab," Holmes said. "Watson and I will follow."

Holmes was in a good mood during the drive. He kept singing over songs which we had heard at the concert that afternoon. Then he explained to me why he brought the two men. "Merryweather is personally interested in this case. Jones is brave and will not let a criminal loose once he has caught him."

We came to our location and sent the cabs away. Mr. Merryweather showed us down a narrow street, winding stone steps and into a large underground room filled with large boxes.

"A strong room," Holmes said.

"Yes," Merryweather said, hitting his stick on the floor. "Why, it sounds quite empty," he said, looking up in surprise.

"I must ask you to be quiet, Mr. Merryweather. Please sit down and be still."

Holmes got down on the floor and began looking at the cracks between the stones. After a few minutes, he jumped up. "We have to wait an hour. After the pawnbroker has gone to bed, they will work fast. Watson, you must know that we are in the basement of one of the largest banks in London. Merryweather is an important man at this bank. He will explain why criminals are interested in this place."

"It is our French gold," Merryweather whispered to me. "Some months ago we were able to buy 30,000 napoleons from the Bank of France. It is known that the money is still in boxes."

"We will have to sit in the dark, now." Holmes told us. "I brought along some cards, hoping that you could still have your game tonight. But it is too dangerous to keep the room lit. When they come, Watson, if they open fire, you must shoot them down."

The dark room was heavy with feeling as we waited for the criminals to come.

"There is only one way of escape. I hope you did as I told you, Jones," Holmes said.

"I sent a chief and two officers to the front door of the house."

"Then we have stopped all the holes. Now we can only wait."

What a wait. It seemed that the whole night passed, but it was only a little more than an hour, I learned later. Suddenly, my eyes caught some light. First it was a spot, then it became a yellow line, then a hand came out of the floor, and went back in again. All was quiet. Soon some stones were thrown aside and a boyish face looked into the room. One knee lifted the body's weight. His companion followed him. He had very red hair.

"It's all clear. Have you got the bags, Archie? Jump!"

"It's no use, John Clay," said Holmes quietly. "You have no chance."

"So I see, although you are only holding my pal by his coat."

"There are three men waiting for him at the door."

"How clever you are. I must compliment you."

"And I, you. Your red-headed idea was new and effective."

"I have kings and queens in my family. May I ask you to address me as "Sir" and to say "Please?""

"All right," said Jones, laughing. "Will your Highness please march upstairs so we can take you to prison."

"That is better," said John Clay and walked off to the police car.

"Really, Mr. Holmes," said Mr. Merryweather. "I don't know how the bank can thank you or repay you. You have defeated one of the biggest bank robberies that I have ever heard of."

"I had my own complaints with John Clay and I am glad he has been brought to the law at last. The story told by Mr. Wilson was also most interesting."

Later that night, Holmes explained the mystery to me. "I could see that the criminals only wanted to get the simple pawnbroker out of the way for a few hours every day. The whole plan was drawn up by John Clay. His friend was the man interviewing the red-headed men. As soon as I heard that the assistant was working for half-wages, I thought he must have a reason."

"But how could you guess what his plan was?"

"When I heard that he spent hours in the basement, then I thought he must be running a tunnel to another building. When I went to the door of the pawnshop, I saw the knees of his trousers. You must have noticed how dark they were from digging in the earth. Then in our walk on the surrounding streets, I saw the bank nearby. After the concert, I called Scotland Yard and the bank director. That is why the two gentlemen came with us."

"But how did you know they would try the crime tonight?"

"Well, this morning they put the sign on the door. They did not care if Mr. Wilson was in his store or not. That meant they had completed their tunnel. But they had to use it as soon as possible, before the gold was moved. Saturday would be best because they had two days when the bank was closed. For these reasons, I expected them tonight."

"Your reasoning is wonderful," I exclaimed.

"It saves me from boredom," he answered, yawning.

"Do you live to help mankind?"

He moved his shoulders. "Well, maybe it is of some little use. *'L'homme c'est rien — l'oeuvre c'est tout,'* as Gustave Flaubert wrote to George Sand."

03

The Boscombe Valley Mystery

ボスコム谷の惨劇

読み始める前に

The Boscombe Valley Mystery ボスコム谷の惨劇

56の短編のうち4番目に発表された
1891年の10月号のストランド・マガジン初出
1892年発行の「シャーロック・ホームズの冒険」に収録

[主な登場人物]

Sherlock Holmes シャーロック・ホームズ 世界的に有名な私立探偵。優れた観察眼と推理力を有する。ロンドンのベーカー街221Bに下宿している。

Watson ジョン・H・ワトソン 医師。ホームズの相棒でこの物語の語り手。かつてベーカー街221Bでホームズと同居していた。

John Turner ジョン・ターナー ボスコム谷の大地主。友人マッカーシーに農場の一つを貸している。

McCarthy マッカーシー ジョンの友人。ボスコム沼のほとりで死体となって発見される。

Lestrade レストレード スコットランド・ヤードの警察官。

James McCarthy ジェームズ・マッカーシー マッカーシーの一人息子。殺人の容疑をかけられ逮捕された。

Alice Turner アリス・ターナー ジョンの一人娘。ジェームズの無実を信じ、ホームズに捜査を依頼する。

[あらすじ]

　ある朝、妻と朝食を楽しんでいたワトソンのところにホームズからの電報が届くところから話は始まる。ボスコム谷で起きた不可解な殺人事件の謎を解くために、協力を求めてきたのだ。事件のあらましはこうである。チャールズ・マッカーシーという男が、最後に「クゥイー」という叫び声と、「ラット」という言葉を残してボスコム沼の近くで死体となって発見される。事件直前に、チャールズと口論をしていたところを目撃された彼の息子、ジェームズ・マッカーシーが殺人犯として逮捕される。しかしジェームズは断固として罪を否定し、恋人のアリス・ターナーも彼の無実を信じていた。

[総単語数] 4,843語

The Boscombe Valley Mystery

I was seated at breakfast with my wife one morning when a telegram came. It was from Sherlock Holmes and went:

Can you give me some time? Have just been wired about the Boscombe Valley tragedy. Would like you to come with me. Air and view perfect. Leave Paddington at 11:15.

"Will you go, dear?" my wife asked me.

"I don't know. There are a lot of people in my clinic."

"Oh, leave them to your assistant. He can do your work for you. And you look pale. I think the change would do you good. Besides, you are always interested in Sherlock Holmes's work."

"Yes, I would like to go, but the train leaves in one hour."

Well, I packed quickly and found Sherlock Holmes already by the train. He looked even taller in his long dark coat and hat.

"I am glad you came, Watson," Holmes said. "You are always a great help to me. I cannot count on anyone else."

We had a large area in the train to ourselves, but Holmes brought many newspapers with him, which kept him very busy as he read and took notes.

"Do you know about the case?" he asked me.

"No, I haven't read the papers carefully lately."

"The London papers have not written much about it. The problem is that the case is so simple that it seems difficult to understand."

"Why is that?"

"Well, the most ordinary crime is often the hardest to bring home. However, the son of a murdered man has a case against him."

"Did he murder his father?"

"As far as I can tell, these are the facts. Boscombe Valley is in the country. The largest landholder was named Mr. John Turner. One of his farms was run by his friend Mr. McCarthy. Turner and McCarthy were good friends. One had a son and one a daughter, both about eighteen years old, but neither man had a wife. Though the two men met often, they did not meet other people much.

"Last Monday, McCarthy left his house in the morning with one of his servants and went to the nearby town of Ross. He told his servant to hurry because he had another meeting at three that afternoon. But he never returned alive from that meeting.

"It is about a quarter of a mile down to the lake, and two people saw him pass that afternoon. Both say that he was walking alone. One says that his son followed him after a few minutes, and that his son carried a gun under his arm. Later that night, they all heard of the tragedy.

"There was a young girl, the daughter of the lodgekeeper, picking flowers in a field near the lake. She says that she saw McCarthy and his son and that they appeared to be quarreling loudly. The father used strong language and then the son raised his hand at his father. She was so frightened that she ran home and told her mother about the two men quarreling near the lake. Just then, the son came to their house and said that he had found his father dead by the lake. He was very excited and he asked for the lodgekeeper to help him. When they all went back to the lake, they found the dead body in the grass. He was badly beaten, as though by a gun. The son was taken by the police immediately, and the judge said that it was murder."

"I do not see why we are going there. Why do you think the son did not kill his father?" I asked my friend.

"It looks as though the son killed his father, but there are also other possibilities. However, many people think that the boy is innocent. The police have asked me to help, and that is why two men are rushing by train to Boscombe Valley instead of finishing their breakfast."

"I wonder if we are wasting our time?"

"Facts are not always so clear as they seem," Holmes replied. "Besides, there are some facts which have not been carefully considered."

"Surely the police would not miss important facts."

"Watson, I will give you an example. Every morning you shave and you are a careful man. You think that you shave your face carefully, but I can see that under your left ear, you have not done a good job. This is because you cannot see that area of your face well. In the same way, when the police cannot understand facts well, they do not consider them carefully.

"When the boy was told that he was going to be taken prisoner, he was not surprised."

"That was his confession."

"No. It was only his knowledge that the picture looked very dark and there was little reason for him to quarrel. If he had been angry, I would have thought him guilty. His quietness means either he is innocent or that he is very strong. Remember that he had argued with his father just before he stood beside his dead body. He felt sorry. This is a sign of a healthy mind, not a sick one."

"What does the young man say for himself?"

Holmes gave me a newspaper with the man's own comments:

"I had been gone for three days. When I came home my father was out. Soon I heard him come past the house. I did not know where he went. I took my gun and walked in the direction of the lake because I thought I would visit a friend on the other side. I was not following my father. But when I was about a hundred yards from the lake, I heard my father's voice call out 'Cooee!' which is a usual signal between my father and myself. I hurried toward him and found him standing beside the lake. He was very angry, which is not unusual. I thought it would be better to leave him alone, but when I had only gone 150 yards, I heard a terrible cry behind me. I ran back and found him lying on the ground with head wounds. I threw down my gun and took him in my arms, but he died almost immediately. I went to the lodgekeeper's to ask for help. I did not see anyone near my father during any of this time. I do not know how he was injured. He was not a popular man and did not have many friends, but I do not know of anyone who disliked him either."

The Coroner: Did your father say anything before he died?

The Witness: A few words, but I could not understand. Something about a rat. I thought he must be losing his mind.

The Coroner: What did you and your father quarrel about?

The Witness: I cannot say.

The Coroner: You must tell us.

The Witness: I cannot. It has nothing to do with the sad tragedy which followed.

The Coroner: We will decide that.

The Witness: I must still refuse.

The Coroner: The call "Cooee" was a common call between you and your father.

The Witness: It was.

The Coroner: But if he did not know you were near, why did he call out to you?

The Witness (confused): I do not know.

The Coroner: Did you see anything else near him?

The Witness: I'm not sure.

The Coroner: What do you mean "not sure"?

The Witness: Well, I was so upset. But there seemed to be a gray coat on the ground behind me after I sat down with my father in my arms. But when I rose and looked for it, it was gone.

"Do you mean that it disappeared before you went for help?"

"Yes, it was gone."

"How far from the body?"

"A dozen yards or so."

"And how far from the edge of the woods?"

"About the same."

"Then it was removed while you were sitting nearby?"

"Yes, but my back was toward it."

This was the end of the newspaper article.

"I see," said I, still looking at the newspaper. "The coroner brings up several problems. They all are very much against the son."

Holmes laughed. "Don't you see that both you and the coroner give the boy credit for both too much imagination and too little? Too little, because he could not think of a cause for a quarrel that would make the jury think kindly of him. Too much imagination to talk about a rat and a disappearing coat. No, Watson, I think we should consider the problem from another angle. But I am going to read Petrarch now. Not another word until we have reached the scene of the action."

It was almost four o'clock when we reached the beautiful country town of Ross. Lestrade, a policeman from Scotland Yard was at the train to meet us. He looked ugly and tricky but he had gotten us a room at a nearby inn.

We went for tea and Lestrade told us, "I have ordered a cab. I knew that you would want to go straight to the scene of the crime."

"Very thoughtful of you, but it is a question of barometric pressure," Holmes replied.

Lestrade looked surprised. "I do not understand."

"There is no wind now and not a cloud in the sky. This room is quite comfortable. I do not think that I will need to use the cab tonight."

Lestrade laughed loudly. He thought Holmes was mad. "The case is very plain, in any case. But a certain lady asked that you be called in. I told her again and again that there was nothing you could do which I had not already done. Well, how do you like that, here she is now."

Just then a most beautiful young woman rushed into the room. Her eyes were violet and her cheeks pink. She was all excitement and concern.

"Oh, Mr. Sherlock Holmes!" she cried, looking between us. Finally she chose me and said, "I am so glad that you have come. I know that James didn't do it. I want you to start upon your work knowing it, too. Never doubt this point. We have known each other since we were little children and I know his faults as no one else does; but he is too tenderhearted to hurt a fly. Such a charge is absurd to anyone who knows him."

"I hope to clear him, Miss Turner," Sherlock Holmes said to her. "I will do everything I possibly can to help him."

"Oh, you are Sherlock Holmes," she said, turning away from me and toward Holmes. "So, you have read the papers. Is there no loophole, no way of helping James? Don't you think he is innocent?"

"Yes, I think he may be."

"There!" she cried throwing back her head and looking at Lestrade. "See, he gives me hope!"

"My friend is too quick, I am afraid," replied Lestrade.

"But he is right," she answered. "I know James never did it. The only reason why he did not speak to the coroner about the argument is that I was concerned."

"In what way?" asked Holmes.

"I will tell you. James' father wanted us to marry. But James is so young. He wanted to wait. So there were quarrels."

"And your father, did he want you two to marry?"

"No, only Mr. McCarthy did." Her face turned red as Holmes looked at her closely.

"Thank you for your help. May I see your father tomorrow?" Holmes asked.

"I am afraid the doctor will not let you."

"The doctor?"

"Yes, since this tragedy, he is completely broken down. He stays in bed and the doctor says he just needs to rest. He is Mr. Turner's only friend, too."

"Now, that is important. Thank you, Miss Turner. You have helped me."

"You will tell me if you have any news?" she asked. "And if you go to the prison, please tell James that I know he is innocent."

"I will, Miss Turner."

"I must go back to my father now. God help you in your work. Thank you for coming here." She hurried from the room and was gone quickly.

"You should not have told her that James is innocent, Holmes. Why gave her hope? You are cruel to tell her that the boy is innocent."

"I think there is hope for his release," Holmes replied. "Do you have a pass to the prison?"

"Yes, just for you and me. It is about two hours from here by train."

"Then I would like to go out today in the cab you have arranged. I am sorry to leave you alone, Watson. You will be all right here."

I walked down to the station with them and then walked through the streets for a while. I tried to read a novel, but fell to thinking about the day's events. If the young man's story were true, how sad that he should be in prison. What had happened between the time he left his father and the time he returned, called by his screams? Bones had been broken by a heavy blow. The bones named in the courtroom were at the back of the head, so he must have been hit from behind. The son was quarreling with his father face to face. And the rat? What did the father mean about a rat? He must have been trying to explain the tragedy. If there was another murderer who dropped his coat, did he come back and carry it away while the son was sitting so near? I could not understand at all, but I had great faith in Sherlock Holmes' powers.

Sherlock Holmes came back to our inn alone. Lestrade was staying at an inn in town. "It is important that it does not rain before we go over the ground where the man died. But we must also be rested. I have seen young McCarthy."

"What did you learn from him?"

"Nothing. I think that he is as puzzled as everyone else. He is good-looking, but not very bright. I think he is good-hearted, though."

"I cannot admire him, if he refused to marry the beautiful Miss Turner," I said.

"Ah, that is the saddest story. He is madly in love with her. But two years ago, while Miss Turner was away at boarding school, he married an older woman who used him. No one knows about it, but he cannot marry the woman he truly loves now. That is why he was so upset when his father kept urging him to marry Miss Turner. He knows it is impossible. On the other hand, his father refused to keep him in the house if he did not marry Miss Turner. For three days before he met his father for the last time, the boy was with the older woman in Bristol. His father did not know where he was. The only good news is that when the older woman read all the reports in the newspaper, she wrote the young McCarthy that she has a new husband in the Bermuda Dockyard and that there is now no tie between them. This has helped young McCarthy, for all he has suffered."

"But if he did not kill his father, who did?"

"Please think of these two points. One is that the murdered man had an appointment with someone at the lake, and that someone could not have been his son, for his son was away, and he did not know when he would return. The second is that the murdered man was heard to cry 'Cooee!' before he knew that his son had returned. These two points are most important. Now, Watson, we will talk about George Meredith and leave these other matters until tomorrow."

There was no rain the next day, just as Holmes had thought. The morning broke bright and cloudless. At nine o'clock, Lestrade joined us and we all went down to the lake together.

"There is no news, except that Mr. Turner is so ill that they think he may go soon."

"An elderly man?" Holmes asked.

"About sixty; his health has been poor for a long time, but this has made him much worse. He was a good friend to McCarthy. I understand he gave him a farm rent free."

"Indeed! That is interesting," said Holmes.

"Yes, everyone says he helped McCarthy in a hundred ways."

"Really! Does it not seem odd that this McCarthy, a poor man, should talk of marrying his son to a rich friend's daughter as though he had every right? It is even more strange since we know that Turner did not want his daughter to marry McCarthy's son. The daughter told us so. Do you not deduce anything from that?"

"We have your deductions, Holmes, but I am having trouble finding the facts," Lestrade replied.

"So you are," Holmes said quietly.

"But I have one fact which you do not."

"And what is that?"

"That the older McCarthy met his death from the younger McCarthy and that all deductions that do not point to this fact are moonshine."

"Well, moonshine is brighter than fog," said Holmes, laughing.

At this point we passed the McCarthy farm. Holmes asked to stop. The maid showed us the older man's boots which he had worn down to the lake. Holmes measured them carefully. Then he asked to be led down to the lake.

Holmes was a changed man when he got involved like this. Those who saw him only on Baker Street would not recognize him here. His eyebrows were two black lines while his eyes glittered. His face was bent and his lips tight. The veins stood out like rope on his neck. He concentrated so that he did not hear a comment or question. Swiftly and silently, he moved across the land down to the lake. Sometimes he hurried, sometimes he stopped dead. Lestrade did not respect Holmes, but I admired every move, as I knew it was all to an extremely important purpose.

From the lake, we could see Mr. Turner's beautiful home and grounds. Lestrade showed us where the body had been found. The ground was wet and we could still see the marks of where the body had fallen. Holmes was able to read many other things on that earth. He ran around like a dog tracking an animal, then he turned to Lestrade,

"Why did you go into the lake?"

"I thought there might be some gun or something. But how did you know...?"

"Oh, I have no time to explain. I wish I had come here before the herd of animals from the police department did. They have covered all the tracks around the body. But there are three separate tracks from the same feet." He took out his magnifying glass and looked at the ground carefully. "These are of young McCarthy. Twice he was walking and once he ran. That supports his story. He ran when he saw his father had fallen. Here are the father's feet as he paced up and down. Ah, and here we have light steps, three sets of light steps as the person came back for the forgotten coat. Now where did they come from?"

Holmes ran up and down from the lake to the forest and then he went under the largest tree in the area. There he lay down on the ground and was there for a long time, turning over the leaves and sticks. He even looked at the covering of the trees. He collected some dirt and also carried a large stone out with him.

"It is a very interesting case," he said calmly when he had come back to join us. "I believe this gray house is the lodge. I will go in and have a word with the lodgekeeper. Then we will drive back for lunch. You may walk to the cab, I will join you in a moment."

Holmes joined us in ten minutes, still carrying the rock. "This may interest you, Lestrade," holding it out. "The murder was done with it."

"I see no marks."

"There are none."

"How do you know, then?"

"Because grass was growing under it so that it has not been there long. I could not see where it had been taken from. It also matches the head injuries on the murdered man. There is no sign of any other weapon."

"And the murderer?"

"He is a tall man, left-handed, limps, wears a gray coat and thick-soled hunting boots, smokes Indian cigarettes, carries a blunt pen-knife in his pocket, and some other details, but I have given you enough to aid us in our search."

Lestrade laughed, "I am sorry I do not believe you, Holmes. Your theories are very interesting, but we can only take facts to the court."

"You work your method. I shall work mine," Holmes replied. "I shall be busy this afternoon and probably return to London this evening."

"And leave your case unfinished?"

"No, finished."

"But the mystery?"

"It is solved."

"Who is the criminal, then?"

"The gentleman I have described to you."

"But who is he?"

"Surely it would not be difficult to find out. Only a few people live in this town."

"I am a serious man. I cannot go over the countryside looking for a left-handed man who limps. All of Scotland Yard would laugh at me."

"All right," said Holmes quietly. "I have given you your chance. Here is your inn. Good-bye. I will write you a note before I leave."

Holmes ate lunch quietly. He looked pained, as though he did not know what to do.

"Watson, please sit still and let me talk to you for a while. I value your advice."

"My pleasure," I replied.

"There are two points which trouble me. One is that the father should call out to his son when he does not know that he is there. The other is the reference to a rat as he died. Let us assume that the boy's story is true."

"Then what about this 'Cooee!'?"

"It was not meant for the son, but for the person with whom he had the appointment."

"And what of the rat?"

Sherlock Holmes took a folded piece of paper out of his pocket. "Last night I sent away for a map of the area where the two men used to live when they were young." Putting his hand over part of the map, he said, "What do you read?"

"ARAT."

"And now?" He raised his hand.

"BALLARAT."

"Exactly. He was trying to say the name of his murderer."

"You are amazing!"

"I am just telling you the facts. The son also told us about the gray coat. Now we know it is a man from Ballarat with a gray coat. Today I also learned several other things from careful observation. The man's height you may judge from the length of his footsteps, and his boots. His right footprint carried less weight, so I said he is lame. He stood behind the tree during the talk between the father and the son. He even smoked there. I found the ash of a cigar, which I can identify as an Indian cigar. I have studied the topic of tobacco, you recall, Watson, and identified 140 different types in that article I wrote. In fact, I can even tell you from the end of the cigar which I found in the leaves that it was rolled in Rotterdam."

"Holmes, you have drawn a rope around the criminal and he cannot escape. You have saved an innocent boy's life. It is almost as though you have cut the rope that was hanging him. The real criminal is —"

"Mr. John Turner," called the hotel waiter, as he opened our door and let in a visitor.

The man who walked into the room before us was very large and strong. He had a beard and thick eyebrows which made him look very respectable. But his face was white. He looked almost dead.

"Please sit down. You received my note?" Holmes asked.

"Yes, you said you would see me here to stop the town talking." But his unhappy look said more than his words.

"I know about McCarthy."

The old man put his face in his hands. "I would have spoken well of the boy if he was taken to court."

"I am glad to hear you say that," said Holmes seriously.

"I would speak now, but it would break my daughter's heart to hear that I am arrested."

"You may not be arrested."

"What?"

"It is your daughter who called me here and, I am acting here in her interests. But young McCarthy must be set free."

"I am an old man. The doctor says I have only a month to live, but I would rather die in my own house than in a prison."

"Just tell me the truth," Holmes said, "and I will write down a few facts. Watson here will be your witness. I promise I will not use this information unless I absolutely need to."

"Yes, all right," said the old man. "I would just like to spare my daughter the shock. I will tell you everything, but it will not take me long.

"You didn't know the dead man, Holmes. He was impossible. He has been holding my life for the last twenty years and darkened every waking moment. It was more than thirty years ago. I drank too much and was unlucky. I began to live a life away from the law. I led five other men and our group was called the Ballarat Gang.

"One day we fought six men for their gold. Three of our boys were killed. I put my gun to their headman, who was this McCarthy. I wish I had shot him then, but I let him go. The other two men and I got away with all the gold. We came back to England without ever meeting the law. Since then I have led a quiet and respectable life. I bought this land. I got married, and though my wife died young, she left me my dear little Alice. Even when she was just a baby, I tried to lead a good life for her sake. I did my best to make up for my past. Then McCarthy came back into my life.

"It was in London that I met him again. He had nothing.

"'Here we are, Jack,' he said to me. 'Just me and my son. We'll be as good as family to you. If you don't take us, well, we have good policemen in England...'

"I brought them down to the west country here, and they have lived on my best land rent-free ever since. He's never given me any peace. Always at my side. It was worse as my daughter grew up. He knew that I did not want her to know about my past. Whatever he wanted, I had to give him. Land, money, houses. At last he asked for a thing which I could not give. He asked for Alice.

"His son was the same age, and he thought that all my property would go to him if he married Alice. I am in poor health, so he would have everything as soon as I was gone. He cared nothing for my daughter's mind or feelings. I was already a dying man. But my girl! I could save her if I could only keep that man quiet. I did it, Mr. Holmes, and I would do it again. As deeply as I have sinned, I have paid for it. I did not want my girl to be mixed up with the son of such a man. I hit him as I would hit a dangerous animal. His cry brought his son, but I escaped into the wood, though I had to go back for my coat. That is the complete story, gentlemen."

"Well, I cannot judge you," Holmes said as the old man signed his statement as recorded by Holmes. "I hope that we never have to show anyone."

"You will have to explain your reasons to a higher court than the court of men, you know. If the boy is condemned by the judge, I shall have to produce your statement. If not, your secret is safe with Watson and myself."

"Farewell, then," said the old man seriously. "Your own deathbeds will be easier because you have given peace to mine." His large body shaking, he left the room.

"God help us," said Holmes after a long silence.

James McCarthy was released from jail after Holmes raised a number of objections at the court hearings. Old Turner lived for seven months after our meeting, but he is now dead. Young McCarthy and Turner's daughter seem headed for a happy marriage. They do not know about the dark cloud that passed over them.

04

The Man with the Twisted Lip

唇のねじれた男

読み始める前に

The Man with the Twisted Lip 唇のねじれた男

56の短編のうち6番目に発表された
1891年の12月号のストランド・マガジン初出
1892年発行の「シャーロック・ホームズの冒険」に収録

［主な登場人物］

Sherlock Holmes シャーロック・ホームズ 世界的に有名な私立探偵。優れた観察眼と推理力を有する。ロンドンのベーカー街221Bに下宿している。

Watson ジョン・H・ワトソン 医師。ホームズの相棒でこの物語の語り手。かつてベーカー街221Bでホームズと同居していた。

Isa Whitney アイザ・ホイットニー セント・ジョージ・カレッジの校長。重度の薬物依存症がある。

Kate Whitney ケイト・ホイットニー ワトソンの妻の友人。アヘン窟から帰ってこない夫アイザの捜索を求めにくる。

Neville St. Clair ネヴィル・セントクレア アヘン窟で行方不明になり、夫人が行方を探している。

Boone ブーン ホームレスの老人男性。唇がねじれている。

［あらすじ］

　ワトソンは妻の友人に頼まれ、数日戻ってこないという彼女の夫を、アヘン窟に探しに行く。しかし、出向いたその場所でワトソンは驚くべき人物、変装したホームズに遭遇する。ホームズは別の事件の捜査でアヘン窟にいたのだ。ホームズの依頼人は偶然、アヘン窟にいる夫の姿を見かけたというセントクレア夫人。夫を探しにアヘン窟に行ってみたものの、そこには夫の姿はなく唇のねじれたヒュー・ブーンという男だけがいたという。いよいよホームズが乗り出し、セントクレア夫人の夫を探すことになるのだが……。

［総単語数］4,026語

The Man with the Twisted Lip

Isa Whitney was head teacher at the College of St. George's. He had a bad drug habit. His habit started in college after he read De Quincey's description of dreams. Whitney found out, however, that starting to take drugs is much easier than stopping. He was a slave to opium for many years. His family and friends felt fear and sadness for him. I can see him now, yellow skin, closing eyes, and his body sinking in a chair. What a man!

One night in June of '89, someone came to my door. My wife was sitting beside me. She was not happy to have a visitor.

"One of your patients. You will have to go out, now."

I groaned. I had just gotten home from a long and tiring day.

Then the stranger opened the door and came into our house. It was a woman wearing a black veil.

"Please excuse me," she said. Then she ran to my wife, threw her arms around her and began to cry loudly. "Oh, I am in such trouble. Please help me."

"Why, Kate. What is it? You gave me such a fright," said my wife.

"I didn't know what to do, so I came straight to you," she replied.

That was always what happened. When anyone was in trouble, they came straight to my wife for help—just like birds to a tree.

"Yes, all right. Let me get you a cup of tea, and you tell us all about it. Or do you want to talk to me alone?"

"Oh, no, no. I want the doctor's advice, too. It is about Isa. He has not been home for two days. I am so worried about him!"

It was not the first time we had heard about Isa's problems. His wife was a schoolfriend of my wife's, and I was a doctor. We tried to quiet her down as best we could. Did she know where he was?

She did. It was an opium den on the eastern side of the City. Until now, he had always come home after one day, very unhappy in the evening. But he had been gone for two days this time, and was still not home. She was sure he was sleeping off the poison at the Bar of Gold in Swandam Lane. But how could she go there alone as a woman and carry her husband away from his bad friends?

I first thought of going with her. But then I decided I would go alone to get him. I promised I would send him home by cab in two hours if he was at the Bar of Gold. So, in ten minutes, I had left my warm house and was sitting in a cab myself, wondering what the future held.

Swandam Lane is a dirty street near the river east of London Bridge. There are a lot of bars on it, and the one I was looking for was as dark as a cave. I asked the cab to wait for me, went down the steps and opened the door.

It was a long, low room. The air was heavy with smoke. Bodies were lying and sitting in strange shapes. Some of them looked at me with unkind looks. Their pipes made little red circles of light in the darkness. I could hear voices though most of the bodies were silent. But there were no conversations, mostly people just talked to themselves. No one listened to anyone else. There was a thin old man sitting in front of the fire. One of the workers brought me a pipe and a supply of the drug as I entered the room.

"Thank you, I have not come to stay," I told him. "I am looking for my friend, Mr. Isa Whitney. Is he here?"

Someone moved near me and I saw that it was Isa. "My God,

Watson! What time is it?" he then asked me. What a state he was in.

"Nearly eleven."

"Of what day?"

"Of Friday, June 19th."

"Good heavens! I thought it was Wednesday. I am sure it is Wednesday. Why are you trying to frighten me by saying that it is Friday?" Then he put his head in his arms and began to cry loudly.

"I tell you that it is Friday, man. Your wife has been waiting for you for two days. You are unkind to her."

"Yes, it's true. But I haven't been here long, just had a few pipes. Anyway, I will go back with you. I don't want my poor little Kate to be unhappy. Give me a hand! Did you come by cab?"

"Yes, I have one waiting for us."

"But I have to pay before I leave. Can you get my bill, Watson?"

I walked further into the room looking for the manager. I passed one thin man who caught my shirt and said, "Take two steps and then turn around and look at me." His words were very clear though his body was bent and weak.

I took two steps and turned back to look at him. He sat up straight and there was the fire of life in his eyes. I almost cried out. For it was Sherlock Holmes. But he hid his face from me and again seemed to be a bent old man lost in drugs.

"Holmes, what are you doing here?" I asked.

"Send your friend home first, and then I will talk with you quietly. Be sure to send a note with him to your wife so that she does not worry. Wait outside for me. I will join you in five minutes."

I could not refuse Sherlock Holmes. I did as he told me with pleasure. I always enjoyed working with him on his cases and helping people. Within five minutes I had paid Whitney's bill, written a note to my wife, taken Whitney out to the cab and seen him carried off.

Sherlock Holmes met me outside. He remained bent over and walked very slowly for a hundred yards. Then he stood up straight like a young and healthy man and gave a loud laugh.

"I suppose you think now that I smoke opium with all my other bad habits, Watson!"

"I was surprised to find you at this place," I replied.

"No more than I to find you here."

"I came to find a friend."

"I came to find an enemy."

"An enemy?"

"Yes, the man who runs this den has said he will kill me. I do not like to see people die there."

"Die?"

"Yes, if we had 1,000 pounds for each cold body that has been carried out of there we would be rich men, Watson. Now, would you like to join me?"

"If I can help you."

"A friend can always help. Especially one who writes good notes."

We jumped in his horse cart and ran through the empty streets, across a river, under a clear sky with a few stars. Holmes drove in silence, lost in thought, while I waited eagerly to hear the story of this case. But I did not want to disturb his thought. We had come into a quiet area of nice homes when he began to talk.

"You can be quiet, Watson. That is good. Please, do you mind if I talk to you? I was wondering what to say to the woman we are going to visit."

"But you still have told me nothing about it."

"I do not have time to tell you much. Just the facts. But I have not understood the problem yet. Perhaps you can explain it to me."

"Well, tell me what you can."

"About five years ago, a man named Neville St. Clair came to town. Two years ago he married a friend's daughter. Now he has two children. He is now thirty-seven years old, he is a good husband and father, very popular with all who know him. He also has savings in the bank, so there is no need for him to worry about money.

"However, last week he went to town earlier than usual, saying he would return a little later than usual, but that he would bring his son a game. On the same day, just after he had left, his wife received a telegram that there was a parcel at the Aberdeen Shipping Company. You may know, Watson, that the Aberdeen Shipping Company office is near Swandam Lane, where you found me tonight. Mrs. St. Clair had her lunch, did some shopping, picked up her parcel, and found herself walking through Swandam Lane at 4:45 that day. Do you understand what I have said so far?"

"Yes, it is very clear."

"Monday was a hot day, you may remember, so she walked slowly, looking for a cab rather than walking through that area. Suddenly, she saw her husband in a window. He looked very upset and she almost cried out. He waved to her with fear, and then he was gone as though someone had pulled him from behind. She also noticed that his tie was missing from his shirt.

"She rushed into that building, it was the same Bar of Gold where we met tonight, and tried to go to the window where she had seen her husband. However, the manager of the club pushed her back into the street. She ran into some policemen there, who agreed to come back with her. They helped her enter the building and go to the window where she had seen her husband. But he was not there. There was no one there except one old man on the second floor. The police thought that maybe Mrs. St. Clair was imagining things when she cried out, ran to the table and picked up the game which her husband had promised to bring their son that evening.

"Now the manager also looked surprised, and the police realized it was a serious problem. The police went back into the room where Mrs. St. Clair had seen her husband. They found blood on the window. Below the window was the harbor, only a few feet of water. All of Mr. St. Clair's clothes were found in the room except for his coat. He must have jumped into the water, but it would be difficult for him to swim if he was bleeding.

"So who did it? I know the manager of the den is a mean man. But he was at the door when Mrs. St. Clair came into the building, which must have been at the same time that her husband jumped from the window. He also could not explain the clothes being in the room. There was only the old man on the second floor. He stands in the street and asks people for money. Everyone there has seen him sitting all day. In a short time, he collects a lot of money from people who feel sorry for him. He is an ugly man, with orange hair and very dark eyes. He also makes a lot of noise, never keeping quiet. This is the last person who saw Mr. Neville St. Clair."

"But an old man, what could he have done?"

"He is strong, though old."

"Please continue the story."

"Mrs. St. Clair fainted when she saw the blood. The police took her home by cab. The old man was not taken to the police station immediately which was a mistake because he may have talked with the manager. The old man had some blood on his shirt, but he also had a cut finger and said that the blood on the window was from his finger. Again and again he said he had never seen Mr. St. Clair and that Mrs. St. Clair was dreaming that she saw her husband in the building. The police took him to the station and one of them waited for the water in the harbor to go down to find more clues.

"They did find one. It was St. Clair's coat, but not the man. His coat pockets were filled with coins so that it was not carried away by the water. But the body might have been washed away if he was dead."

"But all the clothes were in the room. Why would the body be dressed in only a coat?"

"Well, if the old man threw St. Clair out of the window without his coat, and then decided that he should throw out the clothes too, he might have thrown the coat out first, after putting coins in the pocket. But Mrs. St. Clair was coming in the building to look for her husband, then she brought back the police. The old man maybe didn't have time to get rid of all of them, though he might have liked to."

"Sounds possible."

"Well, I can think of no other possibility. The old man, Boone, was arrested. But nothing could be brought against him. His life was quiet and innocent, just asking people for money in the street every day. That is the problem. And there are many questions. Why was St. Clair in an opium den? What has happened to him? Where is he now? I have never had such a difficult case."

We had now left the city and were passing through streets where houses had lights in their windows here and there.

"We are near the St. Clair home. Mrs. St. Clair has given me two rooms of her house to work from. I hate to meet her, Watson, when I have no news of her husband. But we are here."

There was a large garden around the house. A boy came out to take our horse. I followed Holmes up to the house. The door flew open, and a little lady greeted us at the door dressed in a pink nightdress. She looked at us with a question in her eyes.

Seeing two of us, she gave a cry, but then she saw that I was not her husband.

"No good news?"

"None," Holmes replied. "No bad, either."

"Thank God for that. Come in. You must be tired."

"This is my friend, Dr. Watson. He is a great help to me on many cases, and it is lucky that we have him here for this one."

"I am delighted to meet you," she said, giving me her hand. "I am sorry I have not made very nice arrangements for your stay."

"Madam, you do not need to apologize to me. I am happy if I can help you or my friend."

Leading us into a dining room and a big dinner, she said, "I would like to ask you one or two simple questions."

"Certainly, madam."

"I mean your real opinion."

"About what?"

"In your heart of hearts, do you think Neville is alive?"

Holmes fell silent. He didn't seem to know what to say.

"Be honest."

"Honestly, I do not."

"You think that he is dead?"

"I do."

"Killed."

"I do not know."

"When did he die?"

"On Monday."

"Then how could I receive a letter from him today?"

Sherlock Holmes jumped from his chair.

"What!" he shouted.

She held up a letter, and he took it from her. Then he laid it on the table and looked at it very carefully.

"This is poor writing. I think it is not your husband's, madam."

"No, but the enclosed ring is his."

"But the person who addressed the envelope did not know your address. The ink of the name and the ink of the address are slightly of different color, which means they were written at different times. Your husband would have written your name and address at the same time. Do you think it is his writing?"

"Yes, when he writes fast it is like this."

"Dearest, do not be afraid. All will be well. There is a huge error which may take some time to make right. Wait in patience.

Neville."

Sherlock Holmes spoke as he looked at the envelope.

"Mailed in town yesterday by a man with a dirty thumb. The letter was sealed by a man who smokes. And you think that your husband wrote this?"

"Yes. Neville wrote those words."

"Well, the clouds are not so dark, but there is still danger, Mrs. St. Clair."

"But at least he is alive."

"Well, he could have written it on Monday, and it was just sent to you today."

"Oh, do not say so, Mr. Holmes. I am so close to him. I would know if he was no longer here on earth."

"Yes, I know how valuable the feelings of a woman are. But if your husband can write you letters, why is he not at home?"

"I cannot understand it."

"He said nothing to you before leaving on Monday?"

"No."

"And you were surprised to see him in Swandam Lane?"

"Very."

"Was the window open?"

"Yes."

"Did he call out to you?"

"I only heard him cry out."

"A call for help?"

"Yes, he waved his arms."

"Maybe he waved his arms in surprise to see you."

"Maybe."

"You thought he was pulled back?"

"He went away so suddenly."

"Perhaps he jumped back. You didn't see anyone else in the room?"

"No, but that old man said he was there."

"Your husband was wearing all of his clothes?"

"Yes, except for his tie."

"Had he ever told you about Swandam Lane?"

"Never."

"Did he ever give signs of using drugs?"

"Never."

"Thank you, Mrs. St. Clair. Those are the questions which I wanted to ask you. Now we will eat and rest. Tomorrow will be a very busy day."

Our room had two beds. I slept quickly. Holmes, however, could continue awake for days when there was a problem he wanted to solve. I saw that he was going to sit up all night. He changed clothes, put a lot of pillows from his bed on the sofa and chairs and made himself a comfortable place to stretch out. I saw him sitting still in the dim light, as I went to sleep. His voice woke me.

"Awake, Watson?" he asked.

"Yes."

"Ready to go for a morning drive?"

"Certainly."

"Then dress." He seemed to be in a good mood.

I looked at my watch. It was only 5 a.m. No wonder the house was still quiet.

"Watson, I am the most stupid man in Europe. At last I think I understand our problem."

"What is it?"

We crossed the river and went through the streets until we were at the central police station.

"Who is here this morning?" Holmes asked.

"Bradstreet," came the reply.

"Ah, I would like to have a word with you, Brad-street."

"Certainly, Mr. Holmes. Come into my room."

"I have come to ask you about Boone, the man who asks for money in the street. I wonder if he is involved in the disappearance of Mr. Neville St. Clair, of Lee."

"We brought him in and asked him questions."

"Is he here?"

"Yes, but he's very dirty and won't wash. His face is black."

"I would like to see him."

"Right, come this way."

We saw him on his bed asleep. He was not only dirty. He was also very ugly. There was a long scar from his lip to his eye.

"He certainly is dirty," Holmes said. "I have brought along some soap and towels to give him a wash."

"You are a funny one," the policeman laughed.

"Please open the door quietly so that I can start," Holmes continued.

"All right. Why not?"

"Let me introduce you to Mr. St. Clair, of Lee," he called out loudly as he washed the man's face.

I have never seen anything like it. The dirt was gone. The scar was gone. The hair was a wig and when taken away we found a handsome young man of good class. He suddenly woke up, gave a scream and threw himself down on the bed.

"Great heavens! It is the missing man of the photograph."

"Yes, all right. What am I charged with?"

"With carrying away Mr. St. Clair," the policeman said, smiling. "I have never seen anything like this in the twenty-seven years I have worked as a policeman," he added.

"No crime," Holmes said, "but a great mistake. You should have trusted your wife."

"I was worried about the children. I did not want them to know the truth about their father. Oh, my God. What can I do?"

Sherlock Holmes sat down next to the young man. "Why don't you tell us what has happened. If you don't, we will have to take you to court and your picture will be in all the newspapers."

"God bless you," the young man cried out. "I would rather die than have my family know this ugly truth. This is the first time I will be telling my story.

"My father was a school teacher. I was given the best education. I traveled when I was young and reported for a London newspaper. One day I was asked to write articles about London. I decided to pretend that I was a poor man living in the streets to get the facts for my writing. I had acted in plays at school and learned how to wear makeup. In this way I made myself look the way you found me in the building and here this morning.

"Later a friend asked me for some money and I gave it to him, but I needed more myself, so I took off work, and went into the street as Boone again. This time I was able to meet the debt in only ten days.

"Now that I had found such an easy way to earn money, it was hard to go back to work. It was a fight in my mind at first but finally the ease of sitting in the street won me, and I quit my job. Only one man knew my secret and that was the manager of the den. I paid him well to use a room to put on my makeup and clothes in the morning, and then dress well to return home in the evening.

"I became rich. I received much more money than other men who sit in the street like I did. It was my way of calling out to people passing by. Then I made plans to marry. I bought a house in the country and had two children. But my job in the street did not change. My dear wife knew only that I worked in the City—nothing else.

"Last week, I saw my wife in the street just before I was getting ready to go home. I quickly changed back into the clothes of the poor old man and left my other clothes in the room. But I thought that I should throw all my clothes in the river. I picked up my coat first because it was on top. But before I could throw the others out, the police started coming in the building. I was glad to be accused of killing Mr. St. Clair instead of having my wife know that I came to such a building every day.

"When the police let me leave, I ran to the manager of the den. I gave him my ring to send to my wife, with the letter, to comfort her."

"That note reached her yesterday," Holmes broke in.

"Good God! What a week she must have spent. The manager must have given it to one of his questionable friends who finally remembered to send it to her."

"You must stop this bad habit now," Bradstreet spoke up.

"Yes, of course. I will stop. I will stop."

"Thank you for all your trouble, Holmes," Bradstreet said as he walked out to the horse with us. "I wish I knew how you figured these things out!"

"I stop sleeping and think of the problem from every angle," Holmes replied. "Come, Watson, if we hurry, we will be in time for breakfast at Baker Street."

05

The Adventure of the Speckled Band

まだらの紐

読み始める前に

The Adventure of the Speckled Band まだらの紐

56の短編のうち8番目に発表された
1892年2月号のストランド・マガジン初出
1892年発行の「シャーロック・ホームズの冒険」に収録

［主な登場人物］

Sherlock Holmes　シャーロック・ホームズ　世界的に有名な私立探偵。優れた観察眼と推理力を有する。ロンドンのベーカー街221Bに下宿している。

Watson　ジョン・H・ワトソン　医師。ホームズの相棒でこの物語の語り手。ベーカー街221Bでホームズと同居している。

Helen Stoner　ヘレン・ストーナー　依頼人の若い女性。双子の姉ジュリアの死に関する調査をホームズに依頼する。

Julia Stoner　ジュリア・ストーナー　ヘレンの双子の姉。ある夜、「まだらの紐」という言葉を遺して亡くなった。

Dr. Roylott　ロイロット博士　医師でストーク・モーラン屋敷の主。義理の娘ヘレンと暮らしている。

［あらすじ］

　ヘレン・ストーナーという若い女性が、身の危険を感じてホームズに助けを求めるところから物語は始まる。ヘレンは、双子の姉ジュリアの死にまつわる不思議な状況を語り、姉が最後に口にした「まだらの紐」という言葉も伝える。ヘレンは結婚式の前夜に姉が使ったのと同じ寝室に眠ることになったが、最近、ジュリアが死ぬ前に聞いたという不気味な口笛が聞こえるようになったという。ヘレンの亡き母が残した遺産について調べたホームズは、ついにヘレンの義父であるロイロット博士と対峙する。

［総単語数］3,999語

The Adventure of the Speckled Band

I have worked with Sherlock Holmes on more than seventy cases in the last eight years. Some were sad, some funny, many only strange, but none ordinary. He always worked for the love of his art rather than for money. However, the most unusual was the case of the Roylott family of Stoke Moran. The case happened when we were both still living on Baker Street. I may have recorded them earlier, but I had to keep many of the facts secret until now. Within the last month, the lady to whom I promised secrecy has died and I think it is best that I bring the secret to light. The rumors about this case are worse than the truth.

It was early in April of 1883 when I found Sherlock Holmes standing next to my bed waiting for me to wake up, though it was still seven o'clock in the morning and he was usually a late sleeper.

"Very sorry to wake you up so early, Watson."

"What? Is there a fire?"

"No, a young lady who needs to see me. When young ladies wake people up early in the morning, I think there must be something very important to talk about. I thought you would like to listen from the beginning, so I am calling you to give you the chance."

"My dear fellow, I would not miss it for anything," I replied, getting up and quickly dressing.

There was no greater pleasure than following Holmes in his work and admiring his quick mind and intuition. The young lady was dressed in black and had a veil over her face. When we entered the room, she stood up.

"Good morning, madam," said Holmes cheerfully. "My name is Sherlock Holmes. This is my close friend, Dr. Watson. You may speak as freely before him as before myself. Oh, I see that you are shivering. Come close to the fire."

"It is not cold which makes me shiver. It is fear, Mr. Holmes. It is terror."

She removed the veil from her face and we could see that her face was pale, with frightened eyes. She looked like a hunted animal. She seemed to be about thirty years old, but she looked even older. Holmes ran his eyes over her, seeing so much.

"You must not fear," he said kindly, touching her arm. "We will make everything all right. I see that you have just arrived by train."

"You know me?"

"No, but I see the half of a return ticket in your glove. You must have left home very early and traveled by dog-cart to the train station."

She looked shocked.

"There is no surprise. Your coat is covered with spots of mud in seven places. Only a dog-cart could make mud come like that on your coat."

"Whatever way you have of finding out, you are quite right," said she. "I left home before six this morning and got the first train to Waterloo. Sir, I cannot be like this any longer. There is only one person who cares for me and he cannot help. I have heard of you, Mr. Holmes, from my friend, Mrs. Farintosh. She said that you help people in their hour of need, and it is from her that I have received your address. Please try to throw a little light on the darkness which surrounds me. I cannot reward you now, but in six weeks I shall be married, with my own income, and I will show you how grateful I am then."

Holmes unlocked his desk and took out a notebook.

"Farintosh," said he. "Ah, yes, I remember. A white opal necklace. I shall be happy to devote as much attention to you as I did to your friend. About payment, my job is my payment. You may cover my expenses as you please. Now please give us the information that will make it possible to help you."

"Oh," she cried. "My fears are based on such small matters. Even that one person who could help me thinks that my problems are only in my own mind. But I believe that you, Mr. Holmes, can see deeply into the unkind human heart. You will be able to tell me how to walk through the dangers I face."

"I will try, madam."

"My name is Helen Stoner. I am living with my stepfather, the oldest member of the Saxon family in England. We were once the richest family in England, but my grandfather, and his father before him wasted our money, so that now we only have a two-hundred-year-old house with a heavy mortgage. My stepfather trained as a doctor and worked in India. After many robberies, he got angry and beat his Indian servant. He was sent to prison and years later returned to England a very unhappy man.

"It was later that my mother married our stepfather; she gave all of her money to him, about 1,000 pounds a year, with a note that some of the money would go to me and my sister at our marriage. My mother died about eight years ago in a train accident, but we had enough money to live comfortably with him. At her death, he took us to live in his family house in the country. My sister and I were twins, so we were always very close and enjoyed each other's company very much there.

"But my stepfather often became very angry. He started to fight with everyone. Twice the police had to come into our house, the fighting was so bad. He was very strong and we were all afraid of him.

"Last week, he hurt a man badly and I had to give him all the money I had to keep him quiet. My stepfather had no friends except the wandering gypsies. Sometimes they came to live on our land in their tents, and other times he even left our home to travel with the gypsies.

"You can understand that my sister and I had little happiness. No servant would stay in our house. We did all the work. Finally, my sister, though she was only thirty years old, died. Her hair was already completely white."

"Your sister is dead, then?"

"She died two years ago. That is what I have come to talk to you about. We had few friends. Occasionally we went to see my mother's sister near Harrow. Julia went there at Christmas two years ago and met a man with whom she became engaged to marry. My father heard of the wedding plans and did not seem displeased. But just before the wedding took place, I lost her."

Until this time, Holmes had had his eyes closed. But at this point, he opened them slightly and looked at his visitor.

"Please explain the details."

"Oh, I can forget none of them. Our house is old, as I said. We lived in only one side of it. There were sitting rooms and then the bedrooms. My father's bedroom was first, my sister's second, and mine, the third. All the doors open into the same hallway."

"I see."

"The windows of the three rooms open out onto a green grassy area. That night, my father had gone to his bedroom early, but my sister could smell cigars which she did not like, from his room, so she came into my room. We talked for a long time about her upcoming wedding, then she stood up to go.

"'Tell me, Helen,' she said, 'have you ever heard anyone whistle in the dead of the night?'

"'Never,' I said.

"'I suppose that you could not whistle in your sleep?'

"'Of course not.'

"'The last few nights, about three o'clock in the morning, I hear someone whistling. It wakes me up. I thought maybe you had heard it, too.'

"'No, it must be the gypsies living on our land.'

"'Yes, maybe.' And she went into her room and turned the lock."

"Did you always lock your doors at night?" Holmes asked her.

"Yes, of course."

"I could not sleep that night. Our souls were so close, being twins. It was raining, and then there was a wild scream of a frightened woman. I knew that it was my sister's voice. I ran from my bed. I heard a whistle, as she had described and then some metal fell. I ran down the hall to my sister's door. It was open. Then my sister appeared in the doorway. Her face was white and her body was shaking. I ran to her and held her in my arms, but she fell to the ground. She looked so strange, but she knew me and said, 'Oh, my God! Helen! It was the band! The speckled band!' She tried to say something else, but could not. She pointed to our father's room, then she was gone. My father came running from his room and tried to help her, but it was too late. That was the end of my dearest sister."

"One moment," said Holmes, "are you sure about this whistle and metallic sound?"

"That is what the coroner asked me. Well, I think I heard it but there was such a terrible storm, maybe it was in my head."

"Was your sister in her clothes?"

"No, in her bedclothes. And in her right hand was a match, and in her left a matchbox."

"So she was lighting a match when the accident happened. What did the coroner say?"

"He could not find any cause for death. I know that the door and the windows were locked. The walls were solid and so were the floors. It is certain that my sister was alone when she met her end. Besides, there were no marks of any violence upon her."

"How about poison?"

"The doctors could find nothing."

"Then what did she die of?"

"Of fear and nervous shock, but I don't know what frightened her."

"Were there gypsies on your land then?"

"Yes, there are almost always some there."

"What do you understand from the 'speckled band' she spoke of?"

"I never knew. Perhaps a band of people, perhaps a kind of hand-kerchief."

Holmes shook his head in disagreement.

"Please continue your explanation."

"During the past two years my life has been very lonely. A month ago, a dear friend asked me to marry him. My father is not against our plan. We hope to be married in the spring. We are repairing our house, and two days ago, my room was broken down, so I moved into my sister's bedroom. I was sleeping in her bed last night. Imagine how frightened I was when I heard the whistle which she heard before her death. I lit a lamp, but there was nothing in my room. I got the train first thing this morning to visit you and seek your advice."

"That is good, but have you told me everything?"

"Yes, all."

"Miss Stoner, you have not. You are protecting your father."

"Why, what do you mean?"

Holmes pushed back the arm of her dress and showed black marks from four fingers and one thumb on her arm.

"You have been treated cruelly."

At this, she turned red. "He does not know his own strength."

Holmes looked into the fire. "There are one thousand details I wish I could know now. But we do not have a moment to lose. If we go to your house immediately, we can see the rooms without your father knowing."

"He will be out of the house all day today. No one is there to disturb you."

"Are you coming, Watson?"

"Of course."

"What are you going to do?" Holmes asked Miss Stoner.

"I have one or two things to do in London, and I will return by the noon train to be there in time for your arrival."

"Then you may expect us in the early afternoon. Will you stay now and join us for breakfast?"

"No, I must go. I feel better now that I have talked to you." She dropped the veil over her face and left the room quietly.

"What do you think, Watson?"

"I cannot guess about this unhappy situation."

"If everything is true, her sister must have been alone when she died."

"But what of the whistles and the strange words of the dying woman?"

"I cannot think."

"When you think about the old man and his friendliness with the gypsies, it is possible that he wanted to prevent her marriage. The band could be the gypsies, or the metal band on the window. But I cannot understand anything. That is why we are going to visit the house today."

Just then a huge man entered our room. He had on a top-hat, a long coat, and a horse whip in his hand. He was so tall his hat touched the ceiling, and his face looked evil.

"Which of you is Holmes?" he asked.

"I am," Holmes said quietly.

"I am Dr. Roylott, of Stoke Moran."

"I see," said Holmes without any surprise.

"Why has my daughter been here to see you? What did she say to you?" he screamed.

"The flowers are blooming nicely this year, aren't they?" Holmes replied.

"Ha! You scoundrel. I have heard of you. You cause trouble."

My friend smiled.

"Don't you cause any trouble in my life. I am a dangerous man." He picked up a tool for the fire and bent it in half. "See that this does not happen to you." And he left the room.

"He seems a friendly person," Holmes said, laughing. "Now we will have breakfast, Watson, and then I will go down to the hospital where I will try to get some information to help us before we take the train."

It was almost one o'clock when Holmes returned. He had a blue sheet of paper with a lot of numbers written on it.

"I have seen the will of his late wife. The total income is now only 750 pounds a year, which means that in the case of marriage each daughter can get only 250 pounds. That means that this fine man would have hardly any money if both daughters married. He has the very strongest reasons for preventing the girl marrying. Now, Watson, we must leave immediately. I would be very grateful to you if you would put your gun in your pocket. That and our toothbrushes are, I think, all that we need to take."

We reached the house easily. There was a bright sun, few clouds, and it was a perfect day, in general. There was a strange contrast between the sweet promise of spring and this ugly work we had to do. My friend was resting, lost in deepest thought. Suddenly he touched my shoulder and pointed over the land.

"Look there!" he said.

We could see an old mansion.

"Stoke Moran?" he asked.

"Yes, that is it," said the driver. "And the fastest way to get to it is to walk across the fields, as the lady is doing."

"And the lady is Miss Stoner? Yes, we shall do as you say."

We crossed over the stile, and went across the fields toward her. Her face was full of joy when she saw us.

"I am so glad you could come. Dr. Roylott is away, and he will not be back until evening."

"We have already met the good man," Holmes said, explaining the morning event.

"Good heavens! He has followed me then. What shall I do?"

"You must be very careful. If he is mean to you tonight, we shall take you away to your aunt's at Harrow. But now, we must use our time wisely."

The building was old with broken windows covered with wooden boards, and blue smoke curling above into the sky. Some workmen were present. Holmes walked around the old house slowly.

"These are the bedrooms as you described them?"

"Yes."

"Are there windows?"

"Yes, but too small for anyone to pass."

"I see. Please go into your sister's bedroom and close the windows tight."

Miss Stoner did so. Holmes tried to open the windows but could not. Even a knife could not be passed through. "Hum, I cannot figure out how anyone could enter the room. We must look inside."

It was a nice little room. A small bed and dressing-table. A brown chair and carpet.

"Please excuse me," he said, and he threw himself down on the floor to examine the wood. He examined the walls in the same way. Then he pulled on the rope over the bed, but there was no bell. There was also a hole in the ceiling connecting this room to the stepfather's bedroom.

"This is a very strange rope," Holmes said. "We shall now look at the inner bedroom."

Dr. Roylott's room was larger, but still plainly furnished. There were many books, an armchair beside the bed and a plain wooden chair.

"What's in here?" Holmes asked, touching the safe.

"Only business papers."

"So you have seen inside?"

"Only years ago, there were business papers."

"Not a cat?"

"No, what a strange idea!"

"Well, here is a dish of milk."

Then he examined the chair carefully and noticed a dog leash tied to one corner of the bed. "Very unusual, is it not, Watson?"

"Yes, sir, very strange."

"I have seen enough now, Miss Stoner. Let us walk outside. It is very important that you follow my advice exactly, ma'am."

"Of course, I shall most certainly do so," she replied.

"Both my friend and I must spend the night in your room."

At this, both Miss Stoner and I looked at him in astonishment.

"You must stay in your old room; say that you have a headache when your stepfather returns home. Open the windows and put your lamp in the window, then go to your room even though it is being torn up by the builders. I think you can manage there for one night."

"Oh, yes, easily."

"The rest you will leave in our hands."

"But what will you do?"

"We shall spend the night in your room and investigate the cause of this noise which you have heard."

"I believe that you already know the cause."

"I believe I do."

"Please tell me."

"I will have proof before I speak, please."

"Well, am I right in thinking that she died of fright?"

"No, I do not think so. I think there was a real cause. Now, we must leave you, Miss Stoner. If your father saw us, our visit would be useless. Please excuse us. Be brave, for if you do as I have told you, you may be sure that the danger will soon be over."

Sherlock Holmes and I took a room at a nearby inn and from our window we saw Dr. Roylott pass by at dusk.

As we were waiting at the inn, Holmes turned to me and said, "You know Watson, I am afraid to take you with me. It is a dangerous evening I have planned."

"Can I help you?"

"Very much."

"Then I shall go with you. But I do not know what the danger is you saw."

"It is odd that the rope and hole in the ceiling are added to the room, and shortly afterward the woman who sleeps there dies. Didn't you notice anything odd about the bed?"

"No."

"It was fixed to the floor. Have you ever seen that before?"

"I cannot say that I have... Holmes! I see what you are saying."

"Well, the night will be frightening enough. Let us now think of something more cheerful."

The house became dark about nine o'clock. Two hours passed slowly and then just at eleven, a single bright light appeared in the window.

"We must go," Holmes said.

A moment later we were on a dark road, with a cold wind in our faces. We had no difficulty entering the area of the house. Soon we had taken off our shoes and had climbed into the bedroom.

"We must sit in the dark. Do not go to sleep. Your very life depends on it," Holmes whispered to me. "I will sit on the bed and you sit in that chair."

I did as he said and laid my gun on the table. Holmes laid his cane on the bed.

I will never forget that night. I sat wide awake. I knew that Holmes was a few feet away, also wide awake. We waited in complete darkness. One, two and three o'clock came and went. Nothing happened. Suddenly a light was lit in the doctor's room. There was a smell of hot metal. Then another half hour passed. Suddenly, we heard a very soft sound, like steam from a kettle. At this Holmes sprang from the bed, lit the lamp and began waving his cane at the hole in the ceiling.

"Do you see it, Watson?" he cried out.

But I saw nothing — only that his face was white and frightened.

When he stopped, there was a terrible cry from the next room. We heard later that people in the village got out of their beds, it struck such coldness in the hearts of those who heard.

"What does that mean?" I asked.

"It means it's all over," Holmes replied.

"We are going into the doctor's room, now."

We found the safe door open with Dr. Roylott sitting dead in the chair. He was wearing a strange yellow band, with brownish speckles, around his head.

"The band, the speckled band!" whispered Holmes.

But it was not cloth. It was a yellow snake that had wound itself around the man's head.

"It is a swamp adder!" cried Holmes, "the deadliest snake in India. The doctor died within ten seconds of being bitten. Violence does come back to the violent. The schemer falls into the pit he digs for another. Let us put the snake back in his cage and take Miss Stoner to a safe place. Then we must tell the police what has happened."

These are the facts of the death of Dr. Roylott of Stoke Moran. We took the daughter to her aunt's, who gave her all the care she needed. Then the slow process of the official investigation began. The conclusion was that the doctor met his death while he was playing with a dangerous pet.

On the train back to London the next day, Holmes told me that he had gotten all the wrong ideas to begin with.

"Then I realized that the danger was not from the window or the door, but from the hole in the wall. The bed was fixed to the floor so that the rope could be used as a bridge for something to be passed through the wall and come down to the bed. The idea of a snake instantly occurred to me. Using a poison that is not commonly known to science was the idea that such a cruel man would have. Only a very sharp-eyed coroner would see two little holes made by a snake bite. The doctor trained the snake to return to his bedroom when it had completed its work.

"I had examined his chair. It was clear that he used to stand on it. I had no doubts when I saw the milk, the leash and the safe. The metallic noise Miss Stoner heard was the door of the safe closing as her father replaced the snake into its cage. Then I waited for the snake to come through the hole. When I heard its hiss, as I am sure you did, I lit the lamp and attacked it."

"So it turned back into the doctor's bedroom."

"And attacked him instead of us. In this way, I am responsible for the man's death, but I cannot say that I feel very sad about it or that it will weigh heavily on my conscience."

06

Silver Blaze

シルバー・ブレーズ

読み始める前に

Silver Blaze シルバー・ブレーズ（白銀号事件）

56の短編のうち13番目に発表された
1892年12月号のストランド・マガジン初出
1893年発行の「シャーロック・ホームズの思い出」に収録

［主な登場人物］

Sherlock Holmes シャーロック・ホームズ　世界的に有名な私立探偵。優れた観察眼と推理力を有する。ロンドンのベーカー街221Bに下宿している。

Watson ジョン・H・ワトソン　医師。ホームズの相棒でこの物語の語り手。ベーカー街221Bでホームズと同居している。

John Straker ジョン・ストレーカー　行方不明となった馬シルバー・ブレーズの調教師。のちに遺体で発見される。

Colonel Ross ロス大佐　行方不明となった馬の持ち主。ホームズに調査を依頼する。

Inspector Gregory グレゴリー警部　事件を担当する警部。

Fitzroy Simpson フィッツロイ・シンプソン　ストレーカー殺しの容疑者として逮捕された。

Silas Brown サイラス・ブラウン　対抗馬デズボロの厩舎の調教師。

［あらすじ］

　ロス大佐が所有する有名な競走馬の失踪とその調教師の殺害をめぐる物語。ホームズが相棒のワトソンとともに、この不可解な事件を調査をするため、イギリスのダートムーアへ向かうところから話は始まる。競走馬シルバーブレイズ号が、重要なレースの数日前に厩舎から姿を消した。調教師のジョン・ストレーカーも近くの茂みの中で頭を殴られ、遺体で発見される。遺体の右手には血のついた凶器、左手にはスカーフのようなものが握られていた。警察はそのスカーフをしていた若いフィッツロイ・シンプソンを容疑者として逮捕した。

［総単語数］7,562語

Silver Blaze

"I am afraid, Watson, that I must go," said Holmes as we sat down to breakfast together one morning.

"Go! Where to?"

"To Dartmoor; to King's Pyland."

I was not surprised. Indeed, my only surprise was that Holmes was not yet working on this case. All of England was talking about it. For a whole day my good friend walked around the room, smoking his pipe. He was thinking deeply and didn't hear anything I said. There were many newspapers in the room. He quickly looked through them one at a time. Then he threw them into a corner. He was quiet but I knew what he was thinking about. There was one problem which the public wanted an answer to. The Wessex Cup is a famous horse race in England. The horse expected to win that race had disappeared, and the trainer was murdered. So when Holmes suddenly decided to go to the scene of the crime, I expected it.

"I would be very happy to go down there with you," I said.

"My dear Watson, of course I want you to come. And I think that it will be interesting for you. This case will be different from any other. We must leave now to catch our train at Paddington. I will tell you more as we travel. Oh, please bring your excellent field-glasses."

And so one hour later we were sitting in a first class train to Exeter. Sherlock Holmes was wearing his famous hat with ear covers on top of his famous head. He was quickly looking through a small group of newspapers which he bought at the station. It was after the city of Reading that he finally finished with them. He offered me a cigar.

"We are moving well," said he, looking out the window, then at his watch. "Our present speed is eighty-five and a half kilometers per hour."

"I have not seen the kilometer markers," I said.

"Nor have I. But the distance between the telegraph sticks is sixty meters. Guessing the speed is easy. Tell me, Watson, what do you know of the murder of John Straker and the disappearance of Silver Blaze?"

"Only what the newspapers, the Telegraph and the Chronicle, say about it."

"It is one of those cases where there are few new clues. It requires careful consideration of the facts already known. Most people in this country know something about the case. Everyone has an idea or two about what happened. But mostly they are guessing. The difficulty here will be to separate the truth from the guesses. We must know the true facts of the case before we can form an idea. On Tuesday evening I received two telegrams. One from Colonel Ross, the owner of the horse; and one from Inspector Gregory, the policeman on the case. Both men have asked for my help."

"Tuesday evening!" I said, surprised. "This is Thursday morning. Why didn't you leave yesterday?"

"Because I made a mistake, my dear Watson. I'm afraid I make more mistakes than you realize. I could not believe that the most famous horse in England could not be found. Especially in Dartmoor where there are few people. Yesterday I expected to hear that the horse was found. Also, that the person who took the horse was the murderer of John Straker. However, no horse was found. A young Mr. Fitzroy Simpson was arrested by the police. I decided it was time to take action."

"Do you have any clear ideas about the case?"

"At least I know about the important facts of the case. I will tell them to you, Watson."

I sat back in my seat and smoked. Holmes used his fingers to count the facts.

"Silver Blaze," said he, "is from the Somomy farm. He is a wonderful horse, like his father and grandfather before him. He is now five years old. He has won almost every important race in the country for Colonel Ross, his owner. Before the crime, he was the number one horse to win the Wessex Cup. The racing public loves him and usually bet on him to win. The bet is now three to one that he will win. Of course, where there is money there is danger. Many other people don't want him to race next Tuesday.

"Silver Blaze's stable is at King's Pyland. There are people there to guard him all day long. The trainer, John Straker, is an ex-jockey. He used to ride for Colonel Ross. He has served the colonel for five years as a jockey and for seven as a trainer. He has always been hard-working and honest. There are three young men who work for Straker. They are the stable-boys. The farm is a small one with only four horses. Each night, one of these young men stays up guarding the stable while the others sleep. All three are good, honest men. John Straker was married. He and his wife lived about two hundred meters from the stables. They had no children. However, they had a maid. The country around the stable is very lonely. It is a wild, natural land where no people live. It is called a moor. About one kilometer to the north of King's Pyland there is a small group of houses. The town of Tavistock lies about three kilometers to the west. Across the moor, also about three kilometers, is a larger stable called Mapleton. It belongs to Lord Backwater, and the trainer is Silas Brown. In every other direction there is moor. Only gypsies live there.

"The crime occurred last Monday night. The horses had been run and watered as usual. The stables were locked at nine o'clock. Two of the young men walked to the trainer's house and ate dinner. The third, Ned Hunter, guarded the horses. A few minutes after nine o'clock the maid, Edith Baxter, brought Ned's dinner to the stables. It was a meat dish. She brought nothing to drink. There was water at the stables and the rule is that the person on guard drinks only water. The maid carried a light with her because it was very dark there in the moor.

"Edith Baxter was thirty meters from the stables when she heard a man call her. He came from the darkness and asked her to stop. He came near to her light. She saw that he was a gentleman, well dressed, with a hat. He carried a heavy walking-stick. His manner seemed nervous. She thought he was a man in his thirties.

"'Can you tell me where I am?' he asked. 'I had almost decided to sleep on the moor until I saw your light.'

"'You are close to the King's Pyland training stables,' said she.

"'Oh, really! What luck!' he cried. 'I understand that there is a stable-boy who sleeps there every night. Perhaps you are carrying his dinner to him. I have a favor to ask you. It will be worth a new dress for you.' He took a piece of white note-paper from his coat pocket. Then he said, 'Give this to the boy and you shall have a pretty dress.'

"She was a little afraid of him and ran towards the window at the stable. She usually passed the food through this window. It was already opened and Ned Hunter was sitting at a table inside. She began to tell him what happened with the stranger. Just then, the stranger walked up.

"'Good-evening,' said he, looking through the window. 'I wanted to talk to you.' The maid says that she noticed the white paper in his hand as he spoke to Ned.

"'What business have you here?' asked the young man.

"'It's business that may pay you nicely,' said the other. 'You have two horses in the Wessex Cup — Silver Blaze and Bayard. Give me some information about them and you may become rich. Is it a fact that Bayard's weight is down, and that he's faster than ever?'

"'I'm not going to tell you anything!' cried the boy. 'You're not welcome in King's Pyland. Get out!' He jumped up, ran across the stable and got the guard dog. The girl ran towards the house. While she ran she looked back. She saw the stranger put his hand through the window. A minute later, however, when Hunter ran outside with the dog, the stranger was gone. Hunter looked all around the stable, but found nothing."

"One moment," I asked. "Did the stable-boy, when he ran out with the dog, leave the door open behind him?"

"Excellent, Watson, excellent!" answered my companion. "That is an important point. I sent a wire to Dartmoor yesterday to ask the same question. The boy did lock the door before he left. The window, by the way, was not large enough for a man to get through.

"Hunter waited until the other two boys returned. Then he sent a message to the trainer and told him what happened. Straker was very surprised to hear the story. I don't think he realized how important it was though. He began to feel somewhat uneasy, however. Mrs. Straker woke up that night at one o'clock and found her husband dressing. She asked him what he was doing. He replied that he was thinking about the horses and could not sleep. He wanted to go to the stables to see them. She asked him to stay at home because she could hear the rain falling outside. But he put on his raincoat and walked out.

"Mrs. Straker got up at seven in the morning and saw that her husband had not yet returned. She quickly dressed, called the maid, and went to the stables. The door was open; inside, Hunter seemed to be sleeping in a chair. Silver Blaze was gone, and so was Straker.

"Hunter had been given a powerful drug. The ladies could not wake him. They went to wake the other two boys in another building nearby. These two were deep sleepers and heard nothing during the night. The two ladies and the two young men went to look for the horse and trainer. They hoped that the man and animal were just riding nearby. But when they walked up the hill to look out on the moor they could see no trace of the horse or the trainer. However, a few hundred meters away they saw something moving.

"John Straker's overcoat was hanging on a small tree. It was blowing in the wind. Just beyond the coat was a small valley. At the bottom of this valley lay the dead body of the trainer. His head was broken by a powerful hit from a heavy object. There was also a deep cut in his leg. It appeared that he had fought against someone. In his right hand he held a knife covered in blood. In his left hand was a red and black neck-cloth. The maid remembered that the stranger who came to the stables wore the same neck-cloth. Hunter later recovered from the drug and also remembered the neck-cloth on the stranger. Hunter was also sure that the stranger put the drug into his dinner while standing at the window. As to the missing horse, he was probably there with Straker when the murder happened. There were many marks of the horse's feet in the ground. But he disappeared. Money has been offered for his return. All the gypsies of Dartmoor know about it. Still there has been no news. Finally, police found the drug, called opium, in Hunter's dinner.

"Those are the main facts of the case, Watson. I will now tell you what the police have done.

"Inspector Gregory, who is in charge of this case, is a very good policeman. He does not, however, have the intelligence of a great detective. When he arrived he quickly found and arrested the stranger who visited the stables. His name is Fitzroy Simpson and he came to the moors for a holiday. He is a man from a good, upper-class family in London. However, he has a problem with betting. He has lost much of his family's money by betting on horses. The police looked into his betting-book. They found a five thousand pound bet by him against Silver Blaze. After he was arrested he told police that he only wanted some information about the King's Pyland horses. And also about Desborough, another excellent horse, trained by Silas Brown at the Mapleton stables. His story is the same as that of Hunter and the maid. However, he said he did nothing wrong. He only wanted some good information. When asked about the red and black neck cloth he was wearing, he could not answer. He simply didn't know how it came to be with the murdered man. He was out in the rain because his clothes were wet. And his heavy walking-stick could have been used to hit the trainer and kill him. However, he was not cut or hurt in any way. Nor were his clothes. Yet it seems that Straker cut someone with his knife. And that's everything I know, Watson. If you can help me at all then please do."

I had listened with great interest to what Holmes told me. I knew many of the facts myself. But I still did not have a clear idea.

"Is it not possible," I said, "that the cut on Straker's leg came from his own knife?"

"It is more than possible; it is probable," said Holmes. "That means an important point against Simpson disappears."

"I still don't understand what the police think happened," said I.

"I believe that there are problems with every idea about this murder," said my friend. "The police believe that Simpson drugged the boy. Then he somehow got inside the locked stable. He then took the horse. The piece that a horse wears over his head, called the bridle, is missing from the stable. The police believe Simpson took that too. Then, leaving the door open behind him, he took the horse away across the moor. There he was met by the trainer. They had a fight, naturally. Simpson hit the trainer's head with his heavy stick but was not hurt himself by the knife. Then the thief either took the horse to a secret place or the horse ran away. Perhaps the horse is walking the moor now. This is what the police think, although it does not seem probable to me. However, I shall very quickly try my own ideas when we arrive."

It was evening before we reached the little town of Tavistock. It lies in the middle of Dartmoor. Two gentlemen were waiting for us at the station. One, a big man with large blue eyes, and long, light-colored hair. The other a small man, very well dressed, with eyeglasses. The first was Inspector Gregory, a man becoming quite famous in the English police force. The second was Colonel Ross, the famous sportsman. "I am so happy you have come down, Mr. Holmes," said the colonel. "The inspector here has done a lot already. But I also wanted your help to find poor Straker's murderer and to recover my horse."

"Has there been any fresh news?" asked Holmes.

"I'm sorry to say very little," answered the inspector. "We have an open carriage waiting for you outside. I'm sure you would like to see the place before it gets dark. We can talk along the way."

A minute later we were all seated and rolling through the Devonshire countryside. Inspector Gregory was talking at length about the case. Holmes sometimes asked questions or said something. Colonel Ross sat back in his seat with his arms crossed and listened. I, too, listened to the two detectives. Gregory was telling his idea of the crime, just as Holmes had said in the train.

"There is a good case against Fitzroy Simpson. I believe he is our man. But at the same time I realize that we can't prove anything yet."

"How about Straker's knife?"

"We now believe that he hurt himself while falling."

"My friend Dr. Watson said the same thing to me earlier. It seems to favor Simpson."

"Quite right. He has neither a knife nor any sign of a cut. But there are several facts against him. One, he was betting against Silver Blaze. Therefore he was interested in the horse's disappearing. Two, he probably drugged the stable-boy. Three, he was out in the storm. Four, he carried a heavy walking-stick. And five, his neck-cloth was found in the dead man's hands. I really think we have enough information on him as the murderer."

Holmes disagreed. "No, there are still too many questions," said he. "Why did he take the horse out of the stable? If he wanted to hurt it, he could have hurt it there. And what about a second key? Has one been found? Who sold him the powdered opium? And especially, how could he hide such a famous horse? He is a stranger in this area. And what did he say about the piece of paper he wanted to give to the stable-boy?"

"He says that it was a ten-pound note. We did find one in his pocket. But there are answers to your other questions. He is not a stranger to this area. He has stayed in Tavistock two times in the summer. The opium was probably bought in London. It is easy to hide a key, or throw it away. Also, there are many places to hide a horse on the moor."

"And what does he say about the neck-cloth?"

"He agrees that it is his. He says he lost it. But there is a piece of new information about his taking the horse from the stable."

Holmes listened closely.

"We can prove that a group of gypsies were staying less than a kilometer from the stable on the night of the murder. The next morning they were gone. Surely there was a plan between Simpson and these gypsies. Maybe he took the horse to them and they have the horse now."

"It is possible."

"We are looking all over the moor for these gypsies. I have looked at every stable and house in and around Tavistock."

"There is another training-stable nearby, I understand?"

"Yes, that's true. Mapleton stables. And their horse, Desborough, is racing against Silver Blaze in the Cup. The trainer, Silas Brown, is no friend of John Straker. Also, Brown is known to make very large bets on the race. However, we have looked at the stables very carefully, and found nothing."

Holmes sat back in the carriage, and the detectives stopped talking. A few minutes later we arrived at a small red and white country house by the road. In the distance, across a field, was a long gray building. In every other direction was the moor. The churches of Tavistock and the Mapleton stables could also be seen beyond the hills. We all got out of the carriage, except Holmes. He continued to look at the sky, thinking deeply. Finally, I touched his arm and he jumped up.

"Excuse me," said he, turning to us, "I was just thinking." There was a look in his eye that I knew very well. Holmes probably had a fresh idea about the crime, though I don't know how.

"Perhaps you would like to go at once to the scene of the crime, Mr. Holmes?" asked Gregory.

"I think I would rather stay here and ask a question or two. Straker was brought back here, right?"

"Yes, his body lies upstairs in the house."

"He has worked for you many years, Colonel Ross?"

"Yes, he has always been an excellent worker."

"I'm sure you made a list, Inspector, of the belongings he was carrying when he died?"

"Of course. These things are inside if you would like to see them."

"Yes, I'd be glad to." We all walked into the front room and sat around a middle table. The inspector unlocked a square metal box and placed the belongings on the table. There was a pipe, some tobacco, a silver watch, some money, some papers, a pencil case, and a very thin, special knife marked Weiss & Co., London.

"This is an unusual knife," said Holmes, lifting it up and looking at it closely. "Yes, I see the blood. I suppose this is the knife found in the dead man's hand. Watson, what do you know about this kind of knife."

"It is used by doctors to remove very small objects from the body."

"I thought so. A very thin, fine knife for very fine work. It is surely a strange thing for a man to carry, especially as it does not close."

"The knife's end was protected by a piece of wood," said the inspector. "We found the wood near the body. His wife tells us that the knife was on a table in their bedroom. Straker picked it up when he went out that night. It is a poor weapon, but perhaps it is the only weapon he had at that moment."

"Very possibly. How about these papers?"

"Three of them are from sellers of horse food. One is a letter from Colonel Ross. This other is a note from a dressmaker asking for payment of thirty-seven pounds. It is from a Madame Lesurier of Bond Street, to William Derbyshire. Mrs. Straker tells us that Derbyshire is a friend of her husband's. Sometimes his letters were sent here."

"It appears that Mrs. Derbyshire likes expensive clothes," said Holmes, looking at the note. "That is a lot of money for a single dress. Well, there seems to be nothing more to learn here. Let's continue to the scene of the crime."

As we left the sitting-room, a woman appeared. She stepped forward and put her hand on the inspector's arm. Her face was thin, tired-looking, and fearful.

"Have you got them? Have you found them yet?" she cried.

"No, Mrs. Straker. But Mr. Holmes has come from London to help us. We shall do everything possible."

"Surely I met you in Plymouth at a garden party a short time ago, Mrs. Straker?" said Holmes.

"No, sir; you are mistaken."

"Dear me! Why, I was sure it was you. You wore a fancy white dress with bird and flower figures."

"I never had such a dress, sir," answered the lady.

"Ah, well, my mistake then. I'm sorry," said Holmes, who then followed the inspector outside. A short walk across the moor brought us to the small valley where the body was found. Nearby was the small tree on which the coat was found hanging.

"There was no wind that night, I understand," said Holmes.

"No, only heavy rain."

"In that case, the coat was not blown onto the tree. It was put there."

"Yes, it was laid across the tree."

"The ground here seems pushed down. I suppose that many people have walked here since the crime, Monday night."

"We put a cloth cover on the ground. Everyone stood on that."

"Excellent."

"In this bag I have three shoes. One worn by Straker, one worn by Fitzroy Simpson, and one of the horseshoes worn by Silver Blaze."

"My dear Inspector, well done!" Holmes said taking the bag. He then walked down into the little valley and onto the cover. He lay down on his front side, his face near the ground. He looked very, very carefully at the mud, studying everything. "Oh!" he said suddenly. "What's this?" In his hand was a small candle.

"I don't know why we didn't find it earlier," said the inspector.

"It was in the mud, almost impossible to see. I only saw it because I was looking for it."

"What! You expected to find this little candle?"

"I thought it possible, yes."

He then took the shoes from the bag to see if there were the same marks in the mud. Then he came back up to us and looked around the plants and trees for a few minutes.

"I'm afraid there are no more marks," said the inspector. "My men and I have looked very closely for over a hundred meters in every direction."

"Really!" said Holmes, standing up again. "Well, just the same, I would like to take a little walk over the moor before it becomes dark. This way I will know the area better tomorrow. I also want to take this horseshoe, to bring me luck."

Colonel Ross watched my friend's unusual method of working. He seemed a little nervous and unhappy. He looked at his watch. "Can you come back with me, Inspector? There are several things I'd like to ask you. I also want your opinion about whether or not to take my horse's name out of the race."

"Certainly not!" cried Holmes. "I would leave the horse in."

"Thank you for your opinion, sir," said the colonel. "You will find us at Straker's house when you finish your walk. We can drive together to Tavistock."

He and the inspector walked away. Holmes and I walked slowly over the moor. The sun was setting. The land became rich in brown and gold colors from the evening light. But my friend was not looking at the natural beauty.

"Here's what I think, Watson," he said at last. "For the moment, let's forget the question of who killed John Straker. Instead, let's think only of finding the horse. Now, supposing he ran away after the crime. Where could he have gone? Horses don't like to be alone. On his own he probably decided to return to King's Pyland or go over to

Mapleton. Why should he run wild upon the moor? Surely, someone would have seen him by now. And why should gypsies take him. They don't want trouble with the police. They could never sell such a famous horse."

"Where is he, then?"

"I already said he must have gone to either King's Pyland or Mapleton. He's not at King's Pyland, so he must be at Mapleton. For now, let's believe that he is there, all right. This part of the moor is hard and dry. But over towards Mapleton it is lower and wetter. It was very wet Monday night. If the horse did go over there then we will find his footmarks in the mud."

We were walking along very quickly as we spoke. Soon we came to the wet, low area. Holmes asked me to walk down to the right, while he went left. Two minutes later, I heard him shouting. I ran to him. There was the mark of a horse's foot in the earth. He took the horseshoe from his coat and placed it over the mark. It was the same!

"See the value of intelligence," said Holmes. "We thought this was possible, we acted, and now we find we are right. Let us continue."

We crossed the wet bottom-land and walked several hundred meters across dry, hard ground. Again we found the horse's marks. Then we lost them for half a kilometer. But we found them again very near Mapleton. It was Holmes who saw them first. He pointed to them happily. Next to the horse's mark was the footmark of a man.

"The horse was not alone," I cried.

"Quite right. It was alone before. Oh, what's this?"

The marks of horse and man suddenly turned in the direction of King's Pyland. Holmes and I began to follow it. His eyes were on the ground. My eyes, however, looked over to the side. I was surprised to see a second set of marks coming back again towards us.

"Good eyes, Watson," said Holmes when I showed him. "You saved us a long walk in a big circle. Let's follow those new marks."

We did not go far. The marks ended at the gate of Mapleton stables. As we came near, a stable-boy saw us and ran to us.

"We don't want any visitors here," said he.

"I only wish to ask a question," said Holmes. "Will I find your master, Mr. Silas Brown, here early tomorrow morning?"

"I'm sure you will, sir. He is always the first one up. Oh, there he is now sir. I see him coming."

A moment later a very unfriendly-looking older man arrived with a stick in his hand.

"What's this Dawson!" he cried. "No talking to strangers! Now go back to work." He turned to us. "What do you want here?"

"Ten minutes talk with you, good sir," replied Holmes in a very sweet voice.

"I've no time to talk to every stranger who happens by. Now go away or you may find my dogs following you."

Holmes then spoke very softly in the man's ear. Silas Brown suddenly turned very red and lost control.

"It's not true! It's not true!" he shouted. "It's a lie!"

"Very well. Shall we talk about it here in public or inside your office?"

"All right, come in if you want."

Holmes smiled. "I will only be a few minutes, Watson," said he. "After you, Mr. Brown."

It was twenty minutes. The sun began to set. Soon it became dark. Holmes and the trainer returned. There was a great change in Silas Brown during that time. His face was rather pale and nervous. His hands were shaking a little. He was no longer unfriendly. He was afraid.

"I shall do as you say. I shall do it," said he.

"There must be no mistake," said Holmes, looking at him directly.

"Oh no, there will be no mistake. It will be there. Should I change it first or not?"

Holmes thought a little then suddenly began laughing. "No, don't," he said. "I shall write to you about it. Meanwhile, no games or surprises or — "

"Oh, you can trust me, you can trust me!"

"Yes, I think I can. Well, you will hear from me tomorrow." Holmes quickly turned around and we walked off towards King's Pyland.

"Not a very likeable man," said Holmes as we walked along.

"He has the horse, then?"

"Yes. At first he tried to tell me he didn't. However, I then began to tell him what he had done that morning. I seemed to know all the facts about his actions. Ha ha! He was very surprised, Watson. He really believed that I had been watching him. Did you see the square shape of his shoes? They are the same as the footmarks in the ground. I told him that, as usual, he got up very early in the morning and went outside. In the distance, he saw a strange horse on the moor. He went out to it and was very surprised to see that it was Silver Blaze. At first, he began to walk the horse back towards King's Pyland. But then he changed his mind. He thought that he could hide the horse at Mapleton until the race was over. Then his own horse might win the Cup. He would win his large bet. Of course, he is afraid of the police. He will do anything I ask."

"But the police looked in his stables?"

"Oh, Watson, an old trainer like Brown can easily hide a horse."

"But aren't you afraid to leave the horse with him? He might hurt Silver Blaze."

"Dear Watson, he will guard the horse with his life. He knows that it is his only hope of saving himself from the police."

"I don't think Colonel Ross will be very kind to him if he discovers the truth."

"Colonel Ross will not know. I have my own methods. I tell as much or as little as I please. That is the good thing about being a detective. By the way, did you watch Colonel Ross' manner towards me? He seems not to trust me completely. I feel like playing a little game with the colonel. Please say nothing about the horse."

"I won't."

"Of course, this matter is not as important as the question of who killed John Straker."

"And now you will work on that?"

"Not really, Watson. I think we shall take the night train to London."

I couldn't believe what I heard. We had only been in Dartmoor for a few hours, and the case was starting well. How could we stop now and return? I didn't understand. He said no more until we were back in the trainer's house. The colonel and inspector were waiting for us.

"My friend and I will return to London by the nightexpress," said Holmes. "We have enjoyed the fresh air of Dartmoor."

The inspector opened his eyes in wide surprise. The colonel looked angry.

"So you already stop trying to find poor Straker's murderer?" said the colonel.

"Well, there are some big problems," said Holmes. "However, I have every hope that your horse will race on Tuesday. I also hope your jockey is ready. May I please have a photograph of John Straker?"

The inspector took one from a group of papers and gave it to Holmes.

"Ah, Gregory, you have everything I need. Please wait here just a moment. I have a question I want to ask the maid."

"I must say that I'm not happy about our famous London detective," said Colonel Ross when Holmes had left. "I do not think we are close to solving this crime."

"Well, he has promised that your horse will run," said I.

"Yes, he did say that. But I would rather have the horse."

My friend returned before I could say anything else to the colonel.

"Now, gentlemen," said he, "we are quite ready to go to Tavistock."

As we entered the carriage, a stable-boy held the door open for us. Holmes suddenly had an idea and he asked the boy a question.

"You have some sheep on the farm too. Who takes care of these sheep?"

"I do, sir."

"Have you noticed anything wrong with them lately?"

"Well, sir, there is something. Three of them can't walk anymore."

I could see that Holmes was very happy to learn this. He put his hands together and smiled broadly.

"A guess, Watson, a guess," said he, touching my arm. "Gregory, I believe you should think about the sheep. Go ahead, driver!"

Colonel Ross still looked unhappy with my friend. The inspector, however, was very interested.

"You consider that to be important?" he asked.

"Very much so."

"Is there anything else?"

"The strange action of the dog in the night."

"But the dog did nothing that night."

"Yes, that is the strange part," said Holmes.

Four days later Holmes and I were again in the train. This time we were going to Winchester to see the Wessex Cup race. Colonel Ross met us at the station as planned. We drove in his carriage to the race course outside the town. His face was rather angry and his manner cold.

"I have seen nothing of my horse," said he.

"I suppose that you would know him when you saw him?" asked Holmes.

The colonel became very angry. "What kind of foolish question is that? I have owned horses for over twenty years," said he. "Even a child would know Silver Blaze with the large white spot above his eyes."

"How is the betting?"

"Well, that is the strange part. Yesterday, it was possible to bet at fifteen to one. But the price has become shorter and shorter. Today, it is hardly three to one."

"Hum!" said Holmes. "Somebody knows something, that is clear."

The carriage passed through the crowd and entered the gate. There was a large sign with all the race and betting information.

Wessex Cup   Four and five year olds

Winner, 1000 pounds   Second, 300 pounds

Third, 200 pounds   New Course (Two Kilometers)

1. Mr. Heath Newton's "The Negro." Red cap. Cinnamon jacket.
2. Colonel Wardlaw's "Pugilist." Pink cap. Blue and black jacket.
3. Lord Backwater's "Desborough." Yellow cap and jacket.
4. Colonel Ross's "Silver Blaze." Black cap. Red jacket.
5. Duke of Balmoral's "Iris." Yellow and black stripes.
6. Lord Singleford's "Rasper." Purple cap. Black jacket.

"We took out our other horse, Bayard. We put all our hopes on your promise, Mr. Holmes," said the colonel. "Oh my, what is that? Silver Blaze is favored?"

"Five to four against Silver Blaze!" shouted the betters inside the ring. "Five to four against Silver Blaze! Five to fifteen against

Desborough! Five to four on the field!"

"All six numbers are up," I cried.

"All six there? Then my horse is running," cried the colonel happily. "But I don't see him. He hasn't passed by."

"Only five have gone by. Here is the sixth. It must be him."

"That's not my horse!" cried the owner. "He doesn't have any white hair on his body. What have you done, Holmes?"

"Well, well, let's just wait and see how he does," said my friend softly. For a few minutes he looked through my field-glasses. "Ah, an excellent start to the race!" he cried suddenly. "There they are coming around the turn!"

From our position we had an excellent view of the race. The horses came up the straight. The six horses were all very close together. At one point the yellow colors of the Mapleton Stable were in front. Soon, however, Desborough looked tired and began falling back. Then the colonel's horse began to strongly move ahead of the others. He reached the finish at least six lengths ahead of Desborough. The Duke of Balmoral's Iris came in a distant third.

"We've won, we've won!," shouted the colonel. "I can't believe it. And I don't understand what has happened. Surely Holmes, you can tell me now what is going on."

"Of course, Colonel, you will know everything. Let's all go together to the winner's circle and see your horse." We arrived at the little circle for family and friends. "Here he is, Colonel. If you wash his face and his legs with wine and water, you will see that he is the same Silver Blaze."

"My God, what a surprise!"

"I found him with someone who tried to hide him. I decided to let him race even though his white spots were covered with paint."

"My dear sir, you are wonderful. The horse looks happy and

healthy. He has never run faster. I am so sorry for not believing you could find my horse. I thank you for your service. However, we must still discover John Straker's murderer."

"I have done that," said Holmes quietly.

The colonel and I looked at him in great surprise. "You know who he is! Where is he, then?"

"He is here."

"Here! Where?"

"With me at this moment."

The colonel became angry once again. "Please don't play games, Mr. Holmes. If you think for one minute that I would murder my own..."

Sherlock Holmes laughed. "No, Colonel, I'm not saying that you are the murderer. The real murderer is directly behind you." He stepped to the horse and put his hand on the horse's neck.

"The horse!" cried both the colonel and myself.

"Yes, the horse. I must say, however, that Silver Blaze only protected himself. Your John Straker was not a man to be trusted. But excuse me, please, the next race is beginning and I must place a bet. We shall talk more about this case later."

We took the train back to London that night. Colonel Ross and I listened to Holmes talk about the case during our trip.

"Before going to Devonshire I must say that most of my ideas about the case were wrong. There were clues that I gathered from reading the newspaper, but I didn't understand their importance. I believed that Fitzroy Simpson was the murderer and horse thief. Of course, more information was needed. It was when we arrived at King's Pyland that I first realized an important fact. Do you remember when we were in the car and I seemed lost in thought? Well, I was thinking about the powdered opium being put into the stable-boy's dinner.

Opium has a taste. The food that night was curry. Curry has a strong taste. Most food could not hide the taste of opium, but curry can. It is not possible that Fitzroy Simpson knew about the curry dinner. Therefore I didn't believe that Simpson put the opium in Ned Hunter's dish. Then I began to think about Straker and his wife. They are the only two people who could choose curry for dinner. Everyone in the house ate curry that night. But opium was added only to the stable-boy's dish. How? Did they put in the opium without the maid knowing?

"Before I knew that answer, I thought of something else. What about the dog? He was in the stable when Simpson came. Usually, he makes loud noises when a stranger comes. However, late that night, when Silver Blaze was taken from the stable, the dog was completely quiet. Why? Because the visitor was someone the dog knew well!

"At this point I was almost sure that John Straker went to the stables to get Silver Blaze. His purpose was not good. Yet I didn't know what he wanted. There have been other cases where trainers bet against their own horses in a race. They have made a lot of money. Often, they tell the jockey to go slower. Sometimes they drug the horse. There are many ways to lose a race. But what was it here? I hoped that the belongings found on Straker's body would tell me.

"And they did. That very special knife, used by doctors, was the biggest clue. It was not a weapon, surely. No, it is used to make very careful cuts in the body. And that night it was used to cut the horse. Colonel Ross, you are a man of experience with horses. You know it is possible to make a very, very, small cut beneath the skin on a horse's leg. A cut that is impossible to see. Afterwards, the horse would have a little problem running well. People might think the horse was ill. Later, the horse would recover and be fine again."

"Straker, you devil!" cried the colonel.

"We know why John Straker took the horse out on the moor.

Because the horse would make a loud crying noise when it felt the knife. That would wake up everyone sleeping in the house. It was necessary to do it in the open air."

"I have been a fool!" cried the colonel. "Of course that is why he needed a candle."

"I now knew the method of his crime. While looking through his belongings I also discovered the reason why he did this. There was another clue. It was the note from a dressmaker asking for payment. This note was for a Mr. Derbyshire. Why was Straker carrying this note? The reason, I decided, is because Straker had two lives. There was no Derbyshire. The note told me that there was a lady in the case. A lady with expensive taste. Trainers don't usually have much money. Straker probably was unable to buy twenty pound dresses for his wife. I asked Mrs. Straker about the dress and I believe she knew nothing. I then took a photograph of John Straker along with the street number of the dressmaker.

"After that, all was plain. Straker took the horse to a small valley on the moor where the candle light could not be seen. Simpson, while running from the stable, dropped his neck-cloth. Straker found it later and picked it up. I believe he wanted to use it to tie the horse's leg. In the valley, he got behind the horse and lit the candle. But the horse suddenly became afraid. He sensed that Straker wanted to hurt him. The horse then struck Straker in the head with his horseshoe. Straker had already taken his coat off. As he fell down the knife went into his leg. Do I make it clear?"

"Wonderful!" cried the colonel. "Wonderful! It seems you were there!"

"Finally, I made a guess. Straker was an intelligent man, but he was not a horse doctor. Before he cut the horse he wanted to try cutting some other animals. What could he do? He used the sheep.

"When I returned to London I visited the dressmaker. She knew Straker because he often came to buy dresses there. She said his name was Derbyshire and that he had a very beautiful wife who liked expensive dresses. I'm quite sure that this second woman used all of Straker's money. He badly needed more money. This is why he tried to hurt Silver Blaze then bet against him."

"You have explained all but one thing," said the colonel. "Where was the horse?"

"Ah, he ran away. He was cared for by one of your neighbors. I must ask you to be kind to your neighbor, Colonel. Ah, this is Clapham Junction. We shall be in Victoria Station in less than ten minutes. If you would like to have a smoke in our rooms, Colonel, you are welcome to join us. I will be happy to give you any more information you like."

07

The "Gloria Scott"

グロリア・スコット号

読み始める前に

The "Gloria Scott" グロリア・スコット号
56の短編のうち17番目に発表された
1893年4月号のストランド・マガジン初出
1893年発行の「シャーロック・ホームズの思い出」に収録された

[主な登場人物]

Sherlock Holmes シャーロック・ホームズ 世界的に有名な私立探偵。優れ
た観察眼と推理力を有する。ロンドンのベーカー街221Bに下宿して
いる。

Watson ジョン・H・ワトソン 医師。ホームズの相棒でこの物語の語り手。
ベーカー街221Bでホームズと同居している。

Victor Trevor ヴィクター・トレヴァー ホームズがカレッジ時代につくった
唯一の友人。

Judge Trevor トレヴァー判事 ヴィクターの父親。ある日届いた手紙を読
んで発作を起こし、のちに亡くなる。

Hudson ハドソン ヴィクターの父親の過去を知る老水夫。

[あらすじ]

　ホームズは大学時代の友人、ヴィクター・トレヴァーに招待され、ノー
フォークにある彼の家族を訪ねることになった。そこで、ヴィクターの父
親であるトレヴァー氏と出会う。このトレヴァー氏の過去について推理し
た能力を絶賛されたことが、ホームズが探偵になるきっかけだったことが
わかる話でもある。トレヴァー氏の本当の名前はジェームズ・アーミテー
ジ。数十年前、グロリア・スコット号という船で流刑地に送られる囚人だ
った。その船が囚人たちの反乱で沈没した後、オーストラリアに住み着き、
富を築いたという過去があったのだ。

[総単語数] 5,725語

The "Gloria Scott"

"I have some papers here," said my friend Sherlock Holmes as we sat one winter's night in front of the fire. "I really think, Watson, that it would be a good idea to look at them. These papers are about the case of the Gloria Scott, and this is the note that was given to Judge Trevor. He died of fear when he read it."

He picked up a piece of gray note-paper and handed it to me. I read the note.

'The supply of game for London is going steadily up. Head-keeper Hudson, we believe, has been now told to receive all orders for fly-paper and for preservation of your hen-pheasant's life.'

As I finished reading this strange note I saw Holmes laughing at the look on my face.

"You look a little surprised," said he.

"I cannot understand how such a note could cause fear. It seems to me more strange than fearful."

"Very likely. But this message was like a gun. It killed a good, strong man who read it."

"Of course I'm interested to know why," said I. "But why did you say there are special reasons why I should study this case?"

"Because it was the first case I ever had."

I often wondered why my friend first became interested in crime. I don't know why he never told me. Now he sat forward in his chair and sorted the papers on a table. Then he lit his pipe and began smoking.

"You never heard me talk of Victor Trevor?" he asked. "He was the only friend I made during my two years at college. I was never a very friendly person, Watson. I usually stayed in my room thinking and studying. I didn't go out much with others. There were only two sports I liked, fencing and boxing. The subjects I studied were different from those of the other students, so there was very little chance to meet people. Trevor was the only man I knew. And I knew him only because his dog, called a bull terrier, tried to eat my leg one day as I was walking to church.

"It was an unusual way to become friends, but it worked. I was in bed for ten days and Trevor used to come visit me. At first we only talked for a few minutes. But soon the visits became longer. By the end of the school year we had become close friends. He was a lively, out-going person, very different from me. However, some of our interests were the same, and I learned that he too had few friends. Finally he asked me to come visit his father's place at Donnithorpe, in Norfolk. I accepted and went to spend one month there during the summer.

"Old Trevor, the father, was a man of some money and power in the area. He was a county judge, and he also owned land. Donnithorpe is a very small town to the north of Langmere, in the country of the Broads. The house was an old, large, building of wood and stone. The road leading to it was lined with large trees. There was very good duck-hunting in the fields, and very good fishing in the streams. There was also a library in the house. The cook was excellent too. It would be difficult not to enjoy a pleasant month there.

"The older Trevor lived alone because his wife had died. My friend was his only son.

"There had been a daughter, I heard, but she had died of illness while on a visit to Birmingham. I found the father very interesting. He had studied very little, but he had an intelligent mind and a strong body. He knew few books, but had traveled far and seen much of the world. He remembered all that he had learned. He was a thick-set man, not tall, with light hair. His face was brown from the sun and he had striking blue eyes. His neighbors said he was a kind, giving man. He was an honest judge with a good heart.

"One evening, shortly after I arrived, we were sitting and drinking a glass of port wine after dinner. Young Trevor began to tell some stories about my methods of thinking. At that time, of course, I didn't know I would become a detective. Anyway, old Trevor had difficulty believing one or two of these stories about me.

"'Come now, Mr. Holmes,' said he, laughing. 'I'm an excellent subject. Let's see what you can guess about me.'

"'I don't think there is much,' I answered. 'I might guess that you have been somewhat afraid of something this past year.'

"His smile disappeared, and he looked at me in surprise.

"'Well, that's true enough,' said he. 'You know, Victor,' turning to his son, 'that group of thieves we caught promised they would kill us. And someone did try to hurt Sir Edward Holly. So yes, I have been a little afraid since then. How did you know?'

"'You have a very nice walking-stick,' I answered. 'By the mark I can see that it is not more than a year old. I can also see that you have made a hole in the wood and put in some metal to make it stronger. I think you probably did that because you sensed some danger.'

"'Anything else?' he asked, smiling uneasily.

"'You were a boxer when you were young.'

"'Right again. How did you know it? Is my nose not straight?'

"'No,' I said. 'It is your ears. They appear to have been hit again and again.'

"'Anything else?'

"'Your hands show me that you worked hard in the mines or fields.'

"'Yes, I made all my money in the gold fields.'

"'You have been in New Zealand.'

"'Right again.'

"'You have visited Japan.'

"'Quite true.'

"'And you have been very close to someone whose name begins with the letters J. A. Later you tried very hard to forget this person.'

"Mr. Trevor stood up slowly. His face turned pale. He fixed his large blue eyes on me in a look of shock. Then he suddenly fell forward onto the floor. He had fainted.

"You can understand, Watson, how surprised both his son and I were. We helped Mr. Trevor to recover. We picked him up slowly and gave him some water. Happily, he was O.K. again five minutes later.

"'Ah, boys,' he said, trying to smile. 'I hope I didn't make you afraid. Strong as I look, there is a weak place in my heart. Sometimes this happens to me. Mr. Holmes, you have unbelievable powers. I tell you now that you will become a great detective in your life.'

"The truth is, Watson, that was the first time in my life that I thought of becoming a detective. At that moment, however, I was thinking only of the condition of Mr. Trevor.

"'I hope I have said nothing to pain you?' said I.

"'Well, you certainly surprised me. May I ask how you know, and how much you know?' He spoke now half-smiling and half-afraid.

"'It is quite simple,' I replied. 'Yesterday, when you uncovered your arm to pull that fish into the boat I saw the letters J. A. written on your skin. The letters were still clear, but I could see that an effort had been made to remove them. I knew that this name was once important to you, and that later you wished to forget it.

"'What an eye you have!' he cried out. 'It is just as you say. But let's not talk about it. I'd rather not remember an old love. Come, let's have a smoke in the next room.'

"From that day, Mr. Trevor's manner towards me was different. I don't think he trusted me completely. Even his son noticed it. 'You've given my father quite a turn,' he said. 'He'll never be sure again what you know and what you don't know.' Mr. Trevor tried to hide his uneasiness, but I could see that I was making him nervous. At last I decided it was time to leave. However, on the day before I left, something happened which later proved to be important.

"The three of us were sitting in the garden enjoying the sun and the view across the Broads. A maid came to tell Mr. Trevor that a man had arrived to see him.

"'What's his name?' asked Mr. Trevor.

"'He won't say,' she replied.

"'What does he want?'

"'He says that you know him, and that he only wants to speak with you for a moment.'

"'All right. Please show him in.' A moment later there appeared a little man with a strange manner and way of walking. He wore an open coat, a red and black shirt, dirty pants and old shoes. His face was thin and lined. There was a half-smile on his mouth. His skin was also browned from many years in the sun. He looked like a seaman. As he walked into the garden a strange sound came from Mr. Trevor's mouth. The old man suddenly jumped from his chair and ran into the house. He returned shortly, smelling of whiskey.

"'Well, my man,' he said. 'What can I do for you?'

"The seaman stood looking at him with the same smile on his face.

"'You don't know me?' he asked.

"'Well, dear me, it is surely Hudson,' said Mr. Trevor, acting surprised.

"'Hudson it is, sir,' said the seaman. 'Why, it's more than thirty years since I last saw you. Here you are in your beautiful house, and I'm still eating salted meat on the oceans.'

"'I haven't forgotten old times, Hudson,' cried Mr. Trevor. He walked towards the visitor and said something in a low voice. Then, louder, he said, "Go into the kitchen and you will find food and drink. I'm sure I can help you find what you need.'

"'Thank you, sir,' said the seaman, touching his hair. 'I just finished a hard two-year trip on a slow ship. I need a rest. I thought I could get it with either you or Mr. Beddoes.'

"'Ah!' cried Mr. Trevor. 'You know where Mr. Beddoes is?'

"'Indeed, sir. I know where all my old friends are,' said the little fellow. He then walked off towards the kitchen. Mr. Trevor then told us about being on a ship with Hudson many years ago while going to the gold fields. He, too, then went inside the house. An hour later, we entered the house. Mr. Trevor was lying on a long chair, very drunk from whiskey. Things were becoming most unpleasant. I was not sorry to leave Donnithorpe the next day, although I felt badly for my friend Victor.

"All this happened during the first month of a long holiday. I went back to my rooms in London. There I spent seven weeks studying chemistry. One day, however, towards the end of my holiday, I received a telegram from my friend. He asked me to please return to Donnithorpe because he needed my help. Of course, I went as quickly as I could.

"He met me at the station. I could see that the past two months had been very difficult for him. He had become thin, pale and tired. He looked less happy than usual.

"'My father is dying,' were the first words he said.

"'Impossible!' I cried. 'What is the matter?'

"'It's his heart and his nerves. He's very sick. I doubt we shall find him alive.'

"I was, as you may think, Watson, sadly surprised at this news.

"'What caused it?' I asked my friend.

"'Ah, that is the point. Come quickly and we can talk in the carriage. Do you remember the little man who came to our house the evening before you left?'

"'Perfectly.'

"'Do you know what he is?'

"'I have no idea.'

"'He is evil, Holmes,' he cried.

"My eyes opened wider.

"'He is evil, like the devil himself. We have not had a peaceful moment since he arrived. My father has been unhappy and afraid. Now the life is being taken from his broken heart. All because of Hudson.'

"'What power does this man have?'

"'I wish I knew. My kind, good father—how could he know such a bad man like Hudson? But I'm very glad you're here, Holmes. I trust your judgment. I know you will help me.'

"We were moving fast along the white country road during a beautiful red sunset. To the left I could see the top of the house among the trees.

"'My father made the man our gardener,' said my friend. 'But the man wasn't happy with that position. He wanted to be the butler. He walked through the house doing just what pleased him. He drank whiskey all the time and used bad language with the maids. He went hunting with our boat and my father's best gun. He never once said thank you. Truly, Holmes, I wanted to hit him hard many times. But he is an older man so I controlled myself. Now I wish I had hurt him.

"'Well, matters became very bad with this animal Hudson. One day, after he said a bad word to my father, I pushed him from the room. He walked away with an evil look in his eyes. Later, I'm sure he talked to my father. The next day my father asked me to say I'm sorry to Hudson. Of course I said no. I also asked my father why he allowed this man to stay in our house.

""""Ah, my boy" said he, "you don't know the trouble I'm in. But you will know, Victor, I promise you. In the meantime, please don't make Hudson angry." He then went into his study for the rest of the day. Through the window I could see him writing busily.

"'That evening there was good news. Hudson told us that he was going to leave. He was half-drunk when he told us.

""""I've had enough of Norfolk," said he. "I'll run down to Mr. Beddoes in Hampshire. I'm sure he'll be as happy to see me as you were."

""""I hope you're not going away with unkind feelings, Hudson," said my father, nervously. I thought he was far too nice to this bad man.

""""Well, your son didn't tell me he was sorry yet," said Hudson looking at me.

""""Victor, you will tell this good man that you made a mistake. You acted unkindly towards him," ordered my father.

""""I will not. I believe we have both been much too kind to him," I answered.

""""Oh, you do, do you?" shouted Hudson. "Very well, my young friend. We shall see about that!"

"'He walked angrily out of the room. A half an hour later he left the house. My poor father was really nervous. Night after night I heard him walking around his room. Days later, just as he was beginning to feel a little better, the shock came.'

"'What happened?' I asked.

"'A letter came for my father from a place called Fordingham. My father opened it and read it. He then put both his hands on his head and began to run around the room in small circles. At last he fell into a large chair. I could see that the problem was his heart. Doctor Fordham came over at once. We put him to bed but he is not getting better. He can't move or speak. I am afraid.'

"'This is very bad indeed, Trevor!' I cried. 'What was in this letter which caused such a result?'

"'Nothing. That's what I don't understand. The note did not make sense.'

"At that moment we arrived in front of the house. All the windows were closed. 'Oh my God, it is as I feared!' said my friend. His face became suddenly very pale and sad. We ran to the door just as a man dressed in black was coming out.

"'When did it happen, doctor?' asked Trevor.

"'Just after you left.'

"'Was he able to say anything before he died?'

"'Only a few words.'

"'Anything to me?'

"'Only that the papers were in a drawer in his study.'

"My friend went up with the doctor to his father's bedroom. I felt very sad. I stayed in the study thinking about the whole matter. What was the past of this Trevor, boxer, traveler, and gold-hunter? And why was he under the power of a small, evil seaman? Why did he faint when I told him of the letters J. A. on his arm? And why did he die of fear when he received this letter from Fordingham? Then I remembered that Fordingham was in Hampshire. The seaman talked of going to Hampshire to see a Mr. Beddoes. The letter, then, may have come from either Hudson or Beddoes. The first, possibly, to hurt old Trevor. The second, possibly, to help him. So far it seemed clear. But how could this letter be strange and without meaning as my friend said? Perhaps it was a code which he didn't understand. I must see this letter. I was sure that I could understand it. For an hour I sat in the darkened house until a maid came in with a light. Close behind her was my friend Trevor. His face was very pale and his eyes were wet. He was holding these same papers, Watson, that I am holding now. He sat down in front of me, next to the light, and handed me this piece of gray paper with this note. 'The supply of game for London is going steadily up,' it said. 'Head-keeper Hudson, we believe, has been now told to receive all orders for fly-paper and for preservation of your hen-pheasant's life.'

"Like you, Watson, I understood nothing when I first read the message. Then I reread it carefully. Surely this was a code. The message included the word Hudson, so probably it was Beddoes who wrote the letter. I tried changing the words. I tried reading from back to front. I tried everything, but still didn't understand.

"Then suddenly, I understood the code. By reading every third word, from the beginning, the note was clear. I read it to my friend:

"'The game is up. Hudson has told all. Fly for your life.'

"Victor Trevor put his face into his hands. 'It must be that, I suppose,' said he. 'But what is the meaning of these "head-keepers" and "hen-pheasants"?'

"'It means nothing to the message. But it might be important if we knew who the sender was. You see that he began to write "The... game...is," etc. Later he filled in the rest with the first words he thought of. Probably he enjoys hunting birds. Do you know anything about Beddoes?'

"'Well, in fact, I remember that he used to ask my poor father to come hunting every November.'

"'Then the note must come from him,' I said. 'Now we must find out what this secret was that Hudson used against your father and Beddoes'

"'Oh, Holmes, I fear that it is a very evil secret!' cried my friend. 'But I will tell you all that I know. Here is the letter which my father wrote when he knew of the danger with Hudson. It was in a drawer in his study as the doctor told us. I have not yet read it, because I feel weak and afraid. Please read it to me, Holmes.'

"These are the same papers, Watson, which he handed to me. I will read them to you now just like I read them to Trevor that night. Here on the outside of the letter it says, 'Some facts about the trip of the ship Gloria Scott, from her leaving Falmouth on the 8th October, 1855, to her being destroyed in North Latitude 15° 20' West Longitude 25° 14', on November 6th.' This is what the letter says.

"'My dear, dear son, the truth of my secret begins to darken the last years of my life. I can tell you that it is not the law which I fear, nor the loss of my position here in Norfolk. Nor is it my shame in the eyes of people who know me. Rather, what cuts my heart is that you might suffer for my past—you who love me. If the public learns about my story then I want you to read this so that you will know, from my own hand, what happened. However, if all goes well (with God's help), and if my secret is not known, and if this letter is not yet destroyed, and if by chance you are reading these words, then, my son, please do this: I ask you please, please, remembering your dear mother, to stop reading now, to burn this paper in the fire and never to think of it again.

"'If, then, you are reading this line, I know that it is too late. Either I have been arrested by the police or, probably, because I have a weak heart, I am already dead. In either case, every word I tell you now is God's truth.

"'My name, dear boy, is not Trevor. I was James Armitage in my younger days. You can understand how I was shocked when your friend Holmes seemed to know my secret a few weeks ago. As

Armitage I began working for a London bank. As Armitage I made a bad mistake at the bank. I broke the law, I was caught. Please don't think badly of me, son. It was a matter of honor. I had to pay money to some others. I planned to secretly borrow the money from the bank and replace it later before anyone knew. However, I had some very bad luck. The money I needed never arrived. A short time later my action was discovered. I hoped the judge would deal with me lightly. But thirty years ago the law was harder than today. So, on my twenty-third birthday I found myself on a criminal ship with thirty-seven other criminals. The ship was the Gloria Scott, and we were sailing to Australia.

"'It was the year 1855, at the height of the Crimean War. Most of the criminal ships were being used to carry men to the Black Sea. It was often necessary to use smaller, slower, ships to carry criminals. The Gloria Scott was such a ship. She had been used for trade with China. She was broad and heavy and old. Besides the thirty-eight criminals, she carried twenty-six seamen, eighteen soldiers, a captain, three officers, four guards, a doctor, and a priest. There were nearly a hundred men on her when we sailed from Falmouth.

"'Usually, the walls between the rooms of the criminals are quite thick. But these were rather thin. The man next to me was one I had especially noticed before we came on the ship. He was a young man, with a clear, hairless face, a long, thin nose, and strong bones. He was also one of the tallest men I'd ever seen—no less than two meters. He had the air of a leader. Other criminals were sad and afraid. He was not. He was proud, and very sure of himself. I was glad to find that he was my neighbor. That night I heard his voice in my ear. I was happy to see that he had cut a small hole in the wall between us.

"'"Hello friend!" said he, "what's your name and why are you here?"'"

"'I answered him, and then I asked who he was.

"'"I'm Jack Prendergast," said he, "and by God! you will be glad you know me before this trip is over."

"'I remembered hearing of his case. It was famous throughout England a short time earlier. He was a man of good family and great intelligence but he had the heart of a thief. He had taken large amounts of money from leading London businesses.

"'"Ha, ha! You remember my case!" he said proudly.

"'"Very well, indeed."

"'"Then maybe you remember something strange about it?"

"'"What was strange?"

"'"I had nearly a quarter of a million pounds, didn't I?"

"'"That's what I heard."

"'"But none was found, right?"

"'"No."

"'"Well, where do you think the money is?" he asked.

"'"I have no idea," said I.

"'"Right here in my fingers," he cried. "By God! I have more pounds to my name than you have hairs on your head. With money and intelligence, my boy, you can do anything. Do you think that an important man like me will be kept on a dirty, old China boat like this? No, sir. Such a man will take care of himself and his friends. I promise you that. Just stay with me and you'll be all right."

"'That's how he talked. At first I thought it meant nothing. But later, when he trusted me more, he told me that there was a plan to take control of the ship. Several of the criminals made this plan before they came on the ship. Prendergast was the leader, and his money was the offer.

"'"My best friend," said Prendergast, "is a good man. He will do anything to help me. Where do you think he is right now? Why, he's the priest of this ship! He came with a black coat, the right papers, and a box full of money. He could buy this ship and everyone on it. Fact is, he already paid most of the seamen before we sailed. They're on our side."

""What are we to do, then?" I asked.

""What do you think?" said he. "We'll make the coats of these soldiers red with their own blood."

""But they have guns," said I.

""And so shall we, my boy. There will be a gun for every one of us. Nobody will be able to stop us. Speak to your neighbor on the left tonight, and see if he can be trusted."

"'I did. I found my neighbor to be a young man in much the same position as me. He too, worked for a bank and broke the law. His name was Evans, but he later changed it. Now he is a rich and important man in the south of England. He was willing to join the group because it was the only way to save ourselves. Soon, there were only two criminals who did not know the secret. One was sick of body and one was sick of mind.

"'From the beginning it was possible to take control of the ship. The priest often came to our rooms. He always carried a black bag. He was supposed to have church books. Instead, he carried guns. Two of the guards worked with Prendergast, as did one of the officers. The captain, two officers, two guards, Lieutenant Martin, his eighteen soldiers, and the doctor were the only ones against us. We planned to surprise them at night. Although it seemed safe we decided to wait for the right moment. However, this moment came sooner than we expected.

"'It happened one evening about three weeks after our start. The doctor came down to see a criminal who was ill. He put his hand on the bed and, by chance, touched several guns. He gave a cry of surprise and looked afraid. The criminal quickly jumped on him and several of us tied him to the bed. The door to the upper floor was not locked. We all picked up our guns and ran up the steps. Three soldiers who were guarding our room were quickly shot. Two more soldiers whose guns were not ready to fire were also killed. Then we ran to the captain's room. As we arrived at the door there was the loud shot of a gun. The captain was dead on the floor and the priest stood above him holding a smoking gun. The other two officers were already caught. It seemed that the whole business was finished.

"'Next to the captain's room was another large room. We all went in there, all speaking together. We felt so glad to be free again. We found bottles of wine with glasses and began to drink. Suddenly, at that moment came the loud shots of guns in our ears. The room was full of smoke. When it cleared there were eight criminals lying on the floor, including Wilson, the priest. The sight of the blood and wine made me sick. Most of us were suddenly afraid. Prendergast, however, made a great shout and ran for the door. We followed him. Outside was the lieutenant and ten soldiers. They had opened some small windows from outside the room and fired on us. We jumped on them before they could fire again. In five minutes the fight was over. Prendergast was like a madman. He picked up the soldiers, dead or alive, and threw them into the water. Soon, the only enemies left were the two guards, the officers, and the doctor.

"'About these five men, however, we could not agree. Some of us were happy to be free again and did not want to kill anyone else. It was one thing to kill in battle, it was another to kill in cold blood. Eight of us, five criminals and three seamen, said that we could not do it. But Prendergast and the others said the five must die. No one must know what happened here. We will never be free if those men live to tell about us, they said. Well, we simply could not agree. Finally,

Prendergast told us that we could take a small boat and go if we wanted. We said O.K. because we did not want to see any more killing. We were given clothes, food, water and a map. Prendergast told us our position, Lat. 15 north and Long. 25 west, then said goodbye.

"'Now I come to the most surprising part of my story, my dear son. The wind was light from the north and east. The seamen on the ship raised the sails and the Gloria Scott began to sail away from us. Our boat lay there in the gentle water. Evans and I had the most schooling so we tried to read the map and decide where to go. We had to choose. To the north, about five hundred kilometers, were the Cape Verde islands. To the east, about seven hundred kilometers, was Africa. We decided on Africa because of the wind. Suddenly, in the distance, we heard a loud sound and saw a large cloud of smoke. The Gloria Scott had disappeared. We turned the boat around and went towards the smoke.

"'It took an hour to get there. There were pieces of ship everywhere on the water. At first, we didn't see anyone living. Then we heard a cry for help. In the distance we saw a man lying on a piece of wood. We pulled him into our boat. He was a young seaman named Hudson. He was badly burned, but we saved him. Several days later he told us what happened.

"'After we left, Prendergast and his friends began to kill the five others. The guards were shot and thrown into the water. Also one of the officers. Prendergast then went down below and cut the doctor's neck with his knife. Then there was only the first officer, a strong, intelligent man. When he saw the criminals coming he somehow untied himself and ran into another room. In this room was the powder for the guns. He sat next to a large box of gun-powder, holding a stick of fire. He said he would blow up the ship if someone came near him. More than ten criminals, with guns, were in the room. A moment later the ship blew up. Hudson thought it was caused by one of the guns and not by the officer. Anyway, it was the end of the Gloria Scott.

"'This, my son, is the history of my secret past. The next day we were picked up by another ship, called the Hotspur. She was going to Australia. We told the captain we were businessmen. We told him that a storm had destroyed our ship. He believed us. It was said that the Gloria Scott was lost at sea. Nobody knows the truth about what happened. Later, the Hotspur arrived in Sydney. Evans and I changed our names and went to the gold fields. Nobody knew us. It's not necessary to tell you much more of my story. We found gold, we traveled, and we returned to England with money. We bought country homes. For over twenty years we have had peaceful, useful lives. And the past was forgotten. Until now. Can you understand my shock at seeing this seaman again after all this time? He somehow found us and came to live upon our fears. I tried to keep the peace with him so that he would not talk. But I don't trust him. I only hope that you understand now, my son.'

"There is something else written here, Watson. But the hand is so shaky that it is difficult to read. 'Beddoes writes in code to say H. has told all. God help us!'

"This was the story which I read to young Trevor that night. It was very interesting, Watson, don't you think? Of course, it broke my young friend's heart. He went to Asia, where I hear he is doing well. Nobody knows what happened to Hudson and Beddoes. They both disappeared completely the day after the coded letter was written. It seems that Hudson did not tell the police, or anyone, about the Gloria Scott. The police saw Hudson near Beddoes' house. They think he might have killed Beddoes and run away. However, I believe that Beddoes may have killed Hudson. Beddoes probably believed that Hudson had already talked. So, feeling afraid and angry he killed Hudson then left the country. No doubt he took as much money as possible with him. Those are the facts of the case, Doctor Watson. I hope they are of some use to you."

08

The Musgrave Ritual

マスグレーヴ家の儀式

読み始める前に

> ### *The Musgrave Ritual* マスグレーヴ家の儀式
> 56の短編のうち18番目に発表された
> 1893年5月号のストランド・マガジン初出
> 1893年発行の「シャーロック・ホームズの思い出」に収録された

［主な登場人物］

Sherlock Holmes　シャーロック・ホームズ　世界的に有名な私立探偵。優れた観察眼と推理力を有する。ロンドンのベーカー街221Bに下宿している。

Watson　ジョン・H・ワトソン　医師。ホームズの相棒でこの物語の語り手。ベーカー街221Bでホームズと同居している。

Reginald Musgrave　レジナルド・マスグレーヴ　ホームズと同じカレッジに学ぶ。父の死後、ハールストーンの領地を継ぐ。

Richard Brunton　リチャード・ブラントン　マスグレーヴ家のハールストーンの執事。何でもこなす才覚の持ち主だが、女たらしの問題がある。

Rachel Howells　レイチェル・ハウエルズ　ハールストーンの家政婦。ブラントンと婚約していたが、捨てられて病んでしまった。

［あらすじ］

　ワトソンと出会う前、探偵を始めて間もない頃の回顧録となっている。物語はホームズの大学時代の友人であるレジナルド・マスグレーヴが、執事のブラントンの奇妙な行動と彼の突然の失踪について助けを求めるところから始まる。マスグレーヴ家はイギリスでも最も古い貴族の家柄だ。この家に仕えていたブラントンはある日、忽然と屋敷から姿を消してしまう。すると彼の元婚約者のレイチェルも行方をくらますのだが。

［総単語数］5,676語

The Musgrave Ritual

My friend Sherlock Holmes had many sides to his character. As a detective mind he had no equal in the world. His methods of thinking were direct, intelligent and complete. In appearance he was fairly well-dressed but not at all fancy. However, he was not someone who kept a clean house. There was little order to his rooms and offices. We call this untidy. His clothes were everywhere. He kept tobacco in his shoe. He liked to throw his knife into the door. I always believed that guns should be fired outside in the open air. Once, however, Holmes shot his gun many times into the wall, making a word with the holes. I am not an especially tidy person myself, but I am surely more tidy than Holmes. I often told him that I didn't like the condition of the house.

Our rooms were always full of chemicals and objects from criminal cases. But my biggest problem were Holmes's papers. He never destroyed papers, especially those from old cases. Yet he almost never put these papers in order. Often when he finished a famous case, there were long periods when he stayed in the house doing nothing. He read books, played music on his violin and moved very little. Month after month the small hill of papers grew and grew. One winter's night we sat together by the fire. I asked him to please make our room a little tidier by throwing out some papers. He agreed, though he really didn't want to. He went into his bedroom and returned with a metal box. He put the box in the middle of the floor and sat next to it in a chair. He opened it. It was already half full of papers.

"There are many cases in here, Watson," said he, looking at me. "If you knew all the information in this box I'm sure you would ask me to save it."

"Are these records of your early work?" I asked. "I often wished I had notes of those cases."

"Yes, my boy, these were all done before you started writing about my life." He picked up his papers lovingly. "They are not all successes, Watson," said he. "But there are some pretty little problems among them. Here's the record of the Tarleton murders; and the case of Vamberry, the wine seller; and the story of the old Russian woman; as well as the case of Ricoletti and his bad wife. And here — ah, now, this is really something special."

He reached down into the bottom of the box. He brought up a small wooden box. It had a moveable top, like a child's game. He opened it and pulled out a rolled piece of paper; an old key; a stick of wood with a ball of string around it; and three old, round, pieces of metal.

"Well, my boy, what do you think this is?" he asked, smiling.

"It is a strange group of objects."

"Indeed. And the story of these objects is even stranger."

"So they have a history?"

"In fact, Watson, they are history."

"What do you mean by that?"

Sherlock Holmes picked them up one by one and placed them on the edge of the table. Then he sat down again in his chair. He looked at them with a happiness in his eyes.

"These," said he, "are what I remember about the Musgrave Ritual."

I had heard him speak more than once of the case. However, I had very little information about it. "I would be very glad," said I, "if you would tell me about it."

"And leave the room untidy?" he asked, laughing. "Well, Watson, I suppose we can clean up later. I would be glad to add this case to your records of my detective life. There are some points about this case which make it quite unusual. I believe that a history of my cases would not be complete without this one.

"You may remember the case of the Gloria Scott. It was when I first became interested in my life's work as a detective. Today you know that my name has become famous in this country and elsewhere. The public and the government call upon me to solve the most difficult crimes. You first knew me during the time of 'A Study in Scarlet.' Even then I was becoming well-known in my work, though I had little money. But you don't know how difficult it was for me at the beginning. I had to wait a long time for success.

"When I first came to London I had rooms in Montague Street. They were just around the corner from the British Museum. I had much free time then. I spent most of it studying subjects to help me with my work. Sometimes cases came to me, usually through fellow college students whom I knew. At college people often talked about my work and my methods. The Musgrave Ritual was my third case. There was much general interest in this case, with important questions being asked. This was the first step toward my present position.

"Reginald Musgrave had been in the same college as myself. I knew him, though not well. He was not generally well-liked among fellow-students. Many thought he was too proud. In appearance he was thin, high-nosed, with large eyes. He came from one of the oldest and richest families in the country. His family separated from the northern Musgraves about three hundred years ago. They settled in western Sussex at the Manor House of Hurlstone. When I think of him I think of old English history. Once or twice we had long talks. He seemed very interested in my work.

"For four years I had not seen him. Then one morning he walked into my room in Montague Street. He had changed little. He still dressed in fancy clothes and had the air of a well-to-do young man.

"'How are you these days, Musgrave?' I asked.

"'You probably heard of my poor father's death about two years ago,' said he. 'Since then I have become the owner of the family home and land. My life has been a busy one. I understand, Holmes, that you are using your wonderful detective powers to make a living.'

"'Yes,' said I, 'I'm trying to.'

"'I'm glad to hear it. Because your ideas at this moment would be very valuable to me. We have had some strange doings at Hurlstone. The police aren't able to help much. It really is an especially difficult matter.'

"You can guess, Watson, how interested I was listening to him. This was the chance I had been waiting for all those months. In my heart I believed that I could succeed where others failed. This was my chance to see if I was a good detective.

"'Please tell me the story,' I cried.

"Reginald Musgrave sat down across from me and lit a cigarette.

"'You know,' he said, 'that I am not married. However, I must keep a large group of servants at Hurlstone. It is a large, old place and needs a lot of care. I also have hunting on our land with a big house-party every hunting season. It's important to have enough help. Altogether, there are thirteen servants—eight maids; the cook; the butler; two footmen; and a boy. The garden and the horses have separate servants.

"'The servant who had worked with us for the longest time was Brunton, the butler. He was a young schoolteacher when he was taken in by my father. He was an intelligent man of good character and very lively. He soon became very important to us in the house. He was a good-looking man as well. He has been with us for twenty years though he cannot be more than forty now. Also, he is able to speak several foreign languages and play music. We have been lucky that he has stayed with us for so long. People who visit us at Hurlstone always remember the butler.

"'There is only one problem with him. He likes the ladies perhaps a little too much. We call him a Don Juan. It is rather easy for him in a quiet country home. When he was married it was all right. However, since his wife died we have had a lot of trouble. A few months ago we hoped that he would marry again. He promised to marry Rachel Howells, our second housemaid. But not long ago he changed his mind and began to see Janet Tregellis. She is the daughter of the man who cares for our animals. Rachel is a very good girl from Wales who became very ill after Brunton left her. She walks about the house now—or did until yesterday—only half alive. That was our first problem at Hurlstone. But a second one came along later. It was necessary to tell butler Brunton to leave the house.

"'This is what happened. I said that the man was intelligent. It was his intelligence that caused the problem. He wanted to know everything about everything, even things which were not his business.

"'I have said that the house is a very large one with many rooms. One day last week—on Thursday night—I could not sleep. I was foolish to drink a cup of strong coffee before going to bed. At about two in the morning I got up from bed and turned on the light. I planned to read more of my book. The book, however, was left in another room down on the first floor. I put on my nightcoat and went down the steps to get the book.

"'To reach the billiard-room it was first necessary to pass by the library, then the gun-room. Of course, I was very surprised to see a light coming from the library at this hour. Earlier, I had turned off the light myself before going to bed. Naturally, I thought there might be thieves in the house. There are many weapons on the walls at Hurl-stone. I took a large weapon, called a battle-axe, from the wall and walked quietly towards the library. I slowly looked in the open door.

"'Brunton, the butler, was in the library. He was sitting, fully dressed, in a chair. He was reading a piece of paper. It looked like a map. He was looking down and he was thinking deeply. I was shocked, watching from the darkness. Suddenly, he got up and walked to a table. He unlocked a drawer, and opened it. From this he took another paper and returned to his seat. He began to study the paper closely. At that point I became angry because he was looking at my personal family papers. I took a step forward. He looked up and saw me. He jumped to his feet. His face turned pale with fear. He quickly put the first map-like paper in his pocket.

"'"So!" said I. "This is how you repay our trust in you. You will leave my service tomorrow."

"'He looked shameful and sad. He walked past me without saying a word. I looked at the table to see which paper he had taken from the drawer. To my surprise it was not very important. It was only the questions and answers to something we call the Musgrave Ritual. It is an old family custom. For centuries, each Musgrave goes through the ritual when he becomes old enough. It is really of no interest to anyone outside the family.'

"'We should talk about the paper later,' said I.

"'If you really think it necessary,' he answered. 'To continue, how-ever, I relocked the drawer using the key Brunton had left. I turned to go and was surprised to find that the butler had returned. He was standing in front of me.

"'"Mr. Musgrave, sir," he cried, his voice shaking, "I can't live in shame. I have always been a proud person. Shame would kill me. If you cannot keep me after what has happened, please don't just throw me out. Instead, let me tell you that I plan to leave in a month. Then people will believe that I decided to leave on my own."

"""Why should I be so kind, Brunton?" I answered. "Your action has been shameful. However, you have been with our family a long time. I do not wish to see you shamed in public. A month, however, is too long. I will give you a week. You may tell the others anything you like."

"""Only a week, sir?" he asked sadly. "Please, at least two weeks!"

"""One week," I said again. "And think of yourself as lucky."

"'He walked away, his head hanging down, like a broken man. I put out the light and returned to my room.

"''For two days after this Brunton worked very hard. I said nothing about the matter. I waited to see how he would deal with the problem. On the third morning, however, he did not appear for breakfast. As I left the dining-room, I met Rachel Howells, the maid. I told you that she was just recovering from her illness. She still looked very thin and pale.

"""You should be in bed," I said. "Come back to work when you are stronger."

"'She looked at me with a very strange face.

"""I am strong enough, Mr. Musgrave," said she.

"""We will see what the doctor says," I answered. "You must stop work now and rest. When you go down please tell Brunton that I want to see him."

"""The butler is gone," said she.

"""Gone! Gone where!"

"""He is just gone. No one has seen him. He is not in his room. Oh, yes, he is gone, he is gone!" She fell back against the wall and began laughing very loudly, then crying. I thought she was losing her mind. I called the other servants. The girl was taken to her room while I asked about Brunton. He had indeed disappeared. His bed had not been slept in, and no one had seen him since the night before. But we did not understand how he left the house. Both the windows and door in his room were locked. His clothes, his watch, and his money were still in the room. The black suit he usually wore was missing. His house-shoes were gone too. But his other shoes were in the room. Where could butler Brunton have gone in the night, and where is he now?

"'Of course we searched everywhere. From the top of the house to the bottom. There was no sign of him. There are many rooms in the house but we searched each one. I can't believe he left without taking his belongings. I called in the police, but they were not successful either. It had rained the night before. We looked at the ground and walkways all around the house but found nothing. Some days later, a new problem appeared.

"'Rachel Howells had been ill for two days, sometimes laughing, sometimes crying. We brought in a nurse to take care of Rachel. It was the third night after Brunton disappeared. The nurse was watching Rachel who was at last sleeping quietly. The nurse also began to sleep in her chair. When she woke up in the morning the bed was empty. The window was open and the girl was gone. The nurse woke me up and told me that Rachel was missing. We ran outside and began searching for her. It was easy to see her footmarks. We followed them out to the small lake at the edge of the grounds. The marks stopped there. We were very afraid that the poor girl might be in the lake.

"'Of course, we brought out the boats and searched the bottom of the lake. But we found no body. However, we did find an unusual object in the lake. It was a bag made of cloth. It contained a piece of old metal, and several small, round objects that were either stone or glass. This is all we could find in the lake. We searched everywhere in the county but we know nothing of Rachel Howells or Richard

Brunton. The county police can't help me and I have at last come to you.'

"You can guess, Watson, how interested I was to hear of this matter. I tried to form some idea of what had happened. The butler was gone. The maid was gone. The maid loved the butler, but later had reason not to love him. She was from Wales and had strong Welsh feelings, which grew stronger after the butler disappeared. She had thrown a bag of strange objects into the lake. These were all facts to think about. Yet none of them really solved the matter. Where did these actions start?

"'I must see that paper, Musgrave,' said I. 'This butler of yours considered it to be important. He lost his job because of it.'

"'Well, it is a little foolish, this ritual of ours,' he answered. 'But it goes back many, many years. I have a list here of the questions and answers.'

"He then handed me the same paper which I have here, Watson. These are the strange questions and answers that were given to each master of Hurlstone over the centuries. I will read them to you.

"'Whose was it?'

"'His who is gone.'

"'Who shall have it?'

"'He who will come.'

"'Where was the sun?'

"'Over the oak tree.'

"'Where was the shade?'

"'Under the elm tree.'

"'How was it found?'

"'North by ten and by ten, east by five and by five, south by two and by two, west by one and by one, and so under.'

"'What shall we give for it?'

"'All that is ours.'

"'Why should we give it?'

"'To keep the trust.'

"'The first one has no date, but the writing is from the seventeenth century,' said Musgrave. 'I am afraid, however, that it is little help to you in solving this mystery.'

"'At least,' said I, 'it gives us another mystery. And this one is more interesting than the first. Perhaps by solving one we can solve the other. You know, Musgrave, I believe that your butler was very intelligent indeed. I think he was trying to solve a mystery that his masters couldn't.'

"'I don't think I understand,' said Musgrave. 'The paper seems to be of no importance.'

"'To me it seems very important. I think Brunton had the same opinion. He probably saw it before that night you caught him.'

"'It is very possible. I never tried to hide it.'

"'He wished, I think, to get a clearer idea of the ritual. You say that he had some sort of map. He was looking at the map and the paper at the same time. When you appeared he put the map in his pocket.'

"'That is true. But what could he be doing with this old family custom of ours? What does this ritual mean?'

"'I don't think that will be difficult to find out,' said I. 'I think we should take the first train down to Sussex.'

"The same afternoon we arrived at Hurlstone. Perhaps you have seen pictures and read articles about the famous building, Watson. The building has the shape of an L. The longer part is the newer building, and the shorter part is the old one. Above the door in the old building is a date written in stone, 1607. But many people believe the stonework is much older than that. The walls are very very thick, and the windows very small. That is why the family built the new part.

Now the old part is used to keep supplies. There is a lovely park with beautiful trees all around the house. The lake is about two hundred meters from the building.

"I believed, Watson, that there were not three separate mysteries here. There was only one. If I could understand the meaning of the Musgrave Ritual then I could solve the mystery of the butler and the maid. Why was Brunton so interested in the ritual? Perhaps because he saw something which his masters, after three hundred years, did not. What was it?

"I was sure that the numbers in the ritual were a measurement. They measured the distance to a spot. If we could find that spot then perhaps we could understand the secret of the ritual. We already had two guides—an oak tree and an elm tree. The oak was easy. It was a truly beautiful tree directly in front of the house.

"'That was where your Ritual was written,' said I to Musgrave as we drove past.

"'It was probably there when the Normans came to England,' he answered. 'It is more than seven meters around.'

"I knew this was one of the measuring points.

"'Do you have any old elm trees?' I asked.

"'There used to be a very old one over there. But ten years ago it fell down during a bad storm. We removed it.'

"'Can you see where it used to be?'

"'Oh, yes.'

"'There are no other elm trees?'

"'No old ones, but many beech trees.'

"'I would like to see where it grew.'

"We got out of the carriage and Musgrave took me to the place where the elm tree used to be. It was nearly halfway between the oak tree and the house.

"'Is it possible to know the height of the elm tree?' I asked.

"'Yes, I can tell you that. Twenty meters.'

"'How do you know?' I asked in surprise.

"'As a boy I had a trigonometry teacher here at the house. He always asked me to measure the height of things. I knew the height of every tree and building at Hurlstone.'

"This was an unexpected piece of luck. I was learning facts more quickly than I had hoped.

"'Tell me,' I asked. 'Did your butler ever ask you such a question?'

"Reginald Musgrave looked at me in great surprise. 'As a matter of fact,' he answered, 'Brunton did ask me about the height of the tree some months ago.'

"This was very good news, Watson. It told me that I was asking the right questions. I looked up at the sun. It was low in the sky. I guessed that it would be just above the top of the oak tree in less than one hour. Soon we might understand one part of the Ritual. I also guessed that the shade of the elm tree must mean the far end of the shade. So, I had to find where the far end of the shade would be when the sun was just above the oak tree."

"That must have been difficult, Holmes, when the elm tree was no longer there."

"Well, I knew that if Brunton could do this, then so could I. Besides, it was not so difficult. I went with Musgrave to his study. There I used my knife to shape this little stick which we have here. I tied a long string on to the stick. I then took a longer stick, used for fishing, that measured two meters. We then went back to where the elm tree had been. The sun was just at the top of the oak tree. I put the fishing stick straight up on the ground and measured the shade. It was three meters long.

"Of course it was now easy to know the distances. If a stick of two meters makes shade of three meters, then a tree of twenty meters would make shade of thirty meters. The line of the one would be the line of the other. I measured out the distance. It brought me to a spot near the wall of the house. I put my small stick in the ground at the spot. To my great surprise I could see a small hole in the ground next to my stick. I knew that it was the mark made by Brunton.

"From this starting-point I began to measure by steps. First, I faced the north. I took ten steps with each foot along the wall of the house. I then marked this spot with my stick. From there I carefully made five steps to the east. Then two to the south. It brought me directly to the old door. Two more steps to the west meant that I would be just inside on the stone floor. This was the spot written about in the Ritual.

"However, for a moment I was very unhappy, Watson. I thought I made a mistake because the spot was directly on the stone floor. The stones were heavy and strong. They were held together by cement. It was impossible to move them. I could see that Brunton had not tried to move them either. I hit the stones very lightly and listened. But there was no sign of a hole or a space under them. Luckily, Musgrave was beginning to understand my actions. He too was now very interested. He took the ritual out of his pocket and looked at it.

"'And under,' he cried. 'You have forgotten the "and under".'

"I thought it meant under the floor. But now I realized I was wrong. It meant there was another room below the floor. 'Is there a cellar under this?' I cried.

"'Yes, and it is as old as the house. Down here, through this door.'

"We went down a stone step. It was dark but Musgrave carried a lantern. In a moment I could see that we had found the right spot. I also saw that we were not the first ones.

"The cellar was used as a place to keep wood. In the middle of the floor was a large stone with an iron ring. Tied to the ring was a muffler.

"'By God!' cried Musgrave. 'That's Brunton's muffler. I have seen it before. What has he been doing here?'

"I thought it was a good idea to call the county police. Two of them arrived a short time later. We then tried to lift the stone by pulling on the muffler. It was very heavy. At last we lifted it to one side. We all looked down into a big black hole. Musgrave held the lantern into the darkness.

"It was a small room, about two meters by one and a half meters. To one side was a short, thick wooden box. The top was pushed up and this old key was in the lock. The wood was very old and wet. Some bugs had eaten holes in the box. Several round pieces of metal were on the bottom of the box. They were coins. There was nothing else inside the box.

"At that moment, however, we saw something which shocked us. It was the figure of a man beside the box. He was dressed in a black suit. The front of his head rested on the back of the box. His two arms were around each side of it. He was dead. His skin color had changed, but his height, hair, and clothes had not. Musgrave told us that this was Brunton the butler. He had been dead for several days. We didn't know how he died. There were no marks on his body. Later his body was carried from the cellar. However, we still hadn't solved the family secret.

"At that point, Watson, I was not happy with my search. The Ritual was still a mystery. True, we had found Brunton. But now I had to understand what happened to him, and to the maid. I sat down in the corner of the cellar and thought carefully.

"You know my methods in such cases, Watson. I put myself in the place of the man. I try to think as he would think, to do what he would do. Brunton was a very intelligent man, so the matter was made easier. He knew that something valuable was hidden. He found the place. He found the heavy stone which he could not lift alone. He needed help. What did he do next? He could not ask help from an outside person. It must be someone he could trust from inside the house. Who could he ask? The girl had loved him before. A man always finds it hard to realize that he has lost a woman's love. Perhaps he then tried to make a new peace with Rachel Howells. Together they could lift the stone. So far I could guess their actions.

"But lifting that stone was heavy work for two people. Especially when one was a woman. A strong Sussex policeman and I had a difficult job to lift it. What did they do to make the job easier? Probably what I would do. I stood up and began looking at pieces of wood on the floor. Minutes later I found what I expected. One piece, about one meter long, had a mark on its side. Several other pieces also had marks. It appeared that Brunton and another person had used the wood to lift the stone. Then they used the wood to hold the stone above the hole.

"What else happened that night, I asked myself? Clearly there was space for only one person to fit into the hole. That person was Brunton. The girl must have waited above. Brunton then unlocked the box, and handed the valuables up through the hole. Then what happened?

"What had the girl been thinking? She had very strong feelings. She had loved Brunton, but then he had broken her heart. Did she want him to suffer too? I was sure that the stone fell back down and covered the hole. But how did it happen? Did the wood break because of the weight of the stone? Or did this young woman move the wood and kill her lover? In my mind I saw her running back up the stairs to her room. She was carrying the valuables from the box. Perhaps she could hear the cries of her lover from the cellar. Soon he would have no more air and would die.

"Yes, this must be the secret to her pale face, and shaken nerves.

This is why she laughed and cried without control. She laughed because she hated him and cried because she loved him. But what was in the wooden box? What did she do with it? Ah, that must have been the bag which was found in the lake. It contained the old metal and the small stones. She threw them in the water to hide her crime.

"For twenty minutes I sat thinking. Musgrave was standing holding the lantern above the cellar hole. His face was pale.

"'These are coins of King Charles the First,' he said. He was holding some in his hand. 'We were right about the date of the Ritual.'

"'We may learn something else of Charles the First,' I said. Suddenly, I realized the meaning of the first two questions of the Ritual. 'Let me see what was in the bag from the lake.'

"We went up to his study. He showed me the objects inside the bag. The metal was almost black and the stones did not shine. I understood why Musgrave thought they were not important. I picked up a cloth and began to clean the metal. Soon it was shining brightly. The metal was in the form of a double ring.

"'We must remember,' I said, 'that the king's family stayed a while in England after Charles the First was killed. Later they escaped from the country. They left behind many valuable things in secret places. Probably they planned to return later and get them.'

"'One of my family, Sir Ralph Musgrave, was close to Charles the Second. He escaped England with the king,' said my friend.

"'Ah, indeed!' I answered. 'Well, I think that probably explains everything. Sir Ralph was a friend of the king's and they hid many of the king's valuables here in Hurlstone. It is wonderful that you now own this piece of metal. Not only is it valuable, it is part of history.'

"'What is it then?' he cried.

"'It is a very famous object. It is what the king wore on his head. This, my friend, is the crown of English kings.'

"'My god! The crown!'

"'Consider what the Ritual says. "Whose was it?" "His who is gone." That was after Charles the First was killed. Then, "Who shall have it?" "He who will come." That was Charles the Second, of course. I believe there is no question about it. This now old and broken piece of metal once sat upon the heads of the Stuart kings.'

"'And why was it in the lake?'

"'Ah, that question will take time to answer.' I began to explain to him my ideas about what happened. Outside, the sun was setting. The moon was shining in the sky before I finished talking.

"'And why didn't Charles get his crown when he returned?' asked Musgrave.

"'Ah, that is something we will probably never know. Possibly, the Musgrave who knew the secret died before Charles the Second returned. He left this Ritual as a guide. But perhaps he forgot to explain its meaning. From that day to this it has been handed from father to son. At last its secret was almost discovered by your butler. He lost his life for it.'

"And that's the story of the Musgrave Ritual, Watson. They have the crown down at Hurlstone. Of course the government made Musgrave pay a lot of money to keep it. I am sure that you can visit Hurlstone to see the crown. Just tell them you are my friend. By the way, we don't know what ever happened to the young woman. Probably she left England and took the secret of her crime with her."

09

The Reigate Puzzle

ライゲートの謎

読み始める前に

The Reigate Puzzle ライゲートの謎

56の短編のうち19番目に発表された
1893年6月号のストランド・マガジン初出
1893年発行の「シャーロック・ホームズの思い出」に収録された

［主な登場人物］

Sherlock Holmes シャーロック・ホームズ 世界的に有名な私立探偵。優れた観察眼と推理力を有する。極度の過労で倒れ、ライゲートで静養中。

Watson ジョン・H・ワトソン 医師。ホームズの相棒でこの物語の語り手。静養するホームズに付き添っている。

Mr. Acton アクトン氏 ライゲートの有力者の老人。屋敷に泥棒に入られる。

Mr. Cunningham カニンガム氏 ライゲートの大地主。

Alec Cunningham アレック・カニンガム カニンガム氏の息子。

William ウィリアム カニンガム家の御者。何者かに心臓を撃ち抜かれて殺された。

Inspector Forrester フォレスター警部 事件を担当する警部。

［あらすじ］

　日頃の疲れを癒すため、ライゲートで静養していたホームズ。ワトソンも付き添いとして共にこの田舎の街に来ていた。ところが、地元の有力者、アクトン家に強盗が入ったという話を聞く。その直後、今度はカニンガム家で殺人事件が発生する。ワトソンは静養中なのだから事件には関わるなと言うのだが、地元警察から助けを求められたホームズは、体調不良にもかかわらず、鋭い知性を駆使し、不可解な事件を解決していくのだ。

［総単語数］5,899 語

The Reigate Puzzle

It was necessary for my friend, Mr. Sherlock Holmes, to recover his health. He had been very busy and very tired in the spring of 1887. This was the time of the Netherland-Sumatra Company and Baron Maupertuis. The public will surely remember there were very big problems with money and government. One indirect result of this period was a new and difficult problem for my friend.

Looking at my notes, I see that I received a telegram on the 14th of April. It was from Lyons, France, telling me that Holmes was ill in the Hotel Dulong. Within twenty-four hours I was there in his sick-room. I was glad to see that his illness was not bad. Holmes was a strong man. However, he was tired from working on a case for over two months. During that time he never worked less than fifteen hours a day. Several times, he told me, he worked five straight days without rest. His work was successful, but he had no strength left. All of Europe was talking about him. His room was full of thank-you telegrams and letters. He had succeeded where the police in three countries had failed. He had found one of the most famous criminals in Europe. Yet Holmes was still nervous and unhappy.

Three days later we were back in Baker Street together. I could see that my friend needed a holiday. I liked the idea of spending a week of springtime in the country. My old friend, Colonel Hayter, had bought a house near Reigate in Surrey. He often asked me to come down for a visit. The last time we spoke he said that my friend was also welcome.

I talked with Holmes about the idea and he agreed to come with me. One week after we returned from Lyons, we were staying with the colonel. Hayter was a fine old soldier who had seen much of the world. As I expected, he and Holmes had much to talk about.

On the evening of our arrival we were sitting in the colonel's gun-room after dinner. Holmes was seated in a long chair. Hayter and I were looking at some of his Eastern weapons.

"By the way," Hayter said suddenly. "I think I'll take one of these guns to my room with me. There has been some trouble around here lately."

"Trouble?" said I.

"Yes. There was a theft last Monday at the home of Mr. Acton. He's an old, rich businessman in this county. They didn't take much, but nobody has found them yet."

"No clues?" asked Holmes.

"None yet. But this is a small country crime, Mr. Holmes. This matter is much too small for you, especially after your great European case."

Holmes smiled. "Was there anything of special interest?"

"I doubt it. The thieves went through the library, opened everything and threw it all on the floor. But they only took a few things—a book called Homer, candles, a paper-weight made of ivory, a barometer, and a ball of string."

"What a strange group of objects!" I said.

"Oh, these men took everything they wanted, I suppose."

Holmes made a sound from his chair. "The police should be able to find some clues," he said. "It is clear to me that..."

I held up my finger to Holmes. "You are here for a rest, my dear friend. Please don't start on a new problem when your nerves are already destroyed from the last one."

Holmes shrugged his shoulders and smiled at the colonel. We then changed the subject of our talk.

However, the next morning this little problem suddenly became much bigger. We were at breakfast when the colonel's servant ran into the room.

"Have you heard the news, sir?" he cried. "At the Cunninghams, sir!"

"Theft?" said the colonel, holding his coffee cup.

"No, murder!"

"My God!" said Hayter. "Who was killed, then? The old man or his son?"

"Neither, sir. It was William the driver. He was shot through the heart."

"Who shot him, then?"

"The thief, sir. He quickly escaped into the night. He had just entered the kitchen window when William arrived and was killed trying to protect the home."

"What time?"

"It was last night, sir, around twelve o'clock."

"Ah. Then we will go over there after breakfast," said the colonel. He then began to eat his breakfast again. "It's a bad business," he added when the servant had gone. "Old Cunningham is probably the most important man in our county. A very good man, too. I'm sure he's quite sad because William was a good driver for many years. It's probably the same group of criminals who broke into Acton's place."

"And took that unusual group of objects," said Holmes thoughtfully.

"Indeed."

"Hmm! It may be a very simple case. However, at first it does appear to be a little strange, doesn't it? Thieves usually move on to a different place after a theft. They don't break into two well-known houses in the same place. You spoke last night of protecting yourself. I remember thinking that this county is one of the safest in England. It seems unlikely that thieves would attempt to work here. I see that I was wrong."

"I think it is a person who lives here," said the colonel. "Acton and Cunningham have the two largest homes in the area."

"And richest?"

"Probably. But there is a problem of law between them. Acton believes that Cunningham must pay him some money. Cunningham disagrees. They both have lawyers, who work for them. These lawyers are expensive."

"If the thief lives around here then it should not be difficult to find him," said Holmes. "All right, Watson, I will not interest myself in the case."

"Inspector Forrester, sir," said the servant, opening the door.

The inspector was a young, intelligent-looking man. He entered the room. "Good morning, Colonel," said he. "I hope I may come in. I understand that Mr. Holmes of Baker Street is here."

The colonel pointed his hand towards my friend.

"We thought that perhaps you would like to come with us for a moment, Mr. Holmes."

"Well, Watson, it seems that I will never get my rest," he said, laughing. "We were just talking about the matter when you arrived, Inspector. Perhaps you can give us some information." Holmes sat back in his chair, and I knew that he was interested.

"We had no clue in the Acton case. But now we have several clues. There is no doubt that the person is the same in both cases. The man was seen."

"Ah!"

"Yes, sir. But he ran away too quickly after he shot poor William

Kirwan. Mr. Cunningham saw him from the bedroom window. And his son, Mr. Alec Cunningham, saw him from the back of the house.

"It was quarter to twelve when the thing happened. Mr. Cunningham had just gone to bed. Mr. Alec was smoking a pipe in his bed-clothes. They both heard William, the driver, calling for help. Mr. Alec ran down to see what was the matter. The back door was open. He came to the bottom of the steps and saw two men fighting outside. One of them fired a shot, the other dropped on the ground. The murderer then ran across the garden. He jumped over a row of plants and escaped. Mr. Cunningham, looking out from his bedroom, saw the man running. However, he lost sight of him when the man ran down the road. Mr. Alec stopped to help the dying man, so the murderer escaped.

"We only know that he was a middle-sized man, wearing dark clothes. We have no other clues about him. But we are asking questions all across the county. If he is a stranger we shall soon find him."

"What was William doing there? Did he say anything before he died?"

"Not a word. He lived nearby with his mother. We believe that he was there to make sure everything was all right at the house. Of course, this Acton business has made everyone nervous. The thief must have just pushed in the door when William arrived. The lock was broken."

"Did William say anything to his mother before going out?"

"She is old and cannot hear well. We have no information from her. This is a shock for her. There is one very important piece of information, however. Look at this!"

He took a small piece of paper from a notebook and put it on the table.

"This was found in the hand of the dead man. It is a message. It appears to be torn from a larger piece of paper. You will see that the hour written on it is the same time as the murder. Perhaps he pulled this from the murderer or the murderer pulled it from him. It seems like a plan was made."

Holmes picked up the paper. It was handwritten, and said:

- at quarter to twelve
learn what

may

$$\left(\begin{array}{c} \textit{at quarter to twelve} \\ \textit{learn what} \\ \textit{may} \end{array} \right)$$

"If this was a planned meeting," continued the inspector, "then it is possible that William Kirwan was not completely honest. He may have been working with the thief. Perhaps he met him there and helped him to break the door. Then perhaps they had a disagreement and began to fight."

"This writing is really very interesting," said Holmes, who was looking closely at the paper. "This is perhaps deeper than I thought." He put his head in his hands. The inspector realized that the great detective was interested in the case and he smiled.

"You think it possible," said Holmes presently, "that there was an understanding between the thief and the driver. And that this note was perhaps used in their plan. It is, of course, possible. But this writing opens up—" He put his head back in his hands, and stayed for some moments thinking deeply. He raised his head again. I saw that his face had new color and that his eyes were bright. He looked healthy again. He jumped to his feet from the chair.

"Listen," said Holmes, "I would like to have a quiet look into the information of this case. There is something which interests me very much. If you will allow me, Colonel, I will leave my friend Watson with you. I want to go with the inspector to try an idea or two. I'll be back in half an hour."

An hour and a half passed before the inspector returned alone.

"Mr. Holmes is walking up and down the field outside," he said. "He wants all four of us to go up to the house together."

"To Mr. Cunningham's?"

"Yes, sir."

"Why?"

The inspector shrugged his shoulders. "I don't quite know, sir. Just between us, I think that Mr. Holmes is acting rather strangely. Perhaps he has not recovered from his illness."

"Oh, I think he's quite O.K.," said I. "Usually there is a method in his madness."

"Or a madness in his method," replied the inspector. "But he wants us to come quickly, so let's go if you're ready."

We found Holmes walking up and down in the field. He was looking at the ground. His hands were in his coat pocket.

"The matter grows in interest," he said. "Watson, your country trip has been a big success. I have had a most enjoyable morning."

"You have been to the scene of the crime, I understand," said the colonel.

"Yes, the inspector and I have had a good look around together."

"Any success?"

"Well, we have seen some interesting things. I'll tell you as we walk.

First of all, we saw the body of this poor man. He surely died from a gunshot, as reported."

"Did you doubt it?"

"Oh, it is a good idea to doubt everything. We then talked with Mr. Cunningham and his son. They showed us the spot where the murderer ran over the plants to the road. That was of great interest."

"Naturally."

"Then we met this poor man's mother. We could get no information from her, however, because she is very old and weak."

"What is the result of your search?"

"I believe that the crime is a very strange one. Perhaps our visit now may help to clear things. I think the inspector and I agree that the piece of paper is very important. Especially because the very hour of death is written on it."

"It is surely a clue, Mr. Holmes."

"Yes, it is. That note is the reason William Kirwan left his bed at that hour. But where is the rest of the paper?"

"I searched the ground carefully hoping to find it," said the inspector.

"It was taken from the dead man's hand. Why was someone so interested in having it? Because the paper could be used against him. And what did he do with it? Put it in his pocket, probably. He didn't notice that a corner of the note was still in the dead man's hand. The rest of that message would, of course, really help to solve the crime."

"Yes, but how can we get the paper before we get the criminal?"

"Well, it is something to think about. There is another point. The note was sent to William. The man who wrote it did not, of course, carry it to William, because then the writer could have told him by mouth. Who brought the note, then? Or did it come by mail?"

"I have asked some questions," said the inspector. "William

received a letter by the afternoon mail yesterday. He then destroyed the cover."

"Excellent!" cried Holmes. "You've seen the mailman. It is a pleasure to work with you, inspector. Well, here is the home of the dead man. Please come up with me, Colonel, and I will show you the scene of the crime."

We passed the small, pretty house where the dead man had lived. We continued walking up a tree-lined street. There was a fine old Queen Anne house. Holmes and the inspector took us around it until we came to the side gate. This gate is separated from the row of plants by part of the garden. A police officer was standing by the kitchen door.

"Please open the door, officer," said Holmes. "Now, it was on those steps that young Mr. Cunningham was standing. He watched the two men fighting just where we are now. Old Mr. Cunningham was at that window — the second on the left — and he saw the man run away to the left of that plant. So did his son. They are both sure because they remember the plant. Then Mr. Alec Cunningham ran out next to the dying man. The ground is very hard, you see, and there are no footmarks to help us." As he spoke, two men came from around the corner of the house. They walked towards us on the garden walkway. One was an older man, with a strong, deep-lined, heavy-eyed face; the other was a good-looking young man, with a bright, smiling face and expensive clothes.

"Still searching, are you?" said the younger one to Holmes. "I thought you Londoners were perfect. You don't seem so quick though."

"Ah, you must give us a little time," said Holmes, smiling.

"You will need it," said young Alec Cunningham. "I don't see that we have any clue at all."

"There's only one important one," answered the inspector. "We thought that if we could only find—My God, Mr. Holmes! What is the matter?!"

My poor friend's face had suddenly become very ill-looking. His eyes rolled upward, and he seemed to be in great pain. Suddenly, with a low sound from his mouth, he fainted to the ground. We were all shocked by this sudden problem. We carried him to the kitchen and put him on a large chair. Finally, some minutes later he began to get up. He told us he was sorry.

"Watson will tell you that I have just recovered from a bad illness," he explained. "Sometimes I feel suddenly weak and faint."

"Shall I send you home in my carriage?" asked old Cunningham.

"Well, since I am here, there is one point on which I would like to feel sure. We can very easily try it."

"What is it?"

"Well, I think it is possible that poor William arrived here at the house after the thief. You seem to believe that door was forced open but that the thief didn't get in."

"I think that is very true," said Mr. Cunningham. "My son Alec had not yet gone to bed. He would have heard someone moving inside the house."

"Where was he sitting?"

"I was smoking in my dressing-room," said Alec.

"Which window is that?"

"The last on the left, next to my father's."

"Both of your lights were on, of course?"

"Of course."

"There are some unclear points here," said Holmes, smiling. "Isn't it strange that this experienced thief tried to enter the house when he could see lights from both your rooms?"

"He must have been a very good thief," said the old man.

"Well, of course, it is a rather strange case," said young Mr. Alec. "That is why we are asking you to explain it to us. But I don't agree with your idea that the thief took something from the house before William found him. That seems foolish. The house would have been in disorder. We would have seen something was taken."

"Perhaps. Perhaps not," said Holmes. "You must remember that this thief is a strange one. He is difficult to understand. Look at the strange things he took from Acton's—some string, a paperweight, and some other things."

"Well, this case is in your hands, Mr. Holmes," said old Cunningham. "Anything you or the inspector want to do is all right."

"Thank you," said Holmes. "First, I would like you to offer some money to the person who catches the thief. The reward may help us to find him quickly. I have already written the reward note here. Could you please sign it? I think fifty pounds is quite enough."

"I would gladly give five hundred," said the old man. He took the note and the pen which Holmes gave him. "Uh, this is not quite right, however," he added, while looking at the note.

"I wrote it rather quickly," said Holmes.

"See here, you begin, 'at about a quarter to one on Tuesday morning a man tried,' and so on. It was at a quarter to twelve, really."

My friend had made an unusual mistake. Perhaps his recent illness made him uneasy. I could see that he was not quite his perfect self yet. The inspector raised his eyes, and Alec Cunningham laughed quickly. The old gentleman changed the time with his pen and gave the paper back to Holmes.

"I think your idea is excellent," he said.

Holmes put the note carefully into his pocket.

"And now," said he, "let us all go through the house together. We will see if the thief took anything with him."

Before going inside, Holmes looked closely at the door. It had been forced open. Some strong knife or stick was used. The lock was also forced. We could see the marks in the wood.

"You don't use a stronger lock?" he asked.

"We never found it necessary."

"You don't keep a dog?"

"Yes, but he is tied on the other side of the house."

"What time do the servants go to bed?"

"About ten."

"I understand that William was usually in bed also at that hour?"

"Yes."

"It is strange that on this night he was not in bed. Mr. Cunningham, kindly show us around the house."

We followed a stone walkway past the kitchen to some wooden steps. We went up to the first floor of the house. This brought us to a front hall where there was a second set of steps. In that hall there were doors to the living room and to several bedrooms, including Mr. Cunningham's and his son's. Holmes walked slowly, looking at everything. I could see that he knew something, but I didn't know what.

"My good sir," said Mr. Cunningham, a little unhappily, "is this really necessary? That is my room at the end of the stairs, and my son's is beyond that. I really doubt that the thief could have come here without us hearing him."

"Yes, perhaps you should search somewhere else," said the son.

"I must ask you to help me a little more. I want to look out the bedroom windows. This is your son's room?" He pushed open the door. "And that, I suppose, is the dressing-room where he sat smoking? Where does the window look out to?" Holmes stepped across the bedroom, pushed open the door, and looked around the other room.

"I hope you are happy now," said Mr. Cunningham coolly.

"Thank you. I think I have seen all that I wished."

"Then, if it is really necessary, we can go into my room."

"If it is not too much trouble."

The old man rolled his eyes and took us into his own room. It was a plain room. We moved across it toward the window. Holmes pulled me to one side for a moment when the others weren't looking. Near the bed was a small table with a glass of water and a container of fruit. As we passed it Holmes did something shocking. He purposely pushed the water and fruit on to the floor. The glass broke into many pieces and the fruit rolled all over the room.

"Look what you've done, Watson!" said my friend coolly. "You've made the floor very dirty."

I looked at Holmes in surprise, but I could see that this was his plan. I said nothing and began to pick up the fruit. Soon, the others helped me with the table.

"Hey!" cried the inspector. "Where is he?"

Holmes had disappeared.

"Wait here a moment," said young Alec Cunningham. "The man is acting like a fool, in my opinion. Come with me, father, and see where he went!"

They rushed out of the room, leaving the inspector, the colonel, and me. We looked at each other.

"Well, I say, I must agree with Mr. Alec," said the inspector. "It must be his illness, but I think Mr. Holmes is — "

His words were cut short by a sudden shout of "Help! Help! Murder!" I realized that it was the voice of my friend. I rushed madly from the room into the hall. The shouts were coming from the room which we had visited first. I ran into the bedroom, then through to the dressing-room. The two Cunninghams were standing over Holmes, who was lying on the floor. The younger Cunningham had his hands around Holmes's neck. The older man was holding my friend's arms. The three of us quickly pulled the father and son away from him. Holmes slowly got to his feet. He was very pale and very tired.

"Arrest these men, Inspector," he said weakly.

"What is the charge?"

"They murdered their driver, William Kirwan."

The inspector looked at him in complete shock. "Oh, wait a moment Mr. Holmes," he said at last. "I'm sure you don't really believe that—"

"Quiet, man, look at their faces!" cried Holmes coolly.

The looks on their faces proved that they were the criminals. The older man seemed shocked and unsure of himself. The son, however, had the look of a wild animal on his face. He was no longer the happy, smiling, easy-going young man. The inspector said nothing. He walked to the door and called to his men. Two policemen quickly arrived.

"I'm sorry Mr. Cunningham, I have no choice," said the inspector. "I hope this is all a big mistake. You can see that—Ha, would you? Drop it!" The son was pulling a gun from his pocket. The inspector reached out and hit the gun from his hand. It fell to the floor.

"Keep that," said Holmes, quietly putting his foot on it. "You will find it useful when these men are judged for their crime. But this is what we really wanted." He held up a small piece of paper.

"The rest of the note!" cried the inspector.

"Right."

"And where was it?"

"Where I was sure it had to be. I will explain everything to you soon. I think, Colonel, that you and Watson can return home now. I will be with you in about an hour for lunch. But first, the inspector and I must talk with these two."

I was with the colonel in his smoking-room when Sherlock Holmes joined us about an hour later. He was with a little old man. The man's name was Mr. Acton. The first theft happened in his house.

"I wanted Mr. Acton to be here while I showed you all something," said Holmes. "It is natural that he would be interested in this matter. I am sure, my dear Colonel, that I have been a problem to you."

"Not at all," answered the colonel warmly. "I consider it an honor to have you stay here with me. It has been most interesting to see the methods of such a famous detective. They are greater than I thought. And yet, I really don't understand the result of this case at all."

"My methods are never a secret. It is a pleasure to share them with my friend Watson or anyone else who is interested. But first, I am still a little shaken by the attempt to kill me a short while ago. May I have a glass of your whiskey, Colonel? Lately, I'm not feeling as strong as usual."

"I hope you won't faint anymore."

Sherlock Holmes laughed loudly. "Soon I will tell you about that," said he. "I will also give you the facts about the case. You will see the clues which guided me. Please tell me if there is anything you don't understand.

"To solve a crime is an art. One must look at the facts and decide which are important and which are not. This is often difficult. In this case, I knew from the beginning what the most important clue was. It was the piece of paper in the dead man's hand.

"Alec Cunningham said that the murderer shot William Kirwan, then quickly ran away. That man did not have time to tear the paper from the dead man's hand. But if it was not the murderer, then who took the paper? It must have been Alec Cunningham himself. He was the first one to arrive at the scene. When the old man came down from his room, there were already several servants there. This is a simple point, but the inspector did not see it. You see, the Cunninghams are rich and important people in this county. The inspector did not believe that they could commit such a crime. I always try to keep an open mind. I search for the truth and follow the facts only. I found myself with some doubts about Alec Cunningham.

"I then looked carefully at the corner of the paper which the inspector gave us. It was clear to me that this was a special message. Here it is. Do you see something unusual about it?"

"It has a strange look, yes," said the colonel.

"My dear sir," cried Holmes, "there is no doubt that the message is written by two different people. Every second word is written by a different hand. Look closely at the strong t's of 'at' and 'to'. Now look at the t's of 'quarter' and 'twelve'. You will see that one is weak and the other strong. The 'learn' and the 'may' are written in the strong hand, while the 'what' is in the weaker."

"By God, it is true!" cried the colonel. "Why would two men write in such a way?"

"Because this business was not honest. One of the men did not trust the other. He made sure that both had an equal part in the crime. Of the two men, it is clear that the writer of 'at' and 'to' was the leader."

"Why is that?"

"One reason is the strength of character of the writing. But there is another reason. You can see that the man with the stronger writing wrote all his words first. He left spaces for the other man to fill in. These spaces were not always big enough. The second man had to write his 'quarter' between the 'at' and 'to'. Those words were already written. The man who wrote all his words first is the one who planned the crime."

"Excellent!" cried Mr. Acton.

"We come now," said Holmes, "to an even more important point.

You may know that it is possible to know a man's age by studying his handwriting. Usually we can know within about ten years how old someone is. I say usually because bad health or weakness sometimes makes a young man seem older. In this case I looked at the strong hand of the one, and the broken appearance of the other. I could see that one was a young man and the other was advanced in years."

"Excellent!" cried Mr. Acton again.

"There is a further point, however, which is of greater interest. It is possible to see that the two writers are of the same family. There are many letters, like the Greek e's, which are written in the same manner. I have counted about twenty-three such points while studying this writing. They all tell me that the Cunninghams, father and son, wrote the letter.

"Next, I began to search for the small clues of the crime. I went up to the house with the inspector. I saw everything I needed to see. I looked at the dead man and decided he was shot by a gun from about four meters. There was no gunpowder on the clothes. Alec Cunningham said the two men were fighting when the shot was fired. Clearly, he lied.

Next, both father and son agreed as to the place where the man escaped into the road. At that point, however, there is some wet ground. I searched very carefully for footmarks but saw none. I then knew that the Cunninghams were lying. There was never an unknown man who came to the house.

"And now I must consider the reason for this murder. Why? First, I tried to understand reasons for the theft at Mr. Acton's. I learned, from the colonel, that there was a problem between you, Mr. Acton, and the Cunninghams. Of course, my first thought was that they broke into your library to get some important papers."

"That's right," said Mr. Acton. "That is just what they did. The law says that I own almost half their land. The local judge is deciding our case. The Cunninghams wanted those valuable papers so that I would lose my case. Happily, they found nothing because the papers were in the office of my lawyer."

"That explains it," said Holmes, smiling. "It was a dangerous attempt, mainly by young Cunningham. But they found nothing, so they tried to make it look like an ordinary theft. They carried away a few objects of little value. That is all fairly clear. But much was still unclear. Above all, I wanted the missing part of that note. I was sure that Alec had torn it out of the dead man's hand. I also believed that he put it in his pocket. The only question was whether or not it was still there. I tried to find out. That is why we all went to the house.

"The Cunninghams joined us, I'm sure you remember, outside the kitchen door. It was very important, of course, not to say anything about the missing piece of paper. If they knew that we wanted it, they would have destroyed it quickly. The inspector was just going to tell them about the importance of the paper, do you remember? That is when I suddenly became ill and fainted."

"Oh, my!" cried the colonel, laughing. "Do you mean that your illness was not real? That you were just acting?"

"Well done Holmes!" I cried. "I'm a doctor, but I still believed you were truly ill." My friend always continued to surprise me with his actions.

"Sometimes acting can be useful," said Holmes. "When I recovered from my little 'problem' I had another idea. I tried to get old Cunningham to write the word 'twelve'. I wanted to make sure that his writing was the same as the 'twelve' on the paper."

"Oh, what a fool I have been!" I shouted.

"I could see that you felt badly for me, my friend," said Holmes, laughing. "I know you thought that I was losing my mind.

"We then went up the steps together. When we entered the dressing-room of young Cunningham I could see his coat hanging on the door. I had to return to that dressing-room as soon as possible. That is when I pushed over the table. I hoped they would not notice me leave the room. I quickly ran back to the dressing-room and searched the coat pockets. The paper was there. A few seconds later, the Cunninghams saw me. I truly believe that they wanted to kill me. I'm very glad all of you arrived to help me. I can still feel the young man's hands around my neck. And the old man turning my arm in pain trying to get the paper. They saw that I knew everything, and they realized they were in danger.

"Later, I had a little talk with old Cunningham. I asked him the reason for the crime. He was willing to talk. His son, however, was very angry. He would gladly have killed me if he had a gun.

"It seems that William secretly followed his two masters the night they went to Mr. Acton's. He then told them that he knew they were the thieves. He told them he would tell the police unless they gave him some money. Mr. Alec, however, was a dangerous man to play games with. He then made an intelligent plan. He wrote a letter to trick William into meeting him late at night. William was fooled by the letter and was then shot. The Cunninghams' big mistake was the letter. If they had gotten the whole piece of paper, I don't think anybody would know of their crime."

"And the message?" I asked.

Sherlock Holmes placed the paper before us. It was the rest of the letter, with the right side missing.

*If you will only come round
to the east gate you will
will very much surprise you and
be of the greatest service to you and also
to Annie Morrison. But say nothing to anyone
upon the matter*

"It is very much the kind of thing I expected," said Holmes. "Of course, we do not yet know about the business between Alec Cunningham, William Kirwan, and Annie Morrison. The letter worked to bring William Kirwan to the house. I'm sure you can now plainly see that the handwriting of father and son is almost the same. Especially in the p's and the g's. You can also see that the old man does not put the point above his i's. Watson, I think our quiet rest in the country has been a great success. I'm sure I will return to Baker Street tomorrow feeling very healthy."

10

The Final Problem

最後の事件

読み始める前に

The Final Problem 最後の事件

56の短編のうち24番目に発表された
1893年12月号のストランド・マガジン初出
1893年発行の「シャーロック・ホームズの思い出」に収録された

［主な登場人物］

Sherlock Holmes シャーロック・ホームズ 世界的に有名な私立探偵。優れた観察眼と推理力を有する。ロンドンのベーカー街221Bに下宿している。

Watson ジョン・H・ワトソン 医師。ホームズの相棒でこの物語の語り手。かつてベーカー街221Bでホームズと同居していた。

Professor Moriarty モリアーティ教授 ロンドンの暗黒面に君臨する犯罪の名手にして、ホームズの宿敵。

［あらすじ］

　この作品で、ホームズは自らの宿敵、ジェームズ・モリアーティ教授との対決を果たすことになる。ロンドンで悪事を重ねる頭脳明晰な犯罪者であるモリアーティ教授を、ホームズはかなりのところまで追い込むことに成功していた。もう逮捕も間近というところで、教授からの反撃にあったホームズは、身を守るためワトソンと共にスイスに逃亡した。二人を追ってきたモリアーティ教授と、ライヘンバッハの滝で一騎打ちとなり、二人とも滝壺に落ちていく。ワトソンはホームズが死んだものと考える。

［総単語数］4,985語

The Final Problem

It is with a heavy heart that I pick up my pen to write these last words about my friend Sherlock Holmes. He was a man gifted with great intelligence. I don't believe I have done a very good job of it, but I have tried to write about everything that happened to us. From our first meeting long ago during the "Study in Scarlet" period, up to the time of "The Naval Treaty." I planned to stop writing there. I did not want to write about the story which happened two years ago and which has made my life very lonely. However, lately, Colonel James Moriarty has written letters in favor of his brother. Now I must come out and tell the public the complete truth. I alone know all the facts of the matter. I must speak out.

I think there have been only three articles about it in the press: one in the *Journal de Genève* on May 6th, 1891; the Reuter's story in the English papers on May 7th; and finally the last letters of Moriarty which I noted. Of these the first and second were very short and incomplete. The last one, however is far from the truth. It is a lie. It is my purpose to tell for the first time what really happened between Professor Moriarty and Mr. Sherlock Holmes.

After I married, the very close friendship between Holmes and I began to change a little. He still came to me when he wanted a friend during his cases. However, we began to see each other less and less. By the year 1890 there were only three cases which I remember. During the winter of that year and the spring of 1891 there was a very important case on which Holmes was working. It was with the French government. I received two letters from Holmes, from Narbonne and Nimes. I understood that his stay in France would be a long one. I was rather surprised, therefore, when he walked into my office on the evening of April 24th. He looked thinner and more pale than usual.

"Yes, I have been too busy," he said, after I looked at him. "Lately, things have not been easy. May I close your window covers?"

The only light in the room came from the small light on the table. Holmes walked carefully to the windows and looked them. Then he closed the covers.

"Are you afraid of something?" I asked.

"Yes."

"Of what?"

"Of air-guns."

"My dear Holmes, what do you mean?"

"I think you know me very well, Watson. You know that I am not a nervous man. However, I would be a fool not to protect myself from the present danger. May I have a smoke?" He then smoked a cigarette.

"I'm sorry for coming so late," said he. "I know it is strange but I must also leave you soon through your back garden."

"But what does it all mean?" I asked.

He held out his hand. I saw in the light that there were several cuts, and blood.

"This problem is real, you see," he said, smiling. "I think I have broken my hand. Is Mrs. Watson in?"

"She is away on a visit."

"Indeed! You are alone?"

"Yes."

"That makes it easier for me to ask you. I'd like you to come away with me for a week to the Continent."

"Where?"

"Oh, anywhere. It doesn't matter to me."

This was something very strange. It was unlike Holmes to take an unnecessary holiday. Also, his pale, thin face told me that he needed a rest. He saw the question in my eyes. Putting his fingers together and crossing his legs he began to explain.

"You have probably never heard of Professor Moriarty?" said he.

"Never."

"Ah, there is the wonder of the thing!" he cried. "The man controls all of London, yet nobody has heard of him. That is why he is a master criminal. I tell you Watson, that if I could control that man, if I could remove him from our country, then I would be very happy indeed. My life as a detective would be complete. I could then settle down quietly somewhere. In fact, Watson, after my work for the government of France and the king of Sweden, I could stop working now. I could live very quietly, with enough money for the rest of my life. I could study my chemistry, and think no more about crime. But I cannot rest, Watson, knowing that a man like Professor Moriarty is free."

"What has he done?"

"His lifetime work has been unbelievable. He is a man of good family, good schooling and especially intelligent. At the age of twenty-one he wrote a paper about 'binomial theorem' which was well known in Europe. With that paper he became a college teacher. His future looked very bright. But there was a dark, criminal part in him. A desire to do evil instead of good. This evil is especially dangerous because of his great mind. There were dark stories about his actions in the college. He was asked to leave. He came down to London and began working with the army. Many people know about his history. But what I am telling you now is what I discovered myself.

"I know London's higher criminal world very well, Watson. For many years I have had a sense that someone, or something, was controlling this world. I felt that a greater power was protecting criminals from the law. Again and again, in many different kinds of crime I have felt this force. There have been many cases of crime that were never solved. For years I have tried to uncover the secret. At last I saw my chance. I began to enter the underground world of ex-Professor Moriarty.

"He is the Napoleon of crime, Watson. He is the power behind half the evil in this country. He is the most intelligent thinker I know. He has hundreds of people working for him. He has a thousand eyes and ears, which give him all the information he needs. He stays in one place and plans everything. Then his followers do what he tells them. They make the crimes. Sometimes a follower is caught by the police. Usually there is enough money to help him become free again. However, the central power is never caught. This is what I am trying to do now, Watson. I want to catch the mind behind these crimes.

"But the professor is very well protected. No matter what I did to find him, I couldn't get close. You know my powers, Watson. You know that I usually have no trouble discovering the truth. However, after three months of looking for Moriarty, I realized that he was my equal. He is truly an evil man, but he is my equal, Watson. At last, however he made a mistake. It was a very small mistake. But it was enough for me to get closer to him. Now I believe that I can catch him. In three days—that is, next Monday—the time will come. The professor and his important helpers will be arrested by the police. Then we will judge this great criminal. We must not move too soon. We must wait.

"The difficulty is that Professor Moriarty knows what I am doing. He knows every step I have taken to catch him. Again and again he tried to hide. But each time I found him. Ah, my friend, I wish there was a book written about our great battle. It is truly my greatest detective work. But he is an equally great criminal. This morning I prepared the last steps. Only three more days were needed. I was sitting in my room thinking about the matter. Suddenly, the door opened and in walked Professor Moriarty.

"My surprise was complete, Watson. The man I was thinking about so much was suddenly standing before me. It seemed like I knew him. He is very tall and thin. He has a large head, especially in the front. His two eyes are deep in his face. His skin is pale and without much hair. He was as interested to meet me as I was to meet him.

"'You look different than I thought,' he said at last. 'It is dangerous to carry a gun in your pocket.'

"It is true that when he entered the room I quickly took my gun from the table. I knew that he wanted me dead. But when he said this I put the gun back out on the table. He continued to smile, but I was nervous. I did not trust this man at all.

"'Perhaps you don't know me,' said he.

"'Not true,' I answered, 'I know you quite well. Please sit down. I can give you five minutes if you want to say something.'

"'I believe you know what I want to say,' he said.

"'Then you already know my answer,' I replied.

"'You won't change your mind?'

"'No.'

"He put his hand in his coat pocket. I picked up my gun. But he only took out a small notebook. There were some dates written down.

"'On January fourth, you worked against me. On the twenty-third you became a problem; by the middle of February the problem was worse; at the end of March I was very uneasy. Now, at the end of April, my position is impossible.'

"'What would you like me to do?' I asked.

"'You must drop it, Mr. Holmes,' he said, his face moving slowly from side to side. 'You really must.'

"'After Monday,' said I.

"'No!' said he. 'I know that you are an intelligent man. In fact, it has been a pleasure to watch you work against me. I have enjoyed our little game. But now it must stop. You know there is only one possible result to your actions. You are in danger, Mr. Holmes. I really don't want to see you hurt, but you are forcing me.'

"'Danger is part of my work,' I said.

"'This is not just danger,' said he. 'You will be destroyed. You don't yet realize who and what you are against. It is a very powerful group. You must move, Mr. Holmes, or you will be stepped on.'

"'I am afraid, sir,' I said, standing up, 'that I have other business to take care of at this moment.'

"He also stood up and looked at me, shaking his head sadly.

"'Well, well,' he said at last. 'I'm sorry, but I have tried to save you. I know every move of your game. You can do nothing before Monday. You hope to put me into the hands of the police. I tell you that the police will never catch me. You hope to control me. I tell you that you will never control me. If you are intelligent enough to hurt me, you may be sure that I will also hurt you.'

"'It is the public I wish to protect, Mr. Moriarty,' said I. 'I care less about myself.'

"'As you wish,' he said, then turned his back and walked out.

"That was my only meeting with Professor Moriarty. It did not make me happy. He means what he says. I don't think that the police can protect me. I am sure that his followers will try to kill me."

"Have they already tried?" I asked.

"My dear Watson, Professor Moriarty acts quickly. At noon I went out to do some business in Oxford Street. When I came to the corner of Welbeck Street a two-horse carriage suddenly drove towards me.

I jumped to the side and just saved myself. The carriage continued around Marylebone Lane and disappeared. I stayed out of the street after that. But as I walked down Vere Street a brick fell from the top of the building. It missed me by only half a meter and broke on the ground. I called the police and we went up to the top. There were no people but there were many bricks. It seems that the building was being fixed. Of course, I could prove nothing. They said that perhaps the wind blew over one of the bricks. I took a taxi to my brother's office in Pall Mall, where I spent the day. Later, while coming here, a young man tried to hit me with a strong stick. I was able to throw him down. The police have him now. But I am sure that the police will learn nothing of Professor Moriarty from this young man. Now you know, Watson, why I closed the window covers when I arrived here. And why I must leave by the back garden."

I had often thought my friend to be a man of very strong mind. Now, after a day of great fear, his nerves were still strong.

"You will spend the night here?" I said.

"No, my friend, you might find me to be a dangerous visitor. I have made my plans, and all will be well. It is not necessary for me to be here when the police arrest our enemies on Monday. Therefore, the best thing for me to do is to leave for a few days. It would be a great pleasure, Watson, if you could come with me to the Continent."

"Well, business is quiet this week," said I. "And my neighbors will watch the place. I would be glad to come."

"And to start tomorrow morning?"

"If necessary."

"Oh yes, it is most necessary. Here is what I want you to do. Please do everything that I say because we are now playing a dangerous game. Now listen! You will send your bags this evening with someone you trust to Victoria Station. In the morning you will send for a taxi.

But don't take either the first or second which arrives. Get into the taxi and drive to the Lowther Arcade at the end of the Strand. Give the taxi driver the street name and number on a piece of paper. Ask him to keep the paper. When the taxi stops quickly pay the driver and run through the Arcade. You must reach the other side at a quarter-past nine. You will find a small carriage waiting. The driver will be a man with a heavy black coat. Get into the carriage and you will reach Victoria in time for the Continental train."

"Where shall I meet you?"

"At the station. The second first-class train carriage will be ours."

"Then we will meet on the train?"

"Yes."

It was useless to ask Holmes to stay for the night. No doubt he believed that it was dangerous for me. We spoke a little more about plans for the next day. We then walked out into the garden. He jumped over the wall into Mortimer Street.

In the morning I did everything that Holmes asked. I took the third taxi that passed directly to the Lowther Arcade. I ran through it at full speed. A taxi was waiting with a large driver dressed in a black coat. I got in and was taken quickly to Victoria Station. After I got out the driver turned and drove away at full speed.

So far all was well. My bags were waiting for me and I had no trouble finding the train carriage. I waited for Holmes to arrive. The train was due to leave in five minutes. Where was Holmes? I looked at the groups of travelers but didn't see him. An old Italian priest was trying to speak with a train worker about his bags. The priest spoke little English and the worker didn't understand. I tried to help him with his bags. I then looked around once more and returned to my carriage. The Italian priest was sitting in my seat. I tried to explain that I was waiting for my friend. But my Italian was no better than his English. I looked out the window for my friend. Now I was afraid. The doors were closing and the train was just beginning to move, when —

"My dear Watson," said a voice, "you haven't even said good morning."

I turned in complete surprise. The old priest had turned towards me. For a moment his face changed back to someone that I knew. Then, just as quickly, it changed back to the old man.

"My God!" I cried, "what a shock!"

"I must still be very careful," he said softly. "I believe they are following me closely. Ah, look, there is Moriarty himself."

The train was moving slowly. Looking back, I saw a tall man push through the crowd. He raised his hand as if he wanted the train to stop. He was too late, however. We were now going faster, and soon left the station. "Do you see how close that was?" said Holmes, laughing. He stood up and took off the coat and hat. He put them in a small bag.

"Have you seen the morning paper, Watson?"

"No."

"You haven't heard about Baker Street, then?"

"Baker Street?"

"They burned our offices last night. Luckily, the fire was small."

"My God, Holmes, this is too much!"

"I think they lost me completely after the police arrested their man last night. They thought that I had returned home. Clearly, they were watching you. That's why Moriarty came to Victoria. Did you make any mistakes in coming here?"

"I did just what you told me."

"Did you find your taxi at the Lowther Arcade?"

"Yes, it was waiting."

"Did you know the driver?"

"No."

"It was my brother Mycroft. Sometimes it is best to use people you can trust. But now we must make a plan about Moriarty."

"Well, this train goes directly to the ship. I believe we have lost him, haven't we?"

"Watson, perhaps you didn't understand me before. I told you that this man is as intelligent as I am. If I were him, do you think I would stop looking now? Of course not. He will continue to hunt for us."

"What will he do?"

"What I would do."

"And what is that?"

"Take a special train."

"But he will be late."

"No he won't. This train stops at Canterbury. Later, there is always at least a twenty-minute wait at the ship. He will catch us there."

"Now I feel like the criminal. Why don't we have him arrested when he arrives?"

"That would destroy three months of my work. True, we would have the most important man, but the others would escape. On Monday we shall have them all. No, an arrest is impossible."

"What then?"

"We shall get off at Canterbury."

"And then?"

"Well, then we must make the trip by land to Newhaven. From there by ship to Dieppe. Moriarty will do what I would do. He will continue to Paris. He will see our bags there and wait for two days at the station. In the meantime, we shall buy new bags and travel slowly to Switzerland through Luxembourg and Basle."

So at Canterbury we got off the train. However, it was necessary to wait an hour for the next train to Newhaven.

I was still looking for my bags when Holmes pointed into the distance.

"Already, you see," said he.

Far away, above the trees of Kent was a thin cloud of smoke. A minute later a train began to appear from around the turn. We quickly jumped behind a group of bags to hide. The train passed noisily.

"There he goes," said Holmes as we watched the train disappear again in the distance. "You see, Moriarty does make mistakes. He should have known what I was thinking."

"What would he have done to us?"

"I have no doubt that he would murder us. However, two can play this game. Well, shall we take an early lunch now or wait until Newhaven?"

That night we arrived in Brussels. We spent two days there then continued to Strasbourg on the third day. On Monday morning Holmes telegraphed the London police. In the evening we found a reply waiting for us at the hotel. Holmes read it, then became very angry.

"I should have known!" he shouted. "He has escaped!"

"Moriarty?"

"They have everyone else in Moriarty's group of criminals. But they did not catch him. I knew it would be a little difficult, especially with me out of the country. I thought the police would get him. Watson, I think you should return to England."

"Why?"

"Because you will find me a dangerous friend now. Moriarty cannot return to London. I believe he will try very hard to find me and kill me. He told me that in our short talk. I believe he means it. It is best that you go back to your business."

I was his best and oldest friend. Of course, I wanted to stay with

Holmes and help him. We sat in a Strasbourg restaurant for an hour talking about travel plans. The same night we continued our journey towards Geneva.

For a very pleasant week we traveled through Switzerland. Up the Rhone Valley to Leuk, then over the Gemmi Pass, still deep in snow, to Interlaken, then Meiringen. It was a lovely trip, the green of spring in the valleys and the white of winter in the mountains above, but it was clear that Holmes could not forget the dark cloud which followed him. I could see in his eyes that he was still afraid. He looked at every face that passed us. He was sure that danger was very close.

Once, I remember, we passed over the Gemmi, walking along the Daubensee lake. A large rock behind us fell down the mountain. It fell into the lake with a loud sound. Holmes quickly ran to a nearby hill and began looking around in every direction. Our guide told us that this often happened in the spring and that there was no problem. Holmes said nothing.

He was watchful but never sad. In fact, he seemed to be rather happy. Again and again he said that if Moriarty was arrested then he would stop working as a detective.

"I don't think my life has been without purpose, Watson," he told me. "My work has been useful to many people. London is a safer place because of me. I have solved over one thousand cases. My powers have always been on the side of good against evil. Your memoirs will finish, Watson, on the day that I find and arrest the most dangerous criminal in Europe."

I will continue to tell the rest of the story just as it happened. There is no pleasure for me to talk about it but I feel it is my job.

It was on May third that we reached the little town of Meiringen. We stayed at a small mountain hotel called the Englischer Hof. The owner was a man named Peter Steiler. He was an intelligent man who spoke perfect English. Earlier, he had worked for three years at the Grosvenor Hotel in London. He told us that we should cross the mountains and visit the small town of Rosenlaui. He also told us that we must stop along the way to see the beautiful waterfall of Reichenbach. The waterfall is about halfway up the mountain. On the afternoon of May fourth we began our walk.

It was, indeed, a beautiful, fearful place. The snow was quickly turning into water. The rivers were full and powerful. The water came loudly down the mountain into a deep valley. It then went over a rock and fell many meters into other rocks below. We stood watching and listening to this wonderful show of nature.

The small foot-road stopped halfway around the falls. It was necessary to return the way we came. As we turned back we saw a Swiss boy running towards us. He had a letter in his hand. It was from our hotel and was written to me by the owner. He wrote that an English woman arrived at the hotel only a few minutes after we had left. She was ill. She had spent the winter at Davos and was now going on to see friends in Lucerne. But her illness was sudden. She appeared to be dying and wished to see only an English doctor. Mr. Steiler asked me to please help her. He wrote that it would be a great favor to him.

Of course I had to help her. She was an English woman dying in a strange land. Yet I did not want to leave Holmes. We finally agreed, however, that he would stay with the young Swiss boy as a guide. I returned to Meiringen. Holmes planned to stay a short while longer at the falls before continuing to Rosenlaui. I planned to join him there that evening. As I turned to leave I saw Holmes with his back against a rock, his arms crossed. He was looking into the fast moving waters. It was the last time I ever saw him.

Near the bottom of the hill I looked back. I could not see the waterfall from that position. However, I could see the small foot-road going up to the falls. I also saw a man walking very quickly.

I could see his black figure very clearly against the green land behind him. But I quickly forgot about him as I returned to the hotel.

Perhaps an hour later I reached Meiringen. Old Steiler was standing outside.

"Well," said I, hurrying, "I hope she is still alive?"

The Swiss man looked surprised. He did not know what I was talking about. My heart almost stopped.

"You did not write this?" I cried, showing him the note. "There is no sick Englishwoman in the hotel?"

"Of course not!" he cried. "But I see that it is from my hotel. Oh, perhaps it was from that tall Englishman who came after you left. He — "

But I didn't wait for him to explain. I was afraid. I began to run back through the town and up the hill again. It took me one hour to come down. It took me nearly two hours to go back up to the Reichenbach falls. I saw Holmes's walking-stick against the rock. But I could not see my friend anywhere. I shouted his name, but there was no answer. I could only hear my own voice.

I stood for a minute or two. I was completely afraid. Then I began to think of Holmes's own methods. What could I do to find him? Only one thing was possible. I walked towards the end of the foot-road. The soil there was dark brown and always wet from the water. I looked closely for footmarks. There were two sets. Both of them were going away from me. None returned. I followed them. At the end of the foot-road I saw that the soil had become mud from their feet. The plants at the edge of the rocks were destroyed. I lay down on my face and looked over the side of the waterfall. I could see only water and rocks. I shouted again, but there was no answer.

I returned to where Holmes's walking-stick was. I saw something bright just above it upon a rock. It was Holmes's silver cigarette-case. As I picked it up a small piece of paper fell on to the ground. I opened it and found that it was three pages taken from his notebook. It was written by Holmes to me.

MY DEAR WATSON:

I write these few lines here at the waterfall. Mr. Moriarty is here waiting for me. We are having a final talk. We are asking one another many questions. I want to know his methods and he wants to know mine. He is telling me how he escaped from the English police and how he found me here. He is indeed an intelligent criminal. I am happy to think that England will be free of him. However, I fear that it is at a great cost to my dear friends and family. Especially to you my old friend. I already explained to you that my life's work was nearly finished. I believe that this is a good ending. I am pleased.

I must tell you, Watson, that I knew the letter from Meiringen was not true. I allowed you to leave and I knew Moriarty would probably come.

Please tell Inspector Patterson that the papers he needs to use against the criminals are in my office. They are in a small blue box marked "Moriarty." Before leaving England I gave my brother Mycroft all my important papers about belongings and money. Please give my best wishes to Mrs. Watson. I will miss you, my dear friend,

Yours,
Sherlock Holmes

Just a few more words about the rest. What truly happened there at the waterfall is a mystery. However, the police later came to the place.

There is no doubt that the two men had a fight at the edge of the falls. It ended, of course, with both men falling to their death. It was not possible, however, to recover their bodies. Therefore, among those rocks and water will forever stay the world's most dangerous criminal and the world's finest detective. The Swiss boy was never found again. It seems sure that he was one of many people working for Moriarty. As for the group of criminals, the public will always be thankful to Sherlock Holmes. These dangerous men were all arrested and locked up. There are, perhaps, a few people who will not remember my friend. But I am writing this because he is the best and wisest man whom I have ever known.

11

The Adventure of the Empty House

空き家の冒険

読み始める前に

The Adventure of the Empty House 空き家の冒険

56の短編のうち25番目に発表された
1903年10月号のストランド・マガジン初出
1905年発行の「シャーロック・ホームズの帰還」に収録された

［主な登場人物］

Sherlock Holmes シャーロック・ホームズ 世界的に有名な私立探偵。優れた観察眼と推理力を有する。約3年前、ライヘンバッハの滝でモリアーティ教授と対決した。

Watson ジョン・H・ワトソン 医師。ホームズの相棒でこの物語の語り手。かつてベーカー街221Bでホームズと同居していた。

Ronald Adair ロナルド・アデア卿 メイノース伯爵の次男。カード賭博が好きでいくつかのクラブに入っていた。何者かに銃殺された。

Colonel Sebastian Moran セバスティアン・モラン大佐 アデアのカード仲間。かつて英国陸軍に所属していた射撃の名手。

Professor Moriarty モリアーティ教授 ホームズの宿敵。約3年前、ライヘンバッハの滝でホームズと対決した。

Mrs. Hudson ハドソン夫人 ベーカー街221Bの女主人。

Lestrade レストレード スコットランド・ヤードの警部。

［あらすじ］

ワトソンは、ライヘンバッハの滝壺に落ちて死んだと思っていたホームズと劇的な再会を果たす。妻とも離別し、孤独な日々を送っていたワトソンだけに、この再会には驚きを隠せない。宿敵モリアーティ教授の手下が起こしたアデア殺人事件の謎を2人で解き明かすことで、再びホームズとのパートナーシップを確立し、次なる事件解決へと向かうことになる。

［総単語数］6,616語

The Adventure of the Empty House

It was in the spring of the year 1894 that all London was interested in the murder of the Honorable Ronald Adair. Although the public learned much about the crime from the law case reported in the newspapers, a lot was not reported as the police did not need to bring forward all the facts. Only now, at the end of ten years, am I allowed to supply the missing pieces which make the story complete. The crime was of interest in itself, but more interesting was perhaps the most remarkable and surprising thing that ever happened to me. Even now, after all this time, I find my blood racing as I think of it. I would of course have loved to have shared my knowledge with those people who have shown interest in the thoughts and actions of a remarkable man. However, the great man himself would not allow me to speak of it until last month.

My close friendship with Sherlock Holmes had interested me deeply in crime, and even after he went missing I still read about the various problems which came before the public. I even attempted, more than once, to use his methods to find the answer, though without great success. There was no case, however, which interested me as much as the sad story of Ronald Adair. The police knew that Mr. Adair had been murdered but were unable to discover who had done it. Their job was made more difficult because they could find no reason for the crime. There were points about this strange business which would, I was sure, have interested Sherlock Holmes. All day as I went upon my rounds, I thought about the case but could find no answer that seemed to be sensible.

The Honorable Ronald Adair was the second son of the Earl of Maynooth, at that time living in Australia. Adair's mother had returned from Australia to have an eye operation, and she, her son Ronald, and her daughter Hilda were living together at 427 Park Lane. The young man had many good friends in town and, so far as was known, had no enemies and had never upset anyone. Yet it was to this rich, easy-going young man that death came, in the most strange and unexpected way, between the hours of ten and eleven-twenty on the night of March 30, 1894.

Ronald Adair liked playing cards, and played often, but never for an amount that would hurt him. He was a member of several card clubs. After dinner on the day of his death he had played cards at the Bagatelle club. The people who had played with him—Mr. Murray, Sir John Hardy, and Colonel Moran—had said that there was a fairly equal fall of cards. Adair might have lost five pounds, but not more. He had a lot of money and such a loss could not in any way affect him. He had played nearly every day at one club or another, but he was a careful player and usually ended up a winner. It came out in evidence that playing with Colonel Moran, he had actually won as much as four hundred pounds some weeks before from Godfrey Milner and Lord Balmoral.

On the evening of the crime, he returned from the club at ten. His mother and sister were out spending the evening with a friend. The servant reported that she heard him enter the front room on the second floor, generally used as his sitting room. She had made up a fire there and she had opened the window to let the smoke out. No sound was heard from the room until eleven-twenty when Lady Maynooth and her daughter returned. She wanted to say good-night to her son but found his room locked on the inside. He did not reply to their cries. They got help and the door was forced open. Ronald Adair was found lying near the table. It was clear from the state of the body that he had been shot by an expanding bullet, but no gun of any sort was to be found in the room. On the table was some money grouped in different amounts. There were also some figures upon a piece of paper, with the names of some club friends opposite them, from which it was judged that before his death he was trying to make out his losses or winnings at cards.

A further investigation only made the case harder to understand. In the first place, no reason could be given why the young man should have locked the door from the inside. There was the possibility that the murderer had done this, and had afterwards escaped from the window. The drop was at least twenty feet, however, and a bed of flowers lay beneath. Neither the flowers nor the earth showed any sign of someone having landed there, nor were there any marks on the grass which separated the house from the road. It appeared, therefore, that the young man himself had fastened the door. But how did he come by his death? No one could have climbed up to the window without leaving a mark. Suppose a man had fired through the window, it would indeed have been a remarkable shot to have caused so deadly a wound from such a distance. Also Park Lane is a busy road; there are people about at all hours but no one had heard a shot. But there was the dead man, and the soft-nosed bullet, which had expanded on hitting Adair, thereby making a wound which must have caused Adair's death at once. These facts of the Park Lane Mystery made even less sense when no reason could be found for the crime. As I have said, young Adair was not known to have any enemies, and no attempt had been made to remove the money or valuables in the room.

All day I turned these facts over in my mind, trying to find an answer which would make sense of them, as well as the simple idea which Holmes had said was the starting point of every investigation. I must say that I was unsuccessful. In the evening I went for a walk and found myself about six o'clock at the Oxford Street end of Park Lane. There was a group of people all looking up at the same window; this was the house which I had come to see. A tall, thin man with colored glasses, whom I thought to be a plain-clothes detective, was pointing out his answer. The others crowded round to listen to what he said, but his thoughts seemed to me to be rather foolish. As I left the crowd I struck against a man almost doubled up with age and illness, causing him to drop several books which he was carrying. I remember that as I picked them up, I saw the title of one of them, a strange book about trees, and it struck me that the fellow must be some poor booklover, who, either as a trade or as a pastime hunted down unusual books. I tried to say I was sorry but it was clear that these books were very important objects to their owner. With an angry look he turned away, and he made his way through the crowd.

My time spent watching No. 427 Park Lane did little to clear up the problem in which I was interested. The house was separated from the street by a low wall about five feet high. It was perfectly easy, therefore, for anyone to get into the garden. However, the window was a different matter. There was nothing which could help even the best climber to get to it. In fact I was less certain of the answer than ever as I walked back to Kensington. I had not been in my study five minutes when the servant entered to say that a person wanted to see me. Remarkably, it was none other than the strange old booklover, his face looking out from a ring of white hair. His books, twelve of them at least, were under his right arm.

"You're surprised to see me, sir," said he, in a strange, dry voice.

"Yes, I am rather," I replied.

"Well I felt I should say sorry for my manner earlier. There was no ill-feeling meant. I am indeed thankful that you helped to pick up my books."

"It was nothing, good sir," said I. "May I ask how you knew where to find me?"

"Well, sir, I am a neighbor of yours. My little bookshop is at the corner of Church Street, and I'm very pleased to meet you, I am sure. Maybe you like books yourself, sir. Here's *Birds of England* and *Catullus*, and *The Holy War*—a good buy every one of them. With five books you could just fill that space on the second row. It doesn't look quite right, sir."

I moved my head to look at the bookcase behind me. When I turned again Sherlock Holmes was standing smiling at me across my study table. I rose to my feet, stared at him for a few seconds unable to speak. Then it appears that I must have passed out for the first and only time in my life. A gray cloud passed before my eyes, and when it had cleared I found my shirt undone. I had the aftertaste of a strong drink in my mouth. Holmes was bending over my chair.

"My dear Watson," said the well-remembered voice, "I am so sorry. I had no idea that you would be so overcome."

I held him by the arms.

"Holmes!" I cried. "Is it really you? Can it indeed be that you are alive? Is it possible that you succeeded in climbing out of that awful drop?"

"Wait a moment," said he. "Are you sure you are really fit to talk about these things? I have given you a grave upset by my unnecessarily unusual reappearance."

"I am all right, but indeed, Holmes, I can hardly believe my eyes. Good heavens!" Again I held him and felt his thin arm. "Well you are real enough. I'm overjoyed to see you. Sit down and tell me how you got out alive from that fearful mountain."

He sat across from me, and lit a cigarette in his old, carefree manner. He was dressed in the old clothes of the book dealer, but the rest of that person lay among the white hair and old books upon the table. Holmes looked even thinner than of old, and although his eyes were bright, there was a dead-white shade to his face. This told me that his life of late had not been a healthy one.

"I am glad to be able to stand straight, Watson," said he. "It is hard for a tall man to appear so short for such a length of time. Now, my dear fellow, we have, if I may ask for your help, a hard and dangerous night's work in front of us. Perhaps it would be better if I told you the whole story when that work is finished."

"I cannot wait, Holmes. I should much rather know now."

"You'll come with me tonight?"

"When you like and where you like."

"This is, indeed, like the old days. We shall have time for a mouthful of dinner before we go. Well, then, about that fall from the mountain. I had no great difficulty getting out of it, for the very simple reason that I never fell!"

"You never fell?"

"No, Watson, I did not. My note at the time to you was completely true. I had little doubt that I had come to the end of my life when I saw the figure of the dangerous Professor Moriarty standing upon the thin passage-way which led to safety. I saw what he meant to do in his cold, gray eyes. I spoke with him, therefore, and he allowed me to write the short note which you afterwards received. I left it with my cigarette-box and my stick, and I walked along the pass with Moriarty close behind. When I reached the end I stood waiting. He pulled no gun, but he rushed at me and threw his long arms around me. He knew that his own game was up and wanted to take me down with him. We fell together close to the edge, and I faced death. With God's help I was able to shake off his hold; with a fearful shout he wildly tried to regain his feet, threw his arms out to try and catch me, but went over. With my face still over the edge, I saw him fall a long way. Then he struck a rock before falling into the water."

I listened to this remarkable explanation, which Holmes gave as he smoked his cigarette.

"But the tracks!" I cried. "I saw, with my own eyes, that two went along the mountain pass and none returned."

"It came about in this way. The moment that the Professor had disappeared, it struck me what a really extraordinarily good chance Heaven had placed before me. I knew that Moriarty was not the only man who wanted to kill me. There were at least three others who would now be even angrier because of the death of their leader. They were all most dangerous men. One or other would surely get me. On the other hand, if all the world thought that I was dead, they would take chances, these men; they would lay themselves open. Sooner or later I could destroy them. Then it would be time for me to let everyone know that I was still in the land of the living. So quick does the mind act that I believe I had thought this all out before Professor Moriarty had reached the bottom of Reichenbach Fall.

"I stood up and looked at the rocky wall behind me. In your rather pretty account of the matter, which I read with great interest some months later, you said that the wall could not be climbed. That was not quite true. A few small footholds presented themselves, and I thought I could see a resting point higher up. The mountain wall was so high that to climb it all was not a possibility, and I could not have made my way along the wet path without leaving some tracks. I thought, then, it was best that I should chance the climb. It was not a pleasant business, Watson. The fall was beneath me, and although I am not easily fooled,

I give you my word that I seemed to hear Moriarty's voice shouting at me from below. One misplaced foot would have meant my death, for real this time. More than once I thought I was gone. But I kept going upward. At last I reached a point several feet deep and covered with soft green grass, where I could lie unseen. There I lay when you, my dear Watson, and all your following were investigating, in your usual questionable way, the manner of my death.

"At last, when you had come to completely the wrong answer, you left for the hotel and I was alone. I had thought that I had reached the end of my problems, but there were still surprises in store for me. A great rock, falling from above, rushed past me, hit the track, and carried on into the fall. For a moment I thought that it was by chance, but, looking up, I saw a man's head against the darkening sky. Then another rock struck near the place where I was laying. Moriarty had not been alone. One of his men, and it was one of the most dangerous of Moriarty's group, had kept guard while the Professor and I had fought. From a distance, unseen by me, he had watched Professor Moriarty's death and my escape. He had waited, and then making his way round to the top of the mountain, he had tried to succeed where Moriarty had failed.

"I did not take long to think about it, Watson. Again I saw that angry face look over the edge, and I knew that another rock was coming. I raced back down toward the path. I don't think I could have done it in cold blood. It was a hundred times more difficult than getting up. But I had no time to think of the danger, for another stone rushed past me. Halfway down I fell, but, thanks to God, I landed torn and bloody upon the path. I raced away, did ten miles over the mountains in the darkness, and a week later I found myself in Florence, knowing that no one in the world knew what had become of me.

"I told only one person—my brother Mycroft. I must say sorry to you, my dear Watson, but it was all important that I should be thought dead. I am sure that you would not have written so believable report of my unhappy end had you yourself not thought it were true. Several times during the last three years I have taken my pen to write to you, but always I feared that your kind feelings for me should lead you to say something which would give away my secret. For that reason I turned away from you this evening when you upset my books, for I was in danger at the time, and any show of surprise on your part might have led to the most unpleasant results. As to Mycroft, I had to tell him in order to get the money I needed. Things did not go as well in London as I had hoped, for the trial of the Moriarty group left two of its most dangerous members, my own most fearful enemies, still free. I traveled for two years in distant countries. You may have read of the remarkable travels of a Norwegian named Sigerson, but I am sure that you did not know you were receiving news of your friend. I kept myself busy doing various jobs, some for my own pleasure and some of which I cannot speak. Then recently I learned that only one of my enemies was now left in London, I was about to return when my movements were quickened by the news of this very remarkable Park Lane Mystery, which not only interested me on its own, but which seemed to offer me a way in which I could also help myself. I came over at once to London, called as myself at Baker Street, threw Mrs. Hudson into a near fit, and found that Mycroft had kept my rooms and my papers just as they had always been. So it was, my dear Watson, that at two o'clock today I found myself in my old room, and only wishing that I could have seen my old friend Watson in the other chair."

Such was the remarkable story to which I listened on that April evening—a story which would have been unbelievable to me had it not been told by Holmes himself, my oldest friend, whom I had never thought I would see again. In some way he had learned of my own sad loss, and his feelings were shown in his manner rather than his words. "Work is the best way to deal with sorrow, my dear Watson," said he; "and I have a piece of work for us both tonight which, if we can bring it to a successful end, will be reason enough, by itself, for a man to live on this earth." I asked him to tell me more. "You will hear and see enough before morning," he answered. "We have three years of the past to talk about first. And at half past nine, we will start upon the adventure of the empty house."

It was indeed like old times when, at that hour, I found myself seated beside him in a cab, my gun in my pocket, and adventure in my heart. Holmes was quiet and deep in thought. I did not know what we were about to do, but I knew from Holmes's manner that the adventure was a dangerous one.

I had thought that we were going to Baker Street, but Holmes stopped the cab at the corner of Cavendish Square. I noticed that as he stepped out he gave a careful look to left and right, and at every street corner he took the same pains to see that we were not followed. We then took back street after back street as Holmes once again showed his remarkable knowledge of London. In the end we were in a small road, lined with old, dark houses, which led us into Manchester Street, and so to Blandford Street. Here he turned quickly down a small passage, passed through a wooden gate into an empty yard, and then opened the back door of a house with a key. We entered together, and he closed it behind us.

The place was completely dark, but it was clear to me that it was an empty house. Holmes's cold, thin fingers closed round my arm and led me forward down a long hall, until I saw the street light over the front door. Here Holmes turned suddenly to the right, and we found ourselves in a large, square, empty room, very dark in the corners, but with just a little light in the center from the street outside. Even so we could only just see each other from a few feet away and the rest of the room was completely black. My friend put his mouth to my ear.

"Do you know where we are?" he said as quietly as possible.

"Surely that is Baker Street," I answered looking through the window.

"Just so. We are in Camden House, which stands across from our old quarters."

"But why are we here?"

"Because it gives such a good view of our old home. Might I trouble you, my dear Watson, to go a little closer to the window, taking every care not to show yourself, and then to look at our old rooms? We will see if my three years away have completely taken away my power to surprise you."

I inched forward and looked across at the window. As my eyes fell upon it, I gave a cry of surprise. There was a strong light burning in the room and the outline of a man, seated in a chair, was clear to see. It could only be one person; it was a perfect reproduction of Holmes. So surprised was I that I threw out my hand to make sure that the man himself was standing beside me. He was shaking as he tried to stop himself laughing out loud.

"Well?" said he.

"Good heavens!" I cried. "It is remarkable."

"I trust you are suitably pleased," said he, and I heard in his voice the same joy a painter feels in his art. "It really is rather like me, is it not?"

"I can hardly believe it is not you."

"Monsieur Oscar Meunier, of Grenoble, made the likeness, and I set it up myself during my visit to Baker Street this afternoon."

"But why?"

"Because, my dear Watson, I have a reason for wishing some people to think that I was there when I was really elsewhere."

"And you thought the rooms were watched?"

"I knew they were."

"By whom?"

"By my old enemies, Watson. By Moriarty's group. You must remember that they, and only they, knew that I was still alive. Sooner or later they believed that I should come back to my rooms. They watched them continuously, and this morning they saw me arrive."

"How do you know?"

"Because I knew their guard. I saw him when I looked out of my window. He is a harmless enough fellow, Parker by name. I cared nothing for him. But I cared a great deal for the person who was behind him, the best friend of Moriarty, the man who dropped the rocks from the mountain top, the most dangerous criminal in London. That is the man who is after me tonight, Watson, and that is the man who has no idea that we are after him."

My friend's plans were slowly becoming clear. From our position, the watchers were being watched and the trackers, tracked. That outline of the thin face across the road would bring our enemy, and we awaited them. In the quiet darkness we stood together and watched the hurrying figures who passed and repassed in front of us. Holmes did not move; but I could tell that he missed nothing, and that his eyes studied each and every passerby. It was a cold night, and the wind blew down the long street. There were many people about, most of them covered up in coats. Once or twice it seemed to me that I had seen the same figure before, and I noticed with interest two men who appeared to be keeping out of the wind in the doorway of a house some distance up the street. I tried to tell Holmes about them but he shook his head quickly and continued to stare into the street. It was clear to me that he was becoming uneasy and that his plans were not working out altogether as he had hoped. At last as it neared twelve o'clock and the street slowly cleared, he walked up and down the room unable to control his nerves. I was about to say something to him, when I raised my eyes to the lighted window, and felt almost as great a surprise as before. I pointed at it.

"The outline has moved," I cried.

It was indeed no longer the side, but the back, which was now turned towards us.

Three years had not made Holmes feel more kindly to minds less clever than his own.

"Of course it has moved," said he. "Am I such a fool, Watson, that I should place such a clear copy, and expect that some of the men of Moriarty's group would be fooled by it? We have been in this room two hours and Mrs. Hudson has made some change in that figure eight times, or once in every quarter of an hour. She works it from the front so that her outline may never be seen. Ah!"

He breathed deeply. In the low light I saw his head thrown forward, his whole body completely still as he looked. Outside the street was completely empty. Those two men might still be in the doorway, but I could no longer see them. All was still and dark, save only that lighted window in front of us with the black figure outlined upon its center. Again in the quiet I heard that thin note from Holmes which told me something was about to happen. A moment later he pulled me back into the darkest corner of the room, and I knew I must, at all costs, stay completely quiet. Never had I known my friend more moved, and yet the dark street was still empty before us.

But suddenly I noticed that which his senses had already picked up. A low sound came to my ears, not from the direction of Baker Street, but from the back of the very house in which we lay in wait. A door opened and closed. A moment later steps could be heard in the hall.

Holmes moved back against the wall, and I did the same, my hand closing upon my gun as I moved. Looking into the darkness of the hall I could just make out the outline of a man, a shade blacker than the blackness of the open door. He stood for a moment and then came into the room. He was within three yards of us, this dangerous looking figure, and I had readied myself to meet his spring before I realized that he had no idea that we were there. He passed close beside us, over to the window, and noiselessly raised it half a foot. As he dropped to the height of this opening, the light of the street fell full upon his face. In his hand he carried what appeared to be a stick. Then from his coat he pulled a heavy object, and he placed the two pieces together. He straightened and I saw that what he held in his hand was a sort of gun. He opened it, put something in and closed it. Then, bending down, he rested the end of the gun upon the edge of the open window, and I saw his eye shining as it looked along the sights. He held the gun into his shoulder. For a moment he was still. Then he fired his shot. There was very little noise in the room, but the sound of broken glass from the window across the road. At that moment Holmes jumped on to his back, and threw him flat upon his face. He was up again in a moment and held Holmes by the neck, but I struck him on the head with my gun and he dropped again to the floor. I fell upon him and held him, and Holmes gave a loud call. There was the sound of running feet outside and two policemen, with a plain clothes detective, rushed through the front door and into the room.

"That you, Lestrade?" asked Holmes.

"Yes, Mr. Holmes. I took the job myself. It's good to see you back in London, sir."

We had all risen to our feet and I was able at last to get a good look at our prisoner. It was a very strong, dangerous-looking face which was turned toward us. He took no notice of any of us, but kept his eyes fixed upon Holmes's face with a look in which deep dislike and wonder showed equally. "You are too clever," he kept on saying, "far too clever!"

"Colonel," said Holmes, "I don't think I have had the pleasure of seeing you since you tried to kill me as I lay on the mountain above the Reichenbach Fall."

The colonel still stared at my friend like a man unable to believe what had happened. "You have not met Colonel Sebastian Moran, have you gentlemen," said Holmes, "once of the British Army, and one of the best shots that our country has produced. I am surprised that my very simple plan could fool an old soldier like yourself!"

Colonel Moran jumped forward with an angry shout, but the policemen held him back.

"I must say," continued Holmes, "you had one small surprise for me. I did not think that you would yourself make use of this empty house and this very window. I had thought you would work from the street, where my friend Lestrade and his men were awaiting you. With that exception all has gone as I expected."

Colonel Moran turned to Lestrade.

"You may or may not have just cause for holding me," said he, "but at least there can be no reason why I should listen any further to what he has to say. If I am in the hands of the law, let things be done in a lawful way."

"Well, that's reasonable enough," said Lestrade. "Nothing else you have to say, Mr. Holmes, before we go?"

Holmes had picked up the powerful air gun from the floor and was looking at how it worked.

"A strange gun this, none like it," said he. "Noiseless and yet of considerable power. I knew Von Herder, the blind German doctor, who built it to the order of the late Professor Moriarty. For years I have been aware of it, though I have never before had the chance to hold it. I ask you to note it well, Lestrade, and also the bullets which fit it."

"You can trust us to look after that, Mr. Holmes," said Lestrade, as the whole group moved toward the door. "Anything further to say?"

"Only to ask what charge you will make against the colonel."

"What charge, sir? Why, of course, the attempted murder of Sherlock Holmes."

"Not so, Lestrade. I will not appear in the matter at all. You, and you alone, will be famous for this remarkable piece of police work. Yes, Lestrade, you have done well! With your usual method of planning and nerve, you have got him."

"Got him! Got whom, Mr. Holmes?"

"The man that the whole police force has been looking for—Colonel Sebastian Moran, the man who shot the Honorable Ronald Adair with an expanding bullet from an air gun through the open window of the second floor front of No. 427 Park Lane, upon the thirtieth of last month. That's the charge, Lestrade. And now, Watson, if you can stand the cold wind from a broken window, I think that half an hour in my study over a cigarette may be of interest to you."

Our old rooms had been left unchanged on the orders of Mycroft Holmes. Mrs. Hudson smiled broadly at us both as we entered and I saw at once the strange reproduction which had played so important a part in the evening's adventure. The likeness to Holmes was almost perfect. However, part of it had been destroyed by the expanding bullet which had passed through the head, hitting the wall behind. I picked it up from the floor.

"A soft bullet, as you see, Watson. Very clever, who would expect to find such a thing fired from an air gun? All right, Mrs. Hudson. Thank you so much for your help. And now, Watson, let me see you in your old seat once more, for there are several points which I would like to go over with you."

I sat down and Holmes continued.

"The old hunter had not lost his nerve, nor his clear sight," said he, with a laugh, as he looked at the hole in the bust. "Right in the middle of the back of the head. He was the best shot in the army, and I expect there are few better in London. Have you heard the name?"

"No, I have not."

"Well, well! But then I remember that you had not heard the name of Professor Moriarty, one of the best minds of the century. Anyway, Colonel Moran appeared to have a record of honor as a soldier. It is true that up to a point he did well and there are many stories still told about his actions. For some reason, however, Colonel Moran began to go wrong. Without any reported trouble, he was asked to leave India. He left the army, came to London, and once more gained a bad name. It was at this time that he was found by Professor Moriarty, in whose group he was second only to Moriarty himself. Moriarty supplied him with money, and only used him in one or two very high-class jobs, which no normal criminal could have undertaken. You may recall the death of Mrs. Stewart in 1887. No? Well, I am sure Moran was at the bottom of it, but nothing could be proved. So cleverly was the colonel placed that, even when the Moriarty group was broken up, we could find no evidence against him. You remember at that date, when I called upon you in your rooms, how I would not stand in front of a window for fear of air guns? No doubt you thought me foolish. I knew, however, of that gun and that one of the best shots in the world would be behind it. When we were in Switzerland he followed us with Moriarty, and it was undoubtedly he who gave me that bad five minutes on the Reichenbach mountain.

"I read the papers carefully during my stay in France, on the lookout for any chance of catching him. So long as he was free in London, my life would really not have been worth living. Night and day he would have been looking for me, and sooner or later his chance must have come. What could I do? I could not kill him on sight or I would myself have been charged with murder. So I could do nothing. But I watched the criminal news, knowing that sooner or later I should get him. Then came the death of this Ronald Adair. My chance had come at last. Knowing what I did, was it not clear that Colonel Moran had done it? He had played cards with the young man, had followed him home from the club, and had shot him through the open window. There was no doubt of it. The bullets alone are enough to prove it. I came over at once, was seen by the guard, who would, I knew, tell the colonel of my presence. He could not fail to realize that my sudden return was because of his crime. I was sure that he would make an attempt to get me out of the way at once, and would bring round his murderous gun for that purpose. I left him a good mark in the window, and, having told the police that they might be needed — by the way, Watson, you spotted their presence in that doorway — I took up what seemed to me to be a wise position to watch from, never dreaming that he would choose the same spot for his attempt on my life. Now, my dear Watson, does that leave anything to explain?"

"Yes," said I. "You have not made it clear what was Colonel Moran's motive in murdering the Honorable Ronald Adair?"

"My dear Watson, there we must guess, and even a clear mind may get it wrong. Each may form his own answer given the evidence, and yours is as likely to be right as mine."

"You have formed one then?"

"I think that it is not difficult to explain the facts. It came out in evidence that Colonel Moran and young Adair had, between them, won a considerable amount of money. Now, Moran undoubtedly played unfairly — of that I have long known. I believe that on the day of the murder Adair had found out that Moran was not playing by the rules. Very likely he had spoken to him man to man, and had said that he would tell all unless Moran gave up his membership of the club, and promised not to play cards again. Not being able to play cards, however, would be the end of Moran, who lived by his card-gains. He therefore murdered Adair, who at the time was trying to work out how much money he should himself return, since he would not make money from his playing companion's unfair play. He locked the door so that the ladies should not surprise him and ask what he was doing with those names and the money. What do you think?"

"I have no doubt that you have hit upon the truth."

"It will be proved so or not at the trial. Meanwhile, come what may, Colonel Moran will trouble us no more. The famous air gun of Von Herder will be kept by the police, and once again Mr. Sherlock Holmes is free to spend his life investigating those interesting little problems which London so readily presents."

12

The Adventure of the Dancing Men

踊る人形

読み始める前に

The Adventure of the Dancing Men 踊る人形

56 の短編のうち 27 番目に発表された
1903 年 12 月号のストランド・マガジン初出
1905 年発行の「シャーロック・ホームズの帰還」に収録された

［主な登場人物］

Sherlock Holmes　シャーロック・ホームズ　世界的に有名な私立探偵。優れた観察眼と推理力を有する。ロンドンのベーカー街 221B に下宿している。

Watson　ジョン・H・ワトソン　医師。ホームズの相棒でこの物語の語り手。ベーカー街 221B でホームズと同居している。

Hilton Cubitt　ヒルトン・キュービット　リドリング・ソープ荘園に夫人とともに住む。ホームズに「踊る人形」の描かれた紙片を持ち込み、調査を依頼する。

Elsie Patrick　エルシー・パトリック　キュービット氏がロンドンで出会ったアメリカ出身の若い女性。のち、氏と結婚してキュービット夫人となる。

［あらすじ］

　この作品は暗号を巧みに用いたプロットで特に有名だ。物語はノーフォークの田舎町に住むヒルトン・キュービットがホームズに助けを求めロンドンに来るところから始まる。踊っているように見える人形のメッセージを発見したキュービットが、それをアメリカ人の妻に見せると彼女が怯えるというのだ。ワトソンは子供のいたずら書き程度に考えるのだが、ホームズは重要なものだと推理する。

［総単語数］8,795 語

The Adventure of the Dancing Men

Holmes had been seated for some hours quietly working at his papers.

"So, Watson," said he suddenly, "you are not going to put money into that South African company?"

I gave a start of surprise. Although I was used to Holmes's clever mind, this sudden insight into my deep thoughts was not possible to explain.

"How on earth do you know that?" I asked.

He turned round with laughter in his deep-set eyes.

"Now, Watson, say you are completely taken aback," said he.

"I am."

"I ought to make you sign a paper saying that."

"Why?"

"Because in five minutes you will say that it is all so very simple."

"I am sure I will say nothing of the kind."

"You see, my dear Watson, it is not really difficult to take a set of ideas, each subject to the one before and each simple in itself. If, after doing so, one simply removes all the ideas in the middle and gives the listener the starting point and the end result, one may produce a surprised reaction. Now it was not really difficult by looking at your left forefinger and thumb to be sure that you were not going to put your money in the gold fields."

"I see no connection."

"Very likely not; but I can quickly show you a close connection.

Here are the missing ideas of this very simple piece of reasoning: 1. You had chalk on your left forefinger and thumb when you returned from the club last night. 2. You get chalk there when you play billiards. 3. You only play billiards with Thurston. 4. You told me, four weeks ago, that Thurston wanted to buy some South African land, which he wished you to share with him, and that you only had a month to decide. 5. Your bank book is locked in my cupboard and you have not asked for the key. 6. You have decided not to put your money into this plan."

"How very simple!" I cried.

"Quite so!" said he, rather quickly. "Every problem becomes very easy when it is explained to you. Here is an unexplained one. See what you can make of that, friend Watson." He threw a piece of paper upon the table, and turned once more to his work.

I looked with surprise at the marks on the paper. "Why, Holmes, it is a child's picture," I cried.

"That's your idea, isn't it?"

"What else could it be?"

"That is what Mr. Hilton Cubitt, of Riding Thorpe Manor, Norfolk, wants to know. This little problem came by the first mail, and he was to follow by the next train. There's a ring at the bell, Watson. I think this will be him."

A heavy step was heard upon the stairs, and a moment later there entered a tall, healthy looking gentleman, whose clear eyes and red face told of a life led far from the smoke of Baker Street. He seemed to bring a smell of fresh country air with him as he entered. Having shaken hands with each of us, he was about to sit down, when he saw the paper with the strange markings which I had looked at, upon the table.

"Well, Mr. Holmes, what do you make of these?" he cried. "They told me that you liked strange mysteries, and I don't think you can find a stranger one than that. I sent the paper on ahead, so that you might have time to study it before I came."

"It is clearly rather unusual," said Holmes. "At first sight it would appear to be a children's game. It is a number of strange little figures dancing across the paper. Why should you put any importance on something so seemingly meaningless?"

"I never should, Mr. Holmes. But my wife does. For some reason she is afraid of it. She says nothing but I can see the fear in her eyes. That is why I must get to the bottom of this matter."

Holmes held up the paper to the light. It was a page taken from a notebook. The markings were like this:

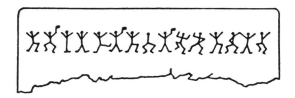

Holmes looked at it for some time and then put it carefully in his pocket book.

"This promises to be a most interesting and unusual case," said he. "You gave me a few facts in your letter, Mr. Hilton Cubitt, but I would like you to go over it all again for my friend, Dr. Watson."

"I'm not much of a storyteller," said our visitor nervously. "You'll have to ask me anything that I don't make clear. I'll begin at the time of my marriage last year, but I want to say this first of all. I'm not a rich man, but my people have been at Riding Thorpe for a matter of five centuries, and there is no better known family in Norfolk. Last year I came up for the summer, and I stopped at a boarding house in Russell Square. Parker, a friend of mine, was staying there. There was an American young lady there — Patrick was the name — Elsie Patrick. In some way we became friends, until before my month was up I was as much in love as a man could be. We were quietly married, and we returned to Norfolk as man and wife. You'll think it very mad, Mr. Holmes, that a man of a good family should marry a wife in this manner, knowing nothing of her past or of her people, but if you saw her and knew her, it would help you to understand.

"She was very straight about it, was Elsie. I can't say that she did not give me every chance of getting out of it if I wished to do so. 'I have known some bad people in my life,' said she. 'I wish to forget all about them. I would rather never talk of the past, for it is very painful for me. If you take me, Hilton, you will take a woman who has done nothing wrong herself, but you will have to be happy with me as I am now, and to allow me to say nothing about all that passed up to the time when I became yours. If these conditions are too hard, then go back to Norfolk, and leave me to the lonely life in which you found me.' It was the day before our marriage that she said those very words to me. I told her that I was content to take her on those conditions, and I have been as good as my word.

"Well, we have been married now for a year, and very happy we have been. But about a month ago, at the end of June, I saw, for the first time, signs of trouble. One day my wife received a letter from America. She turned deadly white, read the letter, and threw it on the fire. She said nothing about it afterwards, and neither did I, for a promise is a promise, but she has never known an easy hour from that moment. There is always a look of fear upon her face. She would do better to trust me, for she would find that I was her best friend. But until she speaks, I can say nothing. Mind you, she is an honorable woman, Mr. Holmes, and whatever trouble there may have been in her past life it has not been caused by her. I am only a simple Norfolk countryman, but there is not a man in England who holds his family honor more highly than I do. She knows it well, and she knew it well before she married me. She would never have married me if she felt she would cause a problem to my family, of that I am sure.

"Well, now I come to the strange part of my story. About a week ago, I found by one of the windows a number of strange little dancing figures like these upon the paper. They were written with chalk. I thought it was the stable-boy who had done them, but he said that he knew nothing about them. Anyhow they had been put there during the night. I had them washed out and only told my wife afterwards. To my surprise, she thought it most grave, and asked me to let her see them if any more come. None did come for a week, and then yesterday morning I found this paper lying on the sunclock in the garden. I showed it to Elsie, and she passed out in front of me. Since then she has looked like a woman in a dream, with fear always in her eyes. It was then that I wrote and sent the paper to you, Mr. Holmes. It was not a thing I could take to the police, for they would have laughed at me, but you will tell me what to do. I am not a rich man but if there is any danger to my little woman, I would spend my last shilling to save her."

He was a fine man, this son of the English soil—simple, straight, and gentle, with his true blue eyes and broad, friendly face. His love for his wife and his trust in her was written on his face. Holmes had listened to his story very carefully, and now he sat for some time quietly thinking.

"Don't you think, Mr. Cubitt," said he at last, "that your best plan would be to directly question your wife, and ask her to share her story with you?"

Hilton Cubitt looked down.

"A promise is a promise, Mr. Holmes. If Elsie wished to tell me, she would. If not, it is not for me to make her. But I must try in some way to help her, and I will."

"Then I will help you with all my heart. In the first place have you heard of any strangers being seen around Riding Thorpe?"

"No."

"I suppose that it is a very quiet place. Any fresh face would be noticed?"

"Around Riding Thorpe Manor, yes. But we have several small watering places not very far away. And the farmers take in people."

"These markings clearly have a meaning. If it is, as I think, a system, I have no doubt that we shall get to the bottom of it. But there are not enough figures in this set to be able to work anything out, and the facts that you bring me give us nothing with which to start an investigation. I would suggest that you return to Norfolk, that you keep a lookout, and that you take a careful copy of any fresh dancing men that may appear. Ask people whether any strangers have been seen in the area. When you have got some fresh evidence, come to me again. That is the best thing that you can do, Mr. Hilton Cubitt. If necessary, I shall always be ready to run down and see you in your Norfolk home."

The meeting left Sherlock Holmes very thoughtful, and several times in the next few days I saw him take the piece of paper from his notebook and look long and hard at the strange figures on it. He said nothing about it, however, until one afternoon two weeks or so later. I was going out when he called me back.

"You had better stay here, Watson."

"Why?"

"Because I had a telegram from Hilton Cubitt this morning. You remember Hilton Cubitt, of the dancing men? He was to reach Liverpool Street at one-twenty. He may be here at any moment. I gather from his telegram that there have been some new turns to this case."

We had not long to wait, for our Norfolk gentleman came straight from the station as fast as a cab could bring him. He was looking upset and unhappy with tired eyes and a lined face.

"It's getting on my nerves, this business, Mr. Holmes," said he, as he dropped into an armchair. "It's bad enough to feel that there are unknown people about you, who have some kind of plan against you, but when, in addition to that, you know that it is killing your wife by inches, then it becomes as much as a man can take. She's wearing away under it, wearing away before my eyes."

"Has she said anything yet?"

"No, Mr. Holmes, she has not. Yet there have been times when the poor girl has wanted to speak, and yet could not quite bring herself to tell me. I have tried to help her, but I suppose I did it badly and put her off. She has spoken about my family and our name in Norfolk, and our pride in our honor, and I always felt it was leading to the point, but somehow it turned off before we got there."

"But have you found out something for yourself?"

"A good deal, Mr. Holmes. I have several fresh dancing men pictures for you to look at, and, what is more important, I have seen the fellow."

"What! The man who makes these marks?"

"Yes, I saw him doing it. But I will tell you everything in order. When I got back after my visit to you, the very first thing I saw next morning was a fresh set of dancing men. They had been drawn in chalk upon the black wooden door of the stable, which is beside the grass in full view of the front windows. I took a careful copy, and here it is." He got out a piece of paper and laid it upon the table. Here is a copy of the figures:

"Very good!" said Holmes. "Very good indeed, please continue."

"When I had taken the copy, I removed the marks, but, two mornings later, a fresh set had appeared. I have a copy of it here":

Holmes laughed with pleasure.

"Our material is quickly increasing," said he.

"Three days later another note was left upon paper, and placed under a stone upon the sunclock. Here it is. The figures are, as you see, the same as the last group. After that I decided to lie in wait, so I got out my gun, and I sat up in my study, which overlooks the garden. About two in the morning I was seated by the window, all being dark save for the moonlight outside, when I heard steps behind me, and there was my wife. She asked me to come to bed. I told her that I wanted to see who it was that played such a strange game with us. She answered that it was all nonsense, and that I should take no notice of it.

"She asked me to come to bed but suddenly I saw her face grow whiter in the moonlight. Something was moving by the stable. I saw a dark figure low to the ground move round the corner in front of the door. Holding my gun, I was about to rush out, when my wife threw her arms around me and held me with all her strength. At last I got clear, but by the time I got into the garden the man was gone. However, on the stable door was the very same set of dancing men which had appeared already, and which I have copied on that paper. There was no sign of the fellow anywhere, though I ran all over the grounds. And yet the remarkable thing is that he must have been there all the time, for when I looked at the door again in the morning, he had done some more of his pictures under the line which I had already seen."

"Have you that fresh set?"

"Yes, it is very short, but I made a copy of it, and here it is."

Again he produced a paper. The new dance was in this form:

"Tell me," said Holmes, and I could see by his eyes that this was important, "was this an addition to the first or did it appear to be separate?"

"It was on a different part of the door."

"Very good! This is by far the most important of all for our purpose. It fills me with hopes. Now, Mr. Hilton Cubitt, please continue your most interesting statement."

"I have nothing more to say, Mr. Holmes, except that I was angry with my wife that night for having held me back when I might have caught the fellow. She said that she feared that I might get hurt. For a moment it had crossed my mind that perhaps what she really feared was that he might be hurt, for I could not doubt that she knew who this man was and what he meant by these strange signs. But when I looked in my wife's eyes, I was sure that it was indeed my safety that was in her mind. There's the whole case, and now I want your opinion as to what I ought to do. My own feeling is to put some of my farm boys in the garden, and when this fellow comes again, to give him such a going-over that he will leave us in peace in the future."

"I fear that it is too deep a case for such simple steps," said Holmes. "How long can you stay in London?"

"I must go back today. I would not leave my wife alone all night for anything. She is very nervous, and asked me to come back."

"I think you are right. But if you could have stopped, I might possibly have been able to return with you in a day or two. Meanwhile, you will leave me these papers, and I think that it is very likely that I shall be able to pay you a visit shortly and to throw some light upon the case."

Sherlock Holmes kept his cool manner until our visitor had left us, although it was easy for me, who knew him so well, to see that he was just waiting to get to work on the problem. The moment that broad back had gone through the door, my friend rushed to the table, laid out all the pieces of paper containing dancing men in front of him, and threw himself into making sense of them. For two hours I watched him as he covered side after side of paper with figures and letters. So taken with his work was he, that he had completely forgotten that I was there. Finally he jumped from his chair with a cry of pleasure, and walked up and down the room looking pleased with himself. Then he wrote a long telegram. "If my answer to this is as I hope, you will have a very pretty case to add to your notebook, Watson," said he. "I expect that we shall be able to go down to Norfolk tomorrow, and to take our friend some news as to what it all means."

I must say that I wanted to know what he had found out, but I knew that Holmes liked to tell things at his own time and in his own way, so I waited until it should suit him to tell me about it.

But the answering telegram did not come for two days, during which time Holmes started at every ring of the bell. On the second evening there came a letter from Hilton Cubitt. A set of dancing men had appeared that morning upon the sunclock. He enclosed a copy of it, which is here reproduced:

Holmes looked at this new statement for some minutes, and then suddenly jumped to his feet with a cry of surprise. His face was white with fear.

"We have let this case go far enough," said he. "Is there a train to North Walsham tonight?"

I looked in the timetable; the last had just gone.

"Then we shall breakfast early and take the very first in the morning," said Holmes. "We must get there as soon as possible. Ah! Here is the telegram I have been waiting for." He tore it open. "This makes it even more necessary that we should not lose an hour in letting Hilton Cubitt know how things stand, for it is a dangerous position in which our simple Norfolk farmer finds himself."

So, indeed, it proved, and we come to the unhappy ending of a story which had seemed at the start to hold no danger. I would like to give some good news, but I must tell my readers the facts that made Riding Thorpe Manor famous throughout England.

We had hardly alighted at North Walsham, when the stationmaster hurried towards us. "I suppose you are the detectives from London?" said he.

A look of fear passed over Holmes's face.

"What makes you think such a thing?"

"Because Inspector Martin from Norwich has just passed through. But maybe you are the doctors. She's not dead—or wasn't the last I heard. You may be in time to save her yet, though it be for the hangman."

Holmes's face darkened.

"We are going to Riding Thorpe Manor, but have heard nothing of what has passed there."

"It's a bad business," said the stationmaster. "They are shot, both Mr. Hilton Cubitt and his wife. She shot him, and then herself, so the servants say. He's dead and it's expected she will follow him. Dear, dear, one of the oldest families in Norfolk, and one of the most liked."

Without a word Holmes hurried to a cab, and during the long drive he did not open his mouth. Never have I seen him so upset. He had been uneasy during the journey from town, and I had noticed that he had looked nervously in the morning newspapers. But now this sudden realization of his worst fears left him in a deep sadness. He sat back in his seat, lost in his unhappy thoughts. Yet there was much around to interest us, for we were passing through one of the most unusual parts of England. A few houses, each one far apart from the next, represented the people who lived there now, while on every side great, square churches reached to the sky from the flat green land and told of the pride and richness of old East Anglia. At last we saw the German Ocean over the green edge of Norfolk, and the driver pointed to an old house set in a wood. "That's Riding Thorpe Manor," said he.

As we drove up to the front door, I saw in front of it, beside the grass, the clock and stables which the late Hilton Cubitt had told us about. A little man with a quick, bright manner had just arrived himself. He told us he was Inspector Martin, of the Norfolk police force, and he was very surprised when he heard the name of my companion.

"Why, Mr. Holmes, the crime only happened at three this morning. How could you hear of it in London and get down here as soon as I?"

"I felt something would happen. I came in the hope of stopping it."

"Then you must have some important evidence that we don't know about for they were said to be a most happy couple."

"I have only the evidence of the dancing men," said Holmes. "I will explain the matter to you later. Meanwhile, as it is too late to save Mr. Hilton Cubitt, I want to make sure that I use what I know to make sure the truth is known. Should I help you in your investigation, or would you like me to work alone?"

"I should be proud to think that we were acting together, Mr. Holmes," said the policeman.

"In that case I should be glad to hear the evidence and to take a look at the house as soon as possible."

Inspector Martin had the good sense to allow my friend to do things in his own manner, and he just carefully noted the results. The doctor, an old, white-haired man, had just come down from Mrs. Cubitt's room, and he reported that her wounds were grave, but he thought that she would live. The bullet had passed through the front of her head and it would probably be some time before she would come round. On the question of whether she had been shot or had shot herself, he would not give an opinion. The bullet had been fired at very close quarters. There was only one gun found in the room, from which two bullets had been fired. Mr. Hilton Cubitt had been shot through the heart. It was equally possible that he had shot her then himself, or that she had been the criminal, for the gun lay upon the floor halfway between them.

"Has he been moved?" asked Holmes.

"We have moved nothing except the lady. We could not leave her lying wounded on the floor."

"How long have you been here, Doctor?"

"Since four o'clock."

"Anyone else?"

"Yes, the policeman here."

"And you have touched nothing?"

"Nothing."

"You have acted with great sense. Who sent for you?"

"The house servant."

"Was it she who called the police?"

"She and Mrs. King, the cook."

"Where are they now?"

"In the kitchen, I believe."

"Then I think we had better hear their story at once."

The old hall had been turned into an office for the police. Holmes sat in a great old chair, his eyes looking all around. I could read in them a set purpose to find out the true story of what had happened at Riding Thorpe Manor, and to clear the family name of Hilton Cubitt. Inspector Martin, the country doctor, myself, and a large policeman made up the rest of that strange company.

The two women told their story clearly enough. They had been awakened from their sleep by a loud noise, which had been followed a minute later by a second one. They rushed out of their rooms and together they had gone downstairs. The door of the study was open and a candle was burning upon the table. Their master lay upon his face in the middle of the room. He was dead. Near the window his wife was lying, her head against the wall. She was badly wounded, and the side of her face was red with blood. She was clearly alive, but was unable to speak. The hall, as well as the room, was full of smoke and the smell of powder. The window was closed and fastened on the inside. Both women were sure about that. They had at once sent for the doctor and the police. Then, with the help of the stable-boy, they had carried the wounded lady to her room. Both she and her husband had been to bed, and they were both still wearing their night-clothes. Nothing had been moved in the study. So far as they knew, there had never been any problem between husband and wife. They had always looked upon them as a very happy couple.

These were the facts of the servants' evidence. In answer to Inspector Martin, they were clear that every door was fastened upon the inside, and that no one could have escaped from the house. In answer to Holmes, they both said they were sure that they could smell powder from the moment that they ran out of their rooms on the top floor. "That is a very important point," said Holmes to Inspector Martin. "And now I think we are in a position to undertake a careful investigation of the room."

The study proved to be a small room, lined on three sides with books, and with a writing table facing a window, which looked out upon the garden. We first looked at the body of Hilton Cubitt which lay stretched across the room. The state of his clothes showed that he had come straight from his bedroom. The bullet had been fired at him from the front, hitting his heart. There was no mark on his back, so the bullet had stayed in his body. His death had been quick and painless. There was no powder-marking either upon his clothes or on his hands. According to the country doctor, the lady had powder marks on her face but not on her hands.

"Having no powder marks means nothing, though having them may mean everything," said Holmes. "Unless the powder from a badly fitting bullet happens to fly backward, one may fire many shots without leaving a sign. I would say that Mr. Cubitt's body may now be removed. I suppose, Doctor, you have not recovered the bullet which wounded the lady?"

"We cannot do that until she recovers a little. But there are still four bullets in the gun. Two have been fired and two wounds made, so that each bullet can be accounted for."

"So it would seem," said Holmes. "Perhaps you can account also for the bullet which has so clearly hit the edge of the window?"

He had turned suddenly, and his long, thin finger was pointing to a hole which had been made just below the lower window.

"By Heaven!" cried Inspector Martin. "How ever did you see that?"

"Because I looked for it."

"Wonderful!" said the country doctor. "You are right, sir. Then a third shot has been fired, and therefore a third person must have been present. But who could that have been, and how could he have got away?"

"That is the question which we are now about to answer," said Sherlock Holmes.

"You remember, Inspector Martin, when the servants said that on leaving their room they noticed at once a smell of powder, I said that the point was a very important one?"

"Yes, Mr. Holmes, but I must say I did not quite follow you."

"It seemed to point to the fact that at the time of the firing, the window as well as the door of the room had been open. Otherwise the smell of powder could not have been blown so quickly through the house. A through wind in the room was necessary for that. Both door and window were only open for a short time, however."

"How do you prove that?"

"Because the candle had burned evenly on all sides."

"Wonderful!" cried Inspector Martin. "Wonderful!"

"Feeling sure that the window had been open at the time of the shots, I thought that there might have been a third person, who stood outside this opening and fired through it. Any shot directed at this person might hit the sill. I looked, and there, sure enough, was the bullet mark!"

"But how came the window to be shut and fastened?"

"The woman's first thought would be to shut and fasten the window. But, look, what is this?"

It was a lady's handbag which stood upon the study table. Holmes opened it and emptied it onto the table. There were twenty fifty-pound notes — and nothing else.

"This must be kept, for it is very likely to be evidence," said Holmes, as he handed the bag and money to Inspector Martin. "It is now necessary that we should try to throw some light upon this third bullet, which has clearly, from the marking of the wood, been fired from inside the room. I should like to see Mrs. King again. You said, Mrs. King, that you were awakened by a loud noise — what we now know to be a gun going off. When you said that, did you mean that it seemed to you to be louder than the second one?"

"Well, sir, it wakened me from my sleep, so it is hard to judge. But it did seem very loud."

"You don't think that it might have been two shots fired almost at the same moment?"

"I am sure I couldn't say, sir."

"I believe that it was undoubtedly so. I rather think, Inspector Martin, that we have now learned all that this room can teach us. If you will kindly step round with me, we shall see what fresh evidence the garden has to offer."

A flowerbed ran up to the study window. All of us except Holmes were surprised to see that the flowers had been stepped on, and the soft soil had many footmarks. Holmes hunted about among the grass and flowers like a dog after a wounded bird. Then, with a cry of pleasure, he picked up a little bullet-case.

"I thought so," said he; "here is the third bullet-case. I really think, Inspector Martin, that our case is almost complete."

The country policeman's face had shown his complete surprise at the fast and masterful way Holmes had run his investigation. At first he had shown some signs of wanting to do things his way, but now he was overcome by Holmes's methods and was ready to follow, without question, wherever Holmes led.

"Who do you think did it?" he asked.

"I'll go into that later. There are several points in this problem that I have not been able to explain to you yet. Now that I have got so far, I had best carry on along my own lines, and then clear the matter up once and for all."

"Just as you wish, Mr. Holmes, so long as we get our man."

"I do not mean to be difficult, but it is not possible, at the moment of action, to enter into long explanations. I now know almost everything about this case. Even if this lady should never recover, we can still work out the events of last night, and ensure that the criminal is caught. First of all, I wish to know if there is any place in this area known as Elrige's?"

The servants were questioned, but none of them had heard of such a place. The stable-boy, however, remembered that a farmer of that name lived some miles off, in the direction of East Rushton.

"Is it a lonely farm?"

"Very lonely, sir."

"Perhaps they have not heard yet of all that happened during the night?"

"Perhaps not, sir."

Holmes thought for a little, then a strange smile played over his face.

"Get a horse ready, my boy," said he, "I wish you to take a note to Elrige's Farm."

He took from his pocket the various pieces of paper that contained the dancing men. With these in front of him, he worked for some time at the study-table. At last he handed a note to the boy, with directions to put it into the hands of the person to whom it was addressed, and to answer no questions of any sort that might be put to him. I saw the outside of the note, written in strange, thin characters, very unlike Holmes's usual writing. It was to Mr. Abe Slaney, Elrige's Farm, East Rushton, Norfolk.

"I think, Inspector Martin," Holmes said, "that you would do well to send for help, as if it works out according to plan, you may have a dangerous man to guard. If there is an afternoon train to town, Watson, I think we should do well to take it, as this investigation draws quickly to a close."

When the young man had been sent with the note, Sherlock Holmes spoke again to the servants. If any visitor were to call asking for Mrs. Hilton Cubitt, nothing should be said as to her condition, but he was to be shown at once into the living room. Then he led the way into the living room, saying that the business was now out of our hands, and that we must while away the time as best we might until we could see what was in store for us. The doctor had already left, and only Inspector Martin and myself were still there.

"I think that I can help you pass an hour in an interesting way," said Holmes, pulling his chair up to the table, and placing out in front of him the various papers upon which were recorded the groups of dancing men. "As to you, friend Watson, I must say sorry for having kept you in the dark for so long. I think, Inspector Martin, that you as a policeman might be very interested in this case. I must tell you, first of all, how we came to be connected with Mr. Hilton Cubitt and this case." He then shortly retold the facts which have already been recorded. "I have here in front of me these unusual pictures, at which one might smile had they not led to such an unhappy ending. I know a lot about all forms of secret writings, and am myself the writer of a small and not very good article upon the subject, in which I analyze many of them, but I must say that this one was new to me. The object of those that thought up the system was to hide that these characters mean something, and to give the idea that they are only pictures done by children.

"Having once realized, however, that the characters stood for letters, and having used the rules which guide us in all forms of secret writings, the answer was easy enough. The first message given to me was so short that all I could safely say was that the character 𝍆 stood for E. As you know, E is the most used letter in the English language, and is used so much more than any other single letter that even in a short passage one would expect to find it most often. Out of fifteen characters in the first group, four were the same, so it was reasonable to set this down as E. It is true that in some cases the figure was holding a flag, and in some cases not, but it was probable, from the way in which the flags were used that they showed the end of a word. I therefore noted that E was represented by 𝍆 .

"But now came the real difficulty of the investigation. The order of the English letters after E is by no means well marked. Speaking generally, T, A, O, I, N, S, H, R, D, and L are the order in which letters are most used; but T, A, O, and I are all used about the same, and it would be an endless job to try each possible set of letters until a meaning was arrived at. I therefore waited for fresh material. In my second meeting with Mr. Hilton Cubitt, he was able to give me three other short groups, one of which appeared—as there were no flags—to be a single word. Here are the characters. Now in the single word I have already got the two E's coming second and fourth in a word of five letters. It came to me that 'never' in reply to a question was quite likely. The position of this group on the stable door made me think that it was a reply written by the lady. Accepting this as right we are now able to say the characters 𝍆𝍇𝍆 stand for N, V, and R.

"Even now I was in considerable difficulty, but a happy thought enabled me to find several other letters. It seemed to me that if these words came, as I expected, from someone who had known the lady in her early life, a word which contained two E's with three letters in between might very well stand for the name 'ELSIE.' Looking at the groups I found that this word formed the end of the set which had been written three times. She was clearly being asked something. Now I had my L, S, and I. But what was she being asked? There were only four letters in the word in front of 'Elsie,' and it ended in E. Surely the word must be 'COME.' I tried all other four letters ending in E, but could find none to fit the case. So now I knew C, O, and M, and I was in a position to try the first group once more, dividing it into words and putting dots for characters which were still unknown. It came out in this way:

. M . ERE . . E SL . NE .

"Now the first letter can only be A, which is most useful, since it comes up no fewer than three times in this short passage, and it must be an H in the second word. Now it becomes:

AM HERE A . E SLANE .

Filling in the name:

AM HERE ABE SLANEY.

I had so many letters now that I could carry on with few problems to the second passage, which worked out in this fashion:

A . ELRI . ES

Here I could only make sense by putting T and G for the missing letters, and supposing that the name was that of some house or farm at which the writer was staying."

Inspector Martin and I had listened with interest to the full and clear account of how my friend had produced the results which had led to so complete an understanding of our difficulties.

"What did you do then, Mr. Holmes?" asked the policeman.

"I had every reason to suppose that this Abe Slaney was an American, since Abe is an American name, and since a letter from America had been the starting point of all the trouble. I had also cause to think, because of what the lady had said of her past, that there was some criminal secret in the matter. I therefore sent a telegram to my friend Wilson Hargreave, of the New York Police Office, who has more than once made use of my understanding of London crime. I asked him whether the name of Abe Slaney was known to him. Here is his reply: 'The most dangerous criminal in Chicago.' On the very evening upon which I had his answer, Hilton Cubitt sent me the last group of figures from Slaney. Working with known letters, it took this form:

ELSIE . RE . ARE TO MEET THY GO .

Adding two P's and a D completed a message that the man had moved on from asking Elsie to meet him to something much more dangerous. I at once came to Norfolk with Dr. Watson, but, unhappily, too late to stop what had happened."

"I am proud to have worked with you on this case," said Inspector Martin, warmly, "but I feel I must now say something. You are answerable only to yourself, but I am not. If this Abe Slaney, staying at Elrige's, is indeed the murderer, and if he has made his escape while I am seated here, I will get into grave trouble."

"You need not be uneasy. He will not try to escape."

"How do you know?"

"If he tried to run, it would tell everyone that he was the criminal."

"Then let us go to arrest him."

"I expect him here any moment."

"But why should he come?"

"Because I have written and asked him."

"But this is unbelievable, Mr. Holmes! Why should he come because you asked him? Would not such a thing make him more careful, or even make him fly?"

"I think I have known how to write the letter in such a way to ensure he comes," said Sherlock Holmes. "In fact I am sure that this is the gentleman himself coming up the drive."

A man was walking up the path which led to the door. He was a tall, good-looking fellow with a big hat. He came up the path as if the place belonged to him, and we heard him ring at the door.

"I think, gentlemen," said Holmes, quietly, "that we had best take up our positions behind the door. Every care must be taken when dealing with such a man. You will need your handcuffs, Inspector Martin. You can leave the talking to me."

We waited quietly for a minute, one of those minutes that one never forgets. Then the door opened and the man stepped in. In a moment Holmes put a gun to his head, and Inspector Martin put the handcuffs over his hands. It was all done so quickly that the fellow was helpless before he knew what had happened. He looked from one to the other with a pair of angry eyes. Then he burst into a strange laugh.

"Well, gentlemen, you have the drop on me this time. But I came here in answer to a letter from Mrs. Hilton Cubitt. Don't tell me that she helped you to catch me."

"Mrs. Hilton Cubitt was gravely wounded, and is at death's door."

The man gave a cry which rang through the house.

"You're mad!" he cried. "It was he that was hurt, not she. Who would have hurt little Elsie? I may have seemed dangerous to her—God help me—but I would never have touched a hair of her pretty head."

"She was found, badly wounded, by the side of her dead husband."

He fell with a cry to the seat, and put his face in his hands. For a few minutes he was quiet. Then he raised his face once more and seemed sad but in control.

"I have nothing to hide from you, gentlemen," said he. "If I shot the man it was because he shot at me, and there's no murder in that. But if you think that I could hurt that woman, then you don't know either me or her. I tell you, there is no man in this world who loved a woman more than I loved her. She was promised to me years ago. Who was this Englishman that he should come between us? I tell you that I had the first right to her, and that I was only trying to get what was mine."

"She broke away from you when she found out what you were really like," said Holmes. "She left America to get away from you, and she married an honorable gentleman in England. You followed her and made problems for her in her new life. You have brought about the death of a good man and driven his wife to attempted suicide. That is your record in this business Mr. Abe Slaney, and you will answer for it to the law."

"If Elsie dies, I care nothing of what becomes of me," said the American. He opened one of his hands and held out a piece of paper. "Look here," he cried with a look of hope in his eyes, "you're not trying to fool me over this, are you? If the lady is as badly hurt as you say, who was it that wrote this note?"

"I wrote it to bring you here."

"You wrote it? There was no one on earth outside our group who knew the secret of the dancing men. How came you to write it?"

"What one man can make up another one can figure out," said Holmes. "There is a cab coming to take you to Norwich, Mr. Slaney. But, meanwhile, you have time to make good some of the trouble you have caused. Do you know that the police thought that Mrs. Hilton Cubitt murdered her husband, and that it was only because of what I know, that they haven't investigated her? The least that you can do is to make it clear to the whole world that she played no part, directly or indirectly, in his sad end."

"I ask nothing better," said the American. "I guess the very best case I can make for myself is to say what truly happened."

"It is necessary for me to tell you that it will be taken down in writing, and may be used in evidence against you," cried Inspector Martin, with the wonderful fair play of British criminal law.

Slaney was unmoved.

"I'll chance that," said he. "First of all, I want you gentlemen to understand that I have known this lady since she was a child. There were seven of us in a group in Chicago, and her father was the chief of it. He was a clever man, was old Patrick. It was he who made up that writing, which would pass as a child's picture unless you happened to have the key to it. Well, Elsie learned some of our ways, but she couldn't stand the business. She had some lawful money of her own, so she ran away to London. She had been promised to me, and she would have married me, I believe, if I had given up my life of crime, but she would have nothing to do with anything against the law. It was only after her marriage to this Englishman that I was able to find out where she was. I wrote to her, but got no answer. After that I came over, and, as letters were of no use, I put my notes where she could read them.

"Well, I have been here a month now. I lived in that farm, where I had a room down below, and could get in and out every night, without anyone knowing. I tried all I could to get Elsie to come away with me. I knew that she read the notes, for once she wrote an answer under one of them. Then my anger got the better of me, and I tried to make her afraid. She sent me a letter then, asking me to go away, and saying that it would break her heart if anything should happen to destroy her husband's name. She said that she would come down when her husband was asleep at three in the morning, and speak with me through the end window, if I would go away afterwards and leave her in peace. She came down and brought money with her, trying to pay me to go. This made me mad, and I caught her arm and tried to pull her through the window. At that moment her husband rushed in with a gun in his hand. Elsie had fallen to the floor, and we were face to face. I had my gun also, and I held it up to show him, still hoping to get away. He fired and missed me. I shot almost at the same moment, and down he dropped. I made away across the garden, and as I went I heard the window shut behind me. They are true words, gentlemen, and I heard no more about it until that lad came riding up with a note which made me come round here and give myself into your hands."

A cab had driven up while the American had been talking. Two policemen sat inside. Inspector Martin rose and touched his prisoner on the shoulder.

"It is time for us to go."

"Can I see her first?"

"No, she has not come round. Mr. Sherlock Holmes, I only hope that, if ever again I have an important case, I shall be able to have you by my side."

We stood at the window and watched the cab drive away. As I turned back my eye caught the piece of paper which Abe Slaney had left on the table. It was the note that had fooled him into coming.

"See if you can read it, Watson," said he, with a smile.

It contained no word, but this little line of dancing men:

"If you use the key which I have explained," said Holmes, "you will find that it simply says, 'Come here at once.' I was sure that he would do it, since he would think that it could only be from the lady. And so, my dear Watson, we have ended by turning the dancing men to good when they have so often been used for bad, and I think that I have kept my promise of giving you something unusual for your notebook. Three-forty is our train, and I think we should be back in Baker Street for dinner."

To finish the story, Abe Slaney was not killed for murder, but was given life in prison in consideration of the fact that Hilton Cubitt had fired the first shot. Of Mrs. Hilton Cubitt, I have heard that she recovered completely, and that she has not remarried, and she spends her whole life caring for the poor and looking after her husband's home and workers.

13

The Adventure of the Priory School

プライオリ・スクール

読み始める前に

The Adventure of the Priory School プライオリ・スクール

56 の短編のうち 29 番目に発表された
1904 年 2 月号のストランド・マガジン初出
1905 年発行の「シャーロック・ホームズの帰還」に収録された

［主な登場人物］

Sherlock Holmes　シャーロック・ホームズ　世界的に有名な私立探偵。優れた観察眼と推理力を有する。ロンドンのベーカー街221Bに下宿している。

Watson　ジョン・H・ワトソン　医師。ホームズの相棒でこの物語の語り手。ベーカー街221Bでホームズと同居している。

Thorneycroft Huxtable　ソーニークロフト・ハクスタブル　プライオリ・スクールの創設者で校長。ホームズに行方不明の生徒の捜索を依頼する。

Duke of Holdernesse　ホールダネス公爵　英国一の偉大かつ裕福な名門貴族。

Lord Saltire　サルタイア卿　ホールダネス公爵の一人息子。プライオリ・スクールで行方不明となった生徒。

James Wilder　ジェームズ・ワイルダー　ホールダネス公爵の秘書。

Heidegger　ハイデッガー　プライオリ・スクールのドイツ人教師。サルタイア卿とともに行方不明となる。

［あらすじ］

　イングランド北部の名門私立校を舞台にした誘拐事件にホームズが挑む。学校の寮からホールダネス公爵の10歳の一人息子ソルタイアの姿が消えた。校内で点呼をすると、ソルタイアと同じ3階に部屋を持つドイツ人教師ハイデッガーも失踪していたことが判明する。彼はその後のホームズの調査で死体となって見つかる。そしてホールダネス公爵の秘書をしているワイルダーは、公爵と愛人の間に生まれたソルタイアの兄であるという事実が出てくることで、事件はさらに複雑になる。

［総単語数］10,105 語

The Adventure of the Priory School

We have seen some strange sights at Baker Street, but I cannot remember anything more sudden and unusual than the first appearance of Thorneycroft Huxtable, M.A., Ph.D., etc. His card came before him by a few seconds, and then he entered himself—so large, so sure of himself that it was unthinkable that he would let any problem upset him. And yet his first action, when the door had closed behind him, was to fall against the table, and then to the floor, and there was that strong figure laying out cold at our feet.

We had jumped to our feet, and for a few moments, we looked at this man and wondered what was the nature of the storm that was causing him such trouble on the ocean of life. Then Holmes got a drink for him and lifted his head. The heavy, white face was covered with lines of trouble, the hanging bags under the closed eyes were gray in color, the loose mouth dropped down at the corners, a beard was just starting on his face. His shirt was dirty from a long journey, and his hair lay uncared for on his head. It was a badly shaken man that lay before us.

"What is it, Watson?" asked Holmes.

"He is completely worn out—possibly from hunger and tiredness," said I, as I listened to his heart.

"Return ticket from Mackleton, in the north of England," said Holmes, drawing it from the watch-pocket. "It is not noon yet. He has certainly been an early starter."

His eyes started to open and a pair of empty gray eyes looked up at us. A moment later the man had jumped to his feet, his face red.

"I am sorry about this weakness, Mr. Holmes, I have been a little upset. If I might have a glass of milk and some bread, I have no doubt that I should be better. I came personally, Mr. Holmes, in order to make sure that you would return with me. I feared that no telegram could tell you how important the case is."

"When you are better——"

"I am quite well again. I cannot think how I came to be so weak. I wish you, Mr. Holmes, to come to Mackleton with me by the next train."

My friend shook his head.

"My friend, Dr. Watson, could tell you that we are very busy at present. I am working on this case about the Ferrers Documents, and the Abergavenny murder is coming up for trial. Only a very important matter could call me from London at present."

"Important!" Our visitor threw up his hands. "Have you heard nothing of the abduction of the only son of the Duke of Holdernesse?"

"What!"

"We had tried to keep it out of the newspapers, but there was some word in the Globe last night. I thought it might have reached your ears."

Holmes looked up the Duke of Holdernesse in one of his books.

"Well, well," he said when he stopped reading, "this man is certainly one of the great men of the nation."

"The greatest and perhaps the richest. I know, Mr. Holmes, that you take a very high line in these matters, and that you are prepared to work for the work's sake. I may tell you, however, that his Grace has already said that five thousand pounds will be handed over to the person who can tell him where his son is, and another thousand if he can name the man or men who have taken him."

"It is a wonderful offer," said Holmes. "Watson, I think that we shall accompany Dr. Huxtable back to the north of England. And now, Dr. Huxtable, when you have finished that milk, you will kindly tell me what has happened, when it happened, how it happened, and, finally, what Dr. Thorneycroft Huxtable, of the Priory School, near Mackleton, has to do with the matter, and why he comes three days after it happened—the state of your face gives the date—to ask for my services."

Our visitor had finished his milk and bread. The light had come back to his eyes and the color to his face, as he set himself to explain the situation.

"The Priory is a school for young boys which prepares them for the best public schools. I am the head of the school. The Priory is, without exception, the best of its sort in England. Lord Leverstoke, the Earl of Blackwater, Sir Cathcart Soames—they all have entrusted their sons to me. But I felt that my school had reached a new height when, three weeks ago, the Duke of Holdernesse sent Mr. James Wilder, his secretary, to say that young Lord Saltire, ten years old, his only son, was about to be sent to my school. Little did I think that this would lead to me being almost destroyed.

"On May 1st the boy arrived. He was a pleasant child, and he soon fell into our ways. I will tell you—given the grave nature of his case—that he was not entirely happy at home. It is an open secret that the Duke's married life had not been a peaceful one, and the matter had ended in a separation, to which both parties agreed, the Duchess living in the south of France. This had happened very shortly before, and the boy was known to have felt strongly for his mother. He was unhappy that she had left Holdernesse Hall, and it was for this reason that the Duke wished to send him to my school. In two weeks the boy was quite at home with us and seemed to be very happy.

"He was last seen on the night of May 13th—that is, the night of last Monday. His room was on the second floor and is entered through another larger room, in which two boys were sleeping. These boys saw and heard nothing, and they are sure that young Saltire did not pass out that way. His window was open, and there is a strong plant leading to the ground. We could find no footmarks below, but it is sure that this is the only possible way out.

"We found out he was missing at seven o'clock on Tuesday morning. His bed had been slept in. He had dressed himself fully in his usual school clothing. There was no signs that anyone had entered the room, and it is quite clear that anything in the nature of cries or a fight would have been heard, since Caunter, the older boy in the outside room, is a very light sleeper.

"When Lord Saltire's disappearance was discovered, I at once made a list of everyone in the building—boys, masters, and servants. It was then that we found that Lord Saltire had not been alone in leaving. Heidegger, the German master, was missing. His room was on the second floor, at the end of the building, facing the same way as Lord Saltire's. His bed had also been slept in, but it seemed he had gone away partly dressed, since his shirt was lying on the floor. He had undoubtedly let himself down by a plant, for we could see the marks of his feet where he had landed on the ground. His bicycle was kept in a small building beside this area of grass, and it also was gone.

"He had been with me for two years, and came with the best reports, but he was a quiet, unhappy man, not really liked by the masters or the boys. No track could be found of the two, and now, on Thursday morning, we have as little to go on as we had on Tuesday. We asked at once, of course, at Holdernesse Hall. It is only a few miles away, and we hoped that some sudden homesickness came upon the lad and he had gone back to his father, but nothing had been heard of him. The Duke is greatly upset, and, as to me, you have seen yourselves the state of my nerves. Mr. Holmes, if ever you put forward your full powers, I ask you to do so now, for never in your life could you have a case which is more worthy of them."

Sherlock Holmes had listened very carefully to the statement of the unhappy schoolmaster. His face showed that he was deep in thought, turning over the facts he had heard. He now drew out his notebook and made one or two notes.

"You have been very remiss in not coming to me sooner," said he, with just a little anger. "My investigation is therefore that much more difficult, for without doubt, the plant and area of grass would have given me some good leads."

"I could not help it, Mr. Holmes. The Duke wanted to make sure this was kept from the general public. He was afraid of his family unhappiness being put out for all to see. He has a deep fear of anything of the kind."

"But there has been a police investigation?"

"Yes, sir, and it has not got very far. A boy and a young man were reported to have been seen leaving a neighboring station by an early train. Only last night we had news that the couple had been found in Liverpool, and they prove to have no connection whatever with the matter in hand. Then it was that in my fear and disappointment, after a sleepless night, I came straight to you by the early train."

"I suppose the investigation was stopped while this lead was being followed up?"

"It was completely dropped."

"So that three days have been lost. This case has been very badly investigated."

"I must agree with you."

"And yet the problem should still give up an answer. I shall be very happy to look into it. Have you been able to find any connection between the missing boy and this German master?"

"None at all."

"Was he in the master's class?"

"No, he had never even spoken to him, so far as I know."

"That is certainly very unusual. Had the boy a bicycle?"

"No."

"Was any other bicycle missing?"

"No."

"Are you sure?"

"Quite."

"Well, now, you do not really mean that this German rode off upon a bicycle in the dead of night, carrying the boy in his arms?"

"Certainly not."

"Then what is the idea in your mind?"

"The bicycle may have been to throw us off the track. It may have been hidden somewhere, and the pair gone off on foot."

"Quite so, but it seems rather a poor attempt at fooling us, does it not? Were there other bicycles in this building?"

"Several."

"Would he not have hidden two, had he wished to give the idea that they had gone off upon them?"

"I suppose he would."

"Of course he would. Your idea won't do. But the bicycle is a good starting point for an investigation. After all, it is not an easy thing to hide or to destroy. One other question. Did anyone call to see the boy on the day before he went missing?"

"No."

"Did he get any letters?"

"Yes, one letter."

"From whom?"

"From his father."

"How did you know it was from his father?"

"The family sign was on the letter, and it was written in the Duke's own unusual handwriting. Besides, the Duke remembers having written."

"When had he a letter before that?"

"Not for several days."

"Had he ever received one from France?"

"No, never."

"You see the point of my questions, of course. Either the boy was carried off by force or he went of his own free will. In the latter case, you would expect that something from outside would be needed to make so young a lad do such a thing. If he has had no visit, that something must have come in a letter. Therefore, I will try to find out who has sent them."

"I fear I cannot help you much. He only received letters, so far as I know, from his own father."

"Who wrote to him on the very day he went missing. Were the feelings between father and son very friendly?"

"His Grace is never very friendly with anyone. He spends his time working on the great public questions, and is not really interested in everyday life. But he was always kind to the boy in his own way."

"But the boy liked his mother more?"

"Yes."

"Did he say so?"

"No."

"The Duke, then?"

"Good heaven, no!"

"Then how could you know?"

"I have spoken with Mr. James Wilder, his Grace's secretary. It was he who told me about Lord Saltire's feelings."

"I see. By the way, that last letter of the Duke's — was it found in the boy's room?"

"No, he had taken it with him. I think, Mr. Holmes, it is time that we were leaving for Euston."

"I will order a cab. In a quarter of an hour, we shall leave with you. If you are sending a telegram home, Mr. Huxtable, it would be well to allow the people in your neighborhood to think that the investigation is still going on in Liverpool. In the meantime I will do a little quiet work at your school, and perhaps the track is not too old, and two old investigators like Watson and myself may still be able to pick it up."

That evening found us in the cold but fresh air of the Peak country, in Dr. Huxtable's famous school. It was already dark when we reached it. A card was lying on the hall table, and a servant said something to Dr. Huxtable, who turned to us clearly upset.

"The Duke is here," said he. "The Duke and Mr. Wilder are in the study. Come gentlemen, and you can meet them."

I was, of course, familiar with the pictures of the famous statesman, but the man himself was very different from these. He was a tall and stately person, well dressed, with a thin face and a nose which was broad and long. His face was white, which showed up even more clearly against his bright red hair. Such was the man who looked icily at us from the center of Dr. Huxtable's room. Beside him stood a very young man, whom I understood to be Wilder, the private secretary. He was a small, good-looking man with light blue eyes. It was he who at once started speaking.

"I called this morning, Dr. Huxtable, too late to stop you from going to London. I learned that you wanted to ask Mr. Sherlock

Holmes to undertake this case. His Grace is surprised, Dr. Huxtable, that you should have taken such a step without asking him."

"When I learned that the police had failed — "

"His Grace is by no means sure that the police have failed."

"But surely, Mr. Wilder — "

"You know very well, Dr. Huxtable, that his Grace does not want a word of this to reach the public. He wants as few people as possible to know about it."

"The matter can be easily put right," said the doctor, clearly afraid. "Mr. Sherlock Holmes can return to London by the morning train."

"Hardly that, Doctor, hardly that," said Holmes, in his quiet voice. "This northern air is healthy and pleasant, so I propose to spend a few days up here, keeping my mind as busy as possible. Whether I stay with you or at the village hotel is, of course, for you to decide."

I could see that the poor doctor did not know what to do or say when he was rescued by the deep voice of the red-haired Duke.

"I agree with Mr. Wilder, Dr. Huxtable, that you would have been wise to talk to me. But since Mr. Holmes already knows our story, it would be foolish if we should not enlist his help. Far from going to the hotel, Mr. Holmes, I should be pleased if you would come and stay with me at Holdernesse Hall."

"I thank your Grace. For the purposes of my investigation, I think that it would be wiser for me to stay at the scene of the mystery."

"Just as you like, Mr. Holmes. Anything you need which Mr. Wilder or I can give you is for the asking."

"It will probably be necessary for me to see you at the Hall," said Holmes. "I would only ask you now, sir, whether you have any explanation in your own mind as to why or how your son went missing?"

"No, sir, I have not."

"Excuse me if I talk about that which is painful to you, but I must if

I am to help in this case. Do you think that the Duchess had anything to do with the matter?"

The great man thought hard and it was clear he was not sure.

"I do not think so," he said, at last.

"The other most simple explanation is that the child has been taken for the purpose of getting money from you. You have not had any demand of the sort?"

"No, sir."

"One more question, your Grace. I understand that you wrote to your son upon the day he went missing."

"No, I wrote the day before."

"Exactly. But he received it on that day?"

"Yes."

"Was there anything in your letter which might have upset him or made him to take such a step?"

"No, sir, not at all."

"Did you post that letter yourself?"

The Duke's reply was cut off by his secretary, who broke in with some heat.

"His Grace does not usually post letters himself," said he. "This letter was put with others upon the study table, and I myself put them in the postbag."

"You are sure this one was among them?"

"Yes, I saw it."

"How many letters did your Grace write that day?"

"Twenty or thirty. I keep in touch with many people. But surely this is not the point?"

"Maybe," said Holmes.

"For my own part," the Duke continued, "I have asked the police to turn their investigation to the south of France. I have already said that I do not believe that the Duchess would take such action, but the lad had the most wrong-headed opinions, and it is possible that he may have run to her, helped by this German. I think, Dr. Huxtable, that we will now return to the Hall."

I could see that there were other questions which Holmes would have wished to put, but the Duke's manner showed that the meeting was at an end. It was clear that his upper-class nature found talking about his family with a stranger most unpleasant, and that he feared that every fresh question would throw more light onto the hidden corners of his life.

When the Duke and his secretary had left, my friend threw himself at once into the investigation.

The boy's room was carefully looked over, and gave us nothing save that it was only through the window that he could have escaped. The German master's room gave nothing further. In this case some of the plant had given way under his weight, and we saw the mark on the grass where his feet had come down. That one mark in the short, green grass was the only evidence left of the night's action.

Sherlock Holmes left the house alone, and only returned after eleven. He had bought a large plan of the neighborhood, and this he brought into my room, where he laid it out on the bed, and, having balanced the lamp in the middle of it, he began to smoke over it, sometimes pointing out objects of interest.

"This case grows upon me, Watson," said he. "There are some unusual points of interest in connection with it. I want you to notice the different types of land shown on this plan. It may have a good deal to do with our investigation.

"This dark square is the Priory School. I'll put a pin in it. Now, this line is the high road. You see that it runs east and west past the school, and you see also that there is no side road for a mile either way. If the two passed away by road, it was this road."

"I see."

"By a happy chance, we are able to some degree to know what passed along this road during the night in question. At this point, where my finger is now resting, a policeman was on duty from twelve to six. It is, as you see, the first crossroad on the east side. This man states that he did not leave his post for a moment, and he is sure that neither boy nor man could have gone that way unseen. I have spoken with this policeman tonight, and he appears to me to be a perfectly trustworthy person. That accounts for this end. We have now to deal with the other. There is a public house here, the Red Bull. The landlady was ill and had sent to Mackleton for a doctor, but he did not arrive until morning, being out on another case. The people at the inn were watching for him all night, and one or other of them seems to have continually had an eye upon the road. They are sure that no one passed. If their evidence is good, then we are fortunate enough to be able to account for the west, and therefore to be able to say that the escapers did not use the road at all."

"But the bicycle?" I objected.

"Quite so. We will come to the bicycle presently. To continue our reasoning: if these people did not go by the road, they must have crossed the country to the north of the house or to the south of the house. That is certain. Let us look at one against the other. On the south of the house is, as you see, a lot of farmland, divided up into smaller areas, with stone walls between them. It is not possible that a bicycle could pass. We turn to the country on the north. Here there lies a group of trees, marked as the 'Ragged Shaw,' and on the far side stretches a great rolling plain, Lower Gill Moor. It goes slowly upward for ten miles. Here, at one side, is Holdernesse Hall, ten miles by road, but only six across the plain. It is a lonely place, this plain.

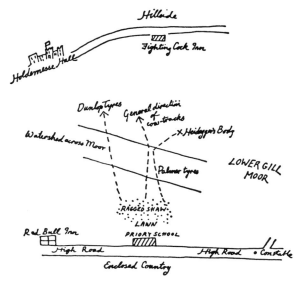

HOLMES'S MAP OF THE NEIGHBORHOOD OF THE SCHOOL

A few farmers have small holdings, where they raise livestock. Except these, birds are the only living things you will find until you come to the Chesterfield high road. There is a church there, a few houses, and a public house. Beyond that, the hills rise quite high. Surely it is here to the north that we must look."

"But the bicycle?" I said again.

"Well, well!" said Holmes, a little quickly. "A good cyclist does not need a high road. The plain has many paths, and the moon was full. Hello! What is this?"

There was a noise outside the door, and a moment afterwards Dr. Huxtable was in the room. In his hand he held a blue school hat.

"At last we have something!" he cried. "Thank heaven! At last we are on the dear boy's track! It is his hat."

"Where was it found?"

"In the van of some travelers who stayed on the plain. They left on Tuesday. Today the police tracked them down and looked through their home. This was found."

"How do they account for it?"

"They lied—said that they found it on the plain on Tuesday morning. They know where he is, all right! Thank goodness, they are all held by the police. Either the fear of the law or the Duke's money will get out of them all that they know."

"So far, so good," said Holmes, when the doctor had at last left the room. "It at least bears out my view that it is on the side of the Lower Gill Moor that we must hope for results. The police have really done nothing, save the arrest of these travelers. Look here, Watson! There is a watercourse across the plain. You see it marked here in the plan. In some parts it is quite wide—as it is in the area between Holdernesse Hall and the school. It is pointless to look elsewhere for tracks in this dry weather, but at that point there is certainly a chance of some record being left. I will call you early tomorrow morning, and you and I will try if we can to throw some little light upon the mystery."

The day was just breaking when I woke to find the long, thin form of Holmes by my bedside. He was fully dressed, and had seemed to have already been out.

"I have done the grass and the bicycle room," said he. "I have also had a walk through the Ragged Shaw. Now, Watson, there is a hot drink ready in the next room. I must ask you to hurry, for we have a busy day before us."

His eyes were shining as he thought of the day before him. A very different Holmes, this busy, alive man, from the thoughtful dreamer of Baker Street. With high hopes we struck across the brown earth of the plain, crossed with a thousand paths, until we came to the broad, light green area which marked the watercourse between us and

Holdernesse. If the lad had gone homeward, he must have passed this, and he could not pass it without leaving a mark. But no sign of him or the German could be seen. With a darkening face my friend strode along the edge, looking at every mark upon the green ground. There were many animal marks, and at one place, some miles down, cows had left their tracks. Nothing more.

"Well, we have found nothing here," said Holmes, looking unhappily over the rolling length of the plain. "There is another watercourse down there, and a narrow space between. Hello! Hello! Hello! What have we here?"

We had come on a small black pathway. In the middle of it, clearly marked on the wet soil, was the track of a bicycle.

"Yes!" I cried. "We have it."

But Holmes was not so pleased, and his face was thoughtful rather than happy.

"A bicycle, certainly, but not the bicycle," said he. "I know of forty-two different tracks left by tires. This, as you see, is a Dunlop, with a mark upon the outer cover. Heidegger's tires were Palmer's, leaving long lined stripes. Aveling, the mathematical master, was sure upon the point. Therefore, it is not Heidegger's track."

"The boy's then?"

"Possibly, if we could prove he took a bicycle. But this we have completely failed to do. This track, as you see, was made by a rider who was going from the direction of the school. It may or may not be connected with our investigation, but we will follow it backwards before we go any further."

We did so, and at the end of a few hundred yards lost the tracks as we came out from the wet part of the plains. Following the path backwards, we picked out another spot, where a spring ran across it. Here, once again, was the mark of the bicycle, though nearly covered by the tracks of cows. After that there was no sign, but the path ran right on into Ragged Shaw, the wood which backed on to the school. The cyclist must have come from this wood. Holmes sat down on a stone and rested his face in his hands. I had smoked two cigarettes before he moved.

"Well, well," said he, at last. "It is, of course, possible that a clever man might change the tires of his bicycle in order to leave strange tracks. A criminal who was capable of such a thought is a man whom I should be proud to do business with. We will leave this question undecided and go back to the plain again, for there is still a lot to investigate."

We continued looking along the edge of the wet part of the plain, and soon our hard work was well rewarded. Right across the lower part of the plain lay a path. Holmes gave a cry of joy as he came up to it. A fine set of lines ran down the center of it. It was the Palmer tires.

"Here is Herr Heidegger, sure enough!" cried Holmes. "My reasoning seems to have been pretty sound, Watson."

"I take my hat off to you."

"But we have a long way still to go. Kindly walk clear of the path. Now let us follow the trail. I fear that it will not lead far."

We found as we moved along that this part of the plain is crossed with soft soil, and though we often lost sight of the track, we always succeeded in picking it up once more.

"Do you see," said Holmes, "that the rider is now undoubtedly going faster? There can be no doubt of it. Look at this mark, where you get both tires clear. The one is as deep as the other. That can only mean that the rider is throwing his weight on to the front, as a man does when he is standing up on the bike to go faster. My God! He has had a fall."

There were broad, uneven marks covering some yards of the track.

Then there were a few footmarks, and the tires reappeared once more.

"A side fall," I suggested.

Holmes held up a branch of a nearby tree. I saw that the yellow flowers were spotted with red. On the path, too, were dark marks of dried blood.

"Bad!" said Holmes. "Bad! Stand clear, Watson! Not an unnecessary footstep! But there is no other track. Cows on this side path. He was surely not wounded by a cow? Not possible! But I see no traces of anyone else. We must push on, Watson. Surely, with blood as well as the track to guide us, he cannot escape us now."

We did not need long. The tracks of the tire began to go from side to side upon the wet path. Suddenly, as I looked ahead, I saw something shiny to the side of the trees. Out of them we pulled a bicycle, Palmer-tired, the front covered with blood. On the other side of the trees, a shoe was sticking out. We ran round, and there lay the poor rider. He was a tall man, with glasses, which were broken. The cause of his death was a fearful blow upon the head. That he could have gone on after receiving such a wound said much for the health and strength of the man. His open coat disclosed a nightshirt beneath it. It was undoubtedly the German master.

Holmes turned the body over with care, and looked at it for some time. He then sat in deep thought for a time, and I could see by his face that this sad find had not, in his opinion, advanced us much in our investigation.

"It is a little difficult to know what to do, Watson," said he, at last. "My own feeling is to push this investigation on, for we have already lost so much time that we cannot lose another hour. On the other hand, we must tell the police and see that this poor fellow's body is looked after."

"I could take a note back."

"But I need your company and help. Wait a bit! There is a fellow in that field. Bring him over here, and he will guide the police."

I brought the farmer across, and Holmes sent him off with a note to Dr. Huxtable.

"Now, Watson," said he, "we have picked up two clues this morning. One is the bicycle with the Palmer tire, and we see what that has led to. The other is the bicycle with the marked Dunlop. Before we start to investigate that, let us try to understand what we do know, so as to make the most of it.

"First of all, the boy left of his own free-will. He got down from his window and he went off, either alone or with someone. That is sure."

I agreed.

"Well, now, let us turn to this poor German master. The boy was fully dressed when he left. Therefore, he knew what he would do. But the German went without his shirt. He acted on very short notice."

"Undoubtedly."

"Why did he go? Because, from his bedroom window, he saw the boy leaving; he wished to overtake him and bring him back. He got on his bicycle, followed the lad, and in following him met his death."

"So it would seem."

"Now I come to the important part. The natural action of a man in following a little boy would be to run after him. He would know that he could overtake him. But the German does not do so. He turns to his bicycle. I am told that he was a good cyclist. He would not do this, if he did not see that the boy had some fast means of escape."

"The other bicycle."

"Let us continue. He meets his death five miles from the school—not by a bullet, mark you, which even a boy might fire but by a heavy blow. The lad, then, had a companion in his escape. And the escape was a fast one, since it took five miles before an expert cyclist could overtake them. Yet we looked at the ground round the body. What do we find? A few cow tracks, nothing more. I took a good look round, and there is no path within fifty yards. Another cyclist could have had nothing to do with the murder, nor were there any human footmarks."

"Holmes," I cried, "this is not possible."

"Good!" he said. "A very useful remark. It is impossible as I state it, and therefore I must in some way have stated it wrong. Yet you saw for yourself. Can you suggest anything I have got wrong?"

I could think of nothing.

"We have had more difficult cases than this. At least we have plenty of clues, if we can only use them. Come then, having followed the Palmer, let us see what the Dunlop with the marked cover has to offer us."

We picked up the track and followed it for some distance, but soon the plain rose into a hill, and we left the watercourse behind us. No further help from tracks could be hoped for. At the spot where we saw the last of the Dunlop tire, it might equally have led to Holdernesse Hall, which we could just see some miles to our left, or to a small town which lay in front of us and marked the position of the Chesterfield high road.

As we approached a rather unpleasant looking public house, Holmes gave a sudden cry, and held me by the shoulder to save himself from falling. He had hurt his foot and was quite helpless. With difficulty he got to the door, where a fat, old man was sitting.

"How are you, Mr. Reuben Hayes?" said Holmes.

"Who are you, and how do you know my name?" the countryman answered, with an angry look from his dark eyes.

"Well, it's written on the sign above your head. It's easy to see a man who is master of his own house. I suppose you haven't such a thing as a wagon in your stables?"

"No, I have not."

"I can hardly put my foot to the ground."

"Don't put it on the ground then."

"But I can't walk."

"Well, don't walk."

Mr. Reuben Hayes's manner was far from pleasant, but Holmes took it remarkably well.

"Look here, my man," said he. "This is really rather a difficult position for me. I don't mind how I get on."

"Neither do I," said the landlord.

"The matter is very important. I would offer you a pound for the use of a bicycle." The landlord looked more interested.

"Where do you want to go?"

"To Holdernesse Hall."

"Friends of the Duke, I suppose?" said the landlord, looking at our mud-covered clothes, trying to make us feel foolish.

Holmes laughed good-naturedly.

"He'll be glad to see us, anyhow."

"Why?"

"Because we bring him news of his lost son."

The landlord looked clearly shaken.

"What, you're on his track?"

"He has been heard of in Liverpool. They expect to get him at any moment."

Again a quick change passed over the heavy face. His manner was suddenly much more friendly.

"I don't like the Duke," said he, "for personal reasons. But I'm glad to hear that the young lord was heard of in Liverpool, and I'll help you to take the news to the Hall."

"Thank you," said Holmes. "We'll have some food first. Then you can bring round the bicycle."

"I haven't got a bicycle."

Holmes held up a pound.

"I tell you, man, that I haven't got one. I'll let you have two horses as far as the Hall."

"Well, well," said Holmes, "we'll talk about it when we've had something to eat."

When we were left alone in the stone-floored kitchen, it was remarkable how quickly Holmes's foot recovered. It was nearly night-fall, and we had eaten nothing since early morning, so that we spent some time over our meal. Holmes was lost in thought, and once or twice he walked over to the window and looked out. It opened on to a yard. In the far corner was a workshop, where a dirty lad was busy. On the other side were the stables. Holmes had sat down again when he suddenly jumped out of his chair with a loud cry.

"By Heaven, Watson, I believe that I've got it!" he cried. "Yes, yes, it must be so. Watson, do you remember seeing any cow-tracks today?"

"Yes, several."

"Where?"

"Well, everywhere. They were at the watercourse, and again on the path, and again near where poor Heidegger met his death."

"Exactly. Well, now, Watson, how many cows did you see on the plain?"

"I don't remember seeing any."

"Strange, Watson, eh?"

"Yes, it is strange."

"Now, Watson, make an effort, throw your mind back. Can you see those tracks upon the path?"

"Yes, I can."

"Can you recall anything unusual about those tracks, Watson?"

"No, I cannot."

"But I can. I am sure, now I think about it, that the tracks showed a cow sometimes walking and sometimes running fast. However, we will go back and see for sure when we have time."

"And what does this mean?"

"Only that it is a remarkable cow which runs in that way, with two feet off the ground. By heaven! Watson, it was no mind of a country landlord that thought out such a thing as that. Let us go out and see what we can see."

There were two large, dirty horses in the old stable. Holmes raised the back leg of one of them and laughed aloud.

"Old shoes, but new nails. This case deserves to be a classic. Let us go across to the workshop."

The lad continued his work without looking at us. I saw Holmes's eye moving quickly to right and left among the pieces of iron and wood which was all over the floor. Suddenly, however, we heard a step behind us, and there was the landlord, his heavy face showing anger and, for us, danger. He held a short, heavy stick in his hand, and he advanced in such a manner that I was glad to feel the gun in my pocket.

"What are you doing there?" the man cried.

"Why, Mr. Reuben Hayes," said Holmes, coolly, "one might think that you were afraid of our finding something out."

The man mastered himself with a great effort, and he gave a dry laugh, which seemed more dangerous than his anger.

"You're welcome to all you can find out in my workshop," said he. "But look here, mister, I don't care for people looking about my place without my leave, so the sooner you pay for your food and get out, the better I shall be pleased."

"All right, Mr. Hayes, we don't want to cause trouble," said Holmes. "We have been having a look at your horses, but I think I'll walk, after all. It's not far, I believe."

"Not more than two miles to the Hall gates. That's the road to the left." He watched us with angry eyes until we had left his land.

We did not go very far along the road, for Holmes stopped the moment that we were out of sight of the landlord.

"The answer is at that public house," said he. "I can't possibly walk away now."

"I am convinced," said I, "that this Reuben Hayes knows all about it. He looks like the criminal sort to me."

"Oh! You think so, do you? There are the horses, there is the workshop. Yes, it is an interesting place, this Fighting Cock. I think we shall have another look without Reuben Hayes knowing about it."

Before we could move I saw a cyclist coming quickly along the path from Holdernesse Hall.

"Get down, Watson!" cried Holmes, with a heavy hand upon my shoulder. We had hardly got out of sight when the man rushed past us on the road. I caught sight of a white face — a face with fear in every line, the mouth open, the eyes looking wildly in front. It was James Wilder, whom we had seen the night before.

"The Duke's secretary!" cried Holmes. "Come, Watson, let us see what he does."

We jumped from rock to rock, until in a few moments we had made our way to a point from which we could see the front door of the house. Wilder's bicycle was against a wall. No one was moving in the house, nor could we see any faces at the windows. Slowly it got dark as the sun went down. Then, in the dark we saw the two sidelights of a wagon light up in the stable-yard, and shortly afterwards heard it move at a rush in the direction of Chesterfield.

"What do you make of that, Watson?" Holmes asked quietly.

"It looks like someone is making a run for it."

"A single man in a wagon, so far as I could see. Well, it was not Mr. James Wilder, for there he is at the door."

The secretary was looking up the road as if he was expecting someone. Then at last there were steps in the road. A second figure came up the road and entered the public house. Five minutes later a light was lit in a room upon the first floor.

"It seems to be a strange business that is done by the Fighting Cock," said Holmes. "Now, what in the world is Mr. James Wilder doing in there at this hour of night, and who is it that comes to meet him there? Come, Watson, we must really take a chance and try to investigate this a little more closely."

Together we went down to the road and keeping our heads low, we crossed to the door of the public house. The bicycle was still against the wall. Holmes held a light to the back wheel, and I heard him laugh as we saw a patched Dunlop tire. Up above us was the lighted window.

"I must have a look through that, Watson. If you bend your back and hold fast to that wall, I think that I can manage."

A moment later, his feet were on my shoulders, but he was hardly up before he was down again.

"Come, my friend," said he, "our day's work has been quite long enough. I think that we have gathered all that we can. It's a long walk to the school, and the sooner we get started the better."

He hardly opened his lips during that tiring walk back across the plain, nor would he enter the school when he reached it, but went on to Mackleton Station, where he could send some telegrams. Late at night I heard him talking to Dr. Huxtable, who was upset by the sorry ending of the brave German teacher. Later still he entered my room as bright and lively as he had been when he started in the morning. "All goes well, my friend," said he. "I promise that before tomorrow evening we shall have reached the end of the mystery."

At eleven o'clock next morning my friend and I were walking up to Holdernesse Hall. We were shown into his Grace's study. There we found Mr. James Wilder, who unlike the previous evening, was quiet and in control of himself, but still showed signs of nervousness in his quick movements.

"You have come to see his Grace? I am sorry, but the fact is that the Duke is far from well. He has been very much upset by the news. We received a telegram from Dr. Huxtable yesterday afternoon, which told us what you found."

"I must see the Duke, Mr. Wilder."

"But he is in his room."

"Then I must go to his room."

"I believe he is in his bed."

"I will see him there."

Holmes's cold manner showed the secretary that it was useless to try and stop him.

"Very good, Mr. Holmes, I will tell him that you are here."

After an hour's delay, the great man appeared. His face was whiter than ever, his shoulders had rounded, and he seemed to me to be an altogether older man than he had been the morning before. He greeted us with a good manner and seated himself at his desk.

"Well, Mr. Holmes?" said he.

But my friend's eyes were upon the secretary, who stood by his master's chair.

"I think, your Grace, that I could speak more freely if Mr. Wilder were not here."

The man turned a shade paler and looked angrily at Holmes.

"If your Grace wishes — "

"Yes, yes, you had better go. Now, Mr. Holmes, what have you to say?"

My friend waited until the door had closed behind the secretary.

"The fact is, your Grace," said he, "that my colleague, Dr. Watson, and myself have been told by Dr. Huxtable that a reward had been offered in this case. I should like to hear this from your own lips."

"It is true, Mr. Holmes."

"It amounted, if I remember, to five thousand pounds to anyone who will tell you where your son is?"

"Yes."

"And another thousand to the man who will name the person or persons who keep him a prisoner?"

"Yes."

"The second point includes, no doubt, not only those who may have taken him away, but also those who keep him in his present position?"

"Yes, yes," cried the Duke, clearly wanting Holmes to continue. "If you do your work well, Mr. Sherlock Holmes, you will find that you will do very well."

My friend looked pleased.

"I fancy that I see your Grace's bankbook upon the table," said he. "I should be glad if you would make me out a bank order for six thousand pounds."

His Grace sat very still and upright in his chair and looked stonily at my friend.

"What are you talking about Mr. Holmes? I hope you are not laughing at me, it is hardly a subject for pleasantry."

"Not at all, your Grace. I mean everything I say."

"What is this about, then?"

"I mean that I should get the reward. I know where your son is, and I know some, at least, of those who are holding him."

The Duke's face had gone a shade whiter still.

"Where is he?" he said breathing hard.

"He is, or was last night, at the Fighting Cock Inn, about two miles from your garden gate."

The Duke fell back in his chair.

"And whom do you say did it?"

Sherlock Holmes's answer surprised even me. He stepped quickly forward and touched the Duke upon the shoulder.

"It was you," said he. "And now, your Grace, I'll trouble you for that money order."

Never shall I forget the Duke's appearance as he jumped up. At first I feared for Holmes's safety. Then, with a remarkable effort of self-control, he sat down and sank his face in his hands. It was some minutes before he spoke.

"How much do you know?" he asked at last, without raising his head.

"I saw you and your son together last night."

"Does anyone else beside your friend know?"

"I have spoken to no one."

The Duke took a pen in his shaking fingers and opened his bank-book.

"I shall be as good as my word, Mr. Holmes. I am about to write your money order, however unwelcome what you have found out may be to me. When the offer was first made, I little thought the way it might end up. Are you and your friend men who can be trusted, Mr. Holmes?"

"I don't understand, your Grace."

"I must put it plainly, Mr. Holmes. If only you two know of this, there is no reason why it should go any farther. I think twelve thousand pounds is the sum that I must give you, is it not?"

But Holmes smiled, shaking his head.

"I fear, your Grace, that matters can hardly be arranged so easily.

There is the death of this schoolmaster to be accounted for."

"But James knew nothing of that. You cannot hold that against him. It was the work of that wild madman whom he employed."

"I must take the view, your Grace, that when a man undertakes a crime, he is guilty of any other crime which may come from it."

"Maybe in the eyes of God, Mr. Holmes, but surely not in the eyes of the law. A man cannot be a murderer if he was not present at the murder. He told me everything, as he was so upset about what had happened. He lost not an hour in breaking completely with the murderer. Oh, Mr. Holmes, you must save him! I tell you that you must save him!" The Duke had dropped the last attempt at self-control, and was walking up and down the room with a red face and with his hands waving wildly in the air. At last he mastered himself and sat down once more at his table. "I must thank you for coming here before you spoke to anyone else," said he. "At least, we may talk about what is the best thing to do from now on."

"Good," said Holmes. "I would like to help your Grace, but, in order to do so, I must understand completely how the matter stands. I realize that your words were about Mr. James Wilder, and that he is not the murderer."

"No, the murderer has escaped."

Sherlock Holmes smiled to himself.

"Your Grace can hardly have heard of me, or you would not think that it is so easy to escape me. Mr. Reuben Hayes was arrested at Chesterfield, at eleven o'clock last night. I had a telegram from the head of the local police before I left the school this morning."

The Duke leaned back in his chair and looked in wonder at my friend.

"You seem to have powers that are hardly human," said he. "So Reuben Hayes is taken? I am glad to hear it, if it will not go against James."

"Your secretary?"

"No, sir, my son."

It was Holmes's turn to look surprised.

"I must say that this is new to me, your Grace. I must ask you to tell me more."

"I will hide nothing from you. I agree with you that telling the truth, however painful it may be to me, is the best way to deal with the situation in which James's foolishness has placed us. When I was a very young man, Mr. Holmes, I loved with a love that comes only once in a lifetime. I offered the lady marriage, but she turned it down on the grounds that such a marriage might not be good for me. Had she lived, I would certainly never have married anyone else. She died, and left this one child, whom for her sake I have looked after. I could not acknowledge I was the father to the world, but I gave him the best of educations, and since he came to manhood I have kept him near my person. He found out my secret, and has tried ever since to get me to honor him as my first born son. He did not like my wife, which caused problems in my marriage, and he could not stand my son — my first son in the eyes of the law. You may well ask me why I still kept James in my house. It was because I could see his mother's face in his, and that for her dear sake I did it. All her pretty ways too — there was not one of them which he could not suggest and bring back to my memory. I could not send him away. But I feared that one day he might do something really bad to Arthur — that is, Lord Saltire — and so I sent the boy to Dr. Huxtable's school.

"James met this fellow Hayes when he worked for me. Hayes was a bad sort, but in a strange way James became friendly with him. When James planned to take Lord Saltire, he asked Hayes for help. You remember that I wrote to Arthur upon that last day. Well, James opened the letter and put in a note asking Arthur to meet him in a little wood called the Ragged Shaw, which is near to the school. He used the Duchess's name, and in that way got the boy to come. That evening James bicycled over, he has told me all this himself, and he told Arthur, whom he met in the wood, that his mother longed to see him, that she was waiting for him, and that if he came back to the wood at midnight he would find a man with a horse who would take him to her. Poor Arthur believed him. He got to the meeting place and found this fellow Hayes. They set off on horse together. It seems — although James only heard this yesterday — that they were followed, that Hayes struck the man with a stick, and that the man died of his wounds. Hayes took Arthur back to his public house, the Fighting Cock, where he was kept in an upper room.

"Well, Mr. Holmes, that was the state of things when I first saw you two days ago. I had no more idea of the truth than you. You will ask me what was James's motive in doing such a deed. He could not think clearly where Arthur was concerned. He felt that he should have my house and position after my death, and wanted to make me change my will to say this. He knew that I would not tell the police as in some way I still loved him. However, before he could put his plan to me, the position had changed. You had found Heidegger's dead body. James was greatly upset by this news. He never thought that anyone would get hurt. He acted so strangely when he heard the news that I asked him if he had anything to do with it. Right away he told me everything. Then he asked me to keep his secret for three more days to give Hayes a chance to get away. I gave in to him, as I always do, and James hurried off to the Fighting Cock to tell Hayes. As soon as night fell I went there to see poor Arthur. I found him safe and well but so upset that he could not talk about the fearful crime he had seen. I kept my promise, against my will, and agreed that he should stay there another three days, under the care of Mrs. Hayes, a good woman, but one who feared her husband. I could not see how the police could be told without the part that James had played becoming known. You have asked for the truth, Mr. Holmes, and there it is. Will you now tell me truthfully what you are going to do?"

"I will," said Holmes. "In the first place, your Grace, I must tell you that you have placed yourself in a grave position in the eyes of the law. You have known about a crime but not told the police. You have also helped the escape of a murderer, for I cannot doubt that any money given to Hayes came from you."

The Duke agreed.

"Worse still, you have left your son with these people for three days."

"They promised—"

"What are promises to such people as these? You cannot be sure that they will not take him away again. To help one son you have endangered the life of your other son."

The proud lord of Holdernesse was not used to being talked to in such a way in his own home. His face went red but he said nothing.

"I will help you, but you must let me do it my way. Please ring for a footman and let me give him such orders as I like."

Without a word, the Duke rang a bell. A servant entered.

"You will be glad to hear," said Holmes, "that your young master is found. It is the Duke's wish that you should go at once to the Fighting Cock Inn to bring Lord Saltire home.

"Now," said Holmes, "we have taken care of the future, so we can think more kindly of the past. As I work only for myself, there is no reason that I should disclose anything that I know. The judge, no doubt, will order Hayes's life to be ended, and I am sure that your Grace can make sure he understands that it would be best for him to say nothing. The police will think that he planned it himself. I must say, though, that if James stays in your house it will lead to trouble."

"I understand that, Mr. Holmes, and it is already decided that he shall leave me forever and go to Australia."

"In that case, your Grace, I would suggest that it might be a good time for your wife to return to the family home."

"That is also going to happen, Mr. Holmes. I wrote to the Duchess this morning."

"In that case," said Holmes, "I think my friend and I can feel quite happy about our little visit to the North. There is one other small point which you might be able to help me with. This fellow Hayes had horses with shoes that looked like cows tracks. Was it from Mr. Wilder that he learned this extraordinary thing?"

The Duke stood in thought for a moment, with a look of surprise on his face. Then he opened a door and showed us into a large room. He led the way to a glass cupboard in a corner and pointed at the writing on the bottom of it.

"These shoes," it ran, "were found near Holdernesse Hall. They are for the use of horses, but they are shaped below with a foot of iron looking like a cow's foot, so as to throw followers off the track. They are believed to have been in use several hundred years ago."

Holmes opened the case, and ran his finger along the shoe. It was still a little wet.

"Thank you," said Holmes, as he closed the cupboard. "It is the second most interesting object that I have seen in the North."

"And the first?"

Holmes held his bank order and then placed it carefully in his notebook. "I am a poor man," said he, as he smiled and pushed the book deep into his pocket.

14

The Adventure of the Six Napoleons

６つのナポレオン像

読み始める前に

The Adventure of the Six Napoleons 6つのナポレオン像

56の短編のうち32番目に発表された
1904年5月号のストランド・マガジン初出
1905年発行の「シャーロック・ホームズの帰還」に収録された

［主な登場人物］

Sherlock Holmes シャーロック・ホームズ 世界的に有名な私立探偵。優れた観察眼と推理力を有する。ロンドンのベーカー街221Bに下宿している。

Watson ジョン・H・ワトソン 医師。ホームズの相棒でこの物語の語り手。ベーカー街221Bでホームズと同居している。

Lestrade レストレード ロンドン警視庁の警部。ホームズに事件の捜査を依頼する。

Morse Hudson モース・ハドソン ケニントン・ロードで画商店を営む。店のナポレオンの石膏像が壊される。

Dr. Barnicott バーニコット医師 ハドソンの店で買った石膏像を盗まれて壊される。ナポレオンに強い関心をもつ。

Horace Harker ホレス・ハーカー 新聞記者。ナポレオンの石膏像を盗まれる。玄関で身元不明の死体を発見する。

Beppo ベッポ 腕のよいイタリア人の職人。

［あらすじ］

　ロンドン警視庁のおなじみレストレード警部が、ナポレオンの石膏像が破壊されるという事件の捜査をホームズに依頼するところから話は始まる。破壊された6つの像は全て同じ画家が制作し、ゲルダー社が販売したものだった。そんな中、ナポレオン像が破壊された現場で殺人事件が起こり、謎はさらに深まっていくのだった。

［総単語数］7,158語

The Adventure of the Six Napoleons

It was not unusual for Mr. Lestrade, of the London police force to look in upon us of an evening. His visits were welcome to Sherlock Holmes, for they enabled him to keep in touch with all that was going on at police headquarters. In return for the news that Lestrade would bring, Holmes was always ready to hear about any case upon which the detective was working. Sometimes with a well-picked word or idea he would point Lestrade in the right direction.

This evening, Lestrade had spoken of the weather and the newspapers. Then he had gone quiet, thoughtfully smoking his cigarette. Holmes looked at him.

"Anything remarkable on hand?" he asked.

"Oh no, Mr. Holmes, nothing very special."

"Then tell me about it."

Lestrade laughed.

"Well, Mr. Holmes, there is something on my mind. And yet it seems so foolish that I did not want to bother you about it. On the other hand, although it does not seem important, it is undoubtedly very strange, and I know that you have a taste for all that is unusual. But, in my opinion, it comes more in Dr. Watson's line than ours."

"Illness?" said I.

"Madness, anyhow. And a strange madness, too. You wouldn't think there was anyone living in this age who had such a feeling about Napoleon the First that he would break any image of him that he could see."

Holmes sat back in his chair.

"This is no business of mine," said he.

"Yes, that's what I thought. But then, when the man commits robbery in order to break images which are not his own, that moves it from the doctor to the policeman."

Holmes sat up again.

"Robbery. This is more interesting. Tell me about it."

Lestrade took out his notebook and started to tell us the story.

"The first case was reported four days ago," said he. "It was at the shop of Morse Hudson, who has a place for the sale of pictures and other artworks in the Kennington Road. He was in the back of the shop, when he heard a noise in the front, and hurrying through, he found a plaster bust of Napoleon, which stood with several other works of art upon the counter, lying broken into pieces. He rushed out into the road, but although several passersby said that they noticed a man run out of the shop, he could not now see the man. It seemed to be one of those senseless acts which happen from time to time, and it was reported to the constable on the beat as such. The plaster cast was not worth more than a few shillings, and the whole thing appeared to be unworthy of any special investigation.

"The second case, however, was more grave, and also more unusual. It happened only last night.

"In Kennington Road, and within only a few hundred yards of Morse Hudson's shop, there lives a well-known doctor, named Dr. Barnicott. His home and office are at Kennington Road, but he also has a branch office at Lower Brixton Road, two miles away. This Dr. Barnicott is very interested in Napoleon, and his house is full of books, pictures, and other things to do with the French Emperor. Some time ago he bought from Morse Hudson two plaster casts of the famous head of Napoleon by the French artist Devine. One of these he placed in his hall in the house at Kennington Road and the other on the table in his office at Lower Brixton. Well, when Dr. Barnicott came down this morning, he was surprised to find that his house had been robbed in the night, but that nothing had been taken save the head from the hall. It had been carried out and had been broken against the garden wall, where it lay in pieces."

Holmes looked even more interested.

"This is certainly very strange," said he.

"I thought it would please you. But I have not got to the end yet. Dr. Barnicott went to his office at twelve o'clock. When he arrived there, he found that the window had been opened in the night and the broken pieces of his second bust were all over the room. It had been broken where it stood. In neither case were there any signs which could give us a clue as to the criminal or madman who had done it. Now, Mr. Holmes, have you got the facts?"

"They are unusual," said Holmes. "Were the two busts broken in Dr. Barnicott's rooms copies of the one which was destroyed in Morse Hudson's shop?"

"They were taken from the same cast."

"Such a fact goes against the idea that the man who breaks them has anything against Napoleon. Considering how many likenesses of the great Emperor there are in London, it is too much to suppose that our criminal friend should chance to begin upon copies of the same bust."

"Well, I thought as you do," said Lestrade. "On the other hand, Morse Hudson is the seller of busts in that part of London, and these three had been in his shop for years. So, although, as you say, there are hundreds of busts and artworks in London, it is very probable that these three were the only ones in that area. Someone from that part of town would begin with them."

Holmes looked as though he doubted Lestrade's ideas.

"That won't do, Lestrade."

"Well, how would you explain it?"

"I don't attempt to do so. I would only note that there is a method in this man's madness. In Dr. Barnicott's house, where a sound might have been heard, the bust was taken outside before being broken, whereas in the office, where there was less danger of being heard, the bust was broken where it stood. The whole thing seems of no importance, and yet I know that some of my most famous cases have had the least promising starts. I shall be very pleased, Lestrade, if you will let me hear of any fresh news about this unusual case."

The news for which my friend had asked came in quicker and was far graver than he could have thought. Holmes entered the living room with a telegram in his hand. He read it out loud:

"Come at once, 131 Pitt Street, Kensington.
"LESTRADE."

In half an hour we had reached Pitt Street, a quiet road in one of the busiest areas of London. No.131 was one of a row of houses, all looking the same. As we drove up, we saw a crowd of people in front of the house. Holmes sat forward in his seat.

"It's attempted murder at the least. Nothing else will hold a London crowd. Look, Watson, the top steps have been washed but the others are dry. There's Lestrade at the front window; we shall know soon enough what is going on."

The policeman received us with a grave face and showed us into a sitting room where an old man was walking up and down, unable to stay still. It was his house; he was Mr. Horace Harker of Central News.

"It's the Napoleon bust business again," said Lestrade. "You seemed interested last night, Mr. Holmes, so I thought perhaps you would be glad to be present now that the matter has taken a very much graver turn."

"What has it turned to then?" I asked.

"To murder. Mr. Harker, will you tell these gentlemen what has happened?"

The old man turned to us with a most unhappy face.

"It's a remarkable thing," said he. "All my life I have been gathering other people's news and now that a piece of real news has come my own way, I am so upset that I can't put two words together. If I had come in here as a newspaperman, I would have questioned myself and had an article in every evening paper. As it is, I am giving away a valuable story by telling it over and over to anyone who asks, and I can make no use of it myself. However, I've heard of your name, Mr. Sherlock Holmes, and if you'll only explain this unusual business, I shall be paid for my trouble in telling you the story."

Holmes sat down and listened.

"It all seems to be about that bust of Napoleon which I bought for this very room about four months ago. I picked it up for a very reasonable price from Harding Brothers, two doors from Kensington Station. A great deal of my work is done at night, and I often write until the early morning. So it was today. I was sitting in my study, which is at the back at the top of the house, about three o'clock, when I was sure that I heard some sounds downstairs. I listened, but could hear nothing more, and I decided that they came from outside. Then suddenly five minutes later there came an almost inhuman cry. It is a sound, Mr. Holmes, that will ring in my ears for as long as I live. I sat unable to move for a minute or two. Then I got hold of my walking stick and went downstairs. When I entered this room I found the window wide open, and I noticed at once that the bust was gone from the writing table. Why any robber should take such a thing passes my understanding, for it was only a plaster cast and of no value whatsoever.

"You can see for yourself that anyone going out through that open window could reach the front doorstep in one long step. This was clearly what the robber had done, so I went round and opened the door. Stepping out into the dark, I nearly fell over a dead man. I ran back for a light, and there was this poor fellow, a great cut in his neck and the whole place awash with blood. I had just time to shout for the police, and then I must have passed out, for I knew nothing more until I found the policeman over me in the hall."

"Well, who was the murdered man?" asked Holmes.

"There's nothing to show who he was," said Lestrade. "You shall see the body later, but we have made nothing of it up till now. He is a tall man, sunburned, very strong, not more than thirty. He is poorly dressed and yet does not appear to be a laborer. A knife was lying in the blood beside. There was no name in his clothing and nothing in his pockets except some fruit, a plan of London, and a photograph. Here it is."

It was a photograph of an unusual, dangerous-looking man. Even from the picture one could tell that he had great strength.

"And what became of the bust?" asked Holmes after a careful study of the picture.

"We had news of it just before you came. It has been found in the front garden of an empty house in Campden House Road. It was broken into pieces. I am going round to see it now. Will you come?"

"Of course. I must just take one look round." Holmes looked closely at the floor and the window. "The fellow either had very long legs or was a very strong man," said he. "It was quite something to reach the window from the steps. Getting back was simple. Are you coming with us to see what is left of your bust, Mr. Harker?"

The unhappy newspaperman had seated himself at his writing table.

"I must try and make something of it," said he, "though I have no doubt that the evening papers are out already with the full story. If I'm not quick I'll be too late with a murder done on my own doorstep."

As we left the room he had already started to write.

The spot where the pieces of the bust had been found was only a few hundred yards away. Holmes picked up several of them and looked at them carefully. I was sure from his purposeful manner that at last we were upon a clue.

"Well?" asked Lestrade.

Holmes's face gave nothing away.

"We have a long way to go yet," said he. "And yet—and yet—we have some important facts to act upon. To have this bust, of little or no value, was worth more, to this strange criminal, than a human life. That is one point. Then there is the fact that he did not break it in the house, or immediately outside the house, if to break it was his only object."

"He was upset by meeting this other fellow. He hardly knew what he was doing," said Lestrade.

"Well, that's likely enough. But I want you to notice the position of this house, in the garden of which the bust was destroyed."

Lestrade looked around him.

"It was an empty house, and so he knew that no one would see him in the garden."

"Yes, but there is another empty house on this road which he must have passed before he came to this one. Why did he not break it there, since it is clear that every yard he carried it increased the chance of someone meeting him?"

"I give up," said Lestrade.

Holmes pointed to the street light above our heads.

"He could see what he was doing here, and he could not there. That was his reason."

"Good Lord! That's true," said the detective. "Now that I come to think of it, Dr. Barnicott's bust was broken not far from his light. Well, Mr. Holmes, what are we to do with that fact?"

"To remember it, to keep it in mind. We may come on something later which will make it more understandable. What steps are you going to take now, Lestrade?"

"The best way of getting at it, in my opinion, is to find out the name of the dead man. There should be no difficulty about that. When we have found who he is and who his friends are, we should have a good start in learning what he was doing in Pitt Street last night, and who it was that met him and killed him on the doorstep of Mr. Horace Harker. Don't you think so?"

"No doubt, and yet it is not quite the way in which I should continue the case."

"What would you do then?"

"Oh, you must not let me change your mind. I think that you should go on your line, and I, on mine. We can trade notes afterwards and each will help the other."

"Very good," said Lestrade.

"If you are going back to Pitt Street, you might see Mr. Horace Harker. Tell him for me that I have quite made up my mind. It is quite clear that a murdering madman, driven out of his mind by likenesses of Napoleon, was in his house last night. It will be quite useful for his article."

Lestrade looked at Holmes in surprise.

"You don't really believe that?"

Holmes smiled.

"Don't I? Well, perhaps I don't. But I am sure that it will interest Mr. Horace Harker and the readers of his article. Now, Watson, I think that we shall find that we have a long and rather tiring day ahead of us. I should be glad, Lestrade, if you could meet us at Baker Street at six o'clock this evening. Until then I should like to keep this photograph found in the dead man's pocket. It is possible that I may have to ask for your company and help tonight, if my reasoning should prove to be right. Until then, good-bye."

Sherlock Holmes and I walked together to the High Street, where we stopped at the shop of Harding Brothers, where the bust had been bought. A young man told us that Mr. Harding would not be there until the afternoon, and that he was himself a newcomer, who could give us no help in our investigation. Holmes's face showed that this was not good news.

"Well, well, we can't expect to have it all our own way, Watson," he said, at last. "We must come back in the afternoon if Mr. Harding will not be here until then. I am, as you have no doubt gathered, trying to find out the supplier of these busts, in order to see if there is not something unusual which may account for these remarkable actions. Let us make for Mr. Morse Hudson, of the Kennington Road. He may be able to throw some light upon the problem."

A drive of an hour brought us to the picture dealer's shop. He was a small, fat man with a red face and an angry manner.

"Yes! In my shop!" said he. "Why we pay so much for the police I do not know, when any criminal can come in and break one's goods. Yes, it was I who sold Dr. Barnicott his two busts. Who did I get the busts from? I don't see what that has to do with it. Well, if you really want to know, I got them from Gelder & Co., of Stepney, where the busts were made. They are a well-known house in the trade and have been for twenty years. How many had I? Three, two of Dr. Barnicott's and one broken in broad daylight in my shop. Do I know that photograph? No, I don't. Yes, I do, though! Why it's Beppo. He was an Italian piece-work man, who made himself useful in the shop. He could do a little bit of everything, and was very good with plaster. The fellow left me last week, and I've heard nothing of him since. No, I don't know where he came from nor where he went to. I had nothing against him while he was here. He was gone two days before the bust was broken."

"Well, that's all we could reasonably expect from Morse Hudson," said Holmes, as we left the shop. "We have this man Beppo connecting Kennington and Kensington, so that was worth a ten-mile drive to find out. Now, Watson, let us make for Gelder & Co., of Stepney, where the busts were made, I shall be surprised if we don't get some help down there."

We traveled to East London where we found the workshop we were looking for. There was a yard full of stone outside, and inside there was a large room in which fifty or so workers were working with plaster. The manager, a big fair German, received us pleasantly and gave a clear answer to all Holmes's questions. His books showed that hundreds of copies had been taken from a cast of Devine's head of Napoleon, but that the three that had been sent to Morse Hudson a year or so before had been half of a group of six, the other three being sent to Harding Brothers. There was no reason why those six should be different from any of the other casts. He could think of no possible cause why anyone should wish to destroy them — in fact, he laughed at the idea. Their wholesale price was six shillings, but the shopkeeper would get twelve or more. The copy was made from two casts from each side of the face, and then the two pieces of plaster were joined together to make the complete bust. The work was usually done by Italians in the room we were in. When finished, the busts were put on a table in the hall to dry, and afterwards stored. That was all he could tell us.

When we showed him the photograph of Beppo, the change in the man was remarkable. His face reddened with anger as he cried, "Him! Yes, indeed, I know him very well. We have never had any trouble here except for one time, and it was over this very fellow. It was more than a year ago now. He knifed another Italian in the street, and then he came to the works with the police after him, and he was taken here. Beppo was his name. I should never have taken on a man with such a face, but he was a good workman, one of the best."

"What happened to him?"

"The other man lived and he got off with a year. I have no doubt that he is out now, but he has not dared to show his nose here. We have a friend of his here, and I daresay he could tell you where he is."

"No, no," cried Holmes, "not a word to the friend, not a word. The matter is very important. I noticed that the date you sold those casts was June 3rd last year. Could you give me the date that Beppo was arrested?"

"I could give you an idea of the date from the pay-list," the manager answered. "Yes," he continued, after looking through the book, "he was last paid on May 20th."

"Thank you," said Holmes. "I don't think that I need use up any more of your time."

As we returned to London, Holmes noticed the newsstand; "Kensington in Fear following Murder by Madman." He read the paper and once or twice laughed out loud.

"This is good, Watson," said he. "Listen to this:

"It is good to know that all are agreed upon this case, since Mr. Lestrade, one of the most experienced members of the police force, and Mr. Sherlock Holmes, the famous investigator, have each decided that the strange set of acts, which have ended in so sad a manner, are the work of a madman rather than a criminal. No explanation except madness can cover the facts.

"Newspapers, Watson, are most valuable things, if only you know how to use them. Now, we will return to Kensington and see what they have to say at Harding Brothers."

The founder of that great shop proved to be a busy little man, but only too pleased to talk to us.

"Yes, I have already read the account in the evening papers. Mr. Horace Harker often visits us. We supplied him with the bust some months ago. We ordered three busts of that sort from Gelder & Co., of Stepney. They are all sold now. To whom? I must look in our sales book. Yes, we have the entries here. One to Mr. Harker, one to Josiah Brown, of Laburnum Lodge, Laburnum Vale, Chiswick, and one to Mr. Sandeford who lives out of London at Lower Grove Road, Reading. No, I have never seen the face in that photograph. You would hardly forget it, would you, for I have seldom seen a more unusual one. Have we any Italians working here? Yes, we have several among our workpeople and cleaners. I daresay they would be able to look at the sales book if they wanted to. There is no reason for keeping a watch upon that book. Well, well, it's a very strange business, and I hope that you will let me know if anything comes of your investigation."

Holmes had taken several notes during Mr. Harding's evidence, and I could see that he was very happy with the way the case was going. He said nothing, however, save that, unless we hurried, we should be late for our meeting with Lestrade. Sure enough, when we reached Baker Street the detective was already there, and we found him walking up and down, clearly wanting to tell us something.

"Well?" he asked. "What news, Mr. Holmes?"

"We have had a very busy day, and not a completely fruitless one," my friend explained. "We have seen both the shopkeepers and also the makers. I now know where each of the busts from that set can be found."

"The busts!" cried Lestrade. "Well, well, you have your own system, Mr. Sherlock Holmes, and it is not for me to say a word against it, but I think that I have done a better day's work than you. I know the name of the dead man."

"You don't say so?"

"And found a cause for the crime."

"Wonderful!"

"I know a policeman, Detective Hill, who knows the Italian Quarter very well. The dead man's appearance made me think he might have been from that part of the world. Hill knew him as soon as he saw the body. His name is Pietro Venucci, from Naples, and he was one of the most feared killers in London. He was connected with the Mafia, which as you know is a criminal group; they often use murder to get their way. Now you see how the case begins to clear up. The other fellow is probably Italian also, and a member of the Mafia. He has broken the rules in some way. Pietro is set upon his track. Probably the photograph we found in his pocket is the man himself, so that he might not knife the wrong person. Pietro follows the fellow, he sees him enter a house, he waits outside for him, and in a fight he receives his own death wound. How is that, Mr. Sherlock Holmes?"

"Well done, Lestrade, well done!" he cried. "But I didn't quite follow your explanation of the reason for destroying the busts."

"The busts! You can't seem to get those busts out of your head. After all, that is nothing, just a small robbery. It is the murder that we are really investigating, and I am gathering all the evidence I need."

"And the next step?"

"It is a very simple one. I shall go down with Hill to the Italian Quarter, find the man whose photograph we have got, and arrest him on the charge of murder. Will you come with us?"

"I think not. I feel that we can get the same result in a simpler way. I can't say for sure because it is beyond our control. But I have great hopes — in fact, the chances are two to one — that if you will come with us tonight I shall be able to help you to catch this man."

"In the Italian Quarter?"

"No, I think Chiswick is an address where he is more likely to be found. If you will come with me to Chiswick tonight, Lestrade, I'll promise to go to the Italian Quarter with you tomorrow, and nothing will be lost by the wait. And now I think that a few hours sleep would do us all good, for I do not want to leave until eleven o'clock, and it is unlikely that we shall be back before morning. You'll eat with us, Lestrade. In the meantime, Watson, I should be glad if you should ring for a boy as I must send a telegram at once."

Holmes spent the evening looking through old newspapers. When he stopped, he had a look in his eyes which told me that he had been successful, but he said nothing to either of us as to the result of his studies. For my own part, I had followed step by step the system by which he had investigated this strange and difficult case, and though I could not yet see the end which we would reach, I understood clearly that Holmes expected this unusual criminal to make an attempt upon the two busts still unbroken. One of them, I remembered, was at Chiswick. No doubt the object of our journey was to catch him in the very act. I could not help but smile as I thought of the clever way in which Holmes had got the wrong idea written up in the evening paper, to make the fellow think that he could continue his plan without danger. I was not surprised when Holmes suggested that I take my gun with me.

A cab was at the door at eleven, and in it we drove to a spot at the other side of Hammersmith Bridge. Here the cabman was told to wait. A short walk brought us to a quiet road with pleasant houses, each standing in its own grounds. By a street light we read "Laburnum Vale" on the gate post of one of them. The people who lived there had clearly gone to bed. All was dark except for a safety-light over the hall door, from which some light fell into the yard. Just inside the wooden fence which separated the grounds from the road was a shaded area, and it was here that we waited.

"I fear we'll have a long wait," said Holmes quietly. "We may thank our stars that it is not raining. I don't think that we can even smoke to pass the time. However, it's a two to one chance that we get something to pay for our trouble."

It proved not to be as long as Holmes had led us to fear, however, and it ended in a very sudden and unusual manner. In a moment, without the least sound beforehand, the garden gate was opened, and a dark figure, strong and quick, rushed up the garden path. We saw him as he passed the light thrown from over the door, and then we lost sight of him against the black background of the house. There was a moment or two of quiet, then we heard a window being opened. The noise stopped, and we knew he was inside the house. We saw a low light, first in one room, then the next.

"Let us get to the open window. We will hold him as he climbs out," Lestrade said quietly.

But before we could move, the man had come out again. As he came out into the light, we saw that he carried something white under his arm. He looked carefully all around him. Feeling he was safe, he turned away from us and laid down what he was carrying. The next moment we heard something being broken. The man was so interested in what he was doing that he did not hear us as we made our way across the grass. With a sudden jump Holmes was on his back, and a second later Lestrade and I had him by either arm and the handcuffs had been fastened. As we turned him over I saw an angry face that I knew from the photograph in the dead man's pocket.

But it was not our prisoner in which Holmes was interested. Bending down on the doorstep he was looking most carefully at that which the man had brought from the house. It was a bust of Napoleon just like the one we had seen this morning, and it too had been broken into many pieces. Carefully Holmes held each separate piece to the light, but in no way was it different to any other piece of plaster. He had just finished looking when the hall lights went on, the door opened, and the owner of the house, a big, happy-looking man, presented himself.

"Mr. Josiah Brown, I suppose?" said Holmes.

"Yes, and you, no doubt, are Mr. Sherlock Holmes? I had the note which you sent by the telegram boy, and I did just what you told me. We locked every door on the inside and waited to see what happened. Well, I'm very glad to see that you've got the man. I hope, gentlemen, that you will come in and have some tea."

However, Lestrade wanted to get his man into safe quarters, so within a few minutes our cab had been called and we were all four upon our way to London. Not a word would our prisoner say, he just looked angrily at each of us in turn. We stayed long enough at the police station to learn that his pockets contained a few shillings and a long knife which was covered in dried blood.

"That's all right," said Lestrade, as we parted. "Hill knows all these people, and he will give a name to him. You'll find that my idea of the Mafia will work out right. But I must thank you, Mr. Holmes, for the workmanlike way in which you laid hands upon him. I don't quite understand it all yet."

"I fear it is rather too late an hour for explanations," said Holmes.

"Besides there are one or two things that are not finished off, and it is one of those cases which we must work out to the very end. If you will come round once more to my rooms at six o'clock tomorrow, I think that I will be able to show you that even now, you have not fully understood the whole meaning of this business, which has one or two points that make it a one-off in the history of crime. If ever I allow you to write up any more of our little problems, Watson, I think that you will enliven your pages with an account of the unusual story of the Napoleonic busts."

When we met again the next evening Lestrade knew a lot more about the prisoner. His name, it appeared, was Beppo, second name unknown. He had a bad name in the Italian Quarter, and had already been to prison twice, once for robbery and once, as we already knew, for knifing a fellow-countryman. He could speak English perfectly well. His reasons for destroying the busts were still unknown, and he would not answer any questions upon the subject, but the police had discovered that these same busts might very well have been made by his own hands, when he was working at a place called Gelder & Co. To all these facts, most of which we already knew, Holmes only half-listened, and I thought he looked a little uneasy. At last he sat forward in his chair, and his eyes brightened. There had been a ring at the bell. A minute later we heard steps upon the stairs, and an old, red-faced man was shown in. In his right hand he carried an old bag, which he placed upon the table.

"Is Mr. Sherlock Holmes here?"

My friend smiled. "Mr. Sandeford of Reading, I suppose?" said he.

"Yes, I fear that I am a little late, but the trains were not on time. You wrote to me about a bust that I have."

"Yes."

"I have your letter here. You said, 'I wish to have a copy of Devine's

Napoleon, and am prepared to pay you ten pounds for the one which you have.' Is that right?"

"Yes, that is right."

"I was very much surprised at your letter, for I could not think how you knew that I had such a thing."

"Of course you must have been surprised, but the explanation is very simple. Mr. Harding, of Harding Brothers, said that they had sold you there last one, and he gave me your address."

"Oh, I see. Did he tell you how much I paid for it?"

"No, he did not."

"Well, I will, even though it may not be in my best interests. I only gave fifteen shillings for the bust, and I think you ought to know that before I take ten pounds from you."

"I am sure your words do you honor, Mr. Sandeford. But I have named my price, and I will stick to it."

"Well, it is very good of you, Mr. Holmes. I brought the bust up with me, as you asked me to do. Here it is!" He opened his bag and at last we saw, placed upon our table, the complete bust, copies of which we had already seen in pieces.

Holmes took a paper from his pocket and laid a ten pound note upon the table.

"You will kindly sign that paper, Mr. Sandeford, in the presence of these good gentlemen. It is simply to say that you give to me every possible right that you ever had in the bust. I am a careful man, you see, and you never know what turn things may take afterwards. Thank you Mr. Sandeford; here is your money. I wish you a very good evening."

When our visitor had gone, Holmes's movements were such that we could not take our eyes off of him. He began by taking a clean white cloth and laying it over the table. Then he placed his newly bought bust in the middle of the cloth. Then, he picked up his hunting stick and gave Napoleon a heavy blow on the top of his head. The figure broke into pieces, and Holmes quickly looked at them. The next moment, with a loud shout of pleasure, he held up one piece in which a round, dark object was fixed.

"Gentlemen," he cried, "let me show you the famous black pearl of the Borgias."

Lestrade and I sat quietly for a moment, and then we both jumped up in wonder. Holmes could not help but look pleased with himself, and at such times his human side took over from the cold thinker. Although he did not want to be famous, he still needed to know that the people close to him understood the power of his mind.

"Yes, gentlemen," said he, "it is the most famous pearl in the world, and it has been my good chance, by connecting a set of facts, to track it from the Prince of Colonna's bedroom at the Dacre Hotel, where it was lost, to the inside of this, the last of the six busts of Napoleon which were made at Gelder & Co., of Stepney. You will remember, Lestrade, the upset caused when the pearl was lost, and the unsuccessful attempts by the police to recover it. I was myself asked about the case, but was unable to throw any light upon it. It was thought that a servant-girl, an Italian, may have been behind it, and it was proved that she had a brother in London, but we failed to find any more evidence against them. The maid's name was Lucretia Venucci, and there is no doubt in my mind that this Pietro, who was murdered two nights ago, was her brother. I have been looking up the dates in the old papers, and I find that the loss of the pearl was two days before the arrest of Beppo, for knifing another Italian. The knifing took place at Gelder & Co., at the very time the busts were being made. Now you clearly see the order of how things happened. Beppo got the pearl somehow. He may have robbed Pietro, he may have been Pietro's helper. It is of no importance to us which is the right answer.

"The main fact is that he had the pearl, and at that moment, when it was on his person, the police were after him. He made for Gelder & Co., and he knew that he only had a few minutes to hide this valuable pearl, which would otherwise be found on him when he was caught. Six plaster casts of Napoleon were drying in the hall. One of them was still soft. In a minute Beppo, who was a good workman, made a small hole in the wet plaster, dropped in the pearl, and with a few touches covered over the hole once more. It was a very good hiding place. No one could possibly find it. But Beppo was given a year in prison, and during that time his busts were sold to people throughout London. Only by breaking them could he tell which contained his pearl. Even shaking would tell him nothing, for as the plaster was still wet it was probable that the pearl had stuck to it. Beppo did not give up, and he carried out his plan with considerable cleverness. Through a friend who works at Gelder & Co., he found out the shops that had bought the busts. He was able to find work with Morse Hudson, and in that way tracked down three of them. The pearl was not there. Then with the help of some Italian friends, he succeeded in finding out where the other three busts had gone. The first was at Harker's. There he was followed by his criminal friend Pietro, who felt Beppo should give back the pearl. In the fight that followed he knifed Pietro and left him on Mr. Harker's doorstep."

"If Pietro knew him, why should he carry his photograph?" I asked.

"As a means of tracking him down, if he wished to ask someone about him. After the murder I felt that Beppo would hurry rather than slow down. He would fear that the police would uncover his plan, and so he rushed on before they should get ahead of him. Of course, I did not know whether he had found the pearl in Harker's bust. I was not even sure that it was the pearl he was looking for, but it was evident to me that he was looking for something, since he carried the bust past the other houses in order to break it in the garden with the light overlooking it. Since Harker's bust was one in three, the chances were, as I told you, two to one against the pearl being inside it. There were still two busts, and it was clear that he would go for the London one first. I told the people who lived in the house to take steps to ensure their safety, and we went down and caught him in the act. By that time, of course, I knew for certain that it was the Borgia pearl that we were after. The name of the murdered man connected the one crime with the other. There was only one bust left—the Reading one—and I knew the pearl must be there. I bought it, in front of you, from Mr. Sandeford, and there it lies."

We sat unable to speak for a few moments.

"Well," said Lestrade, "I've seen you in a good many cases, Mr. Holmes, but I don't know that I ever knew a more workmanlike one than that. We are proud of you at police headquarters, and if you come down tomorrow there's not a man, from the oldest to the youngest, who wouldn't be glad to shake you by the hand."

"Thank you!" said Holmes. "Thank you!" and as he turned away, it seemed to me that he was more clearly moved than I had ever seen him. A moment later he was the cold and reasoning thinker once again. "Put the pearl in the safe, Watson," said he, "and let's get started on our paperwork. Good-bye, Lestrade. If any little problem comes your way, I shall be happy, if I can, to give you an idea or two to help out."

15

The Adventure of the Golden Glasses

金縁の鼻眼鏡

読み始める前に

The Adventure of the Golden Glasses 金縁の鼻眼鏡

56の短編のうち34番目に発表された
1904年7月号のストランド・マガジン初出
1905年発行の「シャーロック・ホームズの帰還」に収録された

［主な登場人物］

Sherlock Holmes シャーロック・ホームズ 世界的に有名な私立探偵。優れた観察眼と推理力を有する。ロンドンのベーカー街221Bに下宿している。

Watson ジョン・H・ワトソン 医師。ホームズの相棒でこの物語の語り手。ベーカー街221Bでホームズと同居している。

Stanley Hopkins スタンリー・ホプキンス ロンドン警視庁の警部。殺人事件の原因追究の助けをホームズに求める。

Professor Coram コーラム教授 ヨックスリー・オールド・プレースという屋敷の主で、謎の多い老人。

Willoughby Smith ウィロビー・スミス コーラム教授の秘書。何者かに首を刺されて殺された。

Mrs. Marker マーカー夫人 屋敷に住み込みの家政婦。

Susan Tarlton スーザン・タールトン 屋敷に住み込みのメイド。

Mortimer モーティマー 庭師。元軍人で性格がよい。

［あらすじ］

　ヨックスリー・オールド・プレースのコーラム教授宅で殺人が起きた。その原因追究の助けを求め、ロンドン警視庁のホプキンス警部がホームズの元を訪れる。教授の秘書、ウィロビー・スミスがナイフで首を刺され殺されたその現場で、被害者は犯人のものと思われる金縁の鼻眼鏡を握っていた。そこからホームズは鼻眼鏡の持ち主の特徴を推理し始める。

［総単語数］7,892語

The Adventure of the Golden Glasses

When I look back at my notebooks which contain our work for the year 1894, it is difficult for me to choose the cases which are interesting in themselves and, at the same time, best show those remarkable powers for which my friend was famous. As I turn over the pages I see many cases of murder and mystery. Most of them are wonderful stories, but on the whole I am of the opinion that none of them bring together so many points of interest as the story of Yoxley Old Place, which includes not only the death of young Willoughby Smith, but highlights how strange the reason for a crime can be.

It was a wild night towards the end of November. Holmes and I sat together quietly all evening. Outside the wind rushed down Baker Street, while the rain fell heavily against the windows. It was strange there, in the very depths of the town, with ten miles of man's handiwork on every side of us, to feel the iron hand of Nature and to know that to the powerful forces all London was no more than a small hill in the countryside.

I walked to the window, and looked out on the quiet street. The lights showed the muddy road. A single cab was making its way from the Oxford Street end.

"Well, Watson, it's as well we do not have to turn out tonight. Hello, what's this?" said Holmes.

Above the wind we could hear the cab stopping outside our door.

"What can he want?" I asked, as a man stepped out of it.

"He wants us! Run down, my dear fellow, and open the door."

When the light of the hall fell upon our midnight visitor, I knew him right away. It was young Stanley Hopkins, a promising detective whom Holmes had helped several times before.

"Is he in?" he asked.

"Come up, my dear sir," said Holmes's voice from above. "I hope you are not going to ask us to accompany you upon such a night."

The detective went up the stairs and I helped him out of his wet coat, while Holmes put more wood on the fire.

"Now, my dear Hopkins, come close and warm your feet," said he. "It must be something important to bring you out in such a storm."

"It is indeed, Mr. Holmes. I've had a busy afternoon. Did you see anything of the Yoxley case in the late newspapers?"

"No."

"Well, it was only a small story, and all wrong at that, so you have not missed anything. It's down in Kent, seven miles from Chatham and three from the railway line. I was sent for at 3:15, reached Yoxley Old Place at 5:00, held my investigation, was back at Charing Cross by the last train, and straight to you by cab."

"Which means, I suppose, that you are not quite clear about your case?"

"It means that I can make neither head nor tail of it. At first it seemed so simple that one couldn't go wrong. There's no reason for the crime, Mr. Holmes. That's the problem, there's no reason. We have a dead man, of that I am sure, but I can find no reason on earth why anyone should want to hurt him."

Holmes lit a cigarette and sat back in his chair.

"Let us hear about it," said he.

"I've got my facts pretty clear," said Stanley Hopkins. "All I want now is to know what they mean. The story, so far as I can make it out, is like this. Some years ago, an old man by the name of Professor Coram moved to a country house, Yoxley Old Place. He was not well, keeping to his bed half the time. He was well liked by the few neighbors who called upon him, and he was known there as a very learned man.

"His household used to consist of an elderly housekeeper, Mrs. Marker, and of a maid, Susan Tarlton. They have both been with him since his arrival, and they seem to be women of good character. The professor was writing a book and he found it necessary, about a year ago, to engage a secretary. The first two that he tried were not successes, but the third, Mr. Willoughby Smith, a young man straight from college, seems to have been just what his employer wanted. In the morning he would write down what the professor told him, and he usually spent the evening looking up books to prepare for the next day's work. This Willoughby Smith has nothing against him, either as a boy at school or as a young man at Cambridge. There is no reason I can find to explain why he should meet his death this morning in the professor's study in a way which can point only to murder."

The wind and rain were still powerful outside. Holmes and I drew closer to the fire, while the young policeman slowly and point by point gave us the full story.

"If you were to look throughout all England," said he, "I don't suppose you could find a household more self-contained. They had very little to do with the outside world. Whole weeks would pass, and not one of them go past the garden gate. The professor lived only for his work. Young Smith knew no one in the neighborhood and lived very much as his employer did. The two women had no reason to leave the house. Mortimer, the gardener, is an ex-army man of good character. He does not live in the house, but in a three-roomed house at the other end of the garden. Those are the only people that you would find within the grounds of Yoxley Old Place. The gate of the garden is a hundred yards from the main London to Chatham road. It is not locked, and there is nothing to prevent anyone from walking in.

"Now I will give you the evidence of Susan Tarlton, who is the only person who can say anything at all about the matter. It was late morning, between eleven and twelve. She was cleaning the upstairs front bedroom. Professor Coram was still in bed, for when the weather is bad he does not rise before midday. The housekeeper was busy with some work in the back of the house.

"Willoughby Smith had been in his bedroom, which he used as a sitting-room, but the servant heard him pass along the hall and down to the study immediately below her. She did not see him, but she says that she knew the sound of his walk and is certain it was him. She did not hear the study door close, but a minute or so later there was a fearful cry in the room below. It was a wild cry, so unnatural that it might have come either from a man or a woman. At the same instant, she heard a noise that sounded like someone falling to the floor, then all was quiet.

"The maid stood still for a moment, then overcame her fear and ran downstairs. The study door was shut; she opened it. Inside, young Mr. Willoughby Smith was on the floor. At first she thought he was all right, but as she tried to raise him she saw the blood on the underside of his neck. He had a very small but deep wound, which had caused his death. The wound had been made by a small knife which was lying on the floor beside him. It was one of those small letter-opening knives often found on old writing-tables. It was part of the fittings of the professor's own table.

"At first the servant thought that young Smith was already dead, but when she put some cold water on his forehead he opened his eyes for a moment. 'The professor,' he said quietly, — 'it was she.' The girl is sure that those were the words. He tried to say something else and held his right hand up in the air. Then he fell back dead.

"In the meantime the housekeeper had also arrived upon the scene, but she was just too late to catch the young man's dying words. Leaving Susan with the body, she hurried to the professor's room. He was sitting up in bed, looking upset, for he had heard enough to know that there had been trouble. Mrs. Marker has stated that the professor was still in his night-clothes and, indeed, it was impossible for him to dress without the help of Mortimer, whose orders were to come at twelve o'clock. The professor says that he heard the distant cry, but that he knows nothing more. He can give no explanation of the young man's last words. 'The professor—it was she,' but thinks only that the poor man was in great pain and not thinking clearly. He believes that Willoughby Smith had not an enemy in the world, and he can give no reason for the crime. His first action was to send Mortimer, the gardener, for the local police. A little later the chief detective sent for me. Nothing was moved before I got there, and orders were given that no one should walk upon the paths leading to the house. It was a great chance to put your ideas into practice, Mr. Sherlock Holmes."

"Well, let us hear about it. What sort of a job did you make of it?" said my companion.

"I must ask you first, Mr. Holmes, to look at this plan, which will give you a general idea of the position of the professor's study and the various points of the case. It will help you in following my investigation."

He showed us the plan, which I reproduce here. I rose, and, standing behind Holmes, studied it over his shoulder.

"It only deals with the points which seem to be important. All the rest you will see later for yourself. Now, first of all, supposing that the murderer entered the house, how did he or she come in? Undoubtedly

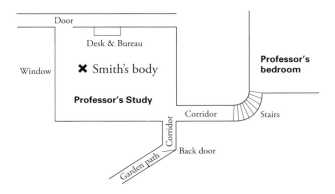

by the garden path and the back door, from which there is a direct way to the study. Any other way would have been very difficult. The escape must have also been made along that line, for of the two other ways out from the room, one was stopped by Susan as she ran downstairs, and the other leads straight to the professor's bedroom. I therefore directed my investigation at once to the garden path, which was still wet with rain and would certainly show any footmarks.

"It was clear to me that I was dealing with a careful and clever criminal. No footmarks were to be found on the path. There could be no question, however, that someone had passed along the grass edge which lines the path, and that he had done so to make sure he did not leave a track. I could not find any clear marks, but someone had undoubtedly passed that way. It could only have been the murderer, since neither the gardener nor anyone else had been there that morning, and the rain had only begun during the night."

"One moment," said Holmes. "Where does this path lead to?"

"To the road."

"How long is it?"

"A hundred yards or so."

"At the point where the path passes through the gate, you could surely pick up the tracks?"

"Unfortunately, the path was too hard at that point."

"Well, on the road itself?"

"No, there were too many marks to see any one of them clearly."

"Tut-tut! Well, then, these tracks upon the grass, were they coming or going?"

"It was impossible to say. There was never any outline."

"A large foot or a small?"

"You could not tell."

Holmes seemed upset.

"It has been raining ever since," said he. "It will be difficult to read now. Well, well, it can't be helped. What did you do, Hopkins, after you had made certain that you had made certain of nothing?"

"I think I made certain of a good deal, Mr. Holmes. I knew that someone had entered the house carefully from without. I looked at the hall next. It was lined with a hard mat, and there were no marks of any kind. This brought me into the study itself. The room contained very little. The largest piece is a large writing-table with a locked cupboard. There were some important papers in that cupboard, but there were no signs that this had been opened, and the professor assures me that nothing was missing. It is certain that no robbery has been committed.

"I come now to the body of the young man. It was found near the writing-table and just to the left of it, as marked upon the plan. The cut was on the right side of the neck and from behind forward, so that it is not possible that he could have done it himself."

"Unless he fell upon the knife," said Holmes.

"True. The idea crossed my mind. But we found the knife some feet away from the body, so that is not possible. Then, of course, there are the man's own dying words. And, finally, there was this very important piece of evidence which was found in the dead man's right hand."

From his pocket Stanley Hopkins drew a small object enclosed in paper. He removed the paper to show us a pair of golden glasses. "Willoughby Smith had good sight," he added. "There can be no question that these came from the face or the person of the criminal."

Sherlock Holmes took the glasses into his hand and looked at them with great interest. He held them on his nose, tried to read through them, went to the window and looked up the road with them, looked at them carefully under a bright light, and finally, with a laugh, seated himself at the table and wrote a few lines upon a piece of paper he handed to Stanley Hopkins.

"That's the best I can do for you," said he. "It may prove to be of some use."

The detective read the note aloud. It ran as follows:

'Wanted, a woman from a good home, dressed like a lady. She has a remarkably thick nose, with eyes that are set close upon either side of it. She has a lined forehead, and probably rounded shoulders. There are indications that she has been to an eye specialist at least twice during the last few months. As her glasses are of remarkable strength, and as there are only a few eye specialists, there should be no difficulty in finding out who she is.'

Holmes smiled at the surprise on Hopkins's face, which must also have been clear on my own.

"Surely my findings are simple enough," said he. "It would be difficult to think of any articles which give as many clues about a person than a pair of glasses, especially so remarkable a pair as these. That they belong to a woman, I can tell from their size, and also, of course, from the last words of the dying man.

"As to her being well-dressed, they are, as you can see, made of solid gold, and it is not reasonable to think that anyone who wears such glasses could be badly dressed in other respects. You will find that the glasses are too wide for your nose, showing that the lady's nose was very broad. My own face is a thin one, and yet I find that I cannot get my eyes in the middle, nor near the middle, of these glasses. Therefore her eyes are set very near to the sides of her nose. You will see, Watson, that the glasses are of unusual strength. A lady whose sight has been this bad all her life is sure to have signs of it in her appearance, namely in the forehead and the shoulders."

"Yes," I said. "I can follow each of your thoughts. I must say, however, that I am unable to understand how you have arrived at the double visit to the eye specialist."

Holmes took the glasses in his hand.

"You will see," he said, "that the sides are lined with small pieces of cloth to soften the feeling upon the nose. One of these is discolored and worn, but the other is new. Clearly, one has fallen off and been replaced. I should judge that the older of them has not been there more than a few months. They are the same apart from their age, so I gather that the lady went back to the same place for the second."

"Good heavens! That's wonderful!" cried Hopkins. "To think that I had all that evidence in my hand and never knew it! I was going to do the round of the London eye specialists however."

"Of course you were. Meanwhile, have you anything more to tell us about the case?"

"Nothing, Mr. Holmes. I think that you know as much as I do now — probably more. We are finding out if any stranger was seen on the country roads or at the train station. We have heard of none. What I still can't understand is the reason for the crime."

"Ah! I am not in a position to help you with that. But I suppose you want us to come out tomorrow?"

"If it is not asking too much, Mr. Holmes. There's a train from Charing Cross to Chatham at six in the morning, and we should be at Yoxley Old Place between eight and nine."

"Then we shall take it. Your case has certainly some points of great interest, and I shall be very happy to look into it. Well, it's nearly one, and we had best get a few hours sleep."

The storm had blown itself out the next day, but it was a cold morning when we started upon our journey. We saw the cold winter sun rise over the river Thames. After a long and tiring journey, we alighted at a small station some miles from Chatham. While we waited for a cab, we had a hurried breakfast, so we were all ready for business when we at last arrived at Yoxley Old Place. A policeman met us at the garden gate.

"Well, Wilson, any news?" asked Hopkins.

"No, sir—nothing."

"No reports of any stranger seen?"

"No, sir. Down at the station they are sure that no stranger either came or went yesterday."

"Well, it's only a short walk to Chatham. Anyone might stay there or take a train without being noticed. This is the garden path of which I spoke, Mr. Holmes."

"On which side were the marks on the grass?"

"This side, sir. This narrow length of grass between the path and the flower bed. I can't see the marks now, but they were clear to me then."

"Yes, yes. Someone has passed along," said Holmes, looking closely at the grass border. "Our lady must have picked her steps carefully, must she not, since on the one side she would leave a track on the path, and on the other an even clearer one on the soft bed?"

"Yes, sir. She must have been very clever."

Holmes was thinking.

"You say that she must have come back this way?"

"Yes, sir, there is no other."

"On this length of grass?"

"Yes, Mr. Holmes."

"I see. It was a very remarkable piece of work — very remarkable. Well, I think that we have finished with the path. Let us go further. This garden door is usually kept open, I suppose? Then this visitor had nothing to do but to walk in. The idea of murder was not in her mind, or she would have brought a weapon with her, rather than having to pick a knife off the writing-table. She advanced along this hall, leaving no marks upon the mat. Then she found herself in this study. How long was she there? We have no means of judging."

"Not more than a few minutes, sir. I forgot to tell you that Mrs. Marker, the housekeeper, had been in there cleaning not very long before — about a quarter of an hour, she says."

"So the most she was here was fifteen minutes. Our lady enters this room, and what does she do? She goes over to the writing-table. What for? It must have been for something in that wooden cupboard. I say! What is that mark on the face of it? Just hold a light, Watson. Why did you not tell me of this, Hopkins?"

The mark which he had been looking at began upon the right hand side of the lock and ran for about four inches, where it had taken the shine from the wood.

"I noticed it, Mr. Holmes, but you'll always find marks around a lock."

"This has not long been made. The wood has not been touched since this mark was made. Look at it closely man! Is Mrs. Marker there?"

A sad-faced, old woman came into the room.

"Did you clean this cupboard yesterday morning?"

"Yes, sir."

"Did you notice this mark?"

"No, sir, I did not."

"I am sure you did not because most of this mark would have been removed if you had cleaned it. Who has the key to this cupboard?"

"The professor keeps it."

"Is it a simple key?"

"No, sir, this is a good lock."

"Very good. Mrs. Marker, you can go. Now we are getting somewhere. Our lady enters the room, advances to the table, and either opens the cupboard or tries to do so. While she is busy at this, young Willoughby Smith enters the room. In her hurry to withdraw the key, she makes this mark upon the door. He holds her, and she, picking up the nearest object, which happens to be this knife, strikes at him to make him let go his hold. The blow is a grave one. He falls and she escapes, either with or without the object for which she has come. Is Susan, the maid, there? Could anyone have got away through that door after the time that you heard the cry, Susan?"

"No, sir, it is not possible. Before I got down the stair, I'd have seen anyone in the hall. Besides, the door never opened, or I would have heard it."

"That settles this way out. Then no doubt the lady went out the way she came in. I understand that this other hall leads only to the professor's room. There is no way out of the house that way?"

"No, sir."

"We shall go down it and meet the professor. Look here, Hopkins! This is very important, very important indeed. The professor's corridor is lined with the same mat as the other hall."

"Well, sir, what of that?"

"Don't you see what this means to the case? Well, well. Maybe I am wrong. And yet it seems to me to be important. Come, lead me to the professor."

We passed down the hall, which was of the same length as that which led to the garden. At the end were a few steps up to a door. Hopkins told the professor of our arrival and then showed us into the professor's bedroom.

It was a very large room, lined with many books. There were too many for the bookcases and they lay on the floor. The bed was in the center of the room, and in it, sitting up, was the professor. Not often have I seen a more remarkable-looking person. It was a thin, bony face which was turned towards us, with clear dark eyes which were hard to see they were so deep set. His hair was white, and his fingers had yellow marks on them. A cigarette was alight in his mouth, and the room was full of the smell of smoke.

"A smoker, Mr. Holmes?" said he, speaking in well-chosen English but with a foreign sound to it. "Please take a cigarette. And you, sir? I think they are good, for I have them especially prepared by Ionides, of Alexandria. He sends me a thousand at a time, and I am sorry to say that I have to have a fresh supply every two weeks. Bad, sir, very bad, but an old man has few pleasures. Cigarettes and my work—that is all that is left to me."

Holmes had lit a cigarette and was looking quickly and often over the room.

"Cigarettes and my work, but now only cigarettes," the old man said sadly. "I cannot continue. Who could have seen such a fearful happening? Such a good young man! I assure you that, after a few months training, he was a most suitable secretary. What do you think of the matter, Mr. Holmes?"

"I have not yet made up my mind."

"I hope you will be able to throw a light where all is so dark to us. To a man as ill as I am such a blow is a hard one. I seem to be unable to think clearly. But you are a man of action — you keep your head in every emergency. It is good to have you at our side."

Holmes was walking up and down one side of the room while the old professor was talking. I noticed that he was smoking remarkably quickly. It was clear that he shared the professor's liking for the fresh Alexandrian cigarettes.

"Yes, sir, it is a hard blow," said the old man. "Those papers on the side table are my life's work. It is my report about the history of our religion. With my poor health I do not know whether I shall ever be able to complete it now that my secretary has been taken from me. Dear me! Mr. Holmes, why, you are even a quicker smoker than I am myself."

Holmes smiled.

"I love cigarettes — and these ones are indeed remarkable," said he, taking another cigarette from the box and lighting it from the one he was just about to finish. "I will not trouble you with any lengthy questioning, Professor Coram, since I gather that you were in bed at the time of the crime and knew nothing about it. I would only ask this: What do you imagine that this poor fellow meant by his last words. 'The professor — it was she'?"

"Susan is a country girl," said the professor, "and you know how foolish that class can be. I think that the poor fellow made some sounds caused by the pain and she formed them into this meaningless statement."

"I see. You have no explanation yourself of what happened?"

"Possibly an accident, possibly — I only speak of it among our-selves — suicide. Young men have their troubles — a broken heart perhaps. It is a more probable answer than murder."

"But the eyeglasses?"

"Ah! I am only a student—a man of dreams. I cannot explain the real world. But still, we know, my friend, that a love-present may take many forms, and it is possible that these glasses belonged to a woman whom Willoughby Smith was sweet on. By all means, take another cigarette. It is a pleasure to see someone enjoy them so much. This gentleman talks of footmarks in the grass, but, after all, it is easy to be wrong on such a point. As to the knife, it might well be thrown far from the poor man as he fell. It is possible that I speak as a child, but to me it seems that Willoughby Smith met his death by his own hand."

Holmes seemed to be interested in the idea put forward by the professor, and he continued to walk up and down for some time, lost in thought and smoking cigarette after cigarette.

"Tell me, Professor Coram," he said at last, "what is in that cupboard by the writing-table?"

"Nothing of value. Family papers, letters from my poor wife, reports from colleges. Here is the key. You can look for yourself."

Holmes picked up the key, looked at it for a moment, then he handed it back.

"No, I hardly think that it would help me," said he. "I would like to go quietly down to your garden and turn the whole thing over in my head. There is something to be said for the idea of suicide which you have put forward. I am sorry to have troubled you, Professor Coram, at this unhappy time and we will leave you now and not return until after you have had your midday meal. Let us say that we will see you at two o'clock."

Holmes was strangely upset, and we walked up and down the garden path for some time without speaking.

"Have you an idea?" I asked at last.

"It is possible that I am wrong. Those cigarettes that I smoked will show me."

"My dear Holmes," I exclaimed, "how on earth——"

"Well, well, you may see for yourself. If not, I will have caused no trouble and we always have the eye specialist clue to fall back upon, but I take a short cut if I can get it. Ah, here is the good Mrs. Marker! Let us enjoy a short talk with her, we may well learn something."

I may have said before that Holmes had, when he liked, a very friendly way with women, and that he very quickly got them to like him. In no time he had got the housekeeper's goodwill and was talking to her as if he had known her for years.

"Yes, Mr. Holmes, it is as you say, sir. He does smoke very bad. All day and sometimes all night, sir. I've seen that room of a morning—well, sir, you'd have thought it was on fire. Poor young Mr. Smith, he was a smoker also, but not as bad as the professor. His health—well, I don't know that it's better nor worse for the smoking."

"Ah!" said Holmes, "but it stops you wanting to eat."

"Well, I don't know about that, sir."

"I suppose the professor eats hardly anything?"

"Well, some days he won't eat, but others he's alright."

"I'll suppose he took no breakfast this morning and won't face his midday meal after all the cigarettes I saw him smoke."

"Well, you're wrong there, sir, as it happens, for he ate a remarkably big breakfast this morning. I don't know when I've known him eat a better one, and he's ordered a good dish of meat for this afternoon. I'm surprised myself, for since I came into that room yesterday and saw young Mr. Smith lying there on the floor, I couldn't stand to look at food. Well, it takes all sorts to make a world, and the professor hasn't let it put him off his food."

We spent the morning in the garden. Stanley Hopkins had gone down to the town to look into some rumors of a strange woman who had been seen by some children on the Chatham Road the morning of the murder. As to my friend, all his usual strength seemed to have left him. I had never known him deal with a case in such a half-hearted manner. Even the news brought back by Hopkins that he had found the children, and that they had undoubtedly seen a woman meeting Holmes's outline and wearing eye-glasses, failed to make him very interested. He was more lively when Susan told us information that she believed Mr. Smith had been out for a walk yesterday morning and that he had only returned half an hour before his death. I could not myself see the importance, but I clearly saw that Holmes was including it into the general plan which he had formed in his mind. Suddenly, he jumped from his chair and glanced at his watch. "Two o'clock, gentlemen," said he. "We must go up and have it out with our friend the professor."

The old man had just finished his lunch, and his empty dish was evidence that he was eating well. He had been dressed and was seated in an armchair by the fire.

"Well, Mr. Holmes, have you an answer to this mystery yet?" He pushed the large case of cigarettes which stood on a table beside him towards my friend. Holmes reached out at the same moment, and between them the case fell over the edge. For a minute or two we were all on the floor picking up the cigarettes which had rolled into the furthest parts of the room. When we rose again, I saw Holmes's eyes were shining and his cheeks colored. These were the signs I have come to expect when Holmes is about to go into action.

"Yes," said he, "I have the answer."

Stanley Hopkins and I looked in wonder. The old professor was smiling and he clearly did not believe Holmes could know the answer.

"Indeed! In the garden?"

"No, here."

"Here! When?"

"This moment."

"This cannot be true, Mr. Sherlock Holmes. I must tell you this is too grave a matter to be dealt with in such a light-hearted way."

"I have looked at my answer most carefully, Professor Coram, and I am now sure that it is sound. What your reasons are, or what part you played in this strange business, I am not yet able to say. In a few minutes I shall probably hear it from your own mouth. Meanwhile I will tell you what happened so that you may tell me what I still need to know.

"A lady entered your study yesterday. She came with the purpose of getting some papers which were in your cupboard. She had a key of her own; I have had the chance to look at yours, and I do not find that small change of color which would have been there if it had been the key that made the mark upon the cupboard. You did not help her, therefore, and she came, so far as I can read the evidence, without your knowledge to rob you."

The professor blew a cloud of smoke from his lips. "This is most interesting, but have you no more to add? Surely having tracked this lady so far, you can also say what has become of her."

"I will try to do so. In the first place she was held by your secretary and stabbed him in order to escape. This, I think, was an unhappy accident, for I am sure that the lady had not meant to cause so grave a wound. A murderer does not come unarmed. She rushed wildly away from the scene of the accident, but she had lost her glasses in the fight, and as she was very short-sighted she was really quite helpless without them. She ran down a hall which she thought to be the one by which she had come—both were lined with the same type of mat—and it was only when it was too late that she realized that she had taken the wrong one and that her escape back was now cut off. What was she to do? She could not go back. She could not stay where she was. She must go on. She went on. She climbed a stair, pushed open a door and found herself in your room."

The old man sat with his mouth open looking wildly at Holmes. Wonder and fear were written on his face. Now, with an effort, he tried to laugh.

"All very fine, Mr. Holmes," said he. "But there is one little problem. I was myself in my room, and I never left it during the day."

"I know that, Professor Coram."

"And you mean to say that I could lie on my bed and not know that a woman had entered my room?"

"I never said that. You did know. You spoke with her. You knew her. You helped her to escape."

Again the professor gave a loud laugh. He had risen to his feet, and his eyes were shining brightly.

"You are mad!" he cried. "You are talking nonsense. I helped her to escape? Where is she now?"

"She is there," said Holmes, and he pointed to a high bookcase in the corner of the room.

I saw the old man throw up his arms, as fear replaced anger on his face, he fell back in his chair. At the same time the bookcase at which Holmes pointed opened outward, and a woman rushed out into the room. "You are right!" she cried, in a strange foreign voice. "You are right! I am here."

She looked just as Holmes had said she would when he first looked through the glasses. What with her poor sight, and the change from dark to light, she stood looking around, rather helplessly, to see where and who we were. And yet, in spite of all this, there was a certain strength in the woman.

Stanley Hopkins had laid his hand upon her arm and claimed her as his prisoner. The old man lay back in his chair with a fearful face and looked at her with angry eyes.

"Yes, sir, I am your prisoner," she said. "From where I stood I could hear everything, and I know that you have learned the truth. I did as you said. It was I who killed the young man. But you are right — you who say it was an accident. I did not even know that it was a knife which I held in my hand, for I picked up anything from the table to strike at him to make him let me go. It is the truth I tell."

"Madam," said Holmes, "I am sure that it is the truth. I fear that you are far from well."

She had turned white. She seated herself on the side of the bed; then she carried on.

"I have only a little time here," she said, "but I would have you to know the whole truth. I am this man's wife. He is not an Englishman. He is a Russian. His name I will not tell."

For the first time, the old man moved. "Thank you, Anna!" he cried. "Thank you!"

She threw him a look which showed that she now felt little for him. "Why should you hold so hard to that sad life of yours, Sergius?" said she. "It has done harm to many and good to none — not even to yourself. However, it is not for me to cause your poor life to end before God's time. I have already done enough since I came into this house. But I must speak or I shall be too late.

"I have said, gentlemen, that I am this man's wife. He was fifty and I a foolish girl of twenty when we married. It was in a city of Russia, a college town — I will not name the place."

"Thank you, Anna!" murmured the old man again.

"We were reformers — planning to overthrow the state, you under-stand. He and I and many more. Then there came a time of trouble;

a police officer was killed; many were arrested; evidence was wanted, and in order to save his own life my husband told the police about his own wife and his friends. Yes, we were all arrested on his evidence. Some were killed, and some sent to prison. I was among these last, but it was not for life. My husband came to England with the money the police paid him and has lived in quiet ever since, knowing that if the Movement knew where he was, not a week would pass before he would be killed."

The old man reached out a shaking hand and helped himself to a cigarette. "I am in your hands, Anna," said he. "You were always good to me."

"I have not yet told you everything," said she. "Among the Movement, there was one who was a friend of my heart. He was kind, selfless, loving—all that my husband was not. He would hurt no one. He wrote many times to try and stop our course. These letters would have saved him, as would my notebook in which, from day to day, I had entered both my feelings toward him and the view which each of us had taken. My husband found and kept both notebook and letters, hoping to see the young man sent to his death. In this he failed, but Alexis was sent a prisoner to the salt mine, where he is to this day. Think of that, you dog!—now, now, at this very moment, Alexis, a man whose name you are not worthy to speak, works and lives like an animal, and yet I have your life in my hands, and I let you go."

Professor Coram kept his eyes on the ground. "You were always a good woman, Anna," he said quietly.

She had risen, but she fell back again with a little cry of pain.

"I must finish," she said. "When they let me out of prison I decided to get the notebook and letters which, if sent to the Russian police, would lead to Alexis being set free. I knew that my husband had come to England. After months of looking, I found out where he was. I knew that he still had the notebook, for when I was in prison I had a letter from him telling me so. Yet I was sure, knowing his nature, that he would not give it to me of his own free will. I had to get it for myself. With this as my purpose I took on someone from a private detective company, who entered my husband's house as secretary — it was your second secretary, Sergius, the one who left you so hurriedly. He found that the papers were kept in the cupboard, and he got a copy made of the key. He would not go further. He gave me a plan of the house and told me that before midday the study was always empty, as the secretary was busy up here. So at last I came down to get the papers for myself. I succeeded; but at what cost!

"I had just taken the papers and was locking the cupboard, when the young man held me. I had seen him already that morning. He passed me on the road, and I had asked him to tell me where Professor Coram lived, not knowing that he was his secretary."

"Yes! Yes!" said Holmes. "The secretary came back and told the professor of the woman he had met. Then, in his last breath, he tried to say that it was she — the she that he had just talked to the professor about."

"You must let me speak," the woman ordered. She looked in pain but she continued, "When he had fallen, I rushed from the room, chose the wrong door and found myself in my husband's room. He spoke of giving me up. I showed him that if he did so, his life was in my hands. If he gave me to the police, I could give him to the Movement. It was not that I wished to live for my own life, but it was that I wished to fulfill my purpose. He knew that I would do what I said — that his own future was tied up with mine. For that reason and for no other, he helped me. He put me in that hiding place. He took his food in his own room, and so was able to give me part of it. It was agreed that when the police left the house I would slip away by night and come back no more. But in some way you have learned our plans." She took from her dress some papers. "These are my last words," said she. "Here are the papers which will save Alexis. I give it to your honor and to your love of fairness. Take them! You must send them to the Russian police. Now, I have done what I had to, and—"

"Stop her!" cried Holmes. He had jumped across the room and had taken a small glass from her hand.

"Too late!" she said, falling back on the bed. "Too late! I took the poison before I came from behind the bookcase. I am going! I charge you, sir, to remember the papers."

I ran to her, but she was already dead.

"A simple case, and yet, in some ways, one from which we can learn," Holmes said as we traveled back to town. "It was all to do with the glasses. But for the fact that the dying man got hold of these, I am not sure that we could ever have reached the answer. It was clear to me, from the strength of the glasses, that the wearer must have had almost no sight without them. When you asked me to believe that she walked along a thin strip of grass without once making a bad step, I said, as you may remember, that it was a noteworthy action. In my mind I set it down as not possible. I therefore had to consider the view that she had stayed within the house. On seeing how alike the two corridors were, it became clear that she might very easily have gone down the wrong one, and, in that case, it was clear that she must have entered the professor's room. I was looking there for evidence to back up my thoughts. I looked in the room for anywhere that might be a hiding place. I thought there might be something behind the books. As you know, there are often hiding places in old studies. I noticed that books were on the floor at all other points, but that one bookcase was left clear. This, then, might be the door. I could see no marks to guide me, but the floor was a dark color, which helped my investigation. I therefore smoked a great number of those remarkable cigarettes, and I dropped the ash all over the space in front of the bookcase. It was a simple plan, but very useful. I then went downstairs, and I found out, while you were present, Watson, without you understanding the importance of my questions, that Professor Coram had been eating more food than usual—as one would expect when feeding a second person. We then returned to the room again, and, by upsetting the cigarette box, I was able to get a good look at the floor, and I saw quite clearly, from the tracks upon the cigarette ash, that the prisoner had come out from her hiding place while we were away. Well, Hopkins, here we are at Charing Cross. Well done for having brought your case to a successful end. You are going to headquarters, no doubt. I think, Watson, that we must have these papers sent to my friend in the Russian police as soon as possible."

16

The Adventure of the Devil's Foot

悪魔の足

読み始める前に

The Adventure of the Devil's Foot 悪魔の足

56の短編のうち40番目に発表された
1910年12月号のストランド・マガジン初出
1917年発行の「シャーロック・ホームズ最後の挨拶」に収録された

[主な登場人物]

Sherlock Holmes シャーロック・ホームズ 世界的に有名な私立探偵。優れた観察眼と推理力を有する。ロンドンのベーカー街221Bに下宿している。

Watson ジョン・H・ワトソン 医師。ホームズの相棒でこの物語の語り手。かつてベーカー街221Bでホームズと同居していた。

Mr. Roundhay ラウンドヘイ氏 村の牧師。

Mortimer Tregennis モーティマー・トリジェニス ホームズたちと同じ別荘の牧師館に下宿する紳士。妹のブレンダが変死し、兄弟のジョージとオーウェンが発狂してしまう。

Brenda Tregennis ブレンダ・トリジェニス モーティマーの美しい妹。自宅の椅子に横たわって亡くなっていた。

Mrs. Porter ポーター夫人 犠牲者たちが住む家の料理人兼メイド。

Dr. Leon Sterndale レオン・スターンデール博士 動物狩りの専門家でアフリカ探検家。別荘の近所に住んでいる。

[あらすじ]

　ホームズが過労のためコーニッシュ海外での静養を勧められた時の出来事を、ワトソンが思い出すところから話は展開する。地元の牧師から恐ろしい出来事についての相談を受けたことで、静かに過ごすはずだった休暇は一転する。事件とは、牧師の隣人であるトリジェニス一家のうち、妹は殺され、二人の兄弟が正気を失っていたというのだ。皆、恐怖の表情を浮かべていたという。

[総単語数] 6,776語

The Adventure of the Devil's Foot

I have often had difficulty recording some of the unusual and interesting cases which I have known about during my long and close friendship with Mr. Sherlock Holmes because he does not want his name to be too well-known. This is why for several years I have not written the stories of any of Holmes's cases—because I knew he would not like it.

So, it was with great surprise that I received a telegram from Holmes last Tuesday saying:

"Why not tell them of the Cornish case— the strangest one I have ever solved?"

I have no idea what made him remember this case or why he suddenly wanted me to write it as a story, but I rushed to take out my notes on it before he had a chance to send another telegram saying he didn't want me to write it.

It was at the end of the winter of the year 1897 that Holmes seemed to be ill. In March that year, Dr. Moore Agar, of Harley Street, had said that the famous private agent must forget all his cases and have complete rest if he wanted to get better. The state of his health was not something which Holmes had any interest in but the doctor made him realize that he really should give himself a little holiday. Thus it was that in the early spring of that year, we went to stay in a cottage near

Poldhu Bay in Cornwall.

Our cottage was on the top of a hill and from it we could see the sea. It was a very wild and windy place and so it was not very welcoming. There were few trees there because of the wind, and it was also a place where you could walk for a long time without seeing anyone—though there were a few villages around. Holmes was happy because he could go for long walks and he also had time to read and study the history of the area. We had a very peaceful time there, until one day we heard of a very strange happening.

I have said that there were some villages around. The nearest of these was Tredannick Wollas, where the cottages of a couple of hundred people were grouped round a very old church. The vicar of the church, Mr. Roundhay, was also interested in the history of the area and so Holmes had met him. He was a middle-aged man, a little bit fat, but very kind, and he knew a lot about the local history. We had had tea with the vicar at his house and had met a Mr. Mortimer Tregennis who also lived in the house. The vicar, being unmarried, was pleased to have someone else in the house. However, he and his lodger were very different people. Mr. Tregennis was a thin, dark man who was very quiet and sad-faced. These were the two men who suddenly came into our little sitting-room on Tuesday, March the 16th, shortly after we had finished our breakfast and were smoking our pipes before going on our daily walk.

"Mr. Holmes," said the vicar in a worried voice, "the strangest and most unbelievable thing has happened during the night. We are so pleased that, by chance, you are here at this time, for you are the man we need most out of all the men in England."

I looked at the vicar with very unfriendly eyes because I didn't want anything to change Holmes's peaceful holiday; but Holmes took his pipe from his mouth and sat up in his chair looking very interested. He told our visitors to sit down, probably because both men were shaking.

"Shall I speak, or you?" Mr. Tregennis asked the vicar.

"Perhaps I should say a few words first," said the vicar, "and then Mr. Holmes can decide whether we should go straight to the place of this strange case or whether we should listen to more of the facts from you, Mr. Tregennis. I will explain that our friend here spent last evening with his two brothers, Owen and George, and his sister Brenda, at their house called Tredannick Wartha. He left them shortly after ten o'clock, playing card games round the dining-room table and seeming to be very happy and healthy. This morning, because he likes getting up early, he went for a walk towards their house before breakfast.

"Suddenly he saw Dr. Richards rushing towards the house. Dr. Richards explained that he had been asked to go to the house as quickly as possible. So Mr. Mortimer Tregennis decided to go with the doctor. When they arrived at Tredannick Wartha, they saw a very strange sight. His two brothers and sister were seated round the table just as he had left them, the cards still on the table. His sister lay back in her chair dead, while the two brothers sat on each side of her laughing, shouting, and singing as if they were completely mad. All three of them looked as if they had had a terrible shock. There was no sign of anyone else in the house except Mrs. Porter, the old cook and maid, who said that she had slept very peacefully and had not heard anything strange in the night. Nothing had been taken or moved, so it was impossible to guess what had frightened a woman to death and made two strong men go mad. If you can help us find out what happened we will be very grateful to you."

I had hoped that in some way I could make my friend forget about all this and continue his holiday; but one look at his face made me realize he would not rest now until the matter was solved. He sat for some time quietly thinking about what we'd heard.

"I will try to solve this matter," he said at last. "From what you have told me I can say that it does sound a very, very strange case. Have you been to Tredannick Wartha yourself, Mr. Roundhay?"

"No, Mr. Holmes. Mr. Tregennis came back to our house and told me what had happened so I at once hurried over with him to talk to you."

"How far is it to the house where this all happened?"

"It is about a mile."

"Then we shall walk there together. But before we go I must ask you a few questions, Mr. Tregennis."

Tregennis had been quiet all this time, but I had seen that his feelings were even stronger than those of the vicar. He sat with a tired, white face looking at Holmes, and he was holding his hands very tightly together. His body was shaking and it seemed to show the shock he had had seeing what had happened to his family.

"Ask what you like, Mr. Holmes," he said. "I don't like thinking about it but I will tell you what happened."

"Tell me about last night."

"Well, Mr. Holmes, I had dinner there, as the vicar told you and then my elder brother George suggested that we play a game of cards. We sat down at about nine o'clock. It was a quarter-past ten when I decided to go. I left them all round the table, and they seemed to be very happy. I shut the doors behind me and saw that the window of the room in which they were was closed, but the curtains were open. There was no change to the door or the window this morning, nor any reason to think that any stranger had been to the house. Yet there they sat, my brothers mad, and Brenda, who had died of fright. I'll never forget what I saw in that room as long as I live."

"The facts, as you tell them to us, are very strange," said Holmes.

"I guess that you have no idea what happened to them?"

"The devil must have made it happen, Mr. Holmes!" cried Mortimer Tregennis. "Something got into that room which has made them mad. What human thing could do that?"

"I fear," said Holmes, "that if the matter is not caused by a human, then I will not be able to solve it. But we will try. It seems, Mr. Tregennis, that you were separated from your family in some way, since they lived together and you lived with the vicar?"

"That is right, Mr. Holmes, though the matter is forgotten now. We used to live at Redruth but we sold our business to a bigger company so that we would have enough money for us all to live without working. It was true that there were some problems dividing the money between us and so we were not friendly to each other for a while, but we soon forgot about the disagreement and we became friends again."

"Thinking about the evening you spent together, do you remember anything unusual? Think carefully, Mr. Tregennis, for any clue which can help me."

"There is nothing at all, sir."

"Your family acted the same as they always do?"

"Yes, they did."

"Did they seem worried about anything— any danger?"

"No."

"You have nothing to tell me then, which could help me?"

Mortimer Tregennis thought hard for a moment.

"There is one thing," he said at last. "As we sat at the table my back was to the window and my brother George was facing it. I saw him once look out of the window for a long time, so I turned round and looked also. The curtains were open and the window shut but I could just see something moving among them. I couldn't see if it was a man or an animal but I just thought there was something there.

When I asked him what he was looking at, he told me that he had seen something but he did not know what. That is all I can say."

"Did you not try and find out if anything was there?"

"No, we did not think it was really important."

"So when you left them, you did not have any idea that anything might happen to them?"

"None at all."

"I do not understand how you heard the news of what had happened so early this morning."

"I always get up early and usually take a walk before breakfast. This morning, I had just started on my walk when the doctor rushed past me. He told me that old Mrs. Porter, their maid, had asked him to go to the house as quickly as possible. When we got there, we looked into that terrible room. They must have been sitting there in the dark until the morning came. The doctor said that Brenda must have been dead for at least six hours. There were no signs of a fight or anything like that. She was just lying back in the chair—dead. George and Owen were singing parts of songs and making noises like animals. Oh, it was terrible to see! The doctor and I both went white. In fact, he fell into a chair in a sort of faint, and so we had to take him out as quickly as possible."

"Strange—very strange!" said Holmes, rising and taking his hat. "I think, perhaps, we should go to Tredannick Wartha now."

We did not discover anything useful that morning to help us solve the case. But we did see something which left us feeling very strange. When we arrived at the house, we saw the two brothers being taken away—their wild faces and mad eyes was a sight I will never forget.

"My brothers!" cried Mortimer Tregennis. "They are taking them away."

We then went into the house. It was large and bright inside with a big garden which already had a lot of flowers even though it was only March. The window of the sitting-room looked onto this garden, and Mortimer Tregennis said that he thought the devilish thing (whatever it was) must have come from the garden. Holmes walked slowly and thoughtfully among the flower pots and all round the garden before we entered the house. He was thinking so hard that he was not looking where he was going. I remember that he fell over the watering can and all our feet and the garden got wet. Inside the house we were met by the elderly maid, Mrs. Porter, who looked after the family. She readily answered all Holmes's questions. She had heard nothing in the night. The family had all been very happy, and she had no feeling of any danger. She had fainted when she went into the room that morning and saw what had happened. When she felt better, she had opened the window to let the air in and had then run down the road to get someone to find the doctor. They had moved Brenda up to her bedroom and said that we could go and see her. Mrs. Porter said she was not going to stay in the house any more and had decided that she would go that afternoon to her family in St. Ives.

We went up the stairs and looked at the body. Miss Brenda Tregennis had been a very beautiful girl though she was now nearing middle age. Her dark face was good-looking, even in death, but there was still a feeling of the terrible thing that had happened to her. We then went down to the sitting-room where this strange thing had happened. The ashes of the fire lay in the fireplace. The cards were still on the table. The chairs had been moved back against the walls, but everything else was just as it had been the night before. Holmes walked all about the room looking very carefully at the chairs where they had all been sitting, seeing how much he could see of the garden and everything else he could think of, but I felt that he had no idea as to what had caused this unpleasant thing.

"Why did they have a fire?" he asked once. "Did they always have a fire in this small room on a spring evening?"

Mortimer Tregennis explained that it had been cold that night and so after his arrival the fire had been lit. "What are you going to do now, Mr. Holmes?" he asked.

My friend smiled and put his hand upon my arm. "I think, Watson, that I shall smoke my pipe," he said. "And I think, if you gentlemen agree, we will return to our cottage, for I do not think I will find out anything else here. I will think about the facts, Mr. Tregennis, and if I have any ideas I will certainly tell you and the vicar. In the meantime, I shall say good-bye to both of you."

It was not until long after we were back in Poldhu Cottage that Holmes said anything to me. He sat in his chair, his face hidden behind the smoke of his pipe. Finally, he put down his pipe and jumped up.

"It won't do, Watson!" said he with a laugh. "Let us go for a walk together. I need some fresh air to help me think.

"Now, let us think about what we know, Watson," he said as we walked. "Two people are mad and one dead because of something a human has done. I do not believe it is possible that anything other than a human caused this. Now, when did this happen? It seems that it must have been very soon after Mr. Mortimer Tregennis left the room. That is a very important point. It was probably within a few minutes. The cards were still on the table. It was already later than their usual hour for going to bed. Yet they had not changed their positions, nor had they moved their chairs back. So it happened not later than eleven o'clock at night.

"I have discovered the movements of Mortimer Tregennis after he left the room. You will remember that I hit the watering can and so your and his feet got wet. That meant I could see his footmark. The footmarks were the same as the ones I saw on the path going away from the cottage. This shows that he left the cottage very quickly and went off in the direction of the vicar's house.

"Since Mortimer Tregennis left the cottage quickly, we have to think if there is any possibility that some other person came and did something. I am sure Mrs. Porter is not guilty of anything. But Mortimer Tregennis and his brother both seemed to notice some movement in the garden. That is surprising because the night was rainy, cloudy, and dark. Anyone who was trying to make these people feel afraid from the outside would have had to put their face right next to the window in order to be seen. But there are no signs of any footmarks outside the window. It is certainly a problem, isn't it Watson?"

"Yes, it is," I answered.

"And yet if we can find out just a few more things we may be able to solve the case. I think we will forget about it this morning and try to enjoy our walk."

It was not until we had returned to our cottage in the afternoon and found a visitor waiting for us that we thought about the case again. Neither of us needed to be told who that visitor was. The large body, the wild-looking face, and the hair that stood up—all these were as well known in London as in Africa, and could only be those of the great animal-hunter and discoverer, Dr. Leon Sterndale.

We had heard that he was in the area and had once or twice seen him on our walks. He had not come to talk to us and we had not gone to talk to him because we knew that he liked to be alone. It was a surprise to me, therefore, to hear him asking Holmes in a lively voice whether he had been able to solve the case.

"Whilst I have lived here I have come to know the Tregennis family very well," he said, "and so I was very worried when I heard what had happened. I may tell you that I had got to Plymouth, as I was on my way to Africa. But the news reached me this morning, and I came straight back to help in the inquiry."

Holmes looked surprised.

"Has your boat sailed to Africa then?"

"Yes, it has, but I can take the next one."

"Dear me! You are a good friend. Were your bags on the ship?"

"Some of them, but the main ones are at the hotel."

"I see. But surely this case was not written about in the Plymouth newspapers."

"No, sir, I had a telegram."

"Might I ask from whom?"

"You ask a lot of questions, Mr. Holmes."

"It is my business."

"I will tell you," he said. "It was Mr. Roundhay, the vicar, who sent me the telegram."

"Thank you," said Holmes. "I may say that I have not solved the case yet but that I am hopeful that I will have some answers soon."

"Perhaps you could tell me what you think happened?"

"No, I'm sorry, I cannot answer that."

"Then I will go, since there is no reason for me stay here any more." The famous doctor walked out of the cottage, and within five minutes Holmes had followed him. I did not see him again until the evening, when he returned with a tired-looking face. I felt that he had not been able to discover much. He looked at a telegram that had arrived while he was away and then threw it into the fire.

"It was from the Plymouth hotel, Watson," he said. "I learned the name of it from the vicar, and I sent a telegram to check that what Leon Sterndale had said was true. The telegram said that he did spend last night in the hotel and that some of his bags have gone on the boat to Africa. What do you think of that, Watson?"

"Well, he seems to be very interested in the case."

"Yes, he is, and we have not yet found out why. When we know, I am sure the case will be a lot easier for us to solve."

Early the next morning, I saw the vicar rush up towards our cottage. Holmes was already dressed, so we both went down to see our visitor.

He was shaking so much that he found it difficult to speak. Finally, he told us his terrible news.

"Mr. Mortimer Tregennis died during the night, and in the same way as his sister."

Holmes jumped up and said, "We will come back with you now and forget about our breakfast. Hurry, hurry, before anyone else gets there and moves anything!"

Mr. Mortimer Tregennis lived in two rooms in the vicar's house. One was a large sitting-room and the other his bedroom. We had arrived before the doctor or the police so nothing had been changed. I will never forget what we saw in that sitting-room.

The servant who had first entered the room had opened the window because the smell was so strong. The dead man sat in his chair, his face turned towards the window, with the same face of fear that we had seen on his sister. He was dressed, but it seemed that he had dressed quickly. We could see that he had slept in his bed, so it seemed that he had died in the early morning.

As soon as Holmes entered the room, he seemed to become happy. His eyes were shining, and I felt that some new ideas had come to him. He went out to the garden, looked in through the window, looked all around the sitting-room and the bedroom. He opened the window in the bedroom, and when he looked out he seemed to see something interesting, because he rushed down and out and then back in again.

He looked at the oil lamp on the table and took some ashes from it and from the fireplace and put them in a bag. Finally, just as the doctor and the police arrived, he asked Mr. Roundhay to come out with us to the garden.

"I am pleased to say that I think I have found something," he said. "I do not have time to stay here and talk about it with the police, but I would be very pleased if you would tell the policeman that I think he will find something interesting, if he looks out of the bedroom window and if he looks at the oil lamp on the table. If he wants to talk to me, he is welcome to come to the cottage. And now, Watson, I think we must leave."

It may be that the police did not like Holmes being in Cornwall, or that they thought they knew the answer to the case, as we heard nothing from them for the next two days. Holmes spent some of this time smoking and resting in the cottage; but a lot more time in country walks, which he went on alone, returning after many hours without saying where he had been. One thing helped me understand what he was thinking about. He had bought a lamp which was the same as the one which Mortimer Tregennis had had in his room. He filled the lamp with the same oil that Tregennis had used and waited to see how long the lamp would burn. He also asked me to help him with something that I am unlikely to forget.

"You will remember, Watson," he said one afternoon, "that there is one thing which was the same in both cases. I am sure you remember that Mortimer Tregennis said that the doctor fell into a chair as soon as he entered the room at his brother's house. Also, Mrs. Porter had said that she fainted when she entered the room and that afterwards she opened the window. In the second case—that of Mortimer Tregennis himself—you cannot have forgotten the strong smell in the room when we arrived, even though the servant had opened the window. That servant, I later heard, was so ill that she had gone to her bed. You will agree, Watson, that these facts are very important. In each case there is a strong smell and in each case something burning. In one case a fire and in the other an oil lamp. The fire was needed, but I know the lamp was lit long after it was daylight because not much oil had been used. Why? Surely something in the fire or in the lamp caused the smell and then the madness or death of these unlucky people. That is clear, is it not?"

"It would seem so."

"It would seem that a poison was placed in the fire in the Tregennis family house and that this is what caused the strong smell. The window was shut and we can guess that some of the smell would go up the chimney so it would not be so strong in the room. That is probably why only the sister died. So when we got to Mortimer Tregennis's house, I looked carefully at the lamp and the fire. As you saw, I took some ashes from both and some brown powder that I saw in the lamp."

"Why did you not take it all?"

"It is not right for me to take anything which might help the police. Now, Watson, we will light our lamp but before we do so we will open the window. We do not want anything to happen to us. You sit in the chair near that window, and I will sit here so that we can see each other and be the same distance from the poison in the lamp. We will leave the door open so that we can leave quickly if something seems to be happening. Now, I will light the lamp and put the powder from Tregennis's lamp on top of it. Now, Watson, let us sit down and wait."

It was not long before I noticed a very strong unpleasant smell. As soon as I smelt it, my head felt very strange — as if I had no control. A thick, black cloud seemed to pass in front of and around my eyes. I felt that my hair was standing up and that my mouth was opened. I tried to shout but was aware that there was only a very quiet sound coming from my voice. Suddenly I saw Holmes's white, fearful face — the face that we had seen on the dead people — and seeing that made me realize what was happening. I jumped up and pulled him out of his chair and together we rushed through the door and out into the garden where we lay down. We were very soon aware of the fresh smell of the garden and the sun and soon we began to feel better.

"I'm sorry, Watson!" said Holmes at last, "I must thank you for helping me, but also I am sorry for making you, my good friend, feel so strange. It was very unfair of me to ask you to help me do something so horrible."

"You know," I answered, "that I am proud to serve you and that working with you is much more interesting than many other jobs would be."

"I must say that I had no idea that we would start feeling strange so quickly and so strongly."

He rushed into the cottage and came out again with the burning lamp, holding it as far away as possible from his body. He then threw it away into the garden. "We must stay out of the room for some time until the air is clear again. I am sure, Watson, that you agree with me that we now know how these deaths happened."

"I do."

"But we do not know who caused this to happen. I think that Mortimer Tregennis was probably the criminal the first time, and we know he was the victim the second time. We must remember that there had been a family disagreement and we do not really know the facts of it. I do not think Mortimer Tregennis is the kind of man who would forgive people after a disagreement. We must remember that he said he and his brother thought they heard someone moving in the garden. But he may have told us that just to stop us discovering that he had done it. However, if he did not throw the poison into the fire, then who did? It all happened just after he had left, and anyhow, in peaceful Cornwall, visitors do not usually arrive after ten o'clock at night. I think we can be sure that Mortimer Tregennis was the criminal in this case."

"Then what about his own death!"

"Well, Watson, there is one person who may be able to help us and I have asked him to come here to tell us the facts. Ah! here he is—a little early."

I looked round and saw Dr. Leon Sterndale just by the garden gate.

"Please come in," Holmes said. "We are sitting out here because we have been doing a little experiment inside and now the room is not really suitable for a visitor."

"You asked me to come, Mr. Holmes. I had your note about an hour ago, and I have come, though I really do not know why I should do what you ask."

"I am very glad you decided to come. I am sorry we have to sit out here but we prefer the fresh air at the moment. It may be better anyhow, since we must talk about personal matters, and if we are here no one can hear us."

The great discoverer looked at my friend.

"I really do not know what you might want to talk about which is personal to me."

"The killing of Mortimer Tregennis," said Holmes.

Sterndale's face suddenly turned red and very, very angry, and he jumped up and went towards Holmes. Suddenly he stopped and seemed to control himself again.

"I have lived so long among wild people that I have got used to being a bit wild myself. But I really don't want to hurt you."

"Nor do I want to hurt you, Dr. Sterndale. Perhaps you can believe that, knowing that I sent for you and not for the police."

Sterndale sat down again—it seemed that Holmes's words and the power in his voice had made him realize that he must listen to Holmes.

"What do you mean?" he asked at last. "I want you to explain in direct words what you are talking about."

"I will tell you," said Holmes, "and the reason why I am telling you is that I hope my directness will enable you to be direct and truthful as well. What I say next will be decided by what reasons you give me for your actions."

"My reasons?"

"Yes, sir."

"My reasons for what?"

"For killing Mortimer Tregennis."

Sterndale put his hand on his head. "You are being direct. Do you always work like this?"

"Only if I know I have good reason to do so. I will tell you some of the facts which made me think you were part of this affair. You came back from Plymouth allowing most of your bags to go to Africa. That made me realize that you must be very interested in what had happened—"

"I came back—"

"I have heard your reasons and do not believe them. We will forget that at the moment. You came down here to ask me who I thought had done it. I would not answer you. You then went to the vicar's house, waited outside it for some time, and finally returned to your cottage."

"How do you know that?"

"I followed you."

"I did not see you."

"That is what you may expect when I follow you. You spent a restless night at your cottage, and you made some plans. In the early morning you left your house. On your way you filled your pocket with some reddish stones that were lying by your gate."

Sterndale looked at Holmes in surprise.

"You then walked quickly to the vicar's house. You were wearing, I may say, the same shoes as you are wearing now. You went to the window of Tregennis's room. It was now daylight, but nobody was up. You threw some of the stones up at the window."

Sterndale jumped up.

Holmes continued. "You had to wait a while before Mortimer Tregennis came to the window. You asked him to come down. He dressed quickly and then let you into his rooms. You talked for a while during which time you walked up and down. Then you left the room making sure the window was closed and stood outside watching what happened. Finally, when you knew he was dead, you left. Now, Dr. Sterndale, can you give me a good reason for these actions? If you do not tell me the truth you can be sure that I will tell the police everything."

Our visitor's face had turned white as he listened to these words. He sat for some time thinking, with his face in his hands. Then he took a photo out of his coat and threw it on to the ground in front of us.

"That is why I did it," he said.

It showed the face of a very beautiful woman. Holmes looked at it.

"Brenda Tregennis," he said.

"Yes, Brenda Tregennis," our visitor repeated. "For years I have loved her. For years she has loved me. That is why I have always come down to Cornwall when I have been in England. Being here brought me close to the one thing on earth that I cared about. I could not marry her, for I have a wife who left me years ago but whom, because of the laws of England, I could not divorce."

He started crying and again he put his head in his hands. Then with an effort he controlled himself and went on speaking:

"The vicar knew. We had told him everything. He would tell you that she was a wonderful woman. That was why he sent me a telegram and I returned. I did not worry about missing the boat when I heard what had happened to my love. Now you can understand all my actions, Mr. Holmes."

"Go on," said my friend.

Dr. Sterndale took out an envelope from his pocket and showed it to us. On the outside was written 'Devil's foot root' and it had a red 'poison' label underneath it. He said to me: "I understand that you are a doctor, sir. Have you ever heard of this?"

"Devil's foot root? No, I have never heard of it."

"It is very unusual so I am not surprised that you do not know of it," said he, "for I believe that there may only be one other sample of it in Europe. The root is shaped like a foot, half human, half animal; that explains its name. It is used as a poison in parts of West Africa and is kept a secret amongst the people there. I was very lucky to be able to get this sample." He opened the envelope as he spoke and showed us the reddish-brown powder that was inside.

"Well, sir?" asked Holmes in a firm voice.

"I am about to tell you, Mr. Holmes, all that happened, for you already know so much that it is best that I tell you everything truthfully. I have already explained how I knew the Tregennis family. I was friendly with the brothers because of Brenda. There was a family disagreement about money which meant that Mortimer moved away from the house, but it was supposed to have been forgotten. However, he seemed to be planning something, but I had no reason to know what or why.

"One day, only a couple of weeks ago, he came down to my cottage and I showed him some of the things I had discovered in Africa. I showed him this powder and I told him what it did to people and how it was not known in Europe so doctors here would not know how some-one had died. I cannot say how he took it because I was in the room all the time, but he certainly took it then. I remember how he asked me many more questions about the devil's foot root than anything else, but I had no idea that he had a personal reason for asking me.

"I forgot about it until the vicar's telegram reached me at Plym-outh. It seems that Mortimer had thought that I would already be on the boat for Africa when the news reached me. But I returned at once. Of course, I could not listen to the facts without knowing that my poison had been used. I came round to see you on the chance that some other explanation had been suggested but there was none. I was sure that Mortimer Tregennis was the murderer and that he had done it to get the family's money and the cottage. But he had killed the one person whom I have ever loved or who has ever loved me. That was his crime and it made me feel very, very angry and unhappy.

"I did not know what to do. I was not sure that the police would believe my story, but I wanted to do something to Mortimer Tregennis because he had killed my loved one. Since I have spent much of my life amongst wild people who do not have laws, I decided that I would make my own law. I decided that he should suffer the same thing that he had made his sister and brothers suffer, and since I do not feel my life has any purpose now, I did not mind if anything happened to me after that.

"Now I have told you everything. You know the rest. I did, as you said, have a restless night and I did set off early from my cottage. I had some stones to throw at the window so that I could wake him up. He let me into his room and I told him what I knew and that I had come to judge him and to punish him. I took out my gun and he was very frightened when he saw it. I put the poison into the lamp and lit it. Then I closed the window and the door and went outside. I told him that I would shoot him if he tried to leave the room. He died in five minutes. It was very difficult to watch his horrible death but my heart was strong because I knew that my loved one had had the same death. There is my story, Mr. Holmes. Perhaps, if you loved a woman, you would have done the same yourself. You can now do what you like with me. I do not fear death now, so I don't care."

Holmes sat quietly for some minutes.

"What were your plans?" he asked at last.

"I had planned to go back to Africa and finish my work there — it is only half finished."

"Go and do the other half," said Holmes. "I, at least, will not stop you."

Dr. Sterndale stood up and walked away. It was clear to us that he was pleased. Holmes lit his pipe.

"I think you will agree that this case is one that we should leave as it is. We were not working with the police so we do not need to tell them what we know. I do not think the man is bad."

"I agree," I answered.

"I have never loved, Watson, but if I did and if the woman I loved had died in that way, I might even have acted as our visitor did. Who knows? Well, Watson, I will not talk about the case any more — we will continue our holiday."

I was very pleased that the case was solved so that my friend could rest again and enjoy his long walks.

17

The Adventure of the Creeping Man

這う男

読み始める前に

The Adventure of the Creeping Man 這う男

56の短編のうち47番目に発表された
1923年3月号のストランド・マガジン初出
1927年発行の「シャーロック・ホームズの事件簿」に収録された

[主な登場人物]

Sherlock Holmes シャーロック・ホームズ 世界的に有名な私立探偵。優れた観察眼と推理力を有する。ロンドンのベーカー街221Bに下宿している。

Watson ジョン・H・ワトソン 医師。ホームズの相棒でこの物語の語り手。かつてベーカー街221Bでホームズと同居していた。

Professor Presbury プレスベリー教授 ヨーロッパで名の知れた教授で、61歳。同僚のモーフィー教授の娘アリスと婚約したのち、奇怪な行動をとるようになる。

Trevor Bennett トレヴァー・ベネット プレスベリー教授の秘書。教授と同居しており、教授の一人娘イーディスと婚約している。

Edith Presbury イーディス・プレスベリー 教授の一人娘。教授の奇怪な行動を目撃して、恐怖に震える。

Roy ロイ ウルフハウンド。プレスベリー教授の飼い犬。

Macphail マクフェイル 御者。

[あらすじ]

プレスベリー教授の秘書のトレヴァー・ベネット氏がホームズのところに依頼に訪れた。教授は名の知れた人物で、妻を数年前に亡くし、一人娘との二人暮らしだった。しかし、同僚の教授の娘との結婚が決まった頃から、プレスベリー教授が奇怪な行動をとるようになったのだという。ホームズは、教授の飼い犬が彼をなんども噛み付いていることに着目していた。

[総単語数] 6,735語

The Adventure of the Creeping Man

Mr. Sherlock Holmes always thought that I should write the facts about Professor Presbury. He thought that there were some untrue stories about the professor which I should make clear. These stories happened some twenty years before in London. There were, however, some problems in the way. The true history of this case stayed in my box with records of other cases. Finally, we were allowed to make the facts public. This is one of the very last cases which Holmes worked on. Even now we must be a little careful in presenting this case to the public.

It was one Sunday evening early in September of the year 1903 when I received one of Holmes' short notes:

Come at once if you can. If you can't, come anyway.

S.H.

The relations between Holmes and I in those days were a little strange. He was a man who did the same things again and again every day. These things are called habits. His habits were playing music on the violin, smoking tobacco from the old black pipe, keeping his record books, and many others. I had become one of these habits. When there was a case of active work, and he needed someone with a good nerve to help him, then he called me. But I also had other uses for him. I was good for his mind, his thoughts. He liked the questions I asked. He would often think out loud while I was there. Of course, he could have been talking to a bed or a chair just as easily. But it was now a habit for me to be there and help in this method. My mind was slower than his. But that served to make his own ideas come faster and brighter. This was my part in our relationship.

When I arrived at Baker Street, I found him sitting in his armchair. His legs were raised, his pipe was in his mouth, and his face deep in thought. It was clear that he was considering some difficult problem. He waved his hand for me to sit down. It was nearly a half hour before he finally looked up. Then he quickly turned to me and smiled. He welcomed me back to what was once my home.

"You will please excuse me, my dear Watson," said he. "Some interesting facts have been given to me in the past twenty-four hours. They have, in turn, made me think of some other ideas. I have serious thoughts of writing a paper about the use of dogs in detective work."

"But surely, Holmes, this idea has already been considered," said I. "Dogs such as bloodhounds, sleuth-hounds . . . "

"No, no, Watson, that side of the matter is well known. But there is another side, less well known. You may remember the case of the Copper Beeches. I was able, by watching the mind of the child, to understand the criminal habits of the father."

"Yes, I remember it well."

"My line of thoughts about dogs is the same. A dog can tell us much about the family life. Whoever saw an active, happy dog in a sad family, or a sad dog in a happy family? Angry people have angry dogs, dangerous people have dangerous dogs. And their passing feelings tell us the feelings of others."

I shook my head. "Surely, Holmes, this is a little too much," said I.

He had refilled his pipe and sat down again. He seemed not to notice my words.

"What I just talked about is very close to the problem I am studying now. It is not an easy problem. There are many things which don't make sense. However, one question I have is: Why does Professor Presbury's dog, a wolfhound named Roy, often try to bite him?"

I sat back in my chair a little unhappily. Was it for such an unimportant question as this that I was called from my work? Holmes looked over at me.

"The same old Watson!" said he. "You never learn that the most important problems may be solved by the smallest things. But is it not a strange situation that this old, famous Camford doctor and professor has been attacked by his own dog two times? What do you think of it?"

"The dog is ill."

"Well, that is possible. But he attacks no one else. And he only attacks his master in very special situations. Strange, Watson—very strange. But I hear someone at the door. Young Mr. Bennett is early if that is him. I had hoped to speak more with you before he came."

There was a quick step outside the door. A moment later the new client walked into the room. He was a tall, good-looking, young man of about thirty. He was well dressed, of a fine manner. However, it seemed more the manner of a student than a man of the world. He shook hands with Holmes, then looked with some surprise at me.

"This matter is very secret, Mr. Holmes," he said. "Consider the relationship I have with Professor Presbury. I really can't speak before a third person."

"Have no fear, Mr. Bennett. Dr. Watson can always be trusted to keep a secret. I am sure to need his help in this matter."

"Very well, Mr. Holmes. You will, I'm sure, understand that I have some doubts about this."

"Watson, I should tell you that this gentleman, Mr. Trevor Bennett, is the great Professor Presbury's secretary. He lives in the same house with the professor and is going to marry the professor's only daughter. The two men clearly have a close and trusting relationship. But this attempt to solve this strange mystery proves that Mr. Bennett is a good friend as well."

"I hope so, Mr. Holmes. That is my one object. Does Dr. Watson know the situation?"

"I have not had time to explain it."

"Then perhaps I should go over the facts again before I tell you of new information."

"I will do that myself," said Holmes, "in order to show that I understand the situation. The professor, Watson, is a man known all over Europe. His life has been given to study. There has never been a problem in his personal life. His wife died some years ago and he has one daughter, Edith. He is a man of strong and forceful character. A few months ago something happened.

"Then the peace in his life was broken. He is sixty-one years old, but he decided to marry the daughter of Professor Morphy. Morphy is a co-worker at the university. It was not the usual relationship between a wise gentleman and a lovely young lady. Rather, the professor acted like a young man in love. The lady, Alice Morphy, was a perfect girl in mind and body. So it is possible to understand the professor's interest. However, many in the family did not think the relationship a good idea."

"We thought it was really too much," said our visitor.

"Exactly. Too much, and too strong and unnatural. Professor Presbury was rich, however, and there was no problem on the part of the father. The daughter, however, had other views. There were already several other young gentlemen interested in marrying her. They were less worldly than the professor, but closer to her own age. The girl liked the professor. It was only age which became a problem.

"At about this time a little mystery clouded the professor's life. He did something he had never done before. He left home and did not say where he was going. He was away for two weeks. He returned looking very tired. He told no one where he had been. Usually, he would talk about anything. Some time later our client here, Mr. Bennett, received a letter from a fellow-student in Prague. He wrote that he was happy to see Professor Presbury there but that he didn't have the chance to talk with him. Only from the letter did the family learn where he had been.

"Now comes the point. After that, a change came over the professor. He became secretive and mysterious. His family and friends felt that they did not know him anymore. He lived under a dark cloud. His mind and his work were still excellent. But always there was something new, unexpected, and fearful. His daughter, who truly loved him, tried again and again to stay close to her father, to understand him. You sir, as I understand, did the same. But it was no use. And now, Mr. Bennett, tell in your own words about the letters."

"You must understand, Dr. Watson, that the professor had no secrets from me. I was like his son, or younger brother. He told me everything. As his secretary I took care of all his papers and letters. Shortly after he returned all this changed. He told me that letters might come to him from London with special markings. Nobody was to look at these letters. Several of them later arrived. I don't know if he answered them or not."

"And the box," said Holmes.

"Ah, yes, the box. The professor brought back a little wooden box from his travels. It was beautiful and looked very German. It had a lock. This he placed on a table with his supplies. One day, while looking for something, I picked up the box. To my surprise he was very angry and shouted at me with harsh words. It was the first time such a thing had happened. I was deeply hurt. I tried to explain that I was sorry and that I didn't mean to touch the box. But the entire evening I could see that he looked at me strangely. He was upset."

Mr. Bennett took out his diary, from his coat. "That was on July 2nd," he said.

"It's good that you have a diary and record these things," said Holmes. "I may need some of these dates which you have noted."

"I learned method, among other things, from my great teacher. From the time I first noticed his strange actions, I felt it was my job to study his case. On that same day, July 2nd, I wrote something else in my diary. Roy, the dog, attacked the professor as he came into the house. Again, on July 11th, there was another attack. And then I note yet another one on July 20th. After that we had to take Roy away from the house. He was a dear, loving animal. I'm afraid I'm making you tired, Mr. Holmes."

Mr. Bennett's voice was a little upset because it was clear that Holmes was not listening. Instead, his eyes were looking up. A moment later he looked down.

"Interesting! Most interesting!" he said softly. "These facts were new to me, Mr. Bennett. I think we have now covered the past, haven't we? You spoke of some fresh news."

The pleasant, open face of our visitor suddenly clouded over. "What I speak of happened the night before last," said he. "I was lying in bed awake about two in the morning. I couldn't sleep. I heard a sound coming from the hall. I opened the door and looked out. I should explain that the professor sleeps at the end of the hall — "

"The date being — ?" asked Holmes.

Our visitor clearly did not think the question was important.

"I have said, sir, that it was the night before last — that is, September 4th."

Holmes smiled.

"Please continue," said he.

"He sleeps at the end of the hall and must pass my door to reach the steps. What I saw was truly terrible, Mr. Holmes. I believe that my nerves are as strong as anyone's. But I still shake when I think about it. The hall was dark except for one window about halfway which let in some light. I could see something coming along the hall floor, dark and creeping. Then suddenly it came into the light and I could see that it was him. He was creeping, Mr. Holmes—creeping! Not quite on his hands and knees, but on his hands and feet. He seemed to move very easily. I was so afraid of the sight that I said nothing until he reached my door. Then I stepped forward and asked if I could help him. His answer was unbelievable. He jumped up and said an especially bad word to me. Then he ran past me down the stairs. I waited for about an hour, but he did not come back. It must have been in the morning when he returned to his room."

"Well, Watson, what do you make of that?" asked Holmes with the air of a doctor presenting an unusual case.

"Possibly a back problem, called lumbago. I knew a man who had lumbago and he walked in such a way."

"Good, Watson! You always keep us on the ground. But it can't possibly be lumbago because he was able to stand up a moment later."

"He was never in better health," said Bennett. "In fact, he is stronger than I have known him for years. But there are the facts, Mr. Holmes. It is not a case in which we can go to the police. Yet we really don't know what to do. We also feel that we are moving towards danger. Edith—Miss Presbury—feels as I do. We cannot wait any longer."

"It is surely a very unusual case. What do you think, Watson?"

"Speaking as a doctor," said I, "it appears to be a case for someone who deals with problems of love. The old gentleman's heart and mind are changed by this new love. He made a journey to the Continent in the hope of clearing his feelings. His letters in the box may be about money matters or other business."

"And I suppose his dog attacked him for reasons of money? No, no, Watson, there is more to this case. Now, my own view is that——"

What Sherlock Holmes was about to say will never be known. For at this moment the door opened and a young lady was shown into the room. As she appeared, Mr. Bennett jumped up and ran forward to her. He took her hands in his.

"Edith, dear! Nothing wrong, I hope?"

"I felt I must follow you. Oh, Jack, I have been so very afraid. It is terrible to be there alone."

"Mr. Holmes, this is the young lady I spoke of. This is the lady I'm going to marry."

"We thought it might be her, did we not, Watson?" Holmes answered with a smile. "I suppose, Miss Presbury, that there is some fresh news in the case, that you thought we should know?"

Our new visitor was a bright, pretty, very English girl. She smiled back at Holmes and sat next to Mr. Bennett.

"When I learned that Mr. Bennett had left his hotel, I thought I should probably find him here. Of course, he told me that he would talk to you. But, oh, Mr. Holmes, can you do nothing for my poor father?"

"I have hopes, Miss Presbury, but the case is still difficult. Perhaps your news will help me."

"It was last night, Mr. Holmes. He had been very strange all day. I am sure that there are times when he does not remember what he does. He lives as in a strange dream. Yesterday was such a day. It was not my father with whom I lived. His body was there, but it was not really him."

"Tell me what happened."

"I was awakened in the night by the dog barking. Poor Roy, he is tied now near the stable. I may say that I always sleep with my door locked. Jack—uh, Mr. Bennett—will tell you that we all have a feeling of coming danger. My room is on the second floor. The window was uncovered and there was a bright moon outside. I lay with my eyes fixed on the light, listening to the dog's mad barking. Then I saw my father's face looking at me. Mr. Holmes, I nearly died of surprise and fear. His face was pressed against the glass. One hand was trying to open the window. If that window had opened, I think I would have gone mad. I really saw this, Mr. Holmes. You must believe me. I looked at his face for about twenty seconds. Then it disappeared. But I could not get out of bed and follow him. I lay cold and afraid until morning. We ate breakfast together. His manner was unchanged. He said nothing of his actions during the night. I said nothing either. However, I told him I had some business in the city—and here I am."

Holmes looked very surprised at Miss Presbury's story.

"My dear young lady, you say that your room is on the second floor. Is there something to climb on in the garden?"

"No, Mr. Holmes, that is the surprising part. There is no possible way of reaching the window—and yet he was there."

"The date being September 5th," said Holmes. "That does make the matter more difficult."

It was the young lady's turn to look surprised. "This is the second time you have said something about the date, Mr. Holmes," said Bennett. "Is it possible that it has some meaning in the case?"

"It is very possible. Yet I don't have all my information at the moment."

"Are you thinking of a relationship between the moon and madness?"

"No, I promise you. It was quite a different line of thought. Possibly you can leave your diary with me, and I will look at the dates. Now I think, Watson, that our next action is perfectly clear. This young lady has told us that her father remembers little or nothing of what happens on some dates. So we will visit him as though we have a meeting with him on such a date. He will not be able to remember. Thus we can get a good close look at him."

"That is excellent," said Mr. Bennett. "However, I must tell you that the professor can become very angry and difficult at times."

Holmes smiled. "There are reasons why we should come at once. I have an idea about this matter. Tomorrow we shall be in Camford. There is, I remember, a small hotel called the Chequers where the rooms are good and the wine is excellent. I think, Watson, that we can spend the next few days there."

Monday morning found us on our way to the famous university town. For Holmes, it was easy to simply leave for a few days. For me, however, it was more of a problem because of my practice as a doctor. Holmes did not talk about the case until we had arrived at the old hotel.

"I think, Watson, that we can catch the professor just before lunch. His class is at eleven and then he will go home for a short while."

"What reason can we give for visiting him?"

Holmes looked at his notebook.

"August 26th was one of those strange days for the professor. I think he will have difficulty remembering his actions on those days. If we tell him that we had a meeting planned for that day, then I don't think he will doubt us. Shall we attempt it?"

"We have to try."

"Excellent, Watson! Let's go."

Holmes and I took a taxi past a row of very old university build-ings. We turned into a street lined with trees and stopped at the door of a lovely house. There were pretty trees and flowers all around it. Professor Presbury appeared to enjoy a very good life. As we arrived we could see an older, gray-haired man watching us from the window. He was wearing eyeglasses. A moment later we were in his study. The mysterious professor was standing before us. There was no sign of strangeness in his manner or his appearance. He was a fairly large man, tall, with a serious look to him. His eyes were the most interesting part of his face. They seemed very intelligent and alive.

He looked at our cards. "Please sit down, gentlemen. What can I do for you?"

Mr. Holmes smiled in a friendly manner.

"It was the question which I was about to ask you, Professor."

"To me, sir!"

"Possibly there is some mistake. A business friend of mine told me that Professor Presbury of Camford needed my services."

"Oh, indeed!" It seemed that there was a look of doubt in his gray eyes. "You heard that, did you? May I have the name of this business friend?"

"I am sorry, Professor, but I cannot tell you the name. If I have made a mistake, there is no problem. I can only say I'm sorry."

"Not at all. I wish to go further into this matter. It interests me. Have you anything in writing, any letter, to prove what you say?"

"No, I have not."

"Is it possible that I myself asked you to come?"

"I would rather answer no questions," said Holmes.

"No, I guess not," said the professor. "However, I can find the answer to that one very easily."

He walked across the room to the bell. Our London friend, Mr. Bennett, answered the call.

"Come in, Mr. Bennett. These two gentlemen have come from

London. They say they were asked to come. You are my secretary. You take care of all my papers. Do you have a note or anything going to a person named Holmes?"

"No, sir," Bennett answered, his voice unsure.

"That is that," said the professor looking angrily at Holmes. "Now, sir, it seems to me that your position is very questionable."

Holmes lifted his shoulders.

"I can only say again that I am sorry a mistake was made."

"That's not enough, Mr. Holmes!" the old man cried in a high voice. His face was red with anger. He moved between us and the door as he spoke. "You cannot leave as easily as that." He was now shouting, and his face looked unnatural. He was becoming mad. It appeared that we would have to fight to get out of the room. Just then, Mr. Bennett stepped in.

"My dear Professor," he cried, "consider your position! Consider the problem at the university! Mr. Holmes is a well-known man. You cannot act this way towards him."

Slowly, the professor cooled down and moved away from the door. We were happy to find ourselves outside the house and in the quiet street. Holmes seemed greatly interested in what had happened.

"Our friend's nerves are out of order," said he. "I am glad that we had the chance to meet him in person. But, dear me, Watson, he seems to be running after us."

There was the sound of running feet behind us. They belonged, however, to Mr. Bennett and not the professor. He ran up to us.

"I am so sorry, Mr. Holmes. I feel very badly about it."

"My dear sir, there is no problem. It is all part of my work."

"I have never seen him in a more dangerous manner. He is becoming worse. You can see now why his daughter and I are afraid. And yet his mind is perfectly clear."

"Too clear!" said Holmes. "That was my bad judgement. He can remember things very well. By the way, can we see the window of Miss Presbury's room?"

Mr. Bennett pushed his way through some plants. We looked at the side of the house.

"It is there. The second on the left."

"Dear me, it seems impossible to climb, doesn't it? Yet there is a small water pipe above the window, and ivy growing below it."

"I could not climb up that wall myself," said Mr. Bennett.

"No, it would be very dangerous for any man."

"There was one other thing I wish to tell you, Mr. Holmes. I have the house number of the man in London to whom the professor writes. He wrote something this morning. I happened to see the note and wrote the information on another piece of paper. It is not an honest thing for me to do as his secretary, but I had no choice."

Holmes looked at the paper and put it inside his coat.

"Dorak—an unusual name. Slavic, I imagine. Well, it is an important piece of information. We will return to London this afternoon, Mr. Bennett. I see no good reason to stay here. We cannot call the police because the professor has done no crime. Nor is he mad. No action is possible yet."

"Then what can we possibly do?"

"We must wait a little longer, Mr. Bennett. Things will happen soon. Unless I am mistaken, next Tuesday may be the day. We will surely be in Camford on that day. Meanwhile, the situation is not very pleasant, I know. If Miss Presbury can stay a while longer in the city—"

"That is easy."

"Then let her stay until we are sure all danger is past. Meanwhile, be nice to the professor and let him have his way. As long as he feels good then all is well."

"There he is!" said Bennett in a surprised voice. Looking between the trees we saw his tall figure come out from the front door. He looked all around him. He stood with his body hanging forward a little. His arms were hanging straight down before him. His head turned from side to side. The secretary said good-bye, then walked back through the trees to join the professor. The two entered the house together. They seemed to be talking very quickly to each other.

"I expect the old gentleman has realized the situation," said Holmes as we walked toward the hotel. "He seems to have a very clear and intelligent mind. His manner, however, changes very quickly. He is easily angered. But from his point of view I can understand. He sees that detectives were called to watch him. And the people he trusts are the ones who called. I'm sure that our friend Bennett will have a difficult time."

Holmes stopped at a post office and sent a telegram. The answer reached us in the evening. He handed it to me.

Have visited the Commercial Road and seen Dorak. Worldly manner, Bohemian, older. He owns a large general store.

Mercer.

"You don't know Mercer," said Holmes. "He helps me from time to time with general information. It was important to know something of the man with whom our professor is secretly writing. His nationality is Czech, so the Prague visit makes sense."

"Thank God something makes sense here," said I. "It seems that we have a long line of actions with no relationship between them. For example, what is the relationship between an angry dog and a visit to Bohemia? Or either of those with a man creeping down a hall at night? As to your dates, they are a real mystery to me."

Holmes smiled and put his hands together. At that moment, we were in the sitting-room of the old hotel. We had a bottle of the famous Portuguese wine which Holmes had spoken of on the table between us.

"Well, now, let us take the dates first," said he, sounding like a professor. "This excellent young secretary keeps a diary. The diary shows that there was trouble on July 2. From then on there was trouble, I believe, every nine days. The last problem was on Friday, September 3, and before that on August 26, and so on. It is not chance."

I agreed.

"Let's form the idea that every nine days the professor takes some strong drug. This drug does something to his character. He began to take this drug while he was in Prague. Now he is supplied with it by a Bohemian businessman in London. This all makes sense, Watson!"

"But the dog, the face at the window, the creeping man in the hall?"

"Well, well, we have made a beginning. I don't expect any fresh new ideas until next Tuesday. In the meantime we can only keep in touch with Mr. Bennett. And we can enjoy this lovely town."

In the morning, Mr. Bennett came by to bring us the latest report. Holmes was right, it had been difficult for the secretary. The professor did not say that he thought Mr. Bennett guilty of calling us. However, he probably thought it. He was unkind in his manner towards the secretary. This morning, however, the professor seemed quite usual once again. He had given an excellent talk to his crowded class of students. "Apart from his strange periods," said Bennett, "he actually is more lively than ever. His mind was never better. But it's not him — it's not the same man we have known."

"I don't think you have anything to fear for at least one week," said Holmes. "I am a busy man, and Dr. Watson has his work to do. Let us agree to meet here at this hour next Tuesday. I am fairly sure we will be able to explain this matter and help you with your troubles. Meanwhile, please let us know what happens."

I did not see my friend for the next few days. But on the following Monday evening I received a short note. He asked me to meet him at the train on the next day. On the train he told me that all was well in Camford according to Mr. Bennett. There was peace in the professor's house. Later, at the Chequers Hotel, Mr. Bennett also gave us the same report. "He heard from his London businessman today. There was a letter and a small box. Each had the small cross signed under it which means I'm not to touch them. There has been nothing else."

"That may be quite enough," said Holmes. "Now, Mr. Bennett, I believe we will have some answers tonight, if my ideas are right. It is necessary to watch the professor very closely. I would like to ask you to stay awake and keep your eyes open. If you hear him pass your door, don't bother him. But follow him if possible. Dr. Watson and I will not be far off. By the way, where is the key to that little wooden box of which you spoke?"

"In his watch-pocket."

"I think we have to find that box. Perhaps it won't be too difficult to open. Is there anyone else at the house who can help us?"

"There is the carriageman, Macphail."

"Where does he sleep?"

"Over the stables."

"We might want him. Well, we can do no more until we see what happens. Good-bye for now, but I think we'll see you before morning."

It was nearly midnight. Holmes and I were hiding among some plants across from the house. It was a fine night, but cool. We were glad to have our warm overcoats. There was a light wind, and clouds were crossing the sky. From time to time we could see the half-moon.

It would have been a lonely night, but we expected interesting things to happen.

"If I am right about this period of nine days, then we shall see the professor tonight," said Holmes. "There are several facts which support my idea—his manner became so strange after his visit to Prague; he writes secretly to a Bohemian businessman in London, who probably works for someone in Prague, and he received a small box in the mail from him today. This all leads to one thing. I believe he takes this drug every nine days. Which drug he takes and why are still beyond my understanding. But there are body signs which I find interesting. Did you see his knuckles?"

I told Holmes that I hadn't.

"They were thick and hard. I've never seen knuckles quite like them. Always look at the hands first, Watson. Then look at other parts of the clothing. But those knuckles were very strange. Their condition can only be explained by the manner of movement which—" Holmes suddenly put his hand to his head. "Oh, Watson, Watson, what a fool I have been! It seems unbelievable, yet it must be true. How could I not see the relationship between all these facts? Those knuckles—how could I have missed those knuckles? And the dog! And the ivy that grows on the house wall! I must be losing my mind as a detective. Look out, Watson! Here he is! We shall have the chance to see for ourselves."

The house door opened slowly. From the low light of the house we could see the tall figure of Professor Presbury. He was dressed in his nightclothes. He stood in the doorway. But he was not completely straight. His body was pushed forward, and his arms were hanging, as we had last seen him. Now he stepped forward into the drive. An unbelievable change came over him. He got down on his hands and feet, like an animal. His movements were very quick and lively. He moved along the front of the house and then around the corner. As he disappeared, Bennett came quietly out through the door and followed him.

"Come, Watson, come!" cried Holmes. We walked as quietly as possible through the plants towards the house. There, in the moonlight, we could see the professor creeping along the bottom of the ivy-covered wall. As we watched, he suddenly began to climb up the ivy. He seemed like a young boy as he jumped from plant to plant. There was joy and speed in his movements. He seemed to have no purpose other than pleasure. With his nightclothes on he looked like a big dark bird against the side of his own house. Soon he seemed to become tired of this game and he climbed back down to the ground. Once again he crept along on his hands and feet towards the stables. Roy the dog was out now, barking loudly. He had a chain around his neck. When he saw his master, the dog almost went mad with barking. The professor stopped just beyond reach of the dog's chain. He began to fool with the dog. He took small rocks from the drive and threw them at Roy. He picked up a stick and touched the dog several times with it. He tried every way to make the dog mad with anger. In all our cases I do not know if I have ever seen anything stranger than this sight.

And then in a moment it happened! It was not the chain that broke. It was the dog's collar, that came off. That collar had been made for a Newfoundland dog with a thick neck. Roy attacked the professor. The dog and the man were rolling around on the ground together. The one was senseless with anger, the other was senseless with fear. The professor's life almost ended there. Roy's mouth was on the professor's neck. He was biting him hard. We tried to pull them apart. It might have been dangerous for us. But Bennett's voice brought the big dog under control. The loud noise had awakened the sleepy carriageman,

Macphail. He came to the scene. "I'm not surprised," said he, shaking his head. "I've seen the professor doing this before to the dog. I knew Roy would get him sooner or later."

The dog was tied up again. Together we carried the professor up to his room. Bennett, who had studied to become a doctor, helped me with the professor. We put bandages around his neck. The dog's bite was very serious and there was much blood. In a half-hour the danger was past. I gave the professor a shot of a drug, called morphine. He was sleeping deeply. Then, and only then, were we able to look at each other and talk of the situation.

"I think a first-class doctor should see him," said I.

"No, please no!" cried Bennett. "At present this problem is known only to our house. It is safe with us. If others learn about this it would be terrible. Consider his position at the university, his name in Europe, his daughter's feelings."

"True," said Holmes. "I think it may be possible to keep the matter quiet. And also to stop it from happening again. I'd like the key for that box, Mr. Bennett. Macphail will guard the professor and let us know if there is any change. Let us see what we can find in the professor's mysterious wooden box."

There was not much, but there was enough — two containers of drugs, a syringe, and several letters written in a foreign hand. The marks on the letters showed that each was dated from the Commercial Road. They were signed "A. Dorak." They were only business letters to show that the material and money was sent and received. There was, however, another letter written in a different hand with a Prague postmark. "Here we have our material!" cried Holmes as he opened the letter.

Honored Professor:

Since your visit I have thought much of your case. In your situation there are some special reasons for using this drug. However, I must tell you that there may be some danger in using it. It is possible that this drug could have been better. You should be careful.

As you know, the drug was made from monkeys. I have used a monkey called the black-faced langur. Langur is, of course, a creeper and a climber. The other kind of monkey I use, called anthropoid, walks straight up and is nearer to human beings.

I ask you to please take care so that the treatment goes well. I have one other client in England, for whom Dorak is also my supplier.

Please send weekly reports.

Sincerely yours,

H. LOWNSTEIN.

Lowenstein! I remembered reading something in the newspaper about him. He was a scientist who was searching for the secret of staying young forever. Lowenstein of Prague! Lowenstein with the wonderous strength-giving drug. Other scientists and doctors would not allow it because he would not tell how he made it. I told Holmes and Bennett what I remembered. Bennett was looking at a university book of animals.

"'Langur,'" he read, "'the great black-faced monkey of the Himalaya mountains, biggest and most human of climbing monkeys.' There is other information here also. Well, thanks to you, Mr. Holmes, it is very clear that we have found the source of the problem."

"The real source," said Holmes, "is, of course, the professor's love affair. It gave him the idea that he could only gain his wish by becoming a much younger man. When one tries to rise above Nature, one often falls below it. The highest type of man may become an animal if he tries to change his natural being." He sat thinking for a moment with the drug container in his hand. "I will write to this man in Prague and tell him that his actions are criminal. I think we will have no more trouble from him. But it may happen again. Others may find a better way. There is danger there—a very real danger to humanity. Consider, Watson, how some would use such a drug for their own powers, to keep their own worthless lives. What sort of place would our world become with such drugs?" Suddenly, Holmes the thinker disappeared, and Holmes, the man of action, jumped from his chair. "I think there is nothing more to be said, Mr. Bennett. Everything can now be understood. The dog, of course, knew of the change far more quickly than you. It was his sense of smell. It was the monkey, not the professor, whom Roy attacked. It was also the monkey, and not the professor, who fooled with Roy. Climbing was a joy to the drugged professor. I think it was just by chance that he climbed to the young lady's window. There is an early train to the city, Watson. But I think we shall have just enough time for a cup of tea at the Chequers before we catch it."

18

The Adventure of
the Illustrious Client

高名な依頼人

読み始める前に

The Adventure of the Illustrious Client 高名な依頼人

56の短編のうち50番目に発表された
1925年2, 3月号のストランド・マガジン初出
1927年発行の「シャーロック・ホームズの事件簿」に収録された

［主な登場人物］

Sherlock Holmes シャーロック・ホームズ 世界的に有名な私立探偵。優れた観察眼と推理力を有する。ロンドンのベーカー街221Bに下宿している。

Watson ジョン・H・ワトソン 医師。ホームズの相棒でこの物語の語り手。かつてベーカー街221Bでホームズと同居していた。

Sir James Damery ジェームズ・デマリー卿 とても裕福で顔が広い大佐。依頼の内容を伝えにホームズのもとを訪れる。

Baron Adelbert Gruner アデルバート・グルーナー男爵 悪名高い危険でハンサムなオーストリア貴族。妻の殺害容疑を含む数々の悪事を働いている。

General de Merville ド・メルヴィル将軍 カイバル戦争で功績をあげた将軍。娘がグルーナー男爵と婚約してしまい、神経をすり減らしている。

Violet de Merville ヴァイオレット・ド・メルヴィル嬢 メルヴィル将軍の娘。グルーナー男爵を溺愛してしまっている。

Kitty Winter キティ・ウィンター ホームズの協力者。グルーナー男爵に恨みをもつ。

［あらすじ］

サー・ジェームズ・デマリー大佐を通じて、名を明かさぬ、ある非常に高名で身分の高い人物から、ド・メルヴィル将軍の娘ヴァイオレット嬢とオーストリアからやってきた悪名高いグルーナー男爵との婚約を解消させる依頼を受けたホームズ。ヴァイオレット嬢は男爵を愛していて、彼の言うことを完全に信じきってしまっている。結婚式は来月に迫っていた。

［総単語数］7,912語

The Adventure of the Illustrious Client

"It can't hurt now," was Mr. Sherlock Holmes's reply when I asked him if I could write about the following mystery. And so I may now begin to tell the reader about a great case in the life of my detective friend.

There is a men's club on Northumberland Avenue where Holmes and I go. There we enjoy the Turkish bath. I often find Holmes more likeable and willing to talk after a hot bath. We sat smoking and talking in the drying-room. It was September 3, 1902, the day my story begins. I asked him if there were any new cases. He reached his arm into his nearby coat pocket and pulled out some papers.

"It may be from some fool who thinks he is important, or it may be a matter of life and death. I know only what this note tells me." He handed me the note.

It was from the Carlton Club and dated the evening before. This is what I read:

> Sir James Damery would like to call upon Mr. Sherlock Holmes tomorrow at 4:30 p.m. Sir James wishes to say that the matter is rather important and secret. He asks Mr. Holmes to please telephone the Carlton Club.

"I have, of course, already telephoned to give my OK," said Holmes as I returned the paper. "Do you know anything of this man Damery?"

"Only that he is very well known in rich and powerful circles."

"Well, I can tell you a little more than that. He is often asked to take care of matters which need to be kept out of newspapers. You may remember his work with Sir George Lewis during the Hammerford Will case. He is a man of the world. That is why I think he really does need our help."

"Our?"

"Well, if you don't mind, Watson."

"It would be my pleasure."

"Good. You have the hour—4:30. We can forget about it until then."

I was living in my own apartment in Queen Anne Street at the time. I arrived at Baker Street before the meeting time. Colonel Sir James Damery arrived just at the half-hour. Many people know what Sir James looked like. He had a broad face, with no beard or moustache. His character was strong and likeable, his voice pleasant and easy. He was a very intelligent man. His Irish eyes were gray and direct, and he often smiled. He was perfectly dressed, from his high hat and long black coat to his shining shoes. He was a man used to being with famous, important people.

"Of course, I expected to find Dr. Watson," he said upon entering. "His help may be very necessary, Mr. Holmes. We are dealing with a very bad criminal who will stop at nothing. I believe there is no more dangerous man in Europe."

"I know several men like that," said Holmes with a smile. "Don't you smoke? Then you will excuse me if I light my pipe. If your man is more dangerous than the late Professor Moriarty, or than the living Colonel Sebastian Moran, then he is certainly worth meeting. May I ask his name?"

"Have you ever heard of Baron Gruner?"

"You mean the Austrian killer?"

Colonel Damery threw up his hands with a laugh. "Ah, very good Mr. Holmes! Wonderful! So you already believe he is a killer?"

"It is my business to follow crime on the Continent. I have no doubt that he was guilty of that famous case in Prague. He had good luck and a good lawyer. I am sure that he killed his wife in the Splugen Pass. She did not die of natural causes. I also knew that he came to England. I had a feeling he would bring trouble with him here. Well, what has he been doing? I suppose it is not this old case again?"

"No, it is more serious than that. To catch the criminal after the crime is important. But to stop it from happening is even more so. It is a terrible thing, Mr. Holmes, to see a crime happen, but to be powerless to stop it. Can a human being be placed in a more difficult position?"

"Perhaps not."

"Then you will be able to understand the situation of my client."

"Oh, I didn't realize that you were only helping someone else. Who is it?"

"Mr. Holmes, I really cannot tell you that. It is important that the name of this honored man be kept a secret. His reasons are good and true but he wants to stay unknown. I promise you that you will be paid very well. Also, you may deal with the case as you like. Surely the name of the man is unimportant?"

"I am sorry," said Holmes. "I am used to having a mystery at one end, but not both ends of my cases. I am afraid, Sir James, that I must say no."

Our visitor looked very sad. His large face was darkened with unhappiness.

"I don't think you know what this will mean, Mr. Holmes," said he. "I am in a very difficult position. I am sure that you would be very proud to take this case. However, I promised not to talk about my client. Please let me give you the facts of the case at least."

"All right, as long as you understand that I may or may not take it."

"That is understood. First, you have no doubt heard of General de Merville?"

"De Merville of the Khyber war? Yes, I know of him."

"He has a daughter, Violet de Merville. She is young, rich, beautiful, and gifted, a wonder-woman. It is this daughter, this lovely young lady whom we are trying to save from a bad man."

"Baron Gruner has some control over her?"

"The strongest control of all for a woman — love. The fellow is, as you may have heard, very good-looking. He also has a manner, voice, and sense of mystery which women like so well. They say he has control over most women and uses that control often."

"But how did such a man come to meet Miss Violet de Merville?"

"It was on a ship in the Mediterranean. Nobody realized the Baron's true character until it was too late. He quickly took an interest in the lady. Soon she was completely in love with him. Even worse, she believes that he is everything in the world. She lives only for him. She will not hear one word against him. In fact, she plans to marry him next month. She is old enough and has a strong will. We don't know how to stop her."

"Does she know what happened in Austria?"

"The Baron has told her everything about his past. But what he tells her is not the whole truth. He says nothing about his guilt. She believes he is an honest man."

"Oh my! But surely you have just told me the name of your client. It is no doubt General de Merville."

Our visitor moved in his chair.

"I could tell you he is, Mr. Holmes, but it is not true. De Merville is a broken man. Because of this problem he is no longer strong. He has lost his nerve and become weak. This Austrian is destroying him. My client, however, is an old friend of the general. They have known each other for many years, since Violet was a little girl. My client wants very much to help the general. He wants to stop this relationship. There is nothing, which the police can do. He has asked that you be called to help. But he cannot tell you who he is. You have great powers of the mind, Mr. Holmes. I'm sure you could find out who my client is if you wanted. However, I must ask you, as a point of honor, not to try."

Holmes smiled.

"I think I can promise you that," he said. "Your problem interests me. I am prepared to help you. How shall I keep in touch with you?"

"The Carlton Club will find me. But in case you need me quickly, I have a telephone number, 'XX.31.'"

Holmes wrote it down. He sat, still smiling, with his datebook upon his leg.

"Where does the Baron live?"

"Vernon Lodge, near Kingston. It is a large house. He has been lucky in making business deals. Some of the deals were not honest. Now he is a rich man, which also makes him more dangerous."

"Is he home at present?"

"Yes."

"Can you give me any more information about him?"

"He likes things which cost much money. He loves horses. For a short time he played the sport of polo at Hurlingham. But then people learned about his situation in Prague and he had to leave. He collects books and pictures. He is a man who enjoys art. He especially knows about Chinese pottery. He has a fine collection of the pottery. He also wrote a book about it."

"A very busy mind," said Holmes. "All great criminals have that. My old criminal friend, Charlie Peace, played great music on the violin. Wainwright was a great artist. I can think of many more. Well, Sir

James, you can tell your client that I will help him with Baron Gruner. I can say no more. I also have some places to look for information. Perhaps we can solve this matter."

Our visitor left us. Holmes sat a long time in deep thought. He seemed to forget that I was there. At last he came back to earth.

"Well, Watson, what's your view?" he asked.

"I think you should see the young lady herself."

"My dear Watson, if her poor old broken father cannot change her mind, how can I? I am a stranger to her. Perhaps we can speak to her later. But I believe we must begin elsewhere. I think Shinwell Johnson might be a help."

I haven't talked about Shinwell Johnson in these stories. That is because I have not often written of my friend's later cases. During the first years of the century, Johnson became a valuable helper. He was, I am sorry to say, a dangerous criminal. Two times he was sent to prison. Later, after prison, he changed his ways and began to work on the side of the law. He helped Holmes by gathering information about London's criminal world. Often, this information was very important. Johnson did not work for the police because he did not want other criminals to know about him. He gave secret information only to Holmes and others. It was easy for him to enter the clubs and bars and meeting places of other criminals. He had a good eye and ear. Sherlock Holmes now planned to find him.

I met my friend later that evening at Simpson's, on the Strand. We had a small table at the front window. We looked down upon the rushing stream of life on that busy street. Holmes told me of his talk with Johnson.

"Johnson is hunting for information in the dark criminal under-world," said he. "It is down there that we must find this Baron's secrets."

"But the lady will not believe what is already known. Why do you think that a fresh discovery of yours will change her mind?"

"Who knows, Watson? Women's hearts and minds are not easy for men to understand. Killing might be explained, but a smaller problem might make her upset. Baron Gruner told me —"

"He told you!"

"Oh, yes, I did not tell you of my plans. Well, Watson, I love to know who I am dealing with. I like to meet him eye to eye and to see what he is made of. After I gave Johnson his orders, I took a taxi to Kingston to see the Baron."

"Did he know who you are?"

"I simply gave him my business card. He is an excellent enemy. He is as cool as ice, but is very pleasant on the outside. His voice and manners make you trust him. But he is deadly. Yes, I am glad I've met Baron Adelbert Gruner."

"You say he was pleasant?"

"Like a hungry cat who sees his food. He is surely a dangerous man. When he met me he said, 'I thought I should see you sooner or later, Mr. Holmes. General de Merville probably asked you to stop my marrying his daughter, Violet. That is so, is it not?'

"I said it was.

"'My dear man,' said he, 'you cannot succeed in this plan. It would only be dangerous for you. I believe you should give up this case at once.'

"'It is strange,' I answered, 'but that is exactly what I was going to tell you. You are a very intelligent man, Baron, and you have a good life. Let me tell you as man to man. No one wants to bring up your past to make your life difficult. The past is over, and you are free. However, if you continue with this relationship you will make many new enemies here in England. Is it worth it? Surely it is wiser to leave the lady alone. It would not be pleasant for you if she knew the facts of your past.'

"The Baron looked at me as if I was not serious. He gave a small laugh.

"'Excuse me, Mr. Holmes,' said he, 'but I laugh because you know nothing. You are trying to fool me. But it will do you no good.'

"'So you think.'

"'So I know. Let me tell you something very clearly. My relations with the lady are very strong indeed. She loves me completely. I have told her everything about my past and she still wants me. I have also told her that there are dishonest people who do not like me. They will come to her and tell her lies about me. You, of course, are one of these people. I told her how to deal with them. You will see, Mr. Holmes, just how she feels about me. I'm sure she would be happy to speak with you. She also loves her father and will do what he likes—except in my case.'

"Well, Watson, there seemed no more to say, so I left. But as I began to open the door, he stopped me.

"'By the way, Mr. Holmes,' said he, 'did you know Le Brun, the French detective?'

"'Yes,' said I.

"'Do you know what happened to him?'

"'I heard he was badly beaten by some criminals in Montmartre. He cannot walk for the rest of his life.'

"'Quite true, Mr. Holmes. Interestingly, he too was trying to find information about me only a week before. Don't do it, Mr. Holmes. It's not a wise thing to do. Several others have learned that already. My last word to you is, go your own way and let me go mine. Good-bye!'

"So Watson, now you know what happened."

"This fellow seems dangerous."

"Very dangerous. I'm sure he is quite serious."

"Is it really necessary to take this case? Does it really matter if he marries the girl?"

"Well, considering that he killed his last wife, I think it matters very much. Besides, our client! But we needn't talk about that. When you finish your coffee, you should come home with me. Shinwell will be there with his report."

We found him there. A very large, red-faced, hard-looking man with deep, black eyes. He had gone down into his old world of crime and brought something back. Sitting next to him was a young, red-haired woman. She was quite thin, very pale and looked much older than she was. It seems that her life was difficult and sad.

"This is Miss Kitty Winter," said Shinwell Johnson, waving his fat hand towards her. "She doesn't know—well, I'll let her speak for herself. I found her about an hour after I got your note, Mr. Holmes."

"I'm easy to find," said the young woman. "Porky Shinwell knows where I am—at the bottom of London. We're old friends, aren't we Porky? But if life was fair there is another who would be lower than all of us. That is the man you are after, Mr. Holmes."

Holmes smiled. "I suppose we have your good wishes, Miss Winter."

"I'll do anything to put that terrible dog where he belongs," said our visitor. There was anger and hate in her pale face. Her eyes burned. "You don't have to know about my past, Mr. Holmes. That's not important. But Adelbert Gruner destroyed my life. If only I could destroy his." She struck the air with both hands. "Oh, if only I could pull him into the same hole where he has pushed so many."

"You know what this matter is about?"

"Porky Shinwell has been telling me. He wants to marry some poor fool this time. You want to stop it. If this girl has any sense she would leave him today."

"She is madly in love. She has been told everything about him. She cares nothing."

"Told about the killings?"

"Yes."

"My God, she must have a nerve!"

"She thinks people are telling lies about the good Baron."

"Can't you show her the truth?"

"Well, can you help us do so?"

"Look at me. If I stood before her and told her how he used me——"

"Would you do this?"

"Would I? Of course, I would!"

"Well, it might be worth trying. But he has told her about his past. She believes he is honest and not guilty. I understand she will not reopen the question."

"I don't think he told her everything," said Miss Winter. "I happened to see one or two other killings of his. He would tell me a story about someone in a kind, friendly way. Then he would look at me seriously and say: 'He died within a month.' It was the truth, too. But I didn't care either because, you see, I loved him myself at the time. Whatever he did was fine with me. Same as this new poor fool. There was just one thing which I hated. I should have left him when I found out about it. But his soft lies changed my mind. It is a book he has—a brown book with a lock and a gold figure on the outside. I think he showed it to me one night because he was drunk."

"What is in this book?"

"I tell you, Mr. Holmes, some men collect bugs or pictures or wine. This man collects women. Everything was in that book. Photos, names, personal information about each woman. It was a terrible book—a book that no man, even a terrible dog like Gruner, could have put together. But it was Adelbert Gruner's book. 'Women I Have

Destroyed' — he should name it that. I don't know if the book would serve you. Anyway, you probably can't get it."

"Where is it?"

"Now I don't know. It's more than a year since I left him. I know where he kept it then. Maybe it is still in the desk in his study. Do you know his house?"

"I've been in the study," said Holmes.

"Have you, already? And you only started the job this morning. Maybe dear Adelbert will be the loser this time. Well, the outer study is the one with his Chinese pottery. The pieces sit on big glass-covered boards between the windows. Then behind his desk is the door that leads to the inner study. It's a small room where he keeps his papers and things."

"Is he not afraid of thieves?"

"Adelbert is not afraid of much. Even his enemies know that. There is an alarm in the house to stop thieves. Besides, what is there for a thief, unless they want his fancy pottery?"

"No good," said Shinwell Johnson, the ex-thief. "No thief will take things that he can't sell."

"Quite so," said Holmes. "Well, now, Miss Winter, perhaps you can come back here tomorrow evening at five. In the meantime I will see about setting up a meeting with you and this lady. I am very, very happy for your help in this matter. I'm also sure that my clients will be very kind to — "

"None of that, Mr. Holmes," cried the young woman. "I am not here for the money. Let me see this man's face in the ground, and I'll be happy. That is my price. I'm always on your side as long as you are trying to stop him. Porky here can always tell you where to find me."

I saw Holmes again the following evening when we dined at our Strand restaurant. I asked him about his talk with Violet de Merville earlier that evening. This is what he told me.

"There was no difficulty with setting up the meeting," said Holmes. "Perhaps it was because the girl feels badly about her father. She now wants to help him if possible. The general telephoned to tell me that all was ready. The fiery Miss Winter and I arrived by taxi outside 104 Berkeley Square, where the old general lives. It is one of those very large gray London buildings. It looks as big and serious as a church. A doorman showed us into a great yellow drawing-room. There was the young lady Violet waiting for us. She was quiet, pure, cool, and distant, like snow on a mountain.

"I don't know quite how to make her clear to you, Watson. Perhaps you may meet her before we are through. Then you can choose your own words. She is beautiful, but it is beauty of another world. I have seen such faces in the pictures of old masters of the Middle Ages. How a terrible man like the Baron can be with her, I don't know.

"She knew why we were there, of course. The Baron had already talked to her. I think she was surprised at Miss Winter's coming. But she asked us to sit down in two chairs.

"'Well, sir,' she said in a voice like an icy wind, 'I know who you are. You have called, as I understand, to speak badly of my lover, Baron Gruner. It is only because of my father's wishes that I am seeing you at all. I will tell you now that nothing you will say can change my opinion.'

"I was sorry for her, Watson. I thought of her then as a daughter of my own. I do not usually speak with great feeling. As you know, I use my head and not my heart. But I really did talk to her with all the warmth of words that I could find. I tried to make her see the terrible situation of the woman who realizes too late about a man's character. She would soon be his helpless wife in his bloody hands. I told her everything—the fear, the pain, the hopelessness. But she seemed not to hear my words. There was no sign in her face or eyes. I thought about the Baron having complete control over her. It seemed like she was in a dream. Yet she spoke to me very directly.

"'I have listened to your every word, Mr. Holmes,' said she. 'It is just as I have told you. I realize that Adelbert has had a stormy life. There have been people who hated him, and talked badly about him. You are only the last of several to do so. You are also a paid detective. Perhaps you are willing to work for the Baron as equally as against him. In any case I want you to understand that I love him and that he loves me. All the opinion of the world means no more to me than that rain outside the window. If his goodness has fallen, then perhaps I am here to raise it again. I don't know' — she turned to Miss Winter — 'who this lady can be.'

"I was about to answer her when Miss Winter spoke out. If ever you saw fire and ice face to face, it was those two women.

"'I'll tell you who I am,' she cried, jumping up from her chair. 'I am his last lover. I am one of a hundred that he has used and destroyed. He will do the same to you. Or, if you are lucky, maybe he will kill you. I promise you, foolish woman, if you marry this man it will end your life. It may be a broken heart or a broken neck, but it will happen. It is not for love of you that I am speaking. I really don't care about you. It's because of hate for him. I want to repay him for what he did to me. Don't look at me like that, my fine rich lady. You may soon be lower than me!'

"'I'd rather not talk about such things,' said Miss de Merville coldly. 'Let me say once and for all that I know of my lover's past relationships. I know that there were three other women. I know that he is sorry for them.'

"'Three others!' cried the other girl. 'You think there were only three! You fool! You terrible fool!'

"'Mr. Holmes, I must ask you and your friend to leave,' said the icy voice. 'I have seen you as my father wanted. But I am not required to listen to this mad woman.'

"Miss Winter said something and jumped forward at Miss de Merville. If I had not caught her arm she might have hit the other. I pulled her towards the door and then outside into the taxi. She was unbelievably angry. In a way, I was also angry, Watson. The young lady we are trying to save simply would not believe us. So now you see the problem once again. Our first move did not work. We must now try something else. I will keep in touch with you, Watson, for I will probably need you. It is possible, however, that they will make the next move."

And they did. They struck their blow, — or rather his blow, because I do not believe the young lady knew of it. I remember exactly where I was standing when my eyes fell upon the newspaper. It was between the Grand Hotel and Charing Cross Station. My heart dropped when I read the terrible headline:

DEADLY ATTACK UPON SHERLOCK HOLMES

I think I stood there in shock for some moments. Then I remember taking a paper and walking to a doorway of a nearby store. This is what I read:

We learn that Mr. Sherlock Holmes, the well-known detective, was the object this morning of an attempt to kill him. He is alive but his condition is very serious. There is little information on the attack which happened at about twelve o'clock in Regent Street, outside the Cafe Royal. The attack was made by two armed men with sticks. Mr. Holmes was beaten about the head and body. He was carried to Charing Cross Hospital and later asked to be taken to his rooms in Baker Street. The criminals who attacked him were said to be well-dressed men. They escaped from the scene by running through Cafe Royal and into the street behind it. No doubt they are among those criminals who are afraid of the great detective.

Of course, I quickly found a taxi and hurried to Baker Street. There I found Sir Leslie Oakshott, the famous doctor, in the hallway.

"He is in no serious danger at the moment," was his report. "Two bad cuts to the head and some other marks on his body. I have given him something for the pain. It is important that he rests quietly. However, you can talk to him for a few minutes."

I then walked into the darkened room. Poor Holmes was not sleeping. I heard him call my name. His head was covered with cloth, bandages. There were some red spots on the bandages from blood. I sat beside him and hung my head.

"All right, Watson. Don't look so afraid," he said in a weak voice. "It's not as bad as it seems."

"Thank God for that!"

"I'm very good at fighting with sticks, as you know. I was able to guard myself pretty well. It was the second man that was too much for me."

"What can I do, Holmes? Of course, it was that terrible Baron who told them to attack you. I'll go and fight him myself if you'd like."

"Good old Watson! No, we can do nothing unless the police find those men. But their escape was well planned. I'm sure of that. Wait a while. I have my plans. The first thing to do is tell the newspapers that I am seriously hurt. I want people to think that my condition is very bad, even that I may not live. You can tell them anything."

"But Sir Leslie Oakshott?"

"Oh, he's all right. He knows me. Don't worry about him."

"Anything else?"

"Yes. Tell Shinwell Johnson to get Miss Winter out of the way. Those men will be looking for her now. They know, of course, that she was with me in the case. It is important to guard her. Do it tonight."

"I'll go now. Anything more?"

"Put my pipe on the table—and the tobacco. Right! Come in each morning, and we will make our plans."

I spoke that evening with Johnson. He planned to take Miss Winter to a quiet place out of the city until the danger passed.

For six days the public believed that Holmes was close to death. The news reports were very serious. I visited him often, however, and knew that he would be fine. He got better each day. In fact, I don't even think he told me how well he felt. My friend liked his secrets. I was the person closest to him in life, yet I never knew everything about him.

On the seventh day the bandages were changed. There was a report in the evening newspaper which I brought to my friend. It said that the Cunard ship *Ruritania* was sailing from Liverpool to America on Friday. Among the people going was Baron Adelbert Gruner. He had some important business to do in New York before marrying Miss Violet de Merville. Holmes listened to the news with a cold look on his white face. I knew he didn't like it.

"Friday!" he cried. "Only three days. I believe this dog Gruner wants to escape from danger. But he won't, Watson! I promise you, he won't! Now, Watson, I want you to do something for me."

"I am here to be used, Holmes."

"Well, then, spend the next twenty-four hours studying about Chinese pottery. Learn as much as you can."

He did not tell me why and I did not ask. Long ago I learned to simply do as he wanted. I left his room and walked down Baker Street. I wondered how I could carry out such a strange order. Finally I drove to the London Library in St. James' Square. There I picked up a large book about pottery and brought it home.

They say that someone who learns too much too soon will quickly forget what he learned. I am certainly no expert on pottery. Yet all that evening and all night and all the next morning I studied and learned names and facts. I learned of the great artists, the dates, the marks of the Hung-wu and the Yung-lo. I read the writing of Tang-ying and the beautiful work of the Sung and Yuan periods. The next evening I went to see Holmes. He was out of bed now. The newspapers, however, said he was still close to death. He sat in his chair, his head upon his hand.

"Why, Holmes," I said, "if one believed the papers, you are dying."

"That," said he, "is just what I want people to believe. And now, Watson, have you learned about Chinese pottery?"

"At least I tried to."

"Good. Do you think you can talk about the subject?"

"I believe I could."

"Then please pass me that little box on the table."

He opened the top and took out a small object. It was covered in a fine material, called silk. He took off the silk and showed me a beautiful piece of deep blue pottery.

"Please be careful with this, Watson. It will easily break. This is real pottery from the Ming Period. There is no finer piece anywhere. A complete set of these cups would be worth millions. In fact, I don't think there is a complete set outside the Imperial Palace of Peking. This piece will make any real expert mad with desire."

"What am I to do with it?"

Holmes handed me a card. It said: "Dr. Hill Barton, 369 Half Moon Street."

"That is your name for this evening, Watson. I want you to visit Baron Gruner. I know something of the man. At half-past eight he will probably be free. He will receive a note telling him you will visit. You will say that you are bringing a wonderful piece of Ming china. You will tell him that you are a collector. This set has come your way. You heard of the Baron's interest in the subject, and you may consider selling for a good price."

"What price?"

"Good question, Watson. It is important to know the value of your own things. This cup was brought to me by Sir James, and comes from the collection of his client. You may say that it has no equal in the world."

"Perhaps the value can be judged by art dealers."

"Excellent, Watson! Say Christie or Sotheby. Tell him that you cannot price it yourself."

"But if he won't see me?"

"Oh, yes, he will see you. He is a mad collector. And he is an expert on this subject. Sit down, Watson, and we will write the letter. No answer needed. You will simply say you are coming, and why."

It was an excellent little letter. It would surely interest a collector like Gruner. A young boy was sent off with the letter. On the same evening, I went to the home of Baron Gruner. The beautiful cup was in my hand and the card of Dr. Hill Barton was in my coat.

As Sir James had said, Baron Gruner was a very rich man. The house and grounds were beautiful. There was a long winding drive, with lovely plants on both sides. In front of the house was an open area. There were valuable Greek and Roman figures all around. The place had been built by a South African gold king many years earlier. The house was long, low, and very large. A butler showed me into the house and brought me to the Baron.

He was standing in front of a great glass case which stood between the windows. It contained part of his Chinese collection. He turned as

I entered the room. In his hand was a small, brown vase.

"Please sit down, Doctor," said he. "I was looking over my own collection and wondering if I really wanted something else. This little Tang vase might interest you. It dates from the seventh century. I'm sure you've never seen more perfection. Do you have the Ming cup you spoke of?"

I carefully took it out and handed it to him. He sat down at his desk and turned on the light. He looked closely at the piece. I was also able to study his face in that light.

He was indeed a very good-looking man. He was neither big nor small. He was built with both power and beauty. He looked almost Oriental. He had large, dark eyes that a woman might fall in love with. His hair was quite black. His moustache was also black. It was short and pointed. His look was pleasing, except for his straight, thin mouth. The moustache did not cover his mouth. I thought it was the mouth of a killer—hard, dangerous and terrible. It was nature's sign of danger to others. His voice was pleasant, and his manners were perfect. In age I guessed him to be not much more than thirty. Later I learned that he was forty-two.

"Very fine—very fine indeed!" he said at last. "And you say you have a complete set of six? I don't understand why I haven't heard of such perfectly beautiful pieces. I only know of one in England like this. And it is not for sale in the market. May I ask you, Dr. Hill Barton, how you got this?"

"Does it really matter?" I asked with a careless air. "You can see that the piece is real. If you like we can ask the opinion of an expert."

"Very strange," he said. There was an unbelieving look in his dark eyes. "In dealing with objects of great value I naturally wish to know all about the earlier business. The piece is real, I know that for sure. But is it yours to sell?"

"I can promise you that there is no problem."

"Then, of course, I would like to know how much your promise is worth."

"My bankers would answer that."

"I see. Yet the whole situation strikes me as very unusual."

"You can do business or not," I said a little nervously. "I have given you the first offer because I understood that you are an expert. But I shall have no difficulty with other buyers."

"Who told you I was an expert?"

"I know that you wrote a book upon the subject."

"Have you read the book?"

"No."

"Dear me, this becomes more and more difficult for me to understand! You are an expert collector with a very valuable piece in your collection. But you never took the time to read the one book which could tell you the true value of what you have here. How do you explain that?"

"I am a very busy man. I am a doctor."

"That is no answer. If you are interested in a subject you will find the time. No matter what your job is. You said in your note that you were an expert."

"So I am."

"Might I ask you a few questions about the subject? I must tell you, Doctor — if you are really a doctor — that it becomes more difficult to believe you. What do you know of Emperor Shomu? And what is his relationship to the Shoso-in near Nara? Ah, is that too difficult for you? Tell me about the Northern Wei Period and its place in the history of pottery."

I jumped from my chair, acting angry.

"I will not stand for this, sir," said I. "I came here to do you a favor, not to be questioned like a schoolboy. I may not know as much as you on the subject, but I will not answer questions in this manner!"

He looked at me for several seconds. The softness was gone from his eyes. They were suddenly hard. I could see his teeth now in that angry mouth.

"What is the game? You are here as a spy, aren't you? You are working for Holmes. He is trying to catch me. The fellow is dying I hear, so he sends his spy to watch me. You were able to enter my house easily enough. But, by God! you may find it very hard to get out again."

He jumped to his feet, and I stepped back. I was ready for an attack. The man was red with anger. It is possible that he did not believe me from the beginning; but after his questions he knew I was no collector. I could not hope to lie to him. He opened his desk and reached inside for something. Then suddenly he heard a sound, for he stood listening.

"Ah!" he cried. "Ah!" and he ran into the room behind him.

In two steps I arrived at the open door and looked in. My mind will forever remember the scene within. The window leading out into the garden was wide open. Beside it stood Sherlock Holmes. His head was still covered with bandages. His face was white and thin. In the next moment he stepped outside. I heard the sound of his body moving through the plants. With a shout the master of the house ran after him to the open window.

And then! It happened so fast, and yet I clearly saw it. An arm—a woman's arm—shot out from among the plants. At the same moment the Baron let out a terrible cry. It was a sound which I shall always recall. His hands covered his face and he rushed around the room. He beat his head against the walls. Then he fell upon the floor, shouting and crying in pain.

"Water! Please dear God, water!" was his cry.

I picked up a bottle of water from a side-table. I rushed to help him. At the same moment the butler and several others ran in from the hall. I remember one of them became sick when he saw the master's face. The face, moments ago so beautiful, was now terrible to look at. The woman had thrown acid in his face. One eye was already white, the other was red and burning. His looks were completely destroyed.

I quickly explained to the others what I had seen. Some had climbed through the window. Others had rushed out to the front of the house. But it was dark and it began to rain. Between his terrible cries, the victim shouted about the woman. "It was that damn woman, Kitty Winter!" he cried. "Oh, damn her! Damn her! She will pay for this! Oh God, this is more pain than I can stand!"

I put oil on his face with cotton. I gave him a strong drug, morphine, to help with the pain. I did everything I could. He held on to me with his hands, trusting me now. I could have cried when I looked into his dead eyes. However, I thought about the pain and sadness he had caused others. I was happy when the family doctor arrived at last. A policeman also came and I handed him my real card. It would have been foolish to lie to him. After all, I was almost as well-known to the police as Holmes himself. Then I left that terrible house. Within an hour I was at Baker Street.

Holmes was seated in his chair, looking very tired. It had been a difficult night for his nerves. He listened to my story of the Baron.

"Terrible, Watson, terrible! I'm very sorry for him. But he was a bad man who often hurt others. God knows, he caused much pain." He then picked up the brown book from the table. "Here is the book the woman spoke of. If this will not stop the marriage, then nothing will. But it will, Watson. It must. No woman could stand it."

"Is it his love life?"

"Yes, and more. Everything is in here. The moment the woman told us of this book I realized that we needed it. I knew we could use it against the Baron. I didn't say anything at the time, but I thought about it. Then the Baron's men attacked me. This gave me a chance because the Baron thought I was dying. I would have waited longer but he was leaving for America. He would never leave without such a valuable book. So we had to act quickly. It would have been impossible to break into his house at night. The house is guarded. But there was a chance in the evening if I could be sure that he was busy. That is why I sent you with the blue cup. While you were meeting with him I planned to find and take the brown book. However, I knew that you are not a pottery expert. It would be difficult to fool the Baron for more than a few minutes. Therefore, I had to be sure of the position of the brown book. And that is why I brought the girl with me at the last moment. Of course, I had no idea that she was carrying the acid under her coat. I thought she was coming just to help me. But it seems she had some of her own ideas."

"Gruner guessed that I worked with you."

"I was afraid he would. But you talked with him just long enough for me to get the book. It wasn't long enough for me to escape without being seen, however. Ah, Sir James, I am very glad you have come."

At that moment Sir James arrived. He had been called earlier by Holmes. He listened very closely as Holmes explained what had happened.

"You have done wonders — wonders!" he cried when Holmes had finished speaking. "Surely the terrible condition of the Baron's face is enough to end the marriage. Violet will no longer be interested in him. It may not be necessary to show this book to her."

Holmes shook his head.

"No, no. Women like Miss De Merville do not act like that.

She would feel sorry for him and love him even more with his face destroyed. It is his character, not his face, which we must destroy. That book will bring her back to earth. There is nothing else that will do the job. It is his own writing. She must believe it."

Sir James carried away both the book and the valuable cup. I too was leaving, so I went down with him into the street. A beautiful carriage was waiting for him. He jumped in, gave an order to the driver and drove away. He tried to cover the gold markings outside the window with his coat. But I had seen them. I was greatly surprised. Then I turned back and ran up the steps to Holmes' room.

"I have found out who our client is," I cried out with the news. "Why, Holmes, it is —"

"It is a good friend and a great gentleman," said Holmes, holding up his hand. "Let that be enough for us, now and forever."

I do not know how the brown book was used. Sir James may have shown it to the young lady. Or, more probably, that job was done by the young lady's father. At any rate, the result was desirable. Three days later the *Morning Post* newspaper wrote that there would be no marriage between Baron Adelbert Gruner and Miss Violet de Merville. The same paper also talked about the police-court case against Miss Kitty Winter. She was charged with the crime of throwing acid. She was guilty. However, because of the situation the court was kind to her. There was talk of charging Sherlock Holmes for being a thief. However, when the objective is a good one, and the client is so illustrious, even the hard British law becomes human. My friend did not go to court.

19

The Adventure of the Blanched Soldier

白面の兵士

読み始める前に

The Adventure of the Blanched Soldier 白面の兵士

56の短編のうち52番目に発表された
1926年11月号のストランド・マガジン初出
1927年発行の「シャーロック・ホームズの事件簿」に収録された

[主な登場人物]

Sherlock Holmes　シャーロック・ホームズ　世界的に有名な私立探偵。優れた観察眼と推理力を有する。ロンドンのベーカー街221Bに下宿している。

Watson　ジョン・H・ワトソン　医師。ホームズの相棒。本作では結婚して不在。

James M. Dodd　ジェームズ・M・ドッド　本件の依頼人。元軍人で戦友のゴッドフリーを探している。

Colonel Emsworth　エムズワース大佐　ゴッドフリーの父。厳格で冷たく、口が荒い。

Godfrey Emsworth　ゴッドフリー・エムズワース　大佐の一人息子。戦争から帰国後、行方不明になっている。

old Ralph　老ラルフ　屋敷の執事。

[あらすじ]

　ボーア戦争終結直後の1月、ホームズはジェームズ・M・ドッドという若い男の訪問を受けた。ボーア戦争のときの彼の戦友、ゴッドフリー・エムズワースが、帰国後音信不通になっていた。ドッドはゴッドフリーの屋敷を訪れ、夜、窓越しに彼の真っ白な顔を発見するが、その後彼の父親から屋敷を追い出されてしまったという。

[総単語数] 6,262語

The Adventure of the Blanched Soldier

My friend Watson is the one who writes about my experiences. He writes in a way that is interesting for the reader. I sometimes tell him that he should include more facts in his stories. "Try it yourself, Holmes!" he answers. So now, with my pen in hand, I will try my old friend's idea and write of a very interesting case.

In January 1903, just after the Boer War, I had a visit from Mr. James M. Dodd. He was a big, fresh, healthy Englishman from a good family. My friend Watson had just gotten married. He was not with me at that time. I usually sit with my back to the window while my visitors sit in front of me in the light. Mr. James M. Dodd was not sure how to begin speaking. I said nothing but looked at him closely. Sometimes I find it is a good idea to tell my clients what I see.

"From South Africa, sir, I believe?"

"Yes, sir," he answered, with some surprise.

"Imperial Yeomanry, I suppose."

"Yes again."

"Middlesex Corps, no doubt."

"That's right, Mr. Holmes. You are a wonder."

I smiled at his surprise.

"You are an English gentleman who is dark from the sun, but not from the English sun. And you wear your neck-cloth on your arm, not in your coat pocket. Also, the beard on your face is cut short, which shows that you were not a walking soldier in the army. No, you appear to be a man who rides horses. As to Middlesex, your card already tells me that you are a businessman from Throgmorton Street."

"You see everything."

"I see no more than you, but I have taught myself to notice what I see. However, Mr. Dodd, I'm sure you didn't come here this morning to talk about my power to notice things. What has happened at Tuxbury Old Park?"

"Mr. Holmes — !"

"My dear sir, there is no mystery. Your letter came with that name on it. Also, you wanted this meeting with me in a hurry. So it was clear that something important and sudden had happened."

"Yes, indeed. But the letter was written in the afternoon, and much has happened since then. If Colonel Emsworth had not thrown me out — "

"Thrown you out!"

"Well, yes. He is a hard and serious man, Colonel Emsworth. When he was in the army he was one of the hardest. I only put up with the colonel because of Godfrey."

I lit my pipe and sat back in my chair.

"Perhaps you will explain what you are talking about."

My client smiled a little.

"I began to think, Mr. Holmes, that you already knew everything without being told," said he. "But I will give you the facts. I hope to God that you will be able to tell me what they mean. I have been awake all night thinking about this problem. I really don't understand it.

"I joined the army in January 1901, just two years ago. Young Godfrey Emsworth had joined the same army group. This group is called a squadron. He was Colonel Emsworth's only son. Colonel Emsworth was a famous officer in the Crimean War. Godfrey had fighting blood in him so it is no surprise that he joined the army. There was not a better young soldier in our squadron. We formed a friendship. It is the kind of friendship you can have only when you live the same life, share the same problems and joys. He was my best friend—and that means a lot in the army. We fought side by side for a year. Then he was shot by a gun in a battle near Diamond Hill outside Pretoria. He was hurt but not killed. I got one letter from the hospital at Cape Town and one from Southampton. Since then, I've heard nothing—not one word. Mr. Holmes, he was my closest friend.

"Well, the war later ended and we all came back to England. I wrote to his father and asked where Godfrey was. No answer. I waited a bit and wrote again. This time I had a short reply. Godfrey had gone on a trip around the world, and he probably wouldn't return for a year. That was all.

"It wasn't enough Mr. Holmes. I didn't believe it. The whole story seemed so unnatural. He was a good boy, and he would not forget his best friend like that. I also knew that he was going to receive a lot of money from his father. However, he and his father did not get along very well. The old man was sometimes too cold and serious. Godfrey didn't like that. I decided that I wanted to learn the truth of the matter. But first I needed to take care of my own business after two years of being away. It is only this week that I have been able to look into Godfrey's case again. However, I don't intend to stop until I find the truth."

Mr. James M. Dodd was the kind of person whom it would be better to have as a friend than an enemy. His blue eyes and his face were serious as he spoke.

"Well, what have you done?" I asked.

"My first move was to go down to his home at Tuxbury Old Park near Bedford. I wanted to see the place for myself. So I wrote to his mother, and told her everything: Godfrey was my best friend; we had shared many interesting experiences in South Africa; I was going to be in Bedford soon; would I be able to visit? Her reply to me was quite friendly and she offered to let me stay for the night. So on Monday, I went down there.

"Tuxbury Old Hall is not easy to get to. It is five miles from anywhere. There was no carriage at the train station. I had to walk carrying my bag. It was nearly dark before I arrived. It is a great big house which sits among many trees. I think it was built over many years, from the Elizabethan to the Victorian Period. The inside was dark wood and old paintings. There was a sense of mystery. There was a butler, old Ralph, who seemed about the same age as the house. And there was the butler's wife, who might be older. She took care of Godfrey as a boy. She was his nurse. I heard Godfrey speak of her with warm feelings, almost like his mother. So I was drawn to this old woman. I also liked Godfrey's mother. She is a small, gentle lady. It was only the colonel himself whom I didn't like.

"He and I had a disagreement soon after I arrived. I thought about returning to the station but changed my mind. After all, I didn't want to play his game. I was shown straight into the study, and there I found him. A very big man with smoky skin and a long gray beard seated at his desk. He had a pointed red nose, like that of a large bird. He also had two angry gray eyes that looked hard at me. I could understand why Godfrey did not speak much about his father.

"'Well, sir,' said he in a strong voice. 'I would like to know the real reasons for your visit.'

"I answered that I had explained them in my letter to his wife.

"'Yes, yes, you said that you knew Godfrey in Africa. We don't know if this is true, however.'

"'I have his letters to me in my pocket.'

"'Please let me see them.'

"He looked at the two which I handed him, and then he gave them back.

"'Well, what then?' he asked.

"'I was best friends with your son Godfrey, sir. I wonder why he is suddenly so quiet. I wish to know what has happened to him.'

"'I believe, sir, that I wrote to you already and told you what happened to him. He has gone on a trip around the world. His health was bad after Africa. Both his mother and I believed that complete rest and a change were needed. Please explain that to any other friends who may be looking for Godfrey.'

"'Of course,' I answered. 'But perhaps you would kindly give me the name of the ship and the date he sailed. I'm sure I can reach him by letter.'

"This made the old man nervous. He closed his eyes for a moment and put his hands together. At last he looked up.

"'Many people, Mr. Dodd,' said he, 'would say you have bad manners.'

"'It is because of my love for your son, sir.'

"'I know. And I have already been fair to you. However, I must ask you to stop these questions. Every family has its own reasons for doing things. Sometimes, these reasons cannot be understood by outsiders. My wife is very interested to hear something of Godfrey's past from you. But please don't talk of the present or future. It would put us in a very difficult position.'

"So that was the end, Mr. Holmes. I could go no further. I had to accept his story and ask no more questions. However, I told myself that I would not stop until I learned the truth about my friend.

"That evening was not interesting. We ate dinner quietly, the three of us, in a dark, sad room. The lady asked me many questions about her son. But the old man did not say a word.

"After dinner, I tried to leave the table as soon as I could. I went to my room. It too was a large, dark, old room with very little in it. But after a year of sleeping on the African ground, Mr. Holmes, I didn't care very much. I walked to the window. I opened the curtains, and looked out into the garden. It was a fine, cold night with a bright half-moon.

"Then I sat down next to the fire, turned on the light and began to read a book. A short time later Ralph, the old butler, came in with some more wood for the fire.

"'I thought you might need this tonight, sir. The weather is very cold right now.'

"He stopped for a moment before leaving the room. When I turned around he was looking at me in a strange way.

"'Excuse me, sir, but I heard what you said about young Godfrey at dinner. You know, sir, that my wife was his nurse and I feel like his second father. It is natural for us to be interested. You say that he was a good soldier, sir?'

"'There was no one better in the squadron. He saved my life once from the Boer guns.'

"The old butler put his hands together.

"'Yes, sir, yes, that is young Godfrey. He was not afraid of danger. There's not a tree in the park, sir, that he has not climbed. Nothing could stop him. He was a fine boy—and oh, sir, he was a fine man.'

"I jumped to my feet.

"'What!' I cried. 'You say he *was*. You speak as if he were dead. What is all this mystery? What has happened to Godfrey Emsworth?'

"I held the old man by the shoulder, but he moved away.

"'I don't know what you mean, sir. Ask the master about Godfrey. He knows. It is not for me to say.'

"He was leaving the room, but I held his arm.

"'Listen,' I said. 'You are going to answer one question before you leave here. Is Godfrey dead?'

"He could not look in my eyes. He was afraid. The answer came slowly from his mouth. It was unexpected.

"'I wish to God he was dead!' he cried. He then pulled away from me and ran out of the room.

"You can be sure, Mr. Holmes, that I returned to my chair in a very unhappy mind. The old man's words seemed to mean only one thing. Clearly my poor friend had done something criminal. Or maybe he had hurt the honor of the family. His hard father had sent his son away to keep him from dishonor.

"It is true that Godfrey was rather careless. He would often do what others wanted. Probably he had been led by others to do something foolish.

"However, I felt it was my job to find him and help him. I began to think about doing that when, suddenly, I looked up and there was Godfrey standing before me."

My client said nothing for a moment or two.

"Please continue," I said. "Your problem seems quite unusual."

"He was outside the window, Mr. Holmes. His face was pressed against the glass. I told you that I looked out at the night. The curtains were partly open. His figure was between them. The window came down to the ground and I could see his whole body. But it was his face which I noticed. It was deadly pale — I have never seen a man so white. Perhaps dead people look like that. But our eyes met, and they were the eyes of a living man. He jumped back when he saw that I was looking at him. He disappeared into the darkness.

"There was something terrible about the man, Mr. Holmes. It wasn't just the face like white cheese in the darkness. There was something else, like fear, in his eyes. He was weak and afraid, not the strong young man I knew.

"But I had been a soldier in a dangerous war. I kept my nerve and acted quickly. I jumped to the window. It was a little difficult to open but a moment later I opened it. I passed through it into the garden. I ran down the path. I thought I was following him but I couldn't be sure.

"It was a long path and the light was not very good. But I thought I saw something moving ahead of me. I ran on and called his name. I came to the end of the path. There were several smaller paths going to various buildings. I stood there looking. Then I heard the sound of a door closing. It came from in front of me in the darkness. I was sure that it was Godfrey.

"There was nothing more I could do. I returned to my room but I couldn't sleep. I tried to understand what was happening. The next day I found the colonel to be a little friendlier. His wife told me of some interesting places to visit nearby. I took a chance and asked them if I might be able to spend one more night with them. The old man was not very happy with the idea but he finally said OK. I was sure that Godfrey was hiding nearby. I needed the day to find out where he was.

"The house was so large and had so many rooms that you could hide a small army inside it. If Godfrey was in the house it would be difficult to find him. But the door which I heard close was not in the house. It was outside in the garden. I must look there and see what I could find. This was not difficult because the old people were busy with their own matters inside the house.

"There were several small wooden buildings at the end of the garden. One of these was bigger than the others. It seemed big enough for a gardener or servant to live in. Could this be the place where I heard the door close? I came near it very slowly. I acted as though I was just looking at the trees and plants. Just then a small, bearded man in a black coat and hat came out of the door. He did not look at all like a gardener. He saw me and seemed very surprised.

"'Are you a visitor here?' he asked.

"I explained that I was a friend of Godfrey's.

"'It's too bad that he is away on his travels for I'm sure he would like to see me,' I continued.

"'Uh, yes. Quite,' he said, rather nervously. 'Surely you can visit him when he returns.' He walked away. But when I turned around a moment later, I could see him watching me from the trees.

"I had a good look at the garden house as I passed it. But the windows had heavy curtains over them. It seemed that nobody was inside. I knew that the little man was still watching me. I slowly continued my walk around the garden. I returned to the house and waited for night. When all was dark and quiet, I went out through the window and quietly walked to the mysterious house.

"I said that there were heavy curtains. However, a little light was breaking through one of them. I put my face to the window and tried to look in. I was able to see a little of the room. There was a bright light and a nice fire burning. I could also see the little man whom I had seen in the morning. He was smoking and reading a paper."

"What paper?" I asked.

My client seemed surprised at my question.

"Does it matter?" he asked.

"It is most important."

"I didn't really notice."

"Perhaps you noticed if it was a broad paper, like a daily, or the smaller kind, like a weekly."

"Well, you know, I believe it was a smaller one. It might have been the *Spectator*. However, I wasn't thinking about that. There was a second man seated with his back to the window. I'm sure it was Godfrey. I could not see his face but I knew his shoulders and arms. He seemed to be sadly looking at the fire. I stood there watching and thinking. Suddenly I felt a hand on my shoulder. It was Colonel Emsworth.

"'Come with me, sir!' he said in a low, angry voice. He walked in silence to the house and I followed him into my own bedroom. He picked up a paper with the train times on it.

"'There is a train to London at 8:30 a.m. You will take it,' he said. 'The taxi will be at the door at eight.'

"He was white with anger. I felt very foolish and tried to tell him I was sorry.

"'There is nothing to say,' he told me. 'You have acted very badly in this matter. You came here as a friend of Godfrey's, but you have become a spy. I have nothing more to tell you, except that I never want to see you again.'

"At this point, Mr. Holmes, I lost my control and spoke out.

"'I have seen your son, and I am sure that for some reason you are hiding him from the world. I have no idea why. But I tell you, Colonel Emsworth, that until I know that my friend is all right, I will not stop in my efforts to uncover this mystery. And I am not afraid of anything you can do or say to me.'

"The old man looked at me with hate in his eyes. I thought he would try to kill me. I said that he was a tall, strong man. I too am strong, but I must say that I was afraid. However, after a long angry look at me he turned and walked out of the room. This morning, I took the train back to London with the plan of coming directly here to see you."

Such was the problem which my visitor put before me. As the reader may notice there are not so many possible solutions. However, there were some facts which made it slightly difficult to solve. I now began to use my methods of thinking to find the solution.

"The servants," I asked; "how many were in the house?"

"To the best of my belief there were only the old butler and his wife. They live in a very simple manner."

"There was no servant, then, in the garden house?"

"None, unless the little man with the beard was one. He didn't appear to be a servant, however."

"That seems interesting. Did you notice if food was brought from the big house to the garden house?"

"As a matter of fact, I did see old Ralph carrying a basket down the path towards the garden house. I didn't think of food at the time."

"Did you speak with anyone else in the neighborhood?"

"Yes, I did. I spoke to the stationmaster and to the keeper of the small hotel in the town. I simply asked if they knew anything about my friend, Godfrey Emsworth. Both of them told me that he was on a trip around the world. He had come home from the war and then left again soon after. Everyone appears to believe that story."

"Did you tell anyone what you thought?"

"Nothing."

"That was wise. We must look into the matter. I will go back with you to Tuxbury Old Park."

"Today?"

At that moment, I was finishing the case which my friend Watson called the Abbey School. I was also working on a very important case with the ruler of Turkey. It was necessary to act quickly on that case. Therefore, I was not able to travel to Bedfordshire with Mr. James M. Dodd until the beginning of the next week. We drove together in a carriage to Euston Station. Along the way we stopped at the home of a man who came with us. He was well-known in his work and was someone I knew.

"This is an old friend," I said to Dodd. "It is possible that he will not be able to help us. However, it is also possible that he will help us very much. At this point I don't think I will say anything more."

The reader knows from reading Dr. Watson's stories of my cases that I don't talk about my thoughts during the case. I don't say much to anyone about the case directly. Dodd seemed a little surprised but said nothing. The three of us continued our ride. In the train I asked Dodd one more question which I wanted my friend to hear.

"You say that you saw your friend Godfrey's face very clearly in the window. You are quite sure it was him?"

"I have no doubt. His nose was pressed against the glass. The light was shining on him."

"It could not have been someone else who looked like him?"

"No, no, it was him."

"But you say he was changed?"

"Only in color. His face was, well, it was white like the underside of a fish. There was no color."

"Was his face equally white all over?"

"I think not. It was only the upper part that I saw clearly."

"Did you call to him?"

"I was too surprised and afraid at that moment. Then I ran after him as I told you."

My case was almost completed. There was only one small part needed to finish it. We finally arrived at the large house after a long drive from the station. It was Ralph, the old butler, who met us. I asked my well-known friend to stay in the carriage until we needed him. Ralph was a little old man who wore the usual clothes of a butler. He was also wearing a pair of gloves. When he saw us, he took the gloves off and laid them on a table in the hallway. My sense of smell is quite good, as Watson has written. I smelled something unusual there in the hallway. As we passed the table I dropped my hat onto the floor. I then put my nose quite close to the gloves as I reached for the hat. Yes, the strange smell came from the gloves. My case was now complete. Ah, I wish it wasn't necessary to tell my own story. Now the reader will probably guess the solution to the case.

Colonel Emsworth arrived quickly after Ralph told him of our arrival. We heard his quick, heavy step in the hall. The door was opened and he rushed in with a very angry look on his face. He held our business cards in his hand. He tore them up and threw them on the floor.

"I told you never to show your damned face in this house again! If you ever do this again, I will kill you! By God, I will! As to you sir," he said turning to me, "I will tell you the same thing. Leave at once and never come back here. I have no use for you in this house."

"I cannot leave here," said my client, "until I hear from Godfrey's own mouth that he is free to go."

The colonel rang a bell.

"Ralph," he said, "telephone the police at once. Tell them there are criminals in the house."

"One moment," said I. "You must know, Mr. Dodd, that Colonel Emsworth has the right to do this. It is against the law for us to be in his house if he doesn't want us here. However, he should know that your actions are taken for the good of his son. Perhaps, if I could speak with the colonel for five minutes, alone, then he would change his mind."

"I do not change my mind so easily," said the old army man. "Ralph, do what I have told you. What are you waiting for? Call the police!"

"No, he won't," I said, putting my back to the door. "If the police come then your problems will become greater. The truth about your son will be known." I took out my notebook and wrote one word on a piece of paper. I handed it to Colonel Emsworth. "That is why we are here."

A look of great surprise came over the colonel's face. He suddenly seemed helpless.

"How did you know?" he said weakly, sitting down in his chair.

"It is my business to know things. That is my job."

"Well, if you want to see Godfrey, you may. I am forced to agree. Ralph, tell Mr. Godfrey and Mr. Kent that we will visit them in five minutes."

Five minutes later, we walked down the garden path to the mystery house at the end. The small man with a beard stood at the door. He too had a look of surprise on his face.

"This is all very sudden, Colonel Emsworth," said he. "This will cause a problem for our plans."

"I'm sorry, Mr. Kent. I have no choice. Can Godfrey see us?"

"Yes, he is waiting inside." He turned and took us into a large, plain room. A man was standing with his back to the fire. My client saw him and ran forward to shake his hand.

"Why, Godfrey, my old friend, it is you!"

But Godfrey put up his hand to stop him.

"Don't touch me, Jimmy. Please stay back. Yes, look at me! I'm not the good-looking Godfrey Emsworth of B Squadron, am I?"

His appearance was very terrible indeed. It was possible to see that he had been a good-looking young man. His skin was browned from the African sun. However, there were areas of white skin all over his face and arms.

"This is why I have no visitors," said he. "I'm glad you're here, Jimmy, but I wish you hadn't brought your friend. Perhaps there is a good reason for it."

"I wanted to be sure that all was well with you, Godfrey. I saw you that night when you looked into my window. I could not rest until the matter was cleared."

"Old Ralph told me you were there. I wanted to have a look at you. I didn't want you to see me. When I heard your window open, I had to run back here."

"But tell me, please, what is the matter?"

"Well, it's not a long story to tell," said he, lighting a cigarette. "You remember that morning fight at Buffelsspruit, near Pretoria, on the Eastern railway line? You heard I was shot?"

"Yes, I heard that but I didn't hear anything else."

"Three of us became separated from the others. It was very rocky and hard country. There was Simpson, Anderson, and me. The Boers surprised us. The other two were killed. I was shot in the shoulder. I stayed on my horse, however. He ran several kilometers before I fell off him.

"It was night when I woke up. I was in great pain and very weak. To my surprise there was a house near me. It was a big house with many windows. It was deadly cold. You remember the kind of terrible cold that came in the evening. Well, my only chance to live was to get to the warm house. Somehow, I reached the house. I can hardly remember how. There was nobody inside. I entered a large room with several beds. I fell on one of the beds and covered myself with the cloth. In a moment I was sleeping deeply.

"It was morning when I woke up again. However, I realized that something there was terribly wrong. The African sun came into the room and I could see everything clearly. In front of me was a very, very small man with a large head. He spoke to me quickly in Dutch. He had the hands of an animal. Behind him was a group of strange-looking people who seemed to enjoy watching us. But as I looked at them I became very afraid. Not one of them was usual. Each one was sick or changed in some terrible way. Many of them were laughing.

"None of them could speak English. The scene became dangerous when the strange man with the large head got angry. He made many strange sounds. Then he touched me with his terrible hands and tried to pull me from the bed. There was also blood coming from my shoulder. The little man was as strong as a horse. By good chance, an older man then walked into the room. He was clearly the leader. He said a few words in Dutch and the little man let me go. Then he looked at me in great surprise.

"'My God, how did you come here?' he asked in English. 'Wait a minute! I see that you are hurt and tired. I am a doctor and I'll try to help you. But, man! you are in greater danger here than you were in battle. You are in a hospital for lepers. And you have slept in a leper's bed.'

"'Do I need to tell you more, Jimmie? Because of the battle these poor people were moved from the hospital. That is when I got there. Then, as the British army passed, they were moved back into the hospital by their doctor. That doctor believed that he was safe from leprosy. But he said that he would never sleep in a leper's bed. He put me in a room alone, cared for me, then sent me to the hospital in Pretoria.

"So now you understand my terrible secret. I hoped that I would not become sick. But soon after I came home, the signs of illness began to appear on my face. What could I do? I was in this lonely house. We had two servants whom we trust. There was a garden house where I could live. Mr. Kent, a doctor, was prepared to stay with me. He promised never to tell anyone about my illness. Staying here alone seemed like a good idea. The other possibility was terrible — to live with other lepers and never see any of my friends or family again. But complete secrecy was necessary. It was important that no one around here know about me. Even you, Jimmie—even you must not know. Truly, I'm very surprised my father let you see me."

Colonel Emsworth pointed to me.

"This is the gentleman who forced me." He took out the piece of paper on which I had written the word "Leprosy." "I thought that if he knew that much already perhaps it was safer that he should know everything."

"And so it was," said I. "Perhaps some good will come from it. I understand that only you, Mr. Kent, have seen Godfrey. May I ask, sir, if you are

a specialist in leprosy?"

"I know what most doctors know about the illness," Mr. Kent replied.

"I have no doubt, sir, that you are a fine doctor. But I'm sure you will agree that a second opinion is valuable. You have not asked for another doctor's opinion because of the need for secrecy. Is that right?"

"That is so," said Colonel Emsworth.

"I understand the problem," I explained, "and I have brought a friend with me who may be trusted completely. He is a doctor who came with me to help. His name is Sir James Saunders."

When Mr. Kent heard the name there was a look of wonder on his face.

"It will be a very great honor," said Kent.

"Then I will ask Sir James to come. He is at present in the carriage outside. Meanwhile, Colonel Emsworth, perhaps the rest of us can gather in your study where I may explain my case."

It is here that I miss having Watson to tell my stories. He is able to use questions and surprises which make my detective work seem more interesting. When I tell my own story I am not able to do that.

Anyway, I talked to that small group, including Mrs. Emsworth, in the study.

"In my work," I said, "I begin with a single rule. If something is impossible then I throw it out. That leaves only the possible as the truth. There may be several possibilities, of course. I try test after test to see which of them is the most likely. In this case I could find only three reasons for Godfrey to be kept secretly in his father's house. One, that he was hiding from a crime. The second that he was mad and that he didn't want to be put in a hospital for madmen. And the third, that he had some serious illness. I could think of no other possibility. I then had to consider each one.

"There were no unsolved crimes reported in this area. I was sure of that. If there was a crime still undiscovered, then the family would send the young man away rather than keep him here.

"Madness was more likely. There was a second person in the garden house who might be the madman's keeper. This keeper always locked the door when he came out. On the other hand, the young man wasn't locked in all the time. He was able to go outside and have a look at his visiting friend. You will remember, Mr. Dodd, that I asked you several questions. I asked about the newspaper Mr. Kent was reading. If it had been the *Lancet* or the *British Medical Journal* it would have helped me. In England it is within the law to keep a madman at home — as long as there is a doctor to watch him. Why, then, all this desire for secrecy? Once again I could not fit the story to the facts.

"There remained the third possibility. Everything seemed to fit. Leprosy is not unusual in South Africa. Somehow this young man might have gotten the illness. His family would be in a difficult position because they would not want to send him away. Great secrecy would be needed so that nobody outside the family would know. A doctor, well paid, could easily be found to care for the sick person. And there is no reason why the leper could not be free after dark. Blanched skin is a usual result of the sickness. Yes, I felt sure that this was a case of leprosy. When I arrived here I noticed that Ralph was wearing gloves. He used these to carry the food to and from the garden house. I noticed that the gloves had the smell of a cleaning material. At that point I was sure. I wrote a single word on a paper, sir, to show you that I could be trusted."

I was finishing this little talk about the case when the door opened. My friend, the famous doctor, walked in. Instead of a serious look there was a warmth in his eyes. He walked up to Colonel Emsworth and took him by the hand.

"It is usually my job to bring bad news to the family," said he. "But this time the news is more welcome. It is not leprosy."

"What?"

"It looks exactly like leprosy but it is not. The name of the illness is ichthyosis. I believe we can make him well again. I am sure this young man has suffered terribly in his thoughts. In his mind, perhaps, he believed that he had the illness. This belief then caused signs of the illness on his body. Anyway, I believe — oh, look, the lady has passed out! I think that Mr. Kent should stay with her until she recovers from her joyful surprise."

20

The Adventure of Shoscombe Old Place

ショスコム荘

読み始める前に

The Adventure of Shoscombe Old Place ショスコム荘

56の短編のうち最後に発表された
1927年4月号のストランド・マガジン初出
1927年発行の「シャーロック・ホームズの事件簿」に収録された

［主な登場人物］

Sherlock Holmes シャーロック・ホームズ 世界的に有名な私立探偵。優れた観察眼と推理力を有する。ロンドンのベーカー街221Bに下宿している。

Watson ジョン・H・ワトソン 医師。ホームズの相棒でこの物語の語り手。ベーカー街221Bでホームズと同居している。

Sir Robert Norberton ロバート・ノーバートン卿 元騎手。ショスコム荘に住んでいる。

John Mason ジョン・メイソン 調教師長。雇い主のロバート卿が発狂したと、ホームズのもとを訪れる。

Lady Beatrice Falder ビアトリス・フォルダー夫人 ロバート卿の妹。ショスコム荘の所有者。

Josiah Barnes ジョサイア・バーンズ 宿屋「グリーン・ドラゴン」の主人。ロバート卿から妹のスパニエル犬をもらう。

Stephens スティーブンズ 執事。

Carrie Evans キャリー・エヴァンス フォルダー夫人のメイド。

［あらすじ］

雇い主のサー・ロバート・ノーバートンが発狂したと、ジョン・メイソンがホームズに依頼に来た。サー・ロバートは名馬を所有し、すべての金をこの馬につぎ込んでいた。妹ビアトリスといさかいがあったらしく、妹は愛していた馬への興味を失い、さらに愛犬を勝手に人に譲られてしまう。またサー・ロバートは真夜中に納骨堂に出入りしているのを執事に目撃されていた。

［総単語数］5,669語

The Adventure of Shoscombe Old Place

Sherlock Holmes had been looking for a long time into a microscope. Now he stood up and looked at me smiling.

"It is glue, Watson," said he. "No doubt about it, glue. Have a look at these various objects in the field."

I looked into the eyepiece.

"Those hairs are pieces of cloth from a coat. The gray pieces are earth. And those brown pieces in the center are surely glue."

"Well," I said, laughing, "I believe you. Is it important?"

"I believe it is," he answered. "In the St. Pancras case you may remember that a hat was found beside the dead policeman. The man who is believed guilty says that it is not his hat. But he is a picture-maker who always works with glue."

"Is it one of your cases?"

"No. My friend Merivale, of Scotland Yard, asked me to look into the case. A while ago, I used the microscope to solve a crime about money. They now think the microscope is useful." He looked at his watch. "I had a new client calling, but he is late. By the way, Watson, do you know anything about horse-racing?"

"I ought to. I lose a lot of money at the races."

"Then I'll make you my 'Racing Guide.' What about Sir Robert Norberton? Does that name mean anything to you?"

"Well, I believe so. He lives at Shoscombe Old Place. I know it well because I spent the summer there once. Norberton and you nearly met each other."

"How was that?"

"It was when he had a fight with Sam Brewer, the well-known Jewish, Curzon Street money-man, on Newmarket Heath. He nearly killed the man."

"Ah, he sounds interesting! Does he often fight with people?"

"Well, they say he is a little dangerous. He is a great rider of horses—he finished second in the Grand National a few years ago. He is one of those men who was born in the wrong century. He should have lived back in the days of the Regency—a boxer, a sportsman, a rider, a lover of fair ladies. They also say he is a very strange character."

"Excellent, Watson! That gives me a good idea of the man. I seem to know him. Now, can you give me some idea of Shoscombe Old Place?"

"Only that it is in the center of Shoscombe Park. The famous horse training center is there."

"And the head trainer," said Holmes, "is John Mason. You should not be surprised by what I know, Watson, for this is a letter from him which I received. But tell me more about Shoscombe. You seem to be an expert."

"There are the Shoscombe dogs, called spaniels," said I. "You hear of them at every dog show. They are the most expensive type of dogs in England. They are the specialty of the lady of Shoscombe Old Place."

"Sir Robert Norberton's wife, I suppose!"

"No, Sir Robert never married. He lives with his sister, Lady Beatrice Falder. Her husband died some years ago."

"You mean they live together?"

"No, no. The estate belonged to her late husband, Sir James. Norberton owns nothing there. When the lady dies, the estate goes back to Sir James' brother. Meantime, she receives rent from those who live on the estate."

"And brother Robert, I suppose, spends this rent money?"

"That's about it. He is a devil of a fellow. It must be difficult for his sister. Yet I have heard that she loves her brother and would do anything for him. What is the problem at Shoscombe?"

"Ah, that is what I want to know. And here, I believe, is the man who can tell us."

The door had opened and the servant showed in a man. He was tall and strong. He had the appearance of a man who has control over horses and boys. Mr. John Mason had many of both in his work. He said hello and seated himself upon the chair in front of Holmes.

"You got my note, Mr. Holmes?"

"Yes, but it explained nothing."

"It was too difficult a situation for me to write down on paper. It was only face to face that I could do it."

"Well, please tell us then."

"First of all, Mr. Holmes, I believe that the man I work for, Sir Robert, has gone mad."

Holmes raised his eyes. "This is Baker Street, not Harley Street," said he. "But why do you say so?"

"Well, sir, when a man does one strange thing, or two strange things, there may be a meaning to it. But when everything he does is strange, then you begin to wonder. I believe Shoscombe Prince and the Derby have changed him."

"Is Shoscombe Prince the name of the horse you will run in the Derby?"

"Yes, the best in England, Mr. Holmes. And I should know. Now, I'll be plain with you, for I know you are gentlemen of honor. Sir Robert must win this Derby. He has spent all his money and has no more. Every cent he has raised or borrowed is on this horse. This is his last chance. And the betting chances, called odds, are good too! The odds are now about 40–1; but they were about 100–1."

"But how can the odds be so high if the horse is so good?"

"That's because the public doesn't know how good this horse is. Sir Robert has been too intelligent for the bettors. He puts the Prince's half-brother out on the track for training. The two horses look the same. You can't tell the difference. But Prince is faster than the other. Sir Robert thinks of nothing but the horse and the race. His whole life is on it. He owes money to the Jews. If the Prince loses the race, Sir Robert is finished."

"It sounds like a difficult situation. But what about the madness?"

"Well, you only have to look at him. I don't believe he sleeps at night. He is at the stables at all hours. His eyes are wild. It has been too much for his nerves. Then there is his manner towards Lady Beatrice!"

"Ah! What is that?"

"They have been the best of friends. They had the same tastes. She loved horses as much as he did. Every day at the same hour she would drive down to see them. Above all, she loved the Prince. He would raise his ears when he heard the wheels on the road. Then he would run out to the carriage for his piece of sugar. But that's all over now."

"Why?"

"Well, she seems to have lost all interest in the horses. For a week now she has driven past the stables without even saying 'Good-morning!'"

"You think there has been a fight?"

"Yes, and a bad one too. Why else would he give away her favorite spaniel? She loved that dog. He gave it to old Barnes a few days ago.

He runs the Green Dragon Inn, three miles away, at Crendall."

"That does seem rather strange."

"She also has a weak heart and is ill. Her brother used to spend about two hours every evening with her in her room. She has been a good friend to him. But now he never goes near her. And it makes her very sad. She is unhappy, and she is drinking a lot—like a fish, Mr. Holmes."

"Did she drink before this disagreement?"

"Well, a little. But now it is often a whole bottle in one evening. This is what Stephens, the butler, told me. It's all changed, Mr. Holmes, and there is something very wrong about it. I'd also like to know why the master goes down to the old church graveyard at night. And who is the man that meets him there?"

Holmes put his hands together.

"Go on, Mr. Mason. This sounds more and more interesting."

"It was the butler who saw him go. It was twelve o'clock at night and raining hard. So the next night I was up at the house and, sure enough, the master was off again. Stephens and I went after him. We were nervous because we didn't want him to see us. He can become very angry and is a good fighter with his hands. But we were able to follow him at a distance. He was going to the grave. There was a man waiting for him there."

"What about this grave?"

"Well, sir, there is an old, small church in the park. It is so old that nobody knows the date it was built. And under the church floor there is a room, a crypt, where the dead are put. Most people believe this crypt is a dangerous place. By day, it is dark, wet, and lonely. By night, few of us would have the nerve to go near it. But the master is not afraid. He never feared anything in his life. But what is he doing there in the night time?"

"Wait a moment!" said Holmes. "You say there is another man there. It must be one of your own stablemen, or someone from the house! Surely you can find out who it is and question him?"

"It's no one I know."

"How can you say that?"

"Because I have seen him, Mr. Holmes. It was on that second night. Sir Robert turned and passed us—me and Stephens—as we were hiding behind the trees. He didn't see us. But we could hear the other man moving around near us. We were not afraid of him. So when Sir Robert was gone we acted as though we were just taking a walk under the moon. We walked up behind him and said, 'Hello there! Who are you?' I guess he didn't hear us coming. He quickly turned around and looked at us like he had seen a dead man. He shouted loudly and ran away as fast as he could into the darkness. And he was fast, I'll tell you. In a minute he was out of sight and hearing. Who he was, or what he was, we still don't know."

"But you saw him clearly in the moonlight?"

"Yes, if I saw him again I would know him. He's not a nice-looking man. What could he be doing with Sir Robert?"

Holmes sat for some time lost in thought.

"Who keeps Lady Beatrice Falder company?" he asked at last.

"There is her maid. Her name is Carrie Evans. She has been with her this five years."

"And she cares for her, no doubt?"

Mr. Mason moved nervously in his chair.

"She cares, yes," he answered. "But I won't say for whom."

"Ah!" said Holmes.

"I can't tell you more than that right now."

"I quite understand, Mr. Mason. Of course, the situation is clear enough. From what Dr. Watson tells me of Sir Robert I can realize that no woman is safe from him. Don't you think that is why the brother and sister disagree?"

"Well, this relationship has been clear for a long time."

"But Lady Beatrice may not have seen it before. Let us suppose that she suddenly found out. She wants to make the woman go away. Her brother will not allow it. The sick lady, with her weak heart, has no power to let the woman go. The hated maid is still tied to her. The lady decides to stop speaking to anyone and begins to drink. Sir Robert, in his anger, takes her spaniel away from her. Does this make sense?"

"Well, yes, as far as it goes."

"Quite! As far as it goes. How does this fit in with the night visits to the old crypt? We can't fit that into our story, can we?"

"No, sir, and there is something more that I can't understand. Why should Sir Robert want to uncover a dead body?"

Holmes sat up quickly.

"We only found it out yesterday, after I had written to you. Yesterday Sir Robert went to London, so Stephens and I went down to the crypt. It was all in order, sir, except that in one corner there were parts of a human body."

"You told the police, I suppose?"

Our visitor smiled sadly.

"Well, sir, I think it would not much interest them. It was just the head and a few bones of a very old body. It may have been a thousand years old. But it wasn't there before. I'm sure of that, and so is Stephens. It was away in a corner and covered over with a board. But that corner had always been empty before."

"What did you do with it?"

"Well, we just left it there."

"That was wise. You say Sir Robert was away yesterday. Has he returned?"

"We expect him back today."

"When did Sir Robert give away his sister's dog?"

"It was just a week ago today. The dog was barking loudly outside the house. Sir Robert was angry that morning. He picked up the dog. I thought he was going to kill it. Then he gave it to Sandy Bain. He's a man who rides race horses. Sir Robert told Bain to take the dog to old Barnes at the Green Dragon, for he never wanted to see the dog again."

Holmes sat for some time in quiet thought. He had lit the oldest and smelliest of his pipes.

"I am not sure yet what you want me to do in this matter, Mr. Mason," he said at last. "Can't you make it clearer?"

"Perhaps this will make it clearer, Mr. Holmes," said our visitor.

He took a paper from his pocket, and carefully uncovered a small piece of bone.

Holmes looked at the piece with interest.

"Where did you get it?"

"There is a furnace under the house below Lady Beatrice's room. It has been off for some time. But Sir Robert was cold and had the furnace turned on again.

"Harvey runs it—he's one of the boys who works for me. This morning he came to me with this. He found it while cleaning the burned wood. He didn't like the look of it."

"Nor do I," said Holmes. "What do you think it is, Watson?

It was burned black, but there was no question as to its importance.

"It's a bone from the upper part of a human leg," said I.

"Exactly!" Holmes had become very serious. "When does this boy take care of the furnace?"

"He makes it up every evening and then leaves it."

"Then, anyone could visit the furnace during the night?"

"Yes, sir."

"Can you enter it from outside?"

"There is one door from outside. There is another which goes up to a hall next to Lady Beatrice's room."

"These are deep waters, Mr. Mason; deep and rather dangerous. You say that Sir Robert was not at home last night?"

"No, sir."

"Then, he did not burn the bones."

"That's true, sir."

"What is the name of that inn you talked of?"

"The Green Dragon."

"Is there good fishing in that part of Berkshire?" The look on the trainer's face was one of surprise. He probably thought Holmes was mad.

"Well, sir, I've heard there is good trout fishing in the small river. And there is good pike fishing in the Hall Lake."

"That's good enough. Watson and I are famous fishermen, aren't we Watson? You may find us in the future at the Green Dragon. We should reach there by tonight. Please don't think me unkind, Mr. Mason, but I think it is best if we don't see you there. We can reach one another by letter. When I have a clearer idea of the matter we will talk again."

And so, on a bright May evening, Holmes and I found ourselves on a train in a first-class carriage. We were going to the very little station of Shoscombe. We had bags and lots of things for fishing. From the station, a short drive took us to the Green Dragon Inn. There, the owner, Josiah Barnes, asked us about our fishing plans.

"What about the Hall Lake and the chance of catching some pike?" asked Holmes.

The face of the innkeeper became cloudy.

"I don't think so, sir. You might find yourself in the water before you were through."

"Why is that?"

"It's Sir Robert, sir. He's very afraid of racing people who spy on his horses. The lake is very near the stables. He wouldn't want to see you so close."

"I've heard he has a horse entered in the Derby."

"Yes, and a good one too. He carries all our money for the race, and all Sir Robert's too. By the way"—he looked at us with thoughtful eyes—"are you two interested in the race?"

"No, indeed. We are just two tired Londoners who badly need some good Berkshire air."

"Well, you are in the right place for that. There is a lot of good air here. But remember what I told you about Sir Robert. He's the kind of man who strikes first then speaks later. Keep clear of the park."

"Surely, Mr. Barnes! We shall. By the way, that was a most beautiful spaniel that was barking in the hall."

"It most surely is. That is the real Shoscombe spaniel. There is no finer dog in England."

"I like dogs very much myself," said Holmes. "Now, if I may ask you, what would a dog like that cost?"

"More than I could pay, sir. It was Sir Robert himself who gave me this one. That's why I have to keep it tied. It would run right away if I took off the tie."

The innkeeper took us to our room and left us. "We are getting some information, Watson," said Holmes. "It's not an easy case to understand yet, but we may know much more in a day or two. By the way, Sir Robert is still in London, I hear. We might enter the estate tonight without fear of being attacked. There are one or two things which I'd like to see about."

"Have you any ideas, Holmes?"

"Only that something happened a week or so ago which has cut deep into the life of the Shoscombe house. What is that something? We can only guess from what Mason has told us. It is an interesting situation. Let us consider the facts. The brother no longer visits the sick sister he loves so much. He gives away her favorite dog. Her dog, Watson! Does that mean nothing to you?"

"Nothing but the brother's angry character."

"Well, it might be that. Or—well, there is another possibility. Now, let's look at the situation since the time that the fight, if there was a fight, began. The lady stays in her room and changes her actions. She is never seen except when she drives out with her maid. She doesn't stop at the stables to see her favorite horse. And she has begun to drink. That covers the case, does it not?"

"Except for the business in the crypt."

"That is another line of thought. We must separate the two. Line A, which is about Lady Beatrice, seems serious, doesn't it?"

"I don't understand it."

"Well, let's take up line B, which is about Sir Robert. He is mad about winning the Derby. He is in the hands of the Jews. At any moment they may sell his racing stables and take away his estate. He is an intelligent man, but he has big problems. His money comes from his sister. His sister's maid is having a relationship with him. So far so good, no?"

"But the crypt?"

"Ah, yes, the crypt! Let us suppose, Watson—and this may or may not be true—that Sir Robert has killed his sister."

"My dear Holmes, it is not possible!"

"Perhaps not, Watson. Sir Robert is a man of honor. But even good men sometimes go bad. Anyway, let us continue this line of thought.

He could not leave the country until he made enough money. He can only make enough money by winning the Derby with Shoscombe Prince. Therefore, he must stay here. To do this he must find a place to put the body. He would also have to find a woman who looks like his sister. With the maid as his friend, that would be possible. The woman's body might be taken to the crypt. It would be safe there because most people are afraid of the place. Then it might be secretly destroyed at night in the furnace. What do you think, Watson?"

"Well, it is all possible if you accept the terrible fact of the sister's death."

"I think there is a small test which we may try tomorrow, Watson. In the meantime, we must keep up our characters as fishermen. I think we should have a glass of wine with our innkeeper and talk about fishing. We may be able to get some more information from him."

In the morning Holmes found that we had forgotten a fishing device, called the spoon-jack. He said we couldn't fish without it. Instead, we went for a walk at about eleven o'clock. We also asked if we could bring the black spaniel with us.

"This is the place," said Holmes as we came to a fence with two high gates. The name Shoscombe was written above them. "About midday, Mr. Barnes tells me, the old lady takes a drive. The carriage must slow down while the gates are opened. When it comes through, I want you, Watson, to stop the driver with some question. Never mind me. I shall hide behind this holly tree and see what I can see."

It was not a long wait. Within fifteen minutes, we saw the big yellow open carriage coming down the long street. It was pulled by two beautiful horses. Holmes stayed behind the trees with the dog. I stood on the road. A man ran out and opened the gates.

The carriage slowed to a walk. I was able to get a good look at the ladies in the carriage. A young woman with golden hair sat on the left.

At her right was an older woman with a rounded back. Her face and shoulders were nearly covered with a coat. When the horses reached the main road I held up my hand for the driver to stop. He did. I then asked if Sir Robert was at Shoscombe Old Place.

At the same moment Holmes stepped out. He let go of the spaniel. With a joyous bark the dog ran forward to the carriage and jumped upon the step. Then in a moment, its happiness turned to anger. It began to bark loudly at the old lady in the black dress above it.

"Drive on! Drive on!" shouted a voice. The carriage driver struck the horses and rode away. We were left standing on the road.

"Well, Watson, I think that is clear enough," said Holmes as he tied up the spaniel. "The dog thought the woman was his owner, and he found it was a stranger. Dogs aren't wrong about those things."

"But it was the voice of a man!" I cried.

"Exactly! We have added another fact to our case, Watson. We must still be careful, though."

My friend seemed to have no further plans for the day. We were able to do a little trout fishing in the small river. The result was that we ate trout that night for dinner. After eating, Holmes seemed interested again in the case. Once more we found ourselves upon the same road outside the estate gates. A tall, dark figure was waiting for us. It was the man we met in London, Mr. John Mason, the trainer.

"Good evening, gentlemen," said he. "I got your note, Mr. Holmes. Sir Robert has not returned yet, but I hear that he is expected tonight."

"How far is this crypt from the house?" asked Holmes.

"About half a kilometer."

"Then I think we don't have to worry about Sir Robert."

"I can't do that, Mr. Holmes. The moment he arrives he will want to ask me about the latest news of Shoscombe Prince."

"I see! In that case we must work without you, Mr. Mason. You can show us the crypt and then leave us."

The night was very dark, without a moon. We followed Mason until we came upon a dark building. It was the old chapel. We entered it through a large hole in the wall. Our guide, stepping on pieces of stone, led us to the corner of the building. There we found the steps down to the grave. Mason lit a fire so that we could see something. The sad, bad-smelling room was old, and the walls were falling down. I felt a little afraid myself. There were many stone coffins with dead people inside them. The coffins were placed one on top of the other from the floor to the top of the room. Holmes carried a lantern. He lit the lantern and we could see all around the crypt. We could read the writing on the coffins.

"You spoke of some bones, Mr. Mason. Could you show them to us before you go?"

"They are here in this corner." The trainer walked across the room then stood in complete surprise. "They are gone," said he.

"So I expected," said Holmes, laughing softly. "I believe the rest of the burned bones might be found in the furnace."

"But why would anyone want to burn the bones of a man who has been dead a thousand years?" asked John Mason.

"That is what we are here to find out," said Holmes. "We may have to look for a long time. We won't keep you any longer. I believe we'll have the answer before morning."

When John Mason left us, Holmes began to work. He looked very carefully at each coffin. There were many of them. One was a very, very old Saxon coffin in the center. Then there were a number of Norman Hugos and Odos. Finally, we reached Sir William and Sir Denis Falder of the eighteenth century. It was an hour or more before Holmes came to a coffin standing on end in front of the doorway. I heard him make a little sound, and I knew he had found something important. He was using a small looking-glass to study the coffin. He took another device from his coat which he then used to open the coffin. There was a loud sound as the top came off. We could see part of what was inside. However, at exactly that moment we had an unexpected surprise.

Someone was walking in the chapel above. It was the fast step of one who knew where he was going. A moment later there was light coming from the top of the steps. We could see the man holding a lantern. He was a terrible figure, very large, and angry looking. He had a large beard. His angry eyes looked around the crypt. He saw us.

"Who are you?" he shouted. "And what are you doing here?" Holmes did not answer so the man took several steps towards us. In his hand was a big, heavy stick. "Do you hear me?" he cried. "Who are you and what are you doing here?" He raised the stick in the air.

But Holmes was not afraid. He walked towards the man.

"I also have a question to ask you, Sir Robert," he said in a serious manner. "Who is this? And what is it doing here?"

He turned and took off the top of the coffin behind him. In the lantern's light I could see a body covered from top to bottom in white cloth. Only parts of the face, the nose and eyes, were uncovered. It was a terrible sight.

Sir Robert had stepped back weakly and was holding himself up against a wall.

"How did you know about this?" he cried. And then, with a little anger he asked, "What business is it of yours?"

"My name is Sherlock Holmes," said my friend. "Perhaps you know the name. In any case, my business is the same as any other good man—to follow the law. It seems to me that you have broken the law."

"Before God, Mr. Holmes, it's all right," said he. "It appears bad, I know, but I had to do this."

"I may believe you, but you will have to explain it to the police."

Sir Robert lifted his shoulders.

"Well, if it must be, it must be. Come up to the house, and you can judge for yourself about this matter."

Fifteen minutes later, we found ourselves in the gun-room of the old house. It was a nice room, and Sir Robert left us there for a few minutes. When he returned, he had two people with him; one, the young woman we had seen in the carriage; the other, a small thin-faced man. Both of them looked completely surprised to be there. Sir Robert did not have time to explain the situation to them.

"There," said Sir Robert, pointing with his hand, "are Mr. and Mrs. Norlett. Mrs. Norlett, under her own name of Evans, has for many years been my sister's maid. I brought them here because I want to explain the true situation to you. They are the two people on earth who know the truth of what I say."

"Is this necessary, Sir Robert? Have you thought about what you are doing?" cried the woman.

"As for me, I want no part of this," said her husband.

Sir Robert gave him an angry look. "It is for me to decide," said he. "Now, Mr. Holmes, listen to a plain statement of the facts.

"It is clear that you know a great deal about me already. Therefore, you probably know that I am running a horse in the Derby. Everything depends on my success. If I win, all is easy. If I lose — well, I don't dare think of that!"

"I understand the situation," said Holmes.

"All the money I have comes from my sister, Lady Beatrice. But it is well known that her interest in the estate is for her own life only. I have borrowed money from the Jews. I have always known that if my sister died then the Jews would take everything I have — my stables, my horses, everything. Well, Mr. Holmes, my sister did die just a week ago."

"And you told no one!"

"What could I do? I would be destroyed if they knew. I had to wait three weeks until the race. Her maid's husband—this man here—is an actor. I had the idea that he could act the part of my sister for that period. He only had to appear daily in the carriage. No one but the maid ever entered her room. It was not difficult to do. My sister died of a heart problem she had had for a long time."

"That will be for the doctors to decide."

"Her own doctor will tell you that this is true."

"Well, what did you do?"

"The body could not stay there. On the first night, Norlett and I carried it out to the old well house. It is never used. We were followed, however, by her spaniel who barked all night at her door. I felt that we had to put the dog somewhere else. We carried the body to the crypt. I do not feel that I have wronged the dead, Mr. Holmes."

"Your actions seem very wrong to me, Sir Robert."

"It is easy for you to say that," said he. "Perhaps you would feel differently if you were in my position. I couldn't just let all my hopes and dreams be destroyed without trying to save them. I thought that the crypt would be a worthy resting place for my dear sister. I put her in the coffin of a very old family member for a short time only. We opened that coffin, took out what was inside and placed her in it. We could not leave the old body on the ground so we decided to burn it in the furnace. There is my story, Mr. Holmes. Though how you know of it is still a surprise to me."

Holmes sat thinking for some time.

"There is one problem with your story, Sir Robert," he said at last. "Your bets on the race and your hope for the future would be good even if the estate was taken."

"No, the horse would be part of the estate. They don't care about my bets. They would probably take the horse out of the race. Unhappily, the man I must pay the most money to is my enemy — a man named Sam Brewer. I once beat him with a stick on Newmarket Heath. He hates me."

"Well, Sir Robert," said Holmes, getting up, "this matter must, of course, be brought to the police. It was my job to find the truth, and there I must leave it. As to the right and wrong of your actions, it is not for me to give an opinion. It is nearly midnight, Watson, and I think we ought to return to our inn."

It is known that this matter ended rather happily for Sir Robert. Shoscombe Prince did win the Derby. The owner won eighty-thousand pounds in bets, and the Jews did wait until the race was over. They were paid in full. There was enough money left over to take care of Sir Robert for life. The police were very easy on him. His only wrong was to wait so long to tell them of his sister's death. And so ends this strange case.

Word List

A

☐ **a ~ or two** 1～か2～, 2, 3の

☐ **aback** 熟 be taken aback（不意を突かれて）まごつく, 面くらう, びっくりする

☐ **abbey** 名 修道院

☐ **abduction** 名 誘拐, 拉致

☐ **Abe Slaney** エイブ・スレイニー《人名》

☐ **Aberdeen Shipping Company** 名 アバディーン汽船会社《社名》

☐ **Abergavenny murder** アバゲーブニーの殺人(事件)《ホームズが手がけた事件》

☐ **about** 熟 be about to まさに～しようとしている, ～するところだ be worried about（～のことで）心配している, ～が気になる[かかる] bring about 引き起こす care about ～を気に掛ける come about 起こる How about ～? ～はどうですか。～しませんか。look about あたりを見回す run about 走り回る speak about ～について話す walk about 歩き回る What about ～? ～についてあなたはどう思いますか。～はどうですか。worry about ～のことを心配する

☐ **above all** とりわけ, 何よりも

☐ **absence** 名 欠席, 欠如, 不在

☐ **absolutely** 副 完全に, 確実に

☐ **absurd** 形 常識に反した, 馬鹿げた

☐ **accent** 名 アクセント, 口調, 特徴

☐ **accept** 動 ①～を受け入れる ②～に同意する, ～を認める

☐ **accident** 名 ①(不慮の)事故, 災難 ②偶然

☐ **accompany** 動 ～についていく

☐ **according to** ～によれば[よると]

☐ **account** 名 報告, 説明, 記述 動 ①《– for ～》～を説明する, ～(の割合)を占める, ～の原因となる, ～の説明をする ②～を…とみなす

☐ **accuse** 動 ～を非難する《– + 人 + of》人を～(の理由)で告訴[非難]する

☐ **acid** 名 酸

☐ **acknowledge** 動 (～として・～を)認める

☐ **across** 熟 go across 横断する, 渡る jump across 飛び越える, 飛んで渡る run across 走って渡る walk across ～を歩いて渡る

☐ **act** 名 行為, 行い catch ～ in the act 人が(犯罪行為などを)している現場をおさえる[見つける] 動 ①行動する ②機能する ③～を演じる act in plays 劇に出演する

☐ **action** 熟 take action 行動を取る[起こす], 取り掛かる, 腰を上げる

☐ **active** 形 ①活動的な ②積極的な ③活動[作動]中の

☐ **Acton** 名 アクトン《人名》

☐ **actor** 名 俳優, 役者

☐ **actually** 副 実際に, 本当に, 実は

☐ **ad** 名 広告

☐ **add** 動 ～を(…に)加える, 足す

☐ **adder** 名 クサリヘビ, マムシ swamp adder 沼マムシ《架空のヘビ種》

☐ **addition** 名 付加, 追加, 添加 in addition 加えて, さらに

☐ **address** 名 住所, アドレス 動 ～にあて名を書く

☐ **Adelbert Gruner** アデルバート・グルーナー《人名》

☐ **Adler** 名 アドラー《人名》

☐ **admirable** 形 賞賛に値する, 見事な

☐ **admire** 動 ～に感心する, ～を賞賛する

☐ **advance** 動 進む, 進める, 進歩する[させる] 形 先行の be advanced in years 年を取っている

☐ **adventure** 名 冒険

☐ **advertisement** 名 広告, 宣伝

☐ **advice** 名 忠告, 助言, 意見

☐ **advise** 動 忠告する, 勧める

☐ **affair** 名 事柄, 事件

☐ **affect** 動 影響する

☐ **afraid** 熟 be afraid of ～を恐れる, ～を怖がる I'm afraid (that) 残念ながら～, 悪いけれど～

☐ **Africa** 名 アフリカ

☐ **African** 形 アフリカ(人)の 名 アフリカ人

☐ **after** 熟 after all やはり, 結局 after that その後 come after ～のあとを追う look after ～の世話をする, ～に気をつける run after ～を追いかける

☐ **aftertaste** 名 後味, 後口

☐ **afterward** 副 その後, のちに

☐ **afterwards** 副 その後, のちに

☐ **again and again** 何度も繰り返して, 再三再四

☐ **against** 熟 against the wall 壁を背にして be brought against 嫌疑[容疑]が晴れる work against ～に反する働きをする, ～に反対する

☐ **Agar** 名 アーガー《人名》

☐ **age** 熟 at the age of ～歳のときに

□ **agent** 名 ①代理人 ②代表者

□ **ago** 熟 long ago ずっと前に，昔

□ **agree with** （人）に同意する

□ **ah** 間《驚き・悲しみ・賞賛などを表して》ああ，やっぱり

□ **ahead** 熟 ahead of ～より先［前］に，～に先んじて get ahead 出世する get ahead of ～の先に出る，前方を行く，(相手)をしのぐ go ahead 先に行く，《許可を表す》どうぞ look ahead 先［将来］のことを考える on ahead 先に

□ **aid** 動 ～を援助する，～を助ける，～を手伝う

□ **air** 熟 open air 戸外，野外 up in the air 空中に

□ **air-gun** 名 空気銃

□ **alarm** 名 警報

□ **Aldergate** 名 アルダーゲート《地名》

□ **Alec Cunningham** アレック・カニンガム《人名》

□ **Alexandria** 名 アレキサンドリア《地名》

□ **Alexandrian** 形 アレキサンドリアの

□ **Alexis** 名 アレクシス《人名》

□ **Alice Morphy** アリス・モーフィー《人名》

□ **Alice Turner** アリス・ターナー《人名》

□ **alight** 動 降りる，飛び降りる 形 燃えて，(火が)灯って

□ **alike** 形 よく似ている

□ **all** 熟 above all 何よりも after all やはり，結局 all day 一日中，明けても暮れても all day long 一日中，終日 all one's life ずっと，生まれてから all over ～中で，全体に亘って，～の至る所で，全て終わって，もうだめで all right 大丈夫で，よろしい，申し分ない，わかった，承知した all round 全体において all the time ずっと，いつも，その間ずっと at all とにかく by all means なんとしても，ぜひとも first of all まず第一に for all ～にもかかわらず not at all 少しも～でない not ～ at all 少しも［全然］～ない once and for all これを最後にきっぱりと over it all 全体にわたって sit up all night 徹夜する That's all right. いいんですよ． with all ～がありながら with all one's heart 心から

□ **allow** 動 ①許す，《－…to～》…が～するのを可能にする，…に～させておく ②与える

□ **alone** 熟 leave ～ alone ～を1人に［そっと］しておく

□ **along** 熟 along the way 途中で，これまでに，この先 along with ～と一緒に bring along 持って行く［来る］ carry along 持ち運ぶ come

□ along ①一緒に来る，ついて来る ②やって来る，現れる ③うまくいく，よくなる，できあがる get along やっていく，はかどる go along ～に沿って行く，(人)について行く look along ～に沿って見る move along ～に沿って動く run along おいとまする，立ち去る walk along (前へ)歩く，～に沿って歩く

□ **aloud** 副 大声で，(聞こえるように)声を出して

□ **alright** 形 ①大丈夫で，申し分ない ②ちゃんとした

□ **altar** 名 祭壇

□ **although** 接 ～だけれども，～にもかかわらず，たとえ～でも

□ **altogether** 副 まったく，全然，全部で

□ **amazement** 名 びっくりすること，驚愕

□ **amazing** 形 驚くべき，見事な

□ **America** 名 アメリカ《国名・大陸》

□ **American** 形 アメリカ(人)の 名 アメリカ人

□ **amongst** 前 ～の間に［を，で］

□ **amount** 名 ①量，額 ②《the－》合計 動 (総計～に)なる

□ **analyze** 動 分析する，解析する，細かく検討する

□ **and** 熟 and so そこで，それだから，それで and so on ～など，その他もろもろ and yet それなのに，それにもかかわらず

□ **Anderson** 名 アンダーソン《人名》

□ **anger** 名 怒り white with anger 怒りで白くなる

□ **angle** 名 ①角度 ②角

□ **angrily** 副 怒って，腹立たしげに

□ **angry** 熟 angry with ～に対して怒る，腹を立てる get angry 腹を立てる

□ **animal-hunter** 名 狩りをする人

□ **Anna** 名 ア(ン)ナ《人名》

□ **Anne** 名 アン《人名》

□ **Annie** 名 アニー《人名》

□ **another** 熟 one another お互い one ～ or another ～かまたはほかの～，どこかの～ yet another さらにもう一つの

□ **answer** 熟 in answer to ～に応じて，～に答えて

□ **answerable** 形 (～に対して)責任のある

□ **anthropoid** 名 類人猿

□ **any** 熟 at any moment 今すぐにも at any rate とにかく if any もしあれば，あったとしても in any case とにかく in any way 決して，

多少なりとも **not in any way** 少しも［全く］〜ない **not 〜 any longer** もはや〜でない［〜しない］**than any other** ほかのどの〜よりも

□ **anybody** 代①《疑問文，条件節で》誰か ②《否定文で》誰も（〜ない）③《肯定文で》誰でも

□ **anyhow** 副①いずれにせよ，ともかく ②どんな方法でも

□ **anyone** 代①《疑問文・条件節で》誰か ②《否定文で》誰も（〜ない）③《肯定文で》誰でも 副《通例否定文，疑問文で》今はもう，これ以上，これから

□ **anything else** ほかの何か

□ **anyway** 副①いずれにせよ，ともかく ②どんな方法でも

□ **anywhere** 副どこかへ［に］，どこにも［へも］，どこにでも

□ **apart** 副①ばらばらに，離れて ②別にして，それだけで **apart from** 〜は別として

□ **apartment** 名アパート

□ **apologize** 動謝る，わびる

□ **appear** 動①現れる，見えてくる ②（〜のように）見える，〜らしい **appear to** 〜するように見える

□ **appearance** 名①現れること，出現 ②外見，印象 **in appearance** 外見は

□ **apply** 動①申し込む，志願する ②あてはまる ③〜に適用する **apply in person** 自分で直接申し込む

□ **appointment** 名（会合などの）約束，予約 **have an appointment with** 〜と約束をする

□ **approach** 動接近する

□ **Arat** 名アラット《地図上に読めた言葉》

□ **Archie** 名アーチー《人名》

□ **argue** 動①〜を論じる，議論する ②〜と主張する

□ **argument** 名①論争，口論 ②論拠，理由

□ **armchair** 名ひじ掛けいす，ひじ置き

□ **army** 名軍隊，《the−》陸軍

□ **around** 熟 **look around** まわりを見回す **move around** あちこち移動する **run around** 走り回る **rush around** 走り回る **show 〜 around** 〜を案内して回る **turn around** 振り向く，向きを変える，方向転換する **walk around** 歩き回る，ぶらぶら歩く

□ **arrange** 動①並べる，整える ②取り決める ③準備する，手はずを整える

□ **arrangement** 名①準備，手配 ②取り決め，協定 ③整頓

□ **arrest** 動逮捕する 名逮捕

□ **arrival** 名①到着 ②到達

□ **arrive at** 〜に着く

□ **arrive in** 〜に着く

□ **art** 熟 **works of art** 芸術作品

□ **Arthur** 名アーサー《人名》

□ **article** 名（新聞・雑誌などの）記事

□ **artist** 名芸術家

□ **artwork** 名アートワーク，芸術作品

□ **as** 熟 **as a matter of fact** 実際は，実のところ **as 〜 as one can** できる限り〜 **as 〜 as possible** できるだけ **as best one can** 精一杯，できるだけ **as far as** 〜と同じくらい遠く，〜まで，〜する限り（では）**as far as one can** できるだけ **as for** 〜に関しては，〜はどうかと言うと **as good as** 〜も同然で，ほとんど〜 **as if** あたかも〜のように，まるで〜みたいに **as it happens** たまたま，偶然にも **as long as** 〜する以上は，〜である限りは **as much as** 〜と同じだけ **as soon as** 〜するとすぐ，〜するや否や **as such** 〜など **as though** あたかも〜のように，まるで〜みたいに **as to** 〜に関しては，〜については，〜に応じて **as usual** いつものように，相変わらず **as well** なお，その上，同様に **as well as** 〜と同様に **as you know** ご存知のとおり **as you wish** 望み通りに **just as**（ちょうど）であろうとおり **see 〜 as …** 〜を…と考える **so as to** 〜するように，〜するため **so far as** 〜に関しては，〜する限り **so long as** 〜する限りは **such as** たとえば〜，〜のような **such 〜 as …** …のような〜 **the same 〜 as …** …と同じ（ような）〜

□ **ash** 名①灰，燃えかす ②《複数形》遺骨，なきがら

□ **ashamed of**《be−》恥ずかしい，恥じている

□ **Asia** 名アジア

□ **aside** 副わきへ（に），離れて **throw aside** わきに投げ捨てる

□ **ask for help** 助けを頼む

□ **ask 〜 if** 〜かどうか尋ねる

□ **asleep** 形眠って（いる状態の）**fall asleep** 眠り込む，寝入る

□ **assistant** 名助手，補佐，店員

□ **assume** 動①〜と仮定する，〜を当然のことと思う ②〜を引き受ける

□ **assure** 動①〜を保障する，請け負う ②（人に）〜と確信をもって言う

□ **astonishment** 名驚き

□ **at** 熟 **at a distance** 少し離れて **at a time** 一

度に, 続けざまに **at all** とにかく **at any moment** 今すぐにも **at any rate** とにかく **at first** 最初は, 初めのうちは **at first sight** 一目見て **at home** 自宅で, 在宅して, くつろいで **at last** ついに, とうとう **at least** 少なくとも **at length** ついに, 長々と, 詳しく **at once** すぐに, 同時に **at present** 今のところ, 現在は, 目下 **at that moment** その時に, その瞬間に **at that time** その時 **at the age of** 〜歳のときに **at the end of** 〜の終わりに **at the moment** 今は **at the time** そのころ, 当時は **at this** これを見て, そこで(すぐに) **at this point** 現在のところ **at this time** 現時点では, このときは **at times** 時には **at what cost!** なんという代償を払ったことでしょうか。

- □ **attack** 動 〜を襲う, 攻める 名 攻撃
- □ **attempt** 動 〜を試みる, 〜を企てる 名 試み, 企て, 努力 **make an attempt to** 〜しようとする [試みる]
- □ **attention** 名 ①注意, 集中 ②配慮, 手当て
- □ **Australia** 名 オーストラリア《国名》
- □ **Austria** 名 オーストリア
- □ **Austrian** 形 オーストリアの 名 オーストリア人
- □ **Aveling** 名 アヴェリング《人名》
- □ **avenue** 名 ①並木道 ②《A-, Ave.》〜通り, 〜街
- □ **average** 名 平均, 並み
- □ **await** 動 待つ, 待ち受ける
- □ **awake** 動 ①目覚めさせる ②目覚める 形 目が覚めて
- □ **awaken** 動 目を覚まさせる, 起こす, 目覚める
- □ **aware** 形 ①気がついて, 知って ②(〜の)認識のある **be aware of** 〜に気がついている
- □ **awash** 形 (〜で)あふれて
- □ **away** 熟 **carry away** 運び去る **carrying away** 拉致 **come away** 〜から離れて行く **drive away** 車で走り去る, 追い払う, 追い散らす **far away** 遠く離れて **get away** 逃げる, 逃亡する, 離れる **get away with** うまく逃れる, やり過ごす **give away** ①ただで与える, 贈る, 譲歩する, 手放す ②(素性・正体を)暴露する, 馬脚を現す **go away** 立ち去る **move away** ①立ち去る ②移す, 動かす **move away from** 〜から遠ざかる **pass away** 過ぎ去る, 終わる, 死ぬ **pull away from** 〜から離れる **right away** すぐに **run away** 走り去る, 逃げ出す **send away** 追い払う, 送り出す, 〜を呼び寄せる **send away for** 手紙で〜を発注する **slip away** すり抜ける, こっそり去る, 静かに立ち去る **take away** ①連れ去る ②取り上げる, 奪い去る

③取り除く **take someone away** (人)を連れ出す **throw away** 〜を捨てる；〜を無駄に費やす, 浪費する **turn away** 向こうへ行く, 追い払う,(顔を)そむける, 横を向く **walk away** 立ち去る, 遠ざかる **wash away** 押し流す

- □ **awful** 形 ①ひどい, 不愉快な ②恐ろしい

B

- □ **back** 熟 **back on to** 〜 背面で〜に接する, 〜と背中合わせになる **back to front** うしろ前に **bring back** 戻す, 呼び戻す, 持ち帰る **bring someone back to earth** (人)を現実に引き戻す **come back** 戻る **come back for** 〜の目的で戻って来る **come back to** 〜へ帰ってくる, 〜に戻る **come back to earth** (夢から目を覚まして)現実に戻る **drive back** (敵などを)追い返す **fall back** 後退する, 戻る, 退却する, 後ろ向きに倒れる **fall back upon** 当てにする **from back to front** 逆さまに **get back** 戻る, 帰る **give back** (〜を)返す **go back to** 〜に帰る[戻る], 〜に遡る,(中断していた作業に)再び取り掛かる **lean back** 後ろにもたれる **look back at** 〜に視線を戻す, 〜を振り返って見る **push back** 押し返す, 押しのける **put back** (もとの場所に)戻す, 返す **stay back** 後に下がっている, 離れている **step back** 後ずさりする, 後に下がる **take back** ①取り戻す ②(言葉, 約束を)取り消す, 撤回する **throw back** (光を)反射する **throw back one's head** 頭をのけぞらせる **turn back** 元に戻る
- □ **back street** 裏通り, 裏道
- □ **background** 名 背景, 前歴, 生い立ち
- □ **backward** 副 後方へ, 逆に, 後ろ向きに
- □ **backwards** 副 後方へ, 逆に, 後ろ向きに
- □ **Backwater** 名 バックウォーター《人名》
- □ **bad luck** 災難, 不運, 悪運
- □ **badly** 副 ①悪く, まずく, へたに ②とても, ひどく **feel badly** 悔やまれる, 気の毒に思う
- □ **Bagatelle club** バガテル・クラブ《カードゲームのクラブの名》
- □ **Bain** 名 ベイン《人名》
- □ **Baker Street** ベーカー街《地名》
- □ **balance** 動 つり合いをとる
- □ **ball of string** 名《a-》一巻きの糸
- □ **Ballarat** 名 バララット《地名》
- □ **Balmoral** 名 バルモラル《地名》
- □ **band** ひも, 帯
- □ **bandage** 名 包帯, 帯具
- □ **bank book** 預金通帳

☐ **banker** 图銀行家[員]

☐ **bar** 图①酒場 ②棒，かんぬき

☐ **Bar of Gold** 金の棒《店の名》

☐ **bark** 動ほえる

☐ **Barnes** 图バーンズ《人名》

☐ **Barnicott** 图《Dr. –》バーニコット博士《人名》

☐ **barometer** 图気圧計，バロメーター，晴雨計

☐ **barometric** 形気圧(計)の

☐ **Baron** 图男爵

☐ **based on** 《be –》～に基づく

☐ **basement** 图地下(室)，基部

☐ **Basle** 图バーゼル《スイスの都市》

☐ **battle** 图戦闘，戦い

☐ **battle-axe** 图戦斧(せんぷ)

☐ **bay** 图湾，入り江

☐ **Bayard** 图ベイヤード《馬の名》

☐ **bear** 動①運ぶ ②支える ③耐える ④(子を)産む **bear out** ～を実証する，支持する

☐ **beard** 图あごひげ

☐ **beat** 動①～を打つ ②～を打ち負かす 图打つこと，鼓動，拍 **on the beat** 巡回[パトロール]中で

☐ **beaten** 動beat (～を打つ，～を打ち負かす)の過去分詞 形打たれた，打ち負かされた，疲れ切った

☐ **Beatrice Folder** 图ビアトリス・フォルダー《人名》

☐ **beauty** 图①美，美しい人[物] ②《the –》美点

☐ **because of** ～のために，～の理由で

☐ **become of** 《whatを主語として》～はどうなるのか

☐ **bed** 熟get out of bed 起きる，寝床を離れる go to bed 床につく，寝る

☐ **bed-clothes** 图寝具

☐ **bedclothes** 图寝具

☐ **Beddoes** 图ベドーズ《人名》

☐ **Bedford** 图ベッドフォード《地名》

☐ **Bedfordshire** 图ベッドフォードシャー州《地名》

☐ **bedroom** 图寝室

☐ **bedside** 图寝台のそば，まくら元

☐ **beech** 图ブナ

☐ **before** 熟the night before 前の晩

☐ **beforehand** 副①あらかじめ，前もって ②早まって

☐ **begin** 熟begin with ～で始まる **to begin with** はじめに，まず第一に

☐ **beginning** 熟at the beginning 最初に，当初は **make a beginning** 糸口を開く，着手する

☐ **behind** 前①～の後ろに，～の背後に ②～に遅れて，～に劣って 副①後ろに，背後に ②遅れて，劣って **close ～ behind** …～の後ろで閉める **leave behind** あとにする，～を置き去りにする **stay behind** 後ろにつく，後に残る，留守番をする

☐ **being** 熟human being 人，人間

☐ **belief** 图信じること，信用 **to the best of my belief** 私が信じる限りでは

☐ **believable** 形信じられる

☐ **believe in** ～を信じる

☐ **bell** 图ベル，鈴，鐘

☐ **belong to** ～に属する，～のものである

☐ **belonging** 图《-s》所有物，所持品

☐ **below** 前①～より下に ②～以下の，～より劣る 副下に[へ]

☐ **bend** 動①曲がる，曲げる ②屈服する[させる] **bend over** かがむ，腰をかがめる，～に身をかがめる

☐ **beneath** 前～の下に[の]，～より低い 副下に，劣って

☐ **Bennett** 图ベネット《人名》

☐ **bent** 動bend (曲がる[曲げる]，屈服する[させる])の過去，過去分詞 形①曲がった **bent over** 腰が曲がっている ②熱中した，決心した

☐ **Beppo** 图ベッポ《人名》

☐ **Berkeley Square** バークリー・スクエア《地名》

☐ **Berkshire** 图バークシャー《地名》

☐ **Bermuda Dockyard** 图バミューダ造船所

☐ **beside** 前①～のそばに，～と並んで ②～と比べると ③～とはずれて

☐ **besides** 前①～に加えて，～のほかに ②《否定文，疑問文で》～を除いて 副その上，さらに

☐ **best** 熟as best one can 精一杯，できるだけ **as best one may** (十分ではないにしても)できるだけ，精いっぱい **do one's best** 全力を尽くす **had best** ～するのが最もよい，～するのがいちばんだ **to the best of my belief** 私が信じる限りでは

☐ **bet** 動賭ける 图賭け，掛け金(の対象)

☐ **better** 熟feel better 気分がよくなる **get better** (病気などが)良くなる **get the better of** ～よりすぐれる，～をしのぐ **had better**

〜したほうが身のためだ, 〜しなさい

☐ **betting** 图賭けること, 賭け事, 賭け率

☐ **betting-book** 图賭け金帳

☐ **bettor** 图賭けをする人

☐ **beyond** 前〜を越えて, 〜の向こうに 副向こうに **beyond reach of** 〜の手の届かない

☐ **bill** 图請求書, 勘定書

☐ **billiard-room** 图玉突き部屋, ビリヤードルーム

☐ **billiards** 图ビリヤード

☐ **binomial** 形二項式の

☐ **Birds of England** 『英国の鳥類』《書名》

☐ **Birmingham** 图バーミンガム《イギリスの都市》

☐ **bit** 图①《a – of》少しの〜, 1つの〜 ②小片 **a bit** 少し, ちょっと

☐ **bite** 動〜をかむ, 〜をかじる 图かむこと, かみ傷

☐ **bitten** 動bite (〜をかむ) の過去分詞

☐ **Black Sea** 《the – 》黒海

☐ **black-faced** 形顔の黒い

☐ **blackness** 图黒さ, 暗さ, 暗黒

☐ **Blackwater** 图《Earl of – 》ブラックウォーター伯《人名》

☐ **blanched** 形白面の

☐ **Blandford Street** ブランドフォード街《地名》

☐ **blazing** 形赤々と燃え上がる

☐ **bleed** 動出血する, 血を流す[流させる]

☐ **bless** 動①神の加護を祈る ②恩恵を受ける, 祝福される **God bless you!** おやまあ

☐ **blew** 動blow (吹く) の過去

☐ **blind** 形視覚障害がある, 目の不自由な

☐ **blood** 图血, 血液 **in cold blood** 冷酷に, 落ち着いて

☐ **bloodhound** 图ブラッドハウンド《警察犬・猟犬》

☐ **bloody** 形血だらけの, 血なまぐさい, むごい

☐ **bloom** 動咲く[咲かせる]

☐ **blow** 動①(風が) 吹く, (風が) 〜を吹き飛ばす ②息を吹く **blow up** 破裂する[させる] 图①(風の) ひと吹き, 突風 ②打撃 **strike a blow** 一撃を加える

☐ **blown** 動blow (吹く) の過去分詞

☐ **blunt** 形鈍い

☐ **board** 图板, 掲示板

☐ **boarding house** (まかないつきの) 下宿屋

☐ **boarding school** 图寄宿[全寮制]学校

☐ **body** 图団体, 集まり

☐ **Boer** 图ボーア人 形ボーア人の

☐ **Boer War** ボーア戦争 (第1次1880–81年, 第2次1899–1902年)

☐ **Bohemia** 图ボヘミア《地名》

☐ **Bohemian** 图ボヘミア人 形ボヘミアの, ボヘミア人の

☐ **Bond Street** ボンド街《ロンドンの商店街》

☐ **bone** 图①骨, 《-s》骨格 ②《-s》要点, 骨組み

☐ **bony** 形①骨のような, 骨質の ②(人が) 骨太の, やせた

☐ **bookcase** 图本箱

☐ **booklover** 图本好き, 愛書家

☐ **bookshop** 图書店, 本屋

☐ **Boone** 图ブーン《人名》

☐ **boot** 图《-s》長ぐつ, ブーツ

☐ **border** 图境界, へり, 国境

☐ **boredom** 图退屈

☐ **Borgia** 图ボルジア《人名》,《-s》ボルジア家

☐ **borrow** 動借りる

☐ **Boscombe** 图ボスコム《地名》

☐ **both of them** 彼ら[それら] 両方とも

☐ **bother** 動〜を悩ます, 〜の邪魔をする

☐ **bottom** 图①底, 下部, すそ野, ふもと, 最下位, 根底 ②尻 **at the bottom of** 〜の根底[裏]に, 〜の黒幕で **get to the bottom of** (事件などの) 原因[真相] を探り当てる, (問題などを) 解決する

☐ **bottom-land** 图 (川沿いの) 低地

☐ **bow** 動〜にお辞儀する

☐ **boxer** 图拳闘家

☐ **boxing** 图ボクシング, 拳闘

☐ **boy** 熟**my boy** 友よ《呼びかけ》

☐ **boyish** 形男の子らしい, 男の子のような

☐ **Bradstreet** 图ブラッドストリート《人名》

☐ **branch** 图①枝 ②支流, 支部

☐ **brave** 形勇かんな

☐ **break** 熟**break away from** 〜とのつながり[関係] を断つ **break in** 押し入る, 侵入する, (会話などに) 突然口を挟む **break into** 〜に押し入る, 急に〜する **break out** 発生する, 急に起こる, (戦争が) 勃発する **break through** 〜を打ち破る **break up** ばらばらになる, 解散させる

- □ **breakfast** 動朝食を食べる
- □ **breath** 名息, 呼吸
- □ **breathe** 動呼吸する
- □ **Brenda Tregennis** ブレンダ・トリジェニス《人名》
- □ **Brewer** 名ブルーアー《人名》
- □ **brick** 名レンガ, レンガ状のもの
- □ **bride** 名花嫁, 新婦
- □ **bridle** 名馬勒《頭部馬具。おもがい・くつわ・手綱》
- □ **brighten** 動輝かせる, 快活にさせる
- □ **brightly** 副明るく, 輝いて, 快活に
- □ **bring** 熟 bring about ～を引き起こす, もたらす bring along ～を持って行く［来る］ bring around ～を連れて［持って］くる bring back ～を連れ戻す bring down 打ち降ろす bring forward ～を公開する bring home 家に持ってくる bring in ～を呼び寄せる bring oneself to ～する気になる bring out (物)をとりだす, 引き出す,（新製品など）を出す bring someone back to earth (人)を現実に引き戻す bring the secret to light 秘密を公表する bring up ～を下から上げる, 上に持ってくる,（問題を）持ち出す
- □ **Bristol** 名ブリストル《地名》
- □ **British** 形イギリスの, 英国人の 名英国人
- □ **British Army** 大英帝国陸軍
- □ **British Museum** 《the –》大英博物館
- □ **broad** 形①幅の広い ②寛大な ③明白な
- □ **broadly** 副大ざっぱに, 露骨に
- □ **Broads** 名《the –》(イギリス, ノーフォーク地方の) 湖沼地方［地帯］
- □ **broken down** 《be –》壊れている
- □ **broken heart** 失意, 絶望, 失恋
- □ **brought against** 《be –》嫌疑［容疑］が晴れる
- □ **brownish** 形茶色がかった
- □ **Brussels** 名ブリュッセル《ベルギーの都市》
- □ **Buffelsspruit** 名バッフェルススプルート《地名》
- □ **bug** 名①小虫 ②細菌, ウイルス
- □ **builder** 名建設者
- □ **bull terrier** ブルテリア《犬種》
- □ **bullet** 名銃弾, 弾丸状のもの
- □ **bullet-case** 名薬莢（やっきょう）
- □ **burned** 形やけどした
- □ **burst into** ～に飛び込む, 急に～する

- □ **busily** 副忙しく, せっせと
- □ **business** 名事件, やっかいなこと,《one's –》～にかかわりのあること bad business ひどいこと, 困ったこと This is no business of mine. これは私には関係のないことだ。
- □ **businessman** 名ビジネスマン, 実業家
- □ **businessmen** 名 businessman (ビジネスマン)の複数
- □ **bust** 名胸像
- □ **busy with** 《be –》～で忙しい
- □ **but** 熟 not ～ but … ～ではなくて… not only ～ but (also) … ～だけでなく…もまた nothing but ただ～だけ, ～にすぎない, ～のほかは何も…ない
- □ **butler** 名執事
- □ **buyer** 名買い手
- □ **by** 熟 by God 神にかけて, 本当に by Heaven 神にかけて by all means なんとしても, ぜひとも by chance 偶然, たまたま by contrast (それと) 対照的に,（それと）比べて by day 昼間は, 日中は by far はるかに, 断然 by name ～という名の, 名前で, 名前だけは by no means 決して～ではない by now 今のところ, 今ごろまでには by oneself 一人で, 自分だけで, 独力で by the side of ～のそばに by the time ～する時までに by the way ところで, ついでに, 途中で By whom? 誰に？ come by やって来る, 立ち寄る followed by その後に～が続いて go by ①（時が）過ぎる, 経過する ②～のそばを通る ③～に基づいて［よって］行う one by one 1つずつ, 1人ずつ pass by ～のそばを通る［通り過ぎる］ point by point 逐一 side by side 並んで stand by そばに立つ, 傍観する, 待機する step by step 一歩一歩, 着実に stop by 途中に立ち寄る, ちょっと訪ねる

C

- □ **cab** 名①タクシー ②馬車
- □ **cabby** 名タクシーの運転手
- □ **cabman** 名馬車の御者
- □ **Cafe Royal** カフェ・ロイヤル
- □ **cage** 名鳥かご, 檻
- □ **call** 熟 call for ～を求める, 訴える, ～を呼び求める, 呼び出す call in ～を呼ぶ, ～に立ち寄る call on 呼びかける, 招集する, 求める, 訪問する call out 叫ぶ, 呼び出す, 声を掛ける call to ～に声をかける call upon 求める, 頼む, 訪問する
- □ **calmly** 副落ち着いて, 静かに

□ **Cambridge** 图ケンブリッジ《地名》

□ **Camden House** カムデン・ハウス《ホームズの家の向かいにある家》

□ **Camford** 图カムフォード《地名》

□ **Campden House Road** カムデン・ハウス通り《通りの名》

□ **can** 勦as ～ as one can できる限り～ as best one can 精一杯, できるだけ as far as one can できるだけ can do nothing どうしようもない can hardly とても～できない can't help 避けられない, ～せずにはいられない I can make neither head nor tail of it. 何が何だかさっぱりわからない。

□ **candle** 图ろうそく

□ **cane** 图(籐製の)杖

□ **cannot count on** 当てにならない

□ **Canterbury** 图カンタベリー《イギリスの都市》

□ **capable** 形①～の能力[資質]がある ②有能な

□ **Cape Town** ケープタウン《地名》

□ **Cape Verde islands** 《the –》ベルデ岬諸島《セネガル西部の, アフリカ大陸最西端にある諸島》

□ **captain** 图長, 船長, 首領, 主将

□ **card-gain** 图トランプによる稼ぎ

□ **care** 勦care about ～を気に掛ける care for ～の世話をする, ～を扱う, ～が好きである, ～を大事に思う take care 気をつける, 注意する take care of ～の世話をする, ～の面倒を見る, ～を管理する under the care of ～の世話になって Who cares for ～. ～はいらない, どうでもよい。

□ **carefree** 形のんきな, 心配のない

□ **careless** 形不注意な, うかつな

□ **carelessly** 副不注意にも, ぞんざいに

□ **Carlton Club** 图カールトン・クラブ

□ **carpet** 图じゅうたん, 敷物

□ **carriage** 图①馬車 ②乗り物, (鉄道の)客車

□ **carriageman** 图(馬車の)御者

□ **Carrie Evans** キャリー・エバンス《人名》

□ **carry** 勦carry along 持ち運ぶ carry away 運び去る carry into ～の中に運び入れる carry off 誘かいする, さらって行く, 運び去る carry on ①続ける ②持ち運ぶ carry out 外へ運び出す, [計画を]実行する

□ **carrying away** 拉致

□ **cart** 图荷馬車, 荷車

□ **case** 图事件 case against ～を相手どった事件 have a case 告訴する in any case とにかく in case ～だといけないので, 念のため, 万が一 in that case もしそうなら in the case of ～の場合は

□ **case of Ricoletti and his bad wife** 《the –》リコレッティとその悪妻の事件《ホームズが手がけた事件》

□ **case of Vamberry** 《the –》ヴァンベリ事件《ホームズが手がけた事件》

□ **cast** 图(型に入れて作られた)像, 型

□ **catch fire** 火がつく

□ **catch sight of** ～を見つける, ～を見かける

□ **Cathcart Soames** キャスカート・ソームズ《人名》

□ **Catullus** 图①カトゥルス《古代ローマの叙情詩人》②『カトゥルス』《書名。カトゥルスの詩集》

□ **Caunter** 图カウンター《人名》

□ **cause** 勦～を引き起こす, ～の原因になる cause someone no harm ～に危害を与えない

□ **cave** 图洞穴, 洞くつ

□ **Cavendish Square** キャベンディッシュ広場《広場の名》

□ **ceiling** 图天井

□ **cellar** 图地下貯蔵室

□ **cement** 图セメント

□ **cent** 图セント《米国などの通貨単位。1ドルの100分の1》

□ **central** 形中央の, 主要な

□ **Central News** セントラル・ニューズ《新聞社の名》

□ **certain** 形①確実な, 必ず～する ②(人が)確信した ③ある ④いくらかの for certain 確かに, 確実に

□ **certainly** 副①確かに, 必ず ②《返答に用いて》そのとおり, 承知しました

□ **chalk** 图チョーク, 白墨

□ **chance** 图by chance 偶然, たまたま I'll chance that. それは運に任せよう。 take chances [a chance] (運に任せて)危険を冒す

□ **change with** ～とともに変化する

□ **changed man** 別人

□ **chapel** 图礼拝堂

□ **character** 图①特性, 個性 ②(小説・劇などの)登場人物 ③文字, 記号 ④品性, 人格

□ **charge** 勦①(代金を)請求する ②(～を…に)負わせる ③命じる ④告発する 图①請求金額, 料金 ②責任 ③非難, 告発, 容疑 in charge of

～を担当して，～の責任を負って **make charge against** ～を告発する，非難する

- [ ] **Charing Cross** チャリング・クロス《地名》
- [ ] **Charles the First** チャールズ1世（1600–49）《イギリス国王》
- [ ] **Charles the Second** チャールズ2世（1630–85）《イギリス国王》
- [ ] **Charlie Peace** チャーリー・ピース《人名》
- [ ] **chat** 動 おしゃべるをする，談笑する
- [ ] **Chatham** 名 チャタム《地名》
- [ ] **check** 動 ～を照合する，～を検査する **check on** ～を調べる
- [ ] **cheek** 名 ほお
- [ ] **cheerful** 形 （人が）上機嫌の，元気のよい，（人を）気持ちよくさせる
- [ ] **cheerfully** 副 楽しそうに，明るく快活に
- [ ] **cheese** 名 チーズ
- [ ] **chemical** 名 化学製品［薬品］
- [ ] **chemistry** 名 化学
- [ ] **Chequers** 名 チェッカーズ《ホテル名》
- [ ] **Chesterfield high road** チェスターフィールド街道《通りの名》
- [ ] **Chicago** 名 シカゴ《アメリカの都市名》
- [ ] **chief** 名 頭，長，親分 形 最高位の，第一の，主要な
- [ ] **chimney** 名 煙突（状のもの）
- [ ] **china** 名 ①陶磁器，瀬戸物 ②《C-》中国
- [ ] **Chinese** 形 中国の，中国人の 名 中国人，中国語
- [ ] **Chiswick** 名 チズウィック《地名》
- [ ] **choice** 名 選択（の範囲［自由］），えり好み
- [ ] **Christie** 名 クリスティー《人名，オークション会社名》
- [ ] **Christmas** 名 クリスマス
- [ ] **chronicle** 名 ①年代記，記録，物語 ②《the C-》クロニクル紙《新聞名》
- [ ] **Church Street** チャーチ街《地名》
- [ ] **cigar** 名 葉巻
- [ ] **cigarette** 名 （紙巻）たばこ
- [ ] **cigarette-box** 名 タバコの箱
- [ ] **cigarette-case** 名 タバコ入れ，シガレットケース
- [ ] **cinnamon** 名 ①シナモン ②淡黄褐色
- [ ] **circle** 名 円，円周
- [ ] **claim** 動 ①～を主張する ②～を要求，請求する

- [ ] **Clair** 名 クレア《人名》
- [ ] **Clapham Junction** クラパム・ジャンクション《ロンドンの駅名》
- [ ] **class** 名 階級
- [ ] **classic** 名 古典
- [ ] **clay** 名 粘土，白土
- [ ] **clean up** ～を掃除する，片付ける
- [ ] **clear** 形 ①はっきりした，明白な ②澄んだ ③（よく）晴れた **keep clear of** ～に近寄らない **stand clear** （～から）離れている 動 ①～をはっきりさせる ②～を片づける ③晴れる **clear up** （疑問，問題を）解決する
- [ ] **clearly** 副 ①明らかに，はっきりと ②《返答に用いて》そのとおり
- [ ] **clever** 形 ①頭のよい，利口な ②器用な，上手な
- [ ] **cleverly** 副 利口に，巧みに，上手に
- [ ] **cleverness** 名 利口さ，巧みさ，上手であること
- [ ] **client** 名 依頼人，顧客
- [ ] **climb into** ～に乗り込む
- [ ] **climb on** ～の上によじ登る
- [ ] **climber** 名 登山者
- [ ] **clinic** 名 診療所
- [ ] **close** 熟 **be close to** ～に近い **close around** ～を握りしめる **close ～ behind** ……を～の後ろで閉める **close to -ing** ～する寸前で **draw to a close** 終りに近づく **get close** 近づく
- [ ] **close friend** 親友
- [ ] **closely** 副 ①密接に ②念入りに，詳しく ③ぴったりと
- [ ] **clothing** 名 装身具
- [ ] **cloud** 動 ～に暗い影を落とす **cloud over** 曇る
- [ ] **cloudless** 形 雲のない
- [ ] **cloudy** 形 曇った，雲の **become cloudy** 曇る
- [ ] **clue** 名 手がかり，糸口
- [ ] **co-worker** 名 協力者
- [ ] **Co.** 略 会社（＝company）
- [ ] **code** 名 コード，暗号
- [ ] **coded** 形 暗号化された
- [ ] **coffin** 名 棺
- [ ] **coldly** 副 冷たく，よそよそしく
- [ ] **coldness** 名 寒さ，冷たさ
- [ ] **collar** 名 えり，首輪

□ **colleague** 图同僚, 仲間, 同業者
□ **collection** 图収集, 収蔵物
□ **collector** 图集める人, 収集家
□ **colonel** 图大佐
□ **Colonna** 图コロンナ《人名》
□ **come** 熟 **come about** 起こる　**come after**
〜のあとを追う　**come along** ①一緒に来る, つ
いて来る ②やって来る, 現れる ③うまくいく,
よくなる, できあがる　**come and 〜** しに行く
come around (人が) 訪れる, ぐるっと遠回り
して来る, (時が) 巡ってくる　**come away** 〜か
ら離れて行く　**come back** 戻る　**come back
for** 〜の目的で戻って来る　**come back to** 〜へ
帰ってくる, 〜に戻る　**come back to earth** (夢
から目を覚まして) 現実に戻る　**come by** やっ
て来る, 立ち寄る　**come down** 下りて来る, 田
舎へ来る　**come for** 〜の目的で来る, 〜を取り
に来る　**come in** 中にはいる, やってくる, 出回
る　**come into** 〜に入ってくる　**come off** 取れ
る, はずれる　**come on** ①いいかげんにしろ, も
うよせ, さあ来なさい ②(人) に偶然出会う
come out 出てくる, 出掛ける, 姿を現す, 発行
される　**come out from** 〜から出てくる　**come
out of** 〜から出てくる, 〜をうまく乗り越える
come over やって来る, 〜の身にふりかかる
come round (人が) 訪れる, 回復する　**come
running** 飛んでくる, かけつける　**come
running out of** 〜から走り出てくる　**come
running over** 駆けつける　**come someone's
way** (人) の手に入る　**come through** 通り抜け
る, 成功する, 期待に沿う　**come to think of it**
考えてみると　**come up** 近づいてくる, 階上に
行く, 浮上する, 水面へ上ってくる, 発生する, 芽
を出す　**come up to** (部屋や家) に立ち寄る, 上
がる　**come up with** 〜に追いつく, 〜を思いつ
く, 考え出す, 見つけ出す　**come upon** (人) に
偶然出会う　**come what may** 何があっても, 何
が起ころうとも　**come with** 〜に付属している,
〜を伴う　**How came you to 〜?** どうして〜す
ることになったのか。
□ **comfort** 動 〜を心地よくする
□ **comfortable** 形快適な, 心地いい
□ **comfortably** 副心地よく, くつろいで
□ **comment** 图論評, 解説 動論評する, 注解す
る
□ **Commercial Road** コマーシャル街
□ **commit** 動 (罪などを) 犯す
□ **commonly** 副一般に, 通例
□ **companion** 图友, 仲間, 連れ
□ **company** 图友人, 仲間, 交わり, 親交　**enjoy
each other's company** 同席を楽しむ　**keep
someone company** (人) のそばにいる

□ **complain** 動①不平 [苦情] を言う, ぶつぶつ
言う ②(病状など) を訴える
□ **complaint** 图①不平, 不満 ②訴状　**have
complaints with** 〜について文句がある
□ **complete** 形完全な, 全くの, 完成した 動
〜を完成させる
□ **completely** 副完全に, すっかり
□ **compliment** 動 (人) をほめる, (人) にお世
辞を言う
□ **concentrate** 動一点に集める [まる], 集中
させる [する]
□ **concern** 動①関係する ②心配させる, 《be
-ed about [for]》 〜を心配する 图関心, 心配
□ **concert** 图音楽 [演奏] 会
□ **conclusion** 图結論, 結末
□ **condemn** 動有罪と判決する
□ **condition** 图①(健康) 状態, 境遇 ②《-s》状況,
様子 ③条件
□ **confession** 图告白, 自白
□ **confuse** 動混同する, 困惑させる, 混乱させ
る
□ **congratulate** 動祝う, 祝辞を述べる
congratulate on 〜を祝う, 褒め称える
□ **congratulations** 圃おめでとう
□ **connect** 動つながる, つなぐ, 関係づける, 《受
身または – oneself》関係がある
□ **connection** 图①つながり, 関係 ②縁故　**in
connection with** 〜に関連して, 〜と一緒に, 〜
に加えて
□ **conscience** 图良心
□ **consider** 動①考慮する ②(〜と) みなす ③
〜を気にかける, 思いやる
□ **considerable** 形相当な, かなりの, 重要な
□ **consideration** 图①考慮, 考察 ②考慮すべ
きこと　**in consideration of** 〜を考慮して,
〜に免じて
□ **consist of** (部分・要素) から成る
□ **constable** 图巡査, 警官
□ **contain** 動①〜を含む, 〜が入っている ②
(感情など) を抑える
□ **container** 图容器, 入れ物
□ **content** 形満足して
□ **continent** 图①大陸, 陸地 ②《the C-》ヨー
ロッパ大陸
□ **continental** 形大陸の
□ **continually** 副継続的に, 絶えず, ひっきり
なしに
□ **continue** 動続ける

□ **continuously** 副連続して, 絶え間なく, 変わりなく

□ **contrast** 名対照, 対比

□ **control** 動①～を管理[支配]する ②～を抑制する, コントロールする 名①管理, 支配(力) ②抑制 **have control over** ～を支配[コントロール]する **in control** 抑えて, 制御して **lose control** 我を忘れる, 自制心を失う **take control of** ～を支配[管理・指揮]する

□ **conversation** 名会話, 会談

□ **convince** 動納得させる, 確信させる

□ **Cooee** 間クーイー《呼び声》

□ **cool down** 冷ます, 涼しくする

□ **coolly** 副冷静に, 冷たく

□ **Copper Beeches** ぶな屋敷《ホームズが解決した事件のひとつ》

□ **copy** 名①コピー, 写し ②(書籍の)一部, 冊 ③広告文 動～を写す, まねる, コピーする

□ **Coram** 名コーラム《人名》

□ **corner** 熟 (just) around the corner from ～のすぐ近くに

□ **Cornish** 形コーンウォール地方の, コーンウォール人の

□ **Cornwall** 名コーンウォール州

□ **coroner** 名検死官

□ **corps** 名部隊, 兵団

□ **corridor** 名廊下

□ **cost** 名①値段, 費用 ②損失, 犠牲 **at all costs** どんな犠牲を払っても, ぜひとも **at what cost!** なんという代償を払ったことでしょうか。 動(金, 費用)がかかる, ～を要する

□ **cottage** 名小別荘, 小さな家

□ **cotton** 名綿

□ **could** 熟 How could ～? 何だって～なんてことがありえようか？ If +《主語》+ could ～できればなあ《仮定法》 could have done ～だったかもしれない《仮定法》

□ **count** 動①～を数える ②～を(…と)みなす ③重要[大切]である **cannot count on** 当てにならない

□ **counter** 名 (店の)売り台, カウンター

□ **countryman** 名①田舎者 ②(ある土地の)出身者, 同郷人

□ **countryside** 名地方, 田舎

□ **county** 名郡, 州

□ **coup** 名予期しないこと, 不意の一撃

□ **couple** 名①2つ, 対 ②夫婦, 一組 ③数個 **a couple of** 2, 3の

□ **course** 名方向, 針路

□ **court** 名①中庭, コート ②法廷, 裁判所 ③宮廷, 宮殿 **court hearing** 法廷審問

□ **courtroom** 名法廷

□ **cover** 動①～をおおう, ～を包む, ～を隠す ②～を扱う, ～にわたる ③代わりを務める **be covered with** ～でおおわれている **cover up** 身をくるむ, すっかり覆う 名おおい, カバー

□ **covering** 名覆い

□ **cow** 名雌牛, 乳牛

□ **cow-track** 名牛の通った跡

□ **crack** 名割れ目, ひび

□ **credit** 名信用, 評判, 名声 **give someone credit for** (人)の～を評価する

□ **creep** 動①這う ②ゆっくり動く

□ **creeper** 名這うもの

□ **creeping** 形這い回る

□ **Crendall** 名クレンダル《地名》

□ **crime** 名①(法律上の)罪, 犯罪 ②悪事, よくない行為

□ **Crimean** 形①クリミア自治共和国の ②クリミア半島の

□ **Crimean War** 《the –》クリミア戦争 (1853–1856年)

□ **criminal** 形犯罪の, 罪深い, 恥ずべき 名犯罪者, 犯人

□ **cross over** (領域・枠などを)越える

□ **crossroad** 名①交差道路, 十字路 ②岐路

□ **crowd** 動群がる, 混雑する 名群集, 雑踏, 多数

□ **crowded** 形混雑した, 満員の 動crowd (群がる, 混雑する)の過去, 過去分詞

□ **crown** 名冠

□ **cruel** 形残酷な, 厳しい

□ **cruelly** 副残酷に

□ **cry out** 泣き叫ぶ

□ **crypt** 名地下聖堂, 納骨堂

□ **Cunard** 名キュナード《人名, 船会社の名前》

□ **Cunningham** 名カニンガム《人名》the Cunninghams カニンガム家

□ **cupboard** 名食器棚, 戸棚

□ **curl** 動カールする, 巻きつく **curl up** 丸まって横になる, 体を丸くする

□ **curry** 名カレー料理

□ **Curzon** 名カーゾン《地名》

□ **cut** 熟 cut deep into ～に深く食い込む cut off 切断する, 切り離す short cut 近道

□ **cyclist** 图自転車乗り
□ **Czech** 形チェコ［人，語］の 图チェコ人［語］

D

□ **Dacre Hotel** デイカー・ホテル《ホテル名》
□ **daily** 形毎日の，日常の 副毎日，日ごとに
□ **Damery** 图デマリー《人名》
□ **damn** 画ちくしょう，くそ《怒り・不満・嫌悪・罵倒》動①～をだめだと判定する ②けなす，罵る
□ **damned** 形くそいまいましい
□ **danger** 熟 be in danger 危険な状態にある walk through the dangers 危険を乗り越える
□ **dangerous-looking** 形物騒［危険］な顔つきの
□ **dare** 動《 – to》思い切って～する 助思い切って～する
□ **daresay** 動たぶん～だと思う
□ **daring** 形大胆な，勇気のある
□ **dark** 熟 after dark 日没後 get dark 暗くなる in the dark 知らずに，わからずに，秘密に
□ **darken** 動～を暗くする
□ **darkened** 形暗い
□ **darkening** 形だんだん暗くなってきた
□ **darkness** 图暗さ，暗やみ
□ **Dartmoor** 图ダートムア《イギリスの地名》
□ **datebook** 图日記，業務日誌
□ **Daubensee** 图ダウベンゼー《スイスの湖》
□ **Davos** 图ダボス《スイスの行楽地》
□ **Dawson** 图ドーソン《人名》
□ **day** 熟 all day 一日中，明けても暮れても all day long 一日中，終日 by day 昼間は，日中に in those days あのころは，当時は one day （過去の）ある日，（未来の）いつか the other day 先日 these days このごろ
□ **daylight** 图①日光，昼の明かり，昼間 ②夜明け
□ **de Merville** 图ド・メルヴィル《人名》
□ **De Quincey** 《Thomas – 》トマス・ド・クインシー《1785–1859，イギリスの評論家。著作：阿片吸引者の告白》
□ **dead** 熟 in the dead of the night 真夜中に stop dead 急に止まる
□ **dead-white** 形真っ白な，蒼白な
□ **deadly** 形命にかかわる，痛烈な，破壊的な

副ひどく，極度に
□ **deal** 動《 – with》～を扱う 图（不特定の）量，額 a great deal of 多量の，大量の great deal 多量に，大いに，ずっと
□ **dealer** 图販売人，ディーラー
□ **dear** 熟 dear, dear《驚き・悲しみ・同情などを表して》いやはや，おや，まあ Dear me! おや！，まあ！《驚きを表す》
□ **death** 图死，死ぬこと，《the – 》終えん，消滅 at death's door 重体で，瀕死の状態で meet one's death 最後を遂げる，死ぬ to death 死ぬまで，死ぬほど
□ **deathbed** 图死の床，臨終
□ **debt** 图借金，負債
□ **decision** 图①決心 ②決定，判決 ③決断（力）
□ **deduce** 動推論する
□ **deduction** 图推論
□ **deed** 图行為，行動
□ **deep** 熟 cut deep into ～に深く食い込む deep waters 危険，困難
□ **deep-lined** 形深いしわの
□ **deep-set** 形深くくぼんだ
□ **deeply** 副深く，非常に
□ **defeat** 動～を打ち破る
□ **degree** 图程度
□ **delay** 图遅延，延期
□ **delighted** 形喜んでいる
□ **demand** 图要求，請求
□ **den** 图巣，ほら穴，巣窟，隠れ家
□ **Denis Folder** デニス・フォルダー《人名》
□ **department** 图部門，課，局
□ **depend on [upon]** ①～を頼る，～をあてにする ②～による
□ **depth** 图深さ，奥行き，深いところ
□ **Derby** 图ダービー，競馬
□ **Desborough** 图デスボロー《馬の名》
□ **describe** 動～を（言葉で）描写する，～の特色を述べる，～を説明する
□ **description** 图（言葉で）記述（すること），描写（すること）description of dreams （夢の描写）《トマス・ド・クインシーによるエッセイの一部》
□ **deserve** 動（～を）受けるに足る，値する，（～して）当然である
□ **desirable** 形望ましい，（望む）価値のある
□ **desire** 图欲望，欲求，願望
□ **destroy** 動～を破壊する，～を絶滅させる，

〜を無効にする

- **detail** 名細部,《-s》詳細
- **detective** 名探偵, 刑事 形探偵の
- **develop** 動①発達する［させる］②現像する
- **device** 名装置, 道具
- **devilish** 形①悪魔のような ②呪わしい, 極悪な
- **Devine** 名ドヴィヌ《人名》
- **Devonshire** 名デボンシャー《イギリスの旧州名》
- **devote** 動〜を(…に)捧げる
- **Diamond Hill** ダイアモンド・ヒル《地名》
- **diary** 名日記
- **die for** 〜が欲しくてたまらない
- **die of** 〜がもとで死ぬ
- **Dieppe** 名ディエップ《フランスの町》
- **different from** 《be –》〜と違う
- **differently** 副〜と異なって, 違って
- **difficulty** 名①難しさ ②難局, 支障, 苦情, 異議
- **dig** 動掘る
- **dim** 形薄暗い, 見にくい
- **dine** 動食事をする, ごちそうする
- **dining room** 食堂
- **dining-room** 名食堂, ダイニングルーム
- **direct** 形まっすぐな, 直接の, 率直な 動①〜を指導する, 〜を監督する ②(目・注意・努力など)を向ける
- **direction** 名①方向, 方角 ②《-s》指示 ③指導, 指揮 **in the direction of** 〜の方向に
- **directly** 副①じかに ②まっすぐに ③ちょうど
- **directness** 名まっすぐさ, 直接さ, 率直さ
- **director** 名管理者, 指導者, 監督
- **dirt** 名①汚れ, 泥, ごみ ②土
- **dirty** 形①汚い, よごれた ②卑劣な, 不正な
- **disagree** 動①意見が合わない ②一致しない
- **disagreeable** 形不愉快な, 付き合いにくい
- **disagreement** 名不一致, 相違, 不適合
- **disappear** 動見えなくなる, 姿を消す, なくなる
- **disappearance** 名見えなくなること, 消失, 失踪
- **disappointment** 名失望
- **disclose** 動(秘密などを)公表する, 暴露する

- **discolored** 形変色した, 色あせた
- **discoverer** 名発見者
- **discovery** 名発見
- **dishonest** 形不誠実な
- **dishonor** 名不名誉, 侮辱
- **dislike** 動〜を嫌う 名反感, 嫌気
- **disorder** 名混乱, 無秩序, 乱雑
- **displease** 動不快にする
- **dissolve** 動消える, 解散する
- **distance** 名距離, 隔たり, 遠方 **at a distance** 少し離れて **in the distance** 遠方に
- **distant** 形①遠い, 隔たった ②よそよそしい, 距離のある
- **disturb** 動かき乱す, 妨げる
- **divide** 動分かれる, 分ける, 割れる, 割る
- **divorce** 動離婚する
- **do** 熟**can do nothing** どうしようもない **do 〜 a favor** 〜の願いを聞く **do evil** 悪事を働く **do 〜 good** 〜のためになる **do good** 善行をする **do one's best** 全力を尽くす **do well** 成績が良い, 成功する **do with** 〜を処理する **have nothing to do with** 〜と何の関係もない **have to do with** 〜と関係がある **Nor do I.**《否定の文に続けて》私も(いや)です。
- **dockyard** 名造船所
- **document** 名書類, 文書, 資料
- **Dodd** 名ドッド《人名》
- **dog** 名①犬 ②下劣なやつ
- **dog-cart** 一頭立て二輪馬車, 犬に引かせる車
- **doings** 名行為, 出来事
- **Don Juan** 名①ドン・ファン《スペインの伝説的貴族》②道楽者, 女たらし, 色男,《a –》ドン・ファンのような男［女たらし］
- **Donnithorpe** 名ドニソープ《イギリスの村》
- **doorman** 名門番, 守衛, ドア係
- **doorstep** 名戸口の上がり段
- **doorway** 名戸口, 玄関, 出入り口
- **Dorak** 名ドラーク《人名》
- **dot** 名点
- **double** 形①2倍の, 二重の ②対の 動①2倍になる［する］②兼ねる **double up**(体を)折り曲げる, 前かがみになる
- **doubt** 名疑い, 不確かなこと **no doubt** きっと, たぶん,《but などとともに》確かに(〜だが) **without doubt** 疑いなく, 確かに 動〜を疑う
- **down** 熟**be broken down** 壊れている

bring down 打ち降ろす **come down** 下りて来る, 田舎へ来る **cool down** 冷ます, 涼しくする **down there** 下の方で[に] **fall down** 落ちる, 転ぶ **get down** 降りる, 着地する, 身をかがめる, ひざまずく **go down** 下に降りる **halfway down** 〜の途中で **hang down** ぶら下がる **lay down** ①下に置く, 横たえる ②裏切る **let down** 期待を裏切る, 失望させる **lie down** 横たわる, 横になる **look down** 見下ろす **look down upon** 見下ろす, 俯瞰する **pass down** (次の世代に)伝える **push down** 押し倒す **put down** 下に置く, 下ろす **reach down** 手を下に伸ばす **run down** (液体が)流れ落ちる, 駆け下りる, (車で人を)ひく **run up and down** かけずり回る **rush down** 猛然と〜に駆け寄る **set down** 〜を下に置く, 〜と見なす **settle down** 落ち着く, 興奮がおさまる **slow down** 速度を落とす **take down** 下げる, 降ろす **throw down** 投げ出す, 放棄する **turn down** (音量などを)小さくする, 弱くする, 拒絶する **up and down** 上がったり下がったり, 行ったり来たり, あちこちと **walk up and down** 行ったり来たりする **write down** 書き留める

☐ **downstairs** 副 下へ[で], 階下へ[で]

☐ **dozen** 名 1ダース, 12(個)

☐ **Dr.** 名 〜博士,《医者に対して》〜先生

☐ **draw** 動 ①引く, 引っ張る ②描く ③引き分けになる[する] **draw out** 引き抜く **draw up** (車を)止める

☐ **drawer** 名 引き出し

☐ **drawing-room** 名 応接間

☐ **drawn** 動 draw (引く[引かれる], 〜を描く)の過去分詞 **be drawn to** 〜に惹かれる

☐ **dreamer** 名 夢を見る人, 夢想家

☐ **dressed in** 《be –》〜を着ている

☐ **dressing-room** 名 (寝室の隣の)化粧室, 洗面所

☐ **dressing-table** 名 化粧机

☐ **dressmaker** 名 仕立屋

☐ **drew** 動 draw (引く[引かれる], 〜を描く)の過去

☐ **drive** 名 (自動車などの)運転, ドライブ 熟 **drive away** [**off**] 車で走り去る **drive back** (敵などを)追い返す **drive out** 車で出かける **drive up** 車でやって来る

☐ **driven** 動 drive (車で行く)の過去分詞

☐ **driver** 名 ①運転手 ②(馬車の)御者

☐ **drop** 名 標高差, 垂直の落差, 落下(距離) **have the drop on** 〜の機先を制する 動 (いすに)どさっと腰を下す **drop in** ちょっと立ち寄る

☐ **drove** 動 drive (車で行く, 運転する)の過去

☐ **drug** 名 薬, 麻薬 動 一服盛る

☐ **drying-room** 名 乾燥室

☐ **Duchess** 名 公爵夫人, 女公爵

☐ **duck-hunting** 名 カモの狩猟場

☐ **due** 形 予定された, 期日のきている, 支払われるべき **due to** 〜することになっている, 〜によって, 〜が原因で

☐ **duke** 名 公爵

☐ **Dulong** 名 ドゥーロン《ホテルの名前》

☐ **Duncan Ross** 名 ダンカン・ロス《人名》

☐ **Dunlop** 名 ダンロップ《タイヤの製造会社名》

☐ **during** 前 〜の間に

☐ **dusk** 名 夕闇, 薄暗がり

☐ **Dutch** 形 オランダ[人, 語]の 名 オランダ人[語]

☐ **duty** 名 ①義務(感), 責任 ②職務, 任務, 関税 **on duty** 勤務(時間)中で, 当番で

☐ **dying** 形 死にかかっている, 消えそうな

E

☐ **each** 熟 **each day** 毎日, 日ごとに **each one** 各自 **each other** お互いに **each time** 〜するたびに **enjoy each other's company** 同席を楽しむ **on each side** それぞれの側に

☐ **eagerly** 副 熱心に, しきりに

☐ **earl** 名 伯爵

☐ **earn** 動 (金)を儲ける, 稼ぐ

☐ **earring** 名 イヤリング

☐ **earth** 熟 **bring someone back to earth** (人)を現実に引き戻す **come back to earth** (夢から目を覚まして)現実に戻る **in the earth** 地中に **on earth** ①いったい ②地球上で, この世で **How on earth 〜?** 一体どうやったら

☐ **ease** 名 安心, 気楽

☐ **easily** 副 ①容易に, たやすく, 苦もなく ②気楽に

☐ **East Anglia** イースト・アングリア《地名》

☐ **East London** イースト・ロンドン《地名》

☐ **East Rushton** イースト・ラシュトン《地名》

☐ **Eastern** 形 東洋の, 東洋風の

☐ **easy-going** 形 あくせくしない, のんびりした, おおような

☐ **edge** 名 ①刃 ②端, 縁 **edge of the woods** 森のはずれ

□ **Edith Baxter** エディス・バクスター《人名》

□ **Edith Presbury** イーディス・プレスベリー《人名》

□ **educate** 動 ～を教育する，～するように訓練する

□ **education** 名 教育，教養

□ **Edward** 名 エドワード《人名》

□ **Edward Holly** エドワード・ホリー《人名》

□ **effect** 名 影響，効果，結果

□ **effective** 形 効果的である，有効である

□ **effort** 名 努力（の成果）

□ **Egria** 名 エグリア《地名》

□ **eh** 間《略式》えっ(何ですか)，～だろう？《驚き・疑いを表したり，相手に確認を求める》

□ **either A or B** A かそれとも B

□ **either side of** ～の両側に

□ **either way** どちらにしても

□ **elbow** 名 ひじ

□ **elder** 形 年上の，年長の

□ **elderly** 形 かなり年配の，初老の

□ **Elizabethan** 形 エリザベス女王時代の

□ **elm** 名 楡(ニレ)

□ **Elrige** 名 エルリッジ《場所・人の名》

□ **Elrige's Farm** エルリッジ農場

□ **else** 熟 anything else ほかの何か　no one else 他の誰一人として～しない

□ **elsewhere** 副 どこかほかの所で

□ **Elsie Patrick** エルシー・パトリック《人名》

□ **embarrass** 動 恥ずかしい思いをさせる，困らせる

□ **embarrassment** 名 当惑，困惑，きまり悪さ

□ **emerald** 名 エメラルド

□ **emergency** 名 非常時，緊急時

□ **emotion** 名 感激，感動，感情

□ **emperor** 名《the –》皇帝，天皇

□ **Emperor Shomu** 聖武天皇

□ **employ** 動 （人を）雇う，使う

□ **employer** 名 雇主，使用（利用）する人

□ **empty** 形 ①からの，空いた　②空虚な，うつろな

□ **Emsworth** 名 エムズワース《人名》

□ **enable** 動 （～することを）可能にする，容易にする

□ **enclose** 動 ①同封する，入れる　②取り囲む

□ **encyclopedia** 名 百科事典

□ **Encyclopedia Britannica** 名 ブリタニカ百科事典

□ **end** 名 突き当たり，周辺地域 Oxford Street end オックスフォード街のはずれ　熟 at the end of ～の終わりに　bring ～ to an end ～を終わらせる　end up 最後には～になる　in the end とうとう，最後には　stand on end 直立して

□ **endanger** 動 危険にさらす，脅かす

□ **endless** 形 終わりのない，無限の

□ **enemy** 名 敵

□ **engage** 動 ①～を約束する，～と婚約する　②～を雇う，従事する［させる］

□ **engagement** 名 婚約，約束

□ **England** 名 ①イングランド　②英国

□ **Englischer Hof** 《the –》英国館《ホテルの名前》

□ **Englishman** 名 イングランド人，イギリス人

□ **Englishwoman** 名 イングランド［イギリス］人女性

□ **enjoy each other's company** 同席を楽しむ

□ **enjoyable** 形 愉快な，楽しい

□ **enlist** 動 （援助を）得る

□ **enliven** 動 活気［元気］づける，生き生きさせる，にぎやかにする

□ **enough** 熟 enough of ～はもうたくさん　have enough of ～はもう十分だ，うんざりだ　sure enough 思ったとおり，確かに

□ **ensure** 動 確実にする，保証する

□ **enter** 熟 enter into ～に入る　upon entering 入った途端

□ **entire** 形 全体の，完全な，全くの

□ **entirely** 副 完全に，まったく

□ **entrust** 動 ゆだねる，任せる，委託する

□ **entry** 名 入ること，入り口

□ **envelope** 名 封筒，包み

□ **equal** 形 等しい，均等な，平等な　have no equal 並ぶ［匹敵する］ものがない　名 同等のもの［人］

□ **equally** 副 等しく，平等に

□ **error** 名 誤り，間違い，過失

□ **escape** 動 （～から）逃げる，免れる，もれる　名 逃亡，脱出，もれ

□ **escaper** 名 逃亡者

□ **estate** 名 不動産，財産，遺産，地所，私有地

□ **etc.** 略 ～など，その他 (= et cetera)

- [ ] **Eton** 名 イートン校《イギリスの名門校》
- [ ] **Europe** 名 ヨーロッパ
- [ ] **European** 名 ヨーロッパ人 形 ヨーロッパ（人）の
- [ ] **Euston** 名 ユーストン（駅）《ロンドンの主要駅の一つ，北部方面行き》
- [ ] **Evans** 名 エヴァンズ《人名》
- [ ] **even if** たとえ〜でも
- [ ] **even then** その時でさえ
- [ ] **even though** 〜であるけれども
- [ ] **evening** 熟 of an evening たいてい毎夕，夕方に
- [ ] **evenly** 副 等しく，均等に，対等に
- [ ] **ever** 熟 ever since それ以来ずっと if ever もし〜ということがあれば
- [ ] **every other** 1つおきの〜，他のすべての
- [ ] **everyday** 形 毎日の，日々の
- [ ] **everyone** 代 誰でも，皆
- [ ] **everything** 代 すべてのこと［もの］，何でも，何もかも
- [ ] **everywhere** 副 どこにいても，いたるところに
- [ ] **evidence** 名 ①証拠，証人 ②形跡 in evidence 証拠［証人］として，目だって，はっきり見えて
- [ ] **evident** 形 明白な，明らかな
- [ ] **evil** 形 ①邪悪な ②有害な，不吉な 名 邪悪
- [ ] **ex-army** 形 元軍人の，元軍隊の
- [ ] **ex-jockey** 名 元騎手
- [ ] **ex-professor** 名 元教授
- [ ] **ex-thief** 名 元泥棒
- [ ] **exact** 形 正確な，厳密な，きちょうめんな
- [ ] **examine** 動 〜を試験する，〜を調査［検査］する，〜を診察する
- [ ] **example** 熟 for example たとえば
- [ ] **excellent** 形 すぐれた，優秀な，すばらしい，（たいへん）結構です
- [ ] **except** 前 〜を除いて，〜のほかは except for 〜を除いて，〜がなければ 接 〜ということを除いて except that 〜であることを除いては
- [ ] **exception** 名 例外，除外，異論 without exception 例外なく
- [ ] **excitement** 名 興奮（すること）
- [ ] **exclaim** 動 ①（喜び・驚きなどで）声をあげる ②声高に激しく言う
- [ ] **excuse me** 失礼ですが
- [ ] **Exeter** 名 エクセター《イギリスの地名》

- [ ] **expand** 動 広げる，拡張［拡大］する
- [ ] **expanding bullet** （命中して）先端が（広がって）平らになった弾
- [ ] **expect** 動 〜を予期［予測］する，（当然のこととして）〜を期待する
- [ ] **expense** 名 出費，費用
- [ ] **experiment** 名 実験，試み
- [ ] **expert** 名 専門家，熟練者，エキスパート 形 熟練した，専門の
- [ ] **explanation** 名 ①説明，解説，釈明 ②解釈，意味
- [ ] **extra** 副 余分に
- [ ] **extraordinarily** 副 異常に，並はずれて，法外に
- [ ] **extraordinary** 形 異常な，並はずれた，驚くべき
- [ ] **extremely** 副 非常に，極度に
- [ ] **eye** 熟 eye to eye 面と向かって，目と目が合う in the eyes of 〜の見地からは roll one's eyes （驚きや不快で）目をぎょろつかせる run one's eyes over 〜にザッと目を通す take one's eyes off 〜から目をそらす
- [ ] **eyebrow** 名 まゆ
- [ ] **eyeglass** 名 単眼鏡，《-es》めがね
- [ ] **eyepiece** 名 接眼レンズ，接眼鏡

F

- [ ] **face to face** 面と向かって
- [ ] **fact** 熟 as a matter of the fact 実は，実際に in fact ①実際に，実は ②《前言を強調・否定して》要するに，つまり，いや実際は fact is 実を言えば
- [ ] **fail** 動 ①失敗する，落第する［させる］ ②《 – to 〜》〜し損なう，〜できない ③失望させる never ［not］fail to 必ず〜する
- [ ] **faint** 動 気絶する
- [ ] **fair** 形 ①正しい，公平［正当］な ②快晴の ③色白の，金髪の ④かなりの ⑤《古》美しい
- [ ] **fair lady** 麗人
- [ ] **fairly** 副 ①公平に ②かなり，相当に
- [ ] **fairness** 名 公平さ，公明正大さ
- [ ] **faith** 名 ①信念，信仰 ②信頼，信用，約束
- [ ] **fall** 熟 fall asleep 眠り込む，寝入る fall back 後退する，戻る，退却する，後ろ向きに倒れる fall back upon 当てにする fall down 落ちる，転ぶ fall in love with 恋におちる fall into 〜に陥る，〜してしまう fall off 落ちる，落ち込

む, 下落する, 減る, 衰退する **fall on** 〜に降り
かかる **fall on to** 〜の上に落ちる **fall over**
〜につまずく, 〜の上に倒れかかる **fall to the
ground** 転ぶ **fall to thinking** 考え始める **fall
upon** 〜の上にかかる

- [ ] **fallen** 動 fall (落ちる, (値段・温度が) 下がる)
の過去分詞
- [ ] **Falmouth** 名 ファルマス《イギリスの都市》
- [ ] **familiar with** 《be –》〜に精通している
- [ ] **famous for** 《be –》〜で有名である
- [ ] **fancy** 形 ①装飾的な, 見事な ②法外な, 高級
な
- [ ] **far** 熟 **as far as** 〜と同じくらい遠く, 〜まで,
〜する限り(では) **as far as one can** できるだ
け **by far** はるかに, 断然 **far away** 遠く離れて
far from 〜から遠い, 〜どころか **far off** ずっ
と遠くに, はるかかなたに **far side** 向こう側,
反対側 **far too** あまりにも〜過ぎる **go far** 遠
くへ行く **how far** どのくらいの距離か **so far**
今までのところ, これまでは **so far as** 〜に関
しては, 〜する限り **So far so good.** これまで
は順調だ。(今後の問題を暗示)
- [ ] **farewell** 名 別れ, 別れのあいさつ, 送別会
- [ ] **Farintosh** 名 ファリントッシュ《人名》
- [ ] **farmer** 名 農民, 農場経営者
- [ ] **farmland** 名 農地
- [ ] **farther** 副 もっと遠く, さらに先に
- [ ] **fashion** 名 ①流行, 方法, はやり ②流行のも
の
- [ ] **fasten** 動 固定する, 結ぶ, 締める
- [ ] **fat** 形 太った
- [ ] **fault** 名 過失, 誤り
- [ ] **favor** 熟 **do someone a favor** (人) に便宜を
図る **have a favor to ask** 〜に頼みがある, お
願いがある **in favor of** 〜を支持して, 〜が有利
になるように
- [ ] **fear** 名 ①恐れ ②心配, 不安 **for fear of** 〜を
恐れて **in fear** おどおどして, ビクビクして
動 ①〜を恐れる ②〜を心配する
- [ ] **fearful** 形 ①恐ろしい ②心配な, 気づかって
- [ ] **feed** 動 〜に食物を与える
- [ ] **feel** 熟 **feel better** 気分がよくなる **feel for**
〜に同情する, 〜を思いやる, 〜を捜し求める
feel like 〜がほしい, 〜したい気がする, 〜の
ような感じがする **feel sorry for** 〜をかわいそ
うに思う
- [ ] **feet** 熟 **get to one's feet** 立ち上がる **jump
to one's feet** 飛び起きる **rise to one's feet** 立
ち上がる **to one's feet** 両足で立っている状態
に

- [ ] **fellow** 名 ①仲間, 同僚 ②人, やつ 形 仲間の,
同士の
- [ ] **fellow-countryman** 名 同国人
- [ ] **fellow-student** 名 学友, 同級生
- [ ] **fence** 名 囲み, さく
- [ ] **fencing** 名 フェンシング, 剣術
- [ ] **Ferrers Documents** フェラーズ文書 (事
件)《ホームズが手がけている事件》
- [ ] **field** 熟 gold field 金鉱地
- [ ] **field-glass** 名 《-es》双眼鏡
- [ ] **fiery** 形 ①火の, 燃えさかる ②激しい, 情熱的
な
- [ ] **fight over** 〜のことで言い争う
- [ ] **fight with** 〜と戦う
- [ ] **fighter** 名 戦士
- [ ] **Fighting Cock (Inn)** 闘鶏亭《宿屋の名》
- [ ] **figure** 名 ①人 (物) の姿, 形 ②図 (形) ③数字
動 ①〜を描写する, 〜を想像する ②〜を計算
する ③目立つ, 〜として現れる **figure out**
〜であるとわかる, 解き明かす, 理解する
- [ ] **fill in** 〜に記入する
- [ ] **filled with** 《be –》〜でいっぱいになる
- [ ] **final** 形 最後の, 決定的な
- [ ] **find oneself** (気がつくと) (ある場所・状態
に) いる
- [ ] **find out** 見いだす, 解明する, (正体を) 見破る,
(謎を) 解く
- [ ] **fine** 立派な, 洗練された
- [ ] **fire** 動 発砲 [砲火] する
- [ ] **fireplace** 名 暖炉
- [ ] **firm** 形 堅い, しっかりした, 断固とした
- [ ] **first** 熟 **at first** 初めは **at first sight** 一目見て
first floor 2階《英》**first of all** 何よりも, まず
第一に **for the first time** 初めて **the first
thing** 何よりもまず, すぐに
- [ ] **first-class** 形 一流の, (乗り物の) 一等の
- [ ] **fishermen** 名 fisherman (漁師) の複数
- [ ] **fishing** 名 釣り, フィッシング **fishing stick**
釣りざお
- [ ] **fit** 形 ①適当な, 相応な ②体の調子がよい 動
合致 [適合] する [させる] 名 発作, けいれん, 一
時的興奮
- [ ] **fittings** 名 (移動可能な) 家具類, 調度品
- [ ] **Fitzroy Simpson** フィッツロイ・シンプソ
ン《人名》
- [ ] **fix** 動 ①(〜を) 固定する [させる] ②〜を修理
する ③(〜を) 決定する ④〜を用意する, 〜を

整える **fix on** 〜にくぎ付けになる

☐ **flame** 動燃え上がる, (顔などが) さっと赤らむ

☐ **flat** 形①平らな ②しぼんだ, 空気の抜けた 副①平らに, 平たく ②きっかり

☐ **Fleet Street** 名フリート街

☐ **floor** 熟 **first floor** 2階《英》 **ground floor** 1階

☐ **Florence** 名①フィレンツェ《イタリアの都市名》②フローレンス《アメリカの地名》

☐ **flower pot** 植木鉢

☐ **flowerbed** 名花壇

☐ **fly open** 熟ぱっと開く

☐ **fly-paper** 名ハエ取り紙

☐ **fog** 名濃霧

☐ **folded** 形折りたたまれた

☐ **follow by** その後に〜が続いて

☐ **follow up** (人) の跡を追う

☐ **follower** 名信奉者, 追随者

☐ **fool** 名ばか者, おろかな人 **make a fool of** 〜をばかにする 動〜をばかにする, 〜をだます, ふざける **fool with** 〜をもてあそぶ, 〜をいじくりまわす

☐ **foolish** 形愚かな, ばかばかしい

☐ **foolishness** 名おろかさ, 愚行

☐ **foot** 熟 **on foot** 徒歩で, 歩いて

☐ **foot-road** 名ふもと道

☐ **foothold** 名足場, 足がかり

☐ **footman** 名従僕

☐ **footmark** 名足跡

☐ **footmen** 名 footman (下男) の複数

☐ **footprint** 名足型, 足跡

☐ **footstep** 名足音, 歩み

☐ **for** 熟 **for a moment** 少しの間 **for a moment or two** ほんの少しの間 **for a time** しばらく, 一時の間 **for a while** しばらくの間, 少しの間 **for all** 〜にもかかわらず **for example** たとえば **for long** 長い間 **for now** 今のところ, ひとまず **for once** 一度だけ **for oneself** 独力で, 自分のために **for some reason** なんらかの理由で, どういうわけか **for some time** しばらくの間 **for sure** 確かに **for the first time** 初めて **for the moment** 差し当たり, 当座は **for the rest of life** 死ぬまで **for 〜 years** 〜年間, 〜年にわたって

☐ **force** 名力, 勢い 動〜に強制する, 力づくで〜する

☐ **forceful** 形力強い, 説得力のある

☐ **Fordham** 名フォーダム《人名》

☐ **Fordingham** 名フォーディンガム《イギリスの村》

☐ **forefinger** 名人差し指

☐ **forehead** 名ひたい

☐ **forgive** 動許す, 免除する

☐ **forgotten** 動 forget (〜を忘れる) の過去分詞

☐ **form** 名①形, 形式 ②書式 **take form** (物事が) 形をとる, 具体化する 動〜を形づくる

☐ **formal** 形正式の, 公式の, 形式的な, 格式ばった

☐ **Forrester** 名フォレスター《人名》

☐ **fortunate** 形幸運な, 幸運をもたらす

☐ **forward** 形①前方の, 前方へ向かう ②将来の ③先の 副①前方に ②将来に向けて ③先へ, 進んで **look forward to [-ing]** 〜を期待する **push forward** 前へ進む, 突き出す **put forward** 提出する, 提案する

☐ **founder** 名創立者, 設立者

☐ **fourth-smartest** 形4番目に抜け目ない

☐ **France** 名フランス《国名》

☐ **free** 熟 **free will** 自由意志 **set free** (人) を解放する, 釈放される, 自由の身になる

☐ **free-will** 名自由意志

☐ **freely** 副自由に, 障害なしに

☐ **French** 形フランス (人 [語]) の 名フランス語, 《the –》フランス人

☐ **friend of mine** 《a –》友人の1人

☐ **friendliness** 名友情, 好意

☐ **friendly** 形親しみのある, 親切な, 友情のこもった 副友好的に, 親切に

☐ **friendship** 名友人であること, 友情

☐ **fright** 名恐怖, 激しい驚き **give someone a fright** (人) を怖がらせる

☐ **frighten** 動〜を驚かせる, 〜をびっくりさせる

☐ **from now on** 今後

☐ **from side to side** 左右に

☐ **from then on** それ以来

☐ **from time to time** ときどき

☐ **front** 熟 **back to front** うしろ前に **in front of** 〜の前に, 〜の正面に

☐ **fruitless** 形成果のない, 実を結ばない, 不毛の

☐ **fulfill** 動 (義務・約束) を果たす, (要求・条件) を満たす

☐ **full of** 《be –》〜で一杯である

- **fully** 副 十分に, 完全に, まるまる
- **funny** 形 ①おもしろい, こっけいな ②奇妙な, うさんくさい
- **fur** 名 毛, 毛皮(製品)
- **furnace** 名 炉, かまど, 暖房炉
- **furnish** 動 (～を)備える, 供給する, 家具をとりつける
- **further** 形 いっそう遠い, その上の, なおいっそうの 副 いっそう遠く, その上に, もっと
- **future** 熟 in the future 将来は

G

- **gain** 動 ～を得る, ～を増す
- **game** 熟 play games いいかげんな[無責任な]態度を取る
- **gang** 名 ①群れ, 一団 ②ギャング, 暴力団
- **gardener** 名 庭師, 園芸家
- **gather** 動 ①集まる[集める] ②生じる, 増す ③～を推測する
- **Gelder & Co.** ゲルダー商会《会社名》
- **Gemmi Pass** ゲンミ峠《スイスの峠》
- **general** 形 ①全体の, 一般の, 普通の ②おおよその ③(職位の)高い, 上級の in general 一般に, たいてい 名 大将, 将軍
- **general store** 雑貨店
- **generally** 副 ①一般に, だいたい ②たいてい speaking generally 一般的に言えば
- **Geneva** 名 ジュネーブ《スイスの都市》
- **gentle** 形 ①優しい, 温和な ②やわらかな
- **gently** 副 親切に, 上品に
- **George** 名 ジョージ《人名》
- **George Lewis** ジョージ・ルイス《人名》
- **George Sand** 名 ジョルジュ・サンド (1804–1876)《仏の女流小説家》
- **German** 形 ドイツの, ドイツ人の, ドイツ語の 名 ドイツ人, ドイツ語
- **German Ocean** 《the –》ゲルマン海《北海の旧称》
- **Germany** 名 ドイツ
- **get** 熟 get a good look at ～をよく見る get ahead 出世する get along やっていく, はかどる get angry 腹を立てる get at 届く, 入手する get away 逃げる, 逃亡する, 離れる get away with うまく逃れる, やり過ごす get back 戻る, 帰る get better (病気などが)良くなる get close 近づく get dark 暗くなる get

down 降りる, 着地する, 身をかがめる, ひざまずく get hold of ～を手に入れる, ～をつかむ get home 家に着く[帰る] get in 中に入る, 乗り込む get into ～に入る, 入り込む, ～に巻き込まれる get into trouble 面倒を起こす, 困った事になる, トラブルに巻き込まれる get off (～から)降りる get on (電車などに)乗る, 気が合う get on one's nerves (物・事が)(人)の神経に障る get out ①外に出る, 出て行く, 逃げ出す ②取り出す, 抜き出す Get out! 出ていけ！ 消えうせろ！ get out of ～から下車する, ～から取り出す, ～から外へ出る[抜け出る] get out of bed 起きる, 寝床を離れる Get ～ out of the way ～を取り除く, どかす get ready 用意[支度]をする get rid of ～を取り除く get someone to do (人)に～させる[してもらう] get started 始める get there そこに到着する, 目的を達成する, 成功する get through 乗り切る, ～を通り抜ける get to (事)を始める, ～に達する[到着する] get to do ～できるようになる, ～できる機会を得る get to one's feet 立ち上がる get to the bottom of ～の真相を突き止める get up 起き上がる, 立ち上がる get used to ～になじむ, ～に慣れる get wet ぬれる
- **gifted** 形 才能のある, 知能のある
- **give** 熟 give a start びくっとする give away ①ただで与える, 贈る, 譲歩する, 手放す ②(素性・正体を)暴露する, 馬脚を現す give back (～を)返す give in 降参する, 屈する, (書類などを)提出する give out 分配する, 発表する, 尽きる give someone a fright (人)を怖がらせる give someone a hand (人)に手を貸す give someone credit for (人)の～を評価する give someone one's word (人)に約束する give up あきらめる, やめる, 引き渡す give way 道を譲る, 譲歩する, 負ける I give you my word. 約束するよ。保証するよ。
- **giving** 形 寛大な, 気の大きい
- **glad to do** 《be –》～してうれしい, 喜んで～する
- **gladly** 副 喜んで, うれしそうに
- **glance** 動 ①ちらりと見る ②かすめる
- **glass-covered** 形 ガラスで覆われた
- **glitter** 動 きらきら輝く, きらめく
- **Globe** 名 《the –》グローブ新聞《新聞名》
- **Gloria Scott** 《the –》グロリア・スコット号《船の名》
- **glue** 名 にかわ, 接着剤
- **go** 熟 go across 横断する, 渡る go against ～に逆らう, 従わない, (人)に不利である, (方針など)に反する go ahead 先に行く, 《許可を表す》どうぞ go along ～に沿って行く, (人)につ

いて行く **go away** 立ち去る **go back** さかのぼる **go back to** 〜に帰る［戻る］，〜に遡る，(中断していた作業に)再び取り掛かる **go by** ①(時が)過ぎる，経過する ②〜のそばを通る ③〜に基づいて［よって］行う **go doing** 〜をしに行く **go down** 下に降りる **go far** 遠くへ行く **go for** 〜に出かける，〜を追い求める，〜を好む **go for a walk** 散歩に行く **go home** 帰宅する **go in** 中に入る，開始する **go into** 〜に入る，(仕事)に就く **go mad** 発狂する **go off** ①出かける，去る，出発する ②始める，突然〜しだす ③(電気が)消える **go on** 続く，続ける，進み続ける，起こる，発生する **go on a trip** 旅行する **go on to** 〜に移る，〜に取り掛かる **go out** 外出する，外へ出る **go over** 〜を越えて行く，〜へ渡る **go over to** 〜の前に［へ］行く，〜に出向いて行く **go red** 赤くなる **go round** 〜の周りを進む，歩き回る，回って行く **go through** 通り抜ける，一つずつ順番に検討する **go to bed** 床につく，寝る **go to sleep** 寝る **go up** ①〜に上がる，登る ②〜に近づく，出かける ③(建物などが)建つ，立つ **go up to** 〜まで行く，近づく **go with** 〜と一緒に行く，〜と調和する，〜にとても似合う **go without** 〜なしですませる **go wrong** 失敗する，道を踏みはずす，調子が悪くなる **let go** 手を放す，行かせる **let go of** 〜から手を離す **ready to go** すっかり準備が整った

☐ **God** by God 神にかけて，本当に，おや，きっと，絶対に God bless you! 神のご加護がありますように。おやまあ。 God help 神よ，〜を哀れみたまえ God's truth 絶対的真実 Good God! おやまあ My God! 信じられない！おやまあ！ Thank God for that. それはありがたい。

☐ **Godfrey Emsworth** ゴッドフリー・エムズワース《人名》

☐ **Godfrey Milner** ゴッドフリー・ミルナー《人名》

☐ **Godfrey Norton** ゴッドフリー・ノートン《人名》

☐ **going-over** 名ひどく打つこと，暴力

☐ **gold** 名金，金貨，金製品，金色 形金の，金製の，金色の

☐ **gold-hunter** 名金鉱採掘家

☐ **golden** 副①金色の ②金製の ③貴重な

☐ **gone** 形見込みのない，絶望的な

☐ **good** as good as 〜も同然で，ほとんど〜 do 〜 good 〜のためになる Good God! おやまあ Good heavens! しまった！，おやまあ！ Good lord! おお，ああ good wishes 好意，厚情 make good 〜を弁償する，〜の埋め合わせをする，〜を完済する So far so good. これまでは順調だ。(今後の問題を暗示で)

☐ **good-bye** 間さようなら 名別れのあいさつ

☐ **Good-evening** 間こんばんは

☐ **good-hearted** 形心のやさしい，親切な

☐ **good-looking** 形顔立ちのよい，ハンサムな，きれいな

☐ **good-morning** 間《午前中の挨拶》おはよう

☐ **good-naturedly** 副人がよさそうに

☐ **good-night** 名おやすみ（の言葉）

☐ **goodness** 名①善良さ，よいところ ②神《婉曲表現》Thank goodness! ありがたい。

☐ **goodwill** 名好意，親切，善意

☐ **got** 助 have got 持っている have got to 〜しなければならない

☐ **gotten** 動 get（〜を得る）の過去分詞

☐ **Gottsreich** 名ゴッツライヒ《人名》

☐ **government** 名政治，政府，支配

☐ **grace** 名①優雅，気品がある ②好意，親切 ③《通例 Your [His] G-》閣下《公爵・大司教に対する尊称》，陛下《君主に対する尊称》

☐ **Grace** 名グレース《人名》

☐ **grand** 形雄大な，壮麗な grand duke 大公

☐ **grass** 名草，牧草(地)，芝生 動草［芝生］でおおう［おおわれる］

☐ **grassy** 形草で覆われた，草のような

☐ **grateful** 形感謝する，ありがたく思う

☐ **grave** 名墓 形重要な，厳粛な，深刻な

☐ **gravely** 副ひどく，深刻に

☐ **graveyard** 名墓地

☐ **gray** 形①灰色の ②どんよりした，憂うつな 名灰色

☐ **gray-haired** 形白髪まじりの

☐ **great deal** 多量に，大いに，ずっと a great deal of 多量の，大量の

☐ **great number of** 《a-》非常に多くの

☐ **Great heavens!** 間なんてこと！

☐ **greatly** 副大いに

☐ **Greek** 形ギリシャ(人)の，ギリシャ語の 名ギリシャ人，ギリシャ語

☐ **Green Dragon Inn** グリーン・ドラゴン《宿屋》

☐ **greet** 動①(人)にあいさつする ②〜を(喜んで)迎える 名《-ing》あいさつ(の言葉)，あいさつ(状)

☐ **Gregory** 名グレゴリー《人名》

☐ **Grenoble** 名グルノーブル《フランスの地名》

☐ **grey** 形①灰色の ②どんよりした，憂うつな 名灰色

□ **groan** 動 ①うめく, うなる ②ブーブー言う

□ **Grosvenor Hotel** 《the –》グロブナー・ホテル《ホテル名》

□ **ground** 名《-s》(建物の周囲の) 庭, 敷地 **fall to the ground** 転ぶ **ground floor** 1 階 **on the ground** 地面に **on the grounds of** [that] ～のため, ～という理由で

□ **group** 熟 **in a group** グループで

□ **grow on** [upon] ～の気に入る [心を引く] ようになる, (不安などが) ～にだんだん募ってくる

□ **grow up** 成長する, 大人になる

□ **Gruner** 名 グルーナー《人名》

□ **guard** 名 ①警戒, 見張り ②番人 動 ～の番をする, ～を監視する, ～を守る

□ **guess** 動 ～と推測する **Guess what.** あのね。何だと思う？知ってるかい？ 名 推測, 推量 **make a guess** 見当をつけてみる, 当て推量をする

□ **guest** 名 客, ゲスト

□ **guid** 形 good (よい) に同じ《スコットランド方言》

□ **guilt** 名 罪, 有罪, 犯罪

□ **guilty** 形 有罪の, やましい

□ **gun** 名 銃, 大砲

□ **gun-powder** 名 火薬

□ **gun-room** 名 銃器室

□ **gunpowder** 名 火薬

□ **gunshot** 名 ①発砲, 射撃 ②発射された弾丸

□ **Gustave Flaubert** 名 ギュスターヴ・フロベール (1821–1880)《仏の小説家》

□ **gypsy** 名 ジプシー

H

□ **ha** 間 ほう, まあ, おや《驚き・悲しみ・不満・喜び・笑い声などを表す》

□ **habit** 名 習慣, 癖, 気質

□ **had better** ～したほうが身のためだ, ～しなさい

□ **hairless** 形 毛のない, ひげのない

□ **half-afraid** 形 半ば怖がって

□ **half-brother** 名 異父 (異母) 兄弟

□ **half-drunk** 形 半ば酔っ払って

□ **half-hearted** 形 気乗りのしない

□ **half-hour** 名 半時間, 30 分

□ **half-listen** 動 いい加減 [適当] に聞く

□ **half-moon** 名 半月

□ **half-past** 名 30 分過ぎ

□ **half-smile** 名 中途半端な笑み

□ **half-smiling** 形 中途半端な笑みを浮かべて

□ **half-wage** 名 半分の賃金

□ **halfway** 副 中間 [中途] で, 不完全に **halfway down** ～の途中で 形 中間 [中途] の, 不完全な

□ **hall** 名 公会堂, ホール, 大広間, 玄関

□ **Hall Lake** ホール湖

□ **hallway** 名 玄関, 廊下

□ **Hammerford** 名 ハマーフォード《人名》

□ **Hammersmith Bridge** ハマースミス橋《橋の名》

□ **Hampshire** 名 ハンプシャー《イギリスの州》

□ **hand** **give someone a hand** (人) に手を貸す **hand in** 差し出す, 提出する **hand over** ～を (人に) ゆだねる [引き渡す], 譲り渡す **hold up one's hand** 片手を挙げる **in hand** 手持ちの, 手元にある **in the hands of** ～の掌中にあって, ～の管理下で **lay hands** (up) **on** ～を捕まえる, 入手する, 見つけ出す **on hand** 手持ちの, 手元にある, さし迫って **on the other hand** 他方で (は) **put ～ in one's hands** ～を…に預ける **put up one's hand** 手を挙げる **shake hands** 握手する **take someone by the hand** (人) の手を取る **throw up one's hands** 降参する

□ **handbag** 名 ハンドバッグ

□ **handcuff** 名 手錠

□ **handiwork** 名 手仕事, 手細工 (品)

□ **handkerchief** 名 ハンカチ

□ **handsome** 形 端正な (顔立ちの), りっぱな, (男性が) ハンサムな

□ **handwriting** 名 ①手書き, 肉筆 ②筆跡, 書体

□ **handwritten** 形 手書きの

□ **hang** 動 かかる, かける, つるす, ぶら下がる **hang down** ぶら下がる **hang on** しがみつく, がんばる, (電話を) 切らずに待つ **hang up** つるす, 電話を切る

□ **hangman** 名 絞首刑執行人

□ **happen** 熟 **as it happens** たまたま, 偶然にも **happen to** たまたま～する, 偶然～する **happen to be** 偶然にも

□ **happily** 副 幸福に, 楽しく, うまく, 幸いにも

□ **happiness** 名 幸せ, 喜び

□ **happy to do** 《be –》～してうれしい, 喜んで～する

happy-looking 形 幸せそうな, 楽しそうな

harbor 名 港, 停泊所

hard to 〜し難い

hard-looking 形 粗野な

hard-working 形 よく働く, 勤勉な

harden 動 固める, 固くする, 頑固にする

Harding Brothers ハーディング兄弟（商会）

hardly 副 ①ほとんど〜でない, わずかに ②厳しく, かろうじて **can hardly** とても〜できない **hardly when** 〜するかしないうちに

Harley 名 ハーレー《地名》

Harley Street ハーレー街《ロンドンの街路の一つ。医者の町として有名》

harm 動 〜を傷つける, 〜をそこなう

harmless 形 無害の, 安全な

harmony 名 調和, 一致, ハーモニー

Harrow 名 ハロー《地名》

harsh 形 厳しい, とげとげしい

Harvey 名 ハーベイ《人名》

hat 熟 **take one's hat off to** 帽子を脱いで［上げて］〜にあいさつする, 〜に脱帽する, 敬意を表する

hate 動 〜を嫌う, 〜を憎む, 〜するのを嫌がる 名 憎しみ

have 熟 **could have done** 〜だったかもしれない《仮定法》 **have a case** 告訴する **have a day off work** 一日休みを取る **have a headache** 頭痛がする **have a nerve** 図太い神経をしている **have been to** 〜へ行ったことがある **have control over** 〜を支配［コントロール］する **have got** 持っている **have got to** 〜しなければならない **have it out with** 話の片をつける, 決着をつける **have no equal** 並ぶ［匹敵する］ものがない **have no idea** わからない **have no time to do** 〜する時間がない **have no use for** 〜には用がない, 〜に我慢できない **have nothing to do with** 〜と何の関係もない **have other uses for** 〜にとって役に立つことがある **have something to do with** 〜と何か関係がある **have the nerve** 勇気がある **have to do with** 〜と関係がある **should have done** 〜すべきだった（のにしなかった）《仮定法》 **should never have done** 〜すべきではなかった（のにしてしまった）《仮定法》 **will have done** 〜してしまっているだろう《未来完了形》 **would have … if** 〜 もし〜だったとしたら…しただろう

Hayter 名 ヘイター《人名》

head 熟 **head for** 〜に向かう, 〜の方に進む **head of** 〜の長 **I can make neither head nor tail of it.** 何が何だかさっぱりわからない。 **throw back one's head** 頭をのけぞらせる

head teacher 名 校長, 学長

head-keeper 名 管理人長

headache 名 頭痛 **have a headache** 頭痛がする

headline 名 (新聞等の)見出し

headman 名 頭, 首長

headquarters 名 本部, 司令部, 本署

healthy 形 健康な, 健全な, 健康によい

hear from 〜から手紙［電話・返事］をもらう

hear of 〜について聞く, 〜のうわさを聞く

heart 熟 **break one's heart** (失恋などで)〜をひどく失望させる **in one's heart of hearts** 内心は **with a heavy heart** 打ち沈んで, 陰気に **with all one's heart** 心を込めて, 喜んで, 心から

heat 名 熱, 暑さ

Heath Newton 名 ヒース・ニュートン《人名》

heaven 名 ①天国 ②天国のようなところ［状態］, 楽園 ③空 ④《H-》神 **By Heaven!** 神にかけて。おや。まあ。 **Good heavens!** まあ。大変だ。なんてことだ。とんでもない。 **Thank heaven!** ありがたい。助かった。

heavily 副 ①重く, 重そうに ②多量に

heavy-eyed 形 沈んだ目をした, 悲しげな目つきの

Heidegger 名 ハイデッガー《人名》

height 名 ①高さ, 身長 ②《the-》絶頂, 真っ盛り ③高台, 丘 **at the height of** 〜の絶頂に［で］, 〜の真っ最中に［で］

Helen Stoner 名 ヘレン・ストーナー《人名》

help 熟 **ask for help** 助けを頼む **can't help** 避けられない, 〜せずにはいられない **cannot [can't] help but** 〜せずにはいられない **help in** 〜に役立つ **help oneself** 自分で取って食べる［飲む］ **help 〜 with** ……を〜の面で手伝う

helper 名 助手, 助けになるもの

helpless 形 無力の, 自分ではどうすることもできない

helplessly 副 ①たよるものもなく, どうしようもなく ②どうすることもできず

hen-pheasant 名 雌のキジ

Hercules 名 《ギリシャ神話》ヘラクレス

herd 名 (大型動物の)一群, 群集, 民衆

here 熟 **here and there** あちこちで **here are** 〜 こちらは〜です。 **here is** 〜 こちらは〜です。 **Here it is.** はい, どうぞ。 **Look**

here. ほら。ねえ。**over here** こっちへ[に]；ほら，さあ《人の注意を引く》

□ **Herr** 名《独語》～氏《＝Mr.》

□ **hey** 間 ①《呼びかけ注意を促して》おい，ちょっと ②へえ，おや，まあ

□ **hid** 動 hide（隠れる，隠す）の過去，過去分詞

□ **hidden** 動 hide（隠れる，隠す）の過去分詞 形 隠れた，秘密の

□ **hide** 動 隠れる，隠す，隠れて見えない，～を秘密にする

□ **high hat** シルクハット

□ **high road** 主要[幹線]道路，本街道

□ **High Street** ハイ・ストリート《通りの名》

□ **high-class** 形 高級の，一流の

□ **high-nosed** 形 鼻が高い

□ **highlight** 動 注目させる，強調する

□ **highly** 副 ①大いに，非常に ②高度に，高位に ③高く評価して，高価で

□ **Highness** 名《通常 His, Her, Your –》殿下

□ **Hilda** 名 ヒルダ《人名》

□ **Hill** 名《Detective –》ヒル警部《人名》

□ **Hill Barton** ヒル・バートン《人名》

□ **Hilton Cubitt** ヒルトン・キュービット《人名》

□ **Himalaya** 名《-s》ヒマラヤ山脈

□ **hiss** 名 シューという音

□ **hit upon** ～に出くわす，～を（偶然に）見つける，～をふと思いつく

□ **hmm** 間（熟考，ためらい，疑問）ふうむ

□ **hold** 熟 **get hold of** ～につかまる **hold back** ～を引き止める **hold in**（動かないように）押さえる **hold on to** ～にしがみつく，～をつかんで放さない **hold oneself up against a wall** 身体を壁で真っすぐに支える **hold out**（手に持ったものを）差し出す **hold up** 持ちこたえる，～を掲げる，（手を）上げる，（指を）立てる **hold up one's hand** 片手を挙げる

□ **Holdernesse** 名《Duke of –》ホールダネス伯爵《人名》

□ **Holdernesse Hall** ホールダネス館

□ **Holland** 名 オランダ《国名》

□ **holly** 名 モチノキ，ヒイラギ《植》

□ **Holmes** 名 ホームズ《人名》

□ **Holy War** 『神聖戦争』《書名》

□ **home** 熟 **at home** 自宅で，在宅して，くつろいで **bring home** 家に持ってくる **get home** 家に着く[帰る] **go home** 帰宅する **take someone home**（人）を家まで送る

□ **Homer** 名 ホメロス《古代ギリシャの詩人》

□ **homesickness** 名 ホームシック

□ **homeward** 副 家（のほう）へ

□ **honest** 形 ①正直な，誠実な，心からの ②公正な，感心な

□ **honestly** 副 正直に

□ **honor** 名 ①名誉，光栄，信用 ②節操，自尊心 **do ～ honor** ～に敬意を表する，～の名誉となる **honor of** ～の名誉 **in honor of** ～に敬意を表して，～を記念して 動 ～を尊敬する，～に栄誉を与える

□ **honorable** 形 ①尊敬すべき，立派な ②名誉ある ③高貴な ④《the H-》～閣下《イギリスの貴族の子息などへの敬称》

□ **honored** 形 名誉ある

□ **hope** 熟 **in the hope of** ～を望んで[期待して]

□ **hopeful** 形 希望に満ちた，望みをいだいて（いる），有望な

□ **hopelessness** 名 絶望

□ **Hopkins** 名 ホプキンス《人名》

□ **Horace Harker** ホレス・ハーカー《人名》

□ **horrible** 形 恐ろしい，ひどい

□ **horse-racing** 名 競馬

□ **horsekeeper** 名 馬の飼育人

□ **horseshoe** 名 てい鉄

□ **Hotspur** 名《the –》ホットスパー号《船の名》

□ **hour of need** 助けが必要なとき

□ **house-party** 名 接待会の滞在客

□ **house-shoe** 名《通例 -s》スリッパ

□ **household** 名 家族，世帯

□ **housekeeper** 名 家政婦

□ **housemaid** 名 家政婦，お手伝いさん

□ **how** 熟 **How about ～?** ～はどうですか。～しませんか。**How could ～?** 何だって～なんてことがありえようか？ **How on earth ～?** 一体どうやったら **how far** どのくらいの距離か **how to** ～する方法 **no matter how** どんなに～であろうとも **tell ～ how to …** ～に…のやり方を教える

□ **however** 副 たとえ～でも 接 けれども，だが

□ **Hudson** 名 ハドソン，《Mrs. –》ハドソン夫人《人名》

□ **huge** 形 巨大な，ばくだいな

□ **Hugo** 名 ユーゴ《人名》

□ **hum** 間 うむ，ふーむ

□ **human being** 人，人間

☐ **humanity** 名 人間性, 人間らしさ

☐ **humdrum** 形 単調な, 平凡な

☐ **hundreds of** 何百もの～

☐ **Hung-wu** 洪武 (帝)《明朝の初代皇帝, 在位 1368–1398 年》

☐ **hunger** 名 空腹, 飢え

☐ **hunt** 動 ～を狩る, 狩りをする, ～を捜し求める

☐ **hunted** 形 追われている

☐ **hunter** 名 ①狩りをする人, 狩人, ハンター ②猟馬, 猟犬

☐ **hunting** 名 ハンティング, 狩猟

☐ **Hurlingham** 名 ハーリンガム《地名》

☐ **Hurlstone** 名 ハールストン《イギリスの地名》

☐ **hurriedly** 副 大急ぎで, あわてて

☐ **hurry** 熟 **hurry off** 急いで立ち去る, 急いで出掛ける **hurry over** ～を慌ててやる **in a hurry** 急いで, あわてて **in one's hurry to** ～しようと慌てて

☐ **hurt** 動 害を与える, 困った事になる **get hurt** 傷つく, 負傷する

I

☐ **ichthyosis** 名《病》魚鱗癬

☐ **icily** 副 冷たく, 冷淡に

☐ **icy** 形 氷の (多い), 氷のように冷たい

☐ **idea** 熟 **have no idea** 全くわからない

☐ **identify** 動 ①～を (本人, 同一と) 確認する, 見分ける ②意気投合する

☐ **if** 熟 **as if** あたかも～のように, まるで～みたいに **ask ～ if** ～かどうか尋ねる **Do you mind if …?** ～したらお邪魔ですか **even if** たとえ～でも **If + 《主語》+ could** ～できればなあ《仮定法》**if any** もしあれば, あったとしても **if ever** もし～ということがあれば **if necessary** もし必要ならば **if only** ～でありさえすれば **if possible** できるなら **see if** ～かどうかを確かめる **wonder if** ～ではないかと思う **would have … if ～** もし…だったとしたら…しただろう

☐ **ill-feeling** 名 悪感情, 敵意

☐ **ill-looking** 名 具合の悪そうな顔つき

☐ **illness** 名 病気

☐ **illustrious** 形 ①傑出した, 有名な ②輝かしい

☐ **image** 名 ①印象, 姿 ②画像, 映像

☐ **imagination** 名 想像 (力), 空想

☐ **imagine** 動 ～を想像する, ～と心に思い描く

☐ **immediately** 副 すぐに, ～するやいなや

☐ **imperial** 形 帝国の, 皇帝の, 皇后の **Imperial Yeomanry** 国防騎兵隊

☐ **importance** 名 重要性, 大切さ **of no importance** 取るに足りない, 重要でない

☐ **impossible** 形 手に負えない

☐ **impress** 動 ～を印象づける, ～を感銘させる

☐ **in** 熟 **in a group** グループで **in a hurry** 急いで, あわてて **in a minute** すぐに **in a moment** ただちに **in a way** ある意味では **in a word** 一言で言うと **in addition** 加えて, さらに **in answer to** ～に応じて **in any case** とにかく **in any way** 決して, 多少なりとも **in case** ～だといけないので, 念のため, 万が一 **in charge of** ～を任されて, ～を担当して, ～の責任を負って **in control** ～を支配として, ～を掌握している **in fact** つまり, 実は, 要するに **in favor of** ～に賛成して, ～を支持して **in fear** おどおどして, ビクビクして **in front of** ～の前に, ～の正面に **in general** 一般に, たいてい **in no time** すぐに, 一瞬 **in no way** 決して～でない **in one's heart of hearts** 内心は **in one's hurry to** ～しようと慌てて **in order** きちんと (整理されて), 順序正しく **in order to** ～するために, ～しようと **in other respects** その他の点では **in peace** 平和のうちに, 安心して **in person** (本人) 自ら, 自身で **in public** 人前で, 公然と **in question** 問題の, 論争中の **in return for** ～に対する見返りとして, ～の交換条件として **in silence** 黙って, 沈黙のうちに **in some way** 何とかして, 何らかの方法で **in spite of** ～にもかかわらず **in store** 蓄えて, 用意されて **in that case** もしそうなら **in the case of** ～の場合は **in the dead of the night** 真夜中に **in the direction of** ～の方向に **in the distance** 遠方に **in the earth** 地中に **in the end** とうとう, 結局, ついに **in the future** 将来は **in the hope of** ～を望んで [期待して] **in the meantime** それまでは, 当分は **in the middle of** ～の真ん中 [中ほど] に **in the presence of** ～の面前で **in the world** 世界中で **in this way** このようにして **in those days** あのころは, 当時は **in time** 間に合って, やがて **in touch with** (～と) 連絡を取って **in trouble** 面倒な状況で, 困って **in turn** 順番に, 立ち代わって **in use** 使用されて **in wonder** 驚いて **in writing** 書面で

☐ **inch** 名 ①インチ《長さの単位。1/12 フィート, 2.54cm》②少量 **by inches** 一寸刻みに, わずか [少し] ずつ 動 少しずつ動く

☐ **include** 動 ～を含む, ～を勘定に入れる

☐ **income** 名 所得, 収入

☐ **incomplete** 形 不完全な, 不十分な, 未完成

の

- [ ] **increase** 動 増加［増強］する，増やす，増える
- [ ] **indeed** 副 実際，本当に，《強意》全く 間 本当に，まさか
- [ ] **India** 名 インド《国名》
- [ ] **Indian** 名 ①インド人 ②（アメリカ）インディアン 形 ①インドの，インド人の ②（アメリカ）インディアンの
- [ ] **indication** 名 ①指示，暗示するもの ②表示，指摘
- [ ] **indirect** 形 間接的な，二次的な
- [ ] **indirectly** 副 間接（的）に，遠回しに
- [ ] **inhuman** 形 人間的でない，人間ならざる
- [ ] **injure** 動 痛める，傷つける
- [ ] **injury** 名 ①けが ②侮辱，無礼
- [ ] **ink** 名 インク
- [ ] **inked** 形 入れ墨［タトゥー］の入った
- [ ] **inn** 名 宿屋，居酒屋
- [ ] **inner** 形 ①内部の ②心の中の
- [ ] **innkeeper** 名 宿屋の主人（経営者）
- [ ] **innocent** 形 ①無害の，潔白な ②無邪気な，無害の
- [ ] **inquiry** 名 ①質問，探求 ②事実を求めること
- [ ] **insane** 形 正気でない，狂気の
- [ ] **insight** 名 洞察，真相，見識
- [ ] **inspector** 名 ①検査する人 ②《英》警部補
- [ ] **instant** 名 瞬間，寸時
- [ ] **instantly** 副 すぐに，即座に
- [ ] **instead** 副 その代わりに **instead of** ～の代わりに，～をしないで
- [ ] **instruct** 動 ①～を教える，教育する ②（人）に（～するように）指図［命令］する
- [ ] **intelligence** 名 ①知能 ②情報
- [ ] **intelligent** 形 頭のよい，聡明な
- [ ] **intelligent-looking** 形 頭のきれそうな，利口そうな
- [ ] **intend to** ～しようと思う，～するつもりである
- [ ] **interest** 熟 **of interest** 興味のある［対象となる］ **of no interest** 興味のない **take an interest in** ～に興味を持つ
- [ ] **interested in** 《be –》～に興味［関心］がある
- [ ] **interestingly** 副 おもしろく，（文を修飾して）おもしろいことに
- [ ] **interfere** 動 ①じゃまをする，干渉する ②衝突する

- [ ] **Interlaken** 名 インターラーケン《スイスの町》
- [ ] **intuition** 名 直感，洞察
- [ ] **investigate** 動 ～を研究する，調査する，捜査する
- [ ] **investigation** 名 （徹底的な）調査，取り調べ
- [ ] **investigator** 名 調査者，捜査官，研究員
- [ ] **invite** 動 招待する，誘う
- [ ] **involve** 動 ①～を含む，伴う ②巻き込む，かかわらせる
- [ ] **Ionides** 名 イオニデス商会
- [ ] **Irene Adler** アイリーン・アドラー《人名》
- [ ] **Iris** 名 アイリス《馬の名》
- [ ] **Irish** 形 アイルランド（人）の
- [ ] **Irish-setter** 名 アイリッシュ・セッター《犬種》
- [ ] **iron** 名 鉄，鉄製のもの 形 鉄の，鉄製の
- [ ] **iron hand** 過酷さ，冷酷な支配
- [ ] **Isa Whitney** アイザ・ホイットニー《人名》
- [ ] **It is ~ for someone to ...** 熟 （人）が…するのは～だ
- [ ] **It takes all sorts to make a world.** 世の中にはあらゆる種類の人やものがいる。《ことわざ》
- [ ] **Italian** 形 イタリア（人・語）の 名 ①イタリア人 ②イタリア語
- [ ] **Italian Quarter** イタリア人街
- [ ] **itself** 代 それ自体，それ自身
- [ ] **Ives** 名 《St. –》セント・アイヴス《イギリス・コーンウォール州にある海辺の街》
- [ ] **ivory** 名 象牙
- [ ] **ivy** 名 ツタ，つる植物
- [ ] **ivy-covered** 形 ツタで覆われた

J

- [ ] **Jabez Wilson** ジェイベズ・ウィルソン《人名》
- [ ] **Jack** 名 ジャック《人名，Mr. Bennett の愛称》
- [ ] **Jack Predergast** ジャック・プレンダガスト《人名》
- [ ] **jacket** 名 短い上着
- [ ] **jail** 名 刑務所
- [ ] **James Armitage** ジェームズ・アーミテイジ《人名》
- [ ] **James Damery** ジェームズ・デマリー《人

名》

□ **James M. Dodd** ジェームズ・M・ドッド《人名》

□ **James McCarthy** ジェームズ・マッカーシー《人名》

□ **James Moriarty** ジェームズ・モリアーティ《人名》

□ **James Saunders** ジェームズ・サーンダーズ《人名》

□ **James Wilder** ジェームズ・ワイルダー《人名》

□ **Janet Tregellis** ジャネット・トリジリス《人名》

□ **Jew** 图 ユダヤ人, ユダヤ教徒

□ **Jewish** 形 ユダヤ人, ユダヤ教の

□ **Jimmie** 图 ジミー《James の愛称》

□ **Jimmy** 图 ジミー《James の愛称》

□ **jockey** 图 騎手, ジョッキー

□ **John Clay** ジョン・クレイ《人名》

□ **John Hardy** ジョン・ハーディ《人名》

□ **John Mason** ジョン・メイソン《人名》

□ **John Straker** ジョン・ストレーカー《人名》

□ **Johnson** 图 ジョンソン《人名》

□ **Jones** 图 ジョーンズ《人名》

□ **Josiah Barnes** ジョサイア・バーンズ《人名》

□ **Josiah Brown** ジョサイア・ブラウン《人名》

□ **journal** 图 新聞, 雑誌

□ **Journal de Genève** 图 ジャーナル・ド・ジュネーブ, ジュネーブ新聞《新聞名》

□ **journey** 图 ①(遠い目的地への)旅 ②行程

□ **joy** 图 喜び, 楽しみ

□ **joyful** 形 (〜を)楽しませる, 喜びに満ちた

□ **joyous** 形 うれしい, 喜びに満ちた

□ **judge** 動 (〜に)判決を下す, 裁く, 判断する 图 裁判官, 判事, 審査員

□ **judgement** 图 ①判断, 意見 ②裁判, 判決

□ **judgment** 图 ①判断, 意見 ②裁判, 判決

□ **Julia Stoner** ジュリア・ストーナー《人名》

□ **jump** 熟 jump across 飛び越える, 飛んで渡る jump into 〜に飛び込む jump on 〜に飛びかかる jump out 飛び出る jump out of 〜から飛び出す jump over 〜の上を飛び越える jump to one's feet 飛び起きる jump up 素早く立ち上がる jump upon 飛び乗る

□ **jury** 图 陪審, 陪審員団

□ **Just a minute.** ちょっと待って。

□ **just as** (ちょうど)であろうとおり

□ **just then** そのとたんに

K

□ **Kate Whitney** ケイト・ホイットニー《人名》

□ **keep** 熟 keep clear of 〜に近寄らない keep in touch 連絡を取り合う keep on そのまま続ける keep on 〜[-ing] 〜し続ける, 繰り返し 〜する keep one's nerve 冷静でいる, ひるまずに自分を保つ keep one's promise 約束を守る keep out of 〜を避ける, 〜に干渉しない keep someone company (人)のそばにいる keep someone from 〜から(人)を阻む keep to 〜から離れない, 〜を守る keep up 続ける, 続く, 維持する, (遅れないで)ついていく, 上げたままにしておく

□ **keeper** 图 番人, 看守

□ **Kennington Road** ケニントン通り《通りの名》

□ **Kensington** 图 ケンジントン《地名》

□ **Kensington Station** ケンジントン駅

□ **Kent** 图 ケント《人名, イギリスの州名》

□ **kept out of** 《be-》加わらせない, 遠ざけておく

□ **kettle** 图 鍋, やかん

□ **Khyber** 图 カイバル峠《地名》

□ **killer** 图 殺人者[犯]

□ **kilometer** 图 キロメートル《長さの単位》

□ **kind of** ある程度, いくらか, 〜のようなもの[人]

□ **kind to** 《be-》〜に親切である

□ **kindliness** 图 優しさ, 思いやりのある行為

□ **kindly** 形 ①親切な, 情け深い, 思いやりのある ②(気候などの)温和な, 快い 副 親切に, やさしく

□ **King** 图《Mrs. 〜》キング夫人《人名》

□ **King's Pyland** キングズ・パイランド《架空の地名》

□ **Kingston** 图 キングストン《地名》

□ **Kirwan** 图 カーワン《人名》

□ **Kitty Winter** キティ・ウィンター《人名》

□ **knee** 图 ひざ

□ **knife** 图 ナイフ, 小刀, 包丁, 短剣

□ **knives** 图 knife (ナイフ, 小刀)の複数

□ **knock** 動 (〜を)ノックする, たたく

□ **know** 熟 as you know ご存知のとおり

know nothing of ～のことを知らない know of ～について知っている you know ご存知のとおり、そうでしょう

☐ **knowledge** 名知識、理解、学問

☐ **known** 動know（知っている）の過去分詞 形知られた be known to ～に知られている

☐ **knuckle** 名指関節

L

☐ **L'homme c'est rien—l'oeuvre c'est tout** 「人間は無──仕事こそがすべて」《仏語》

☐ **label** 名標札、ラベル

☐ **laboratory** 名実験室、研究室

☐ **laborer** 名労働者

☐ **Laburnum Lodge** ラバーナム荘

☐ **Laburnum Vale** ラバーナム・ベイル《地名》

☐ **lad** 名少年、若者

☐ **laid** 動lay（～を置く、～を整える、卵を産む）の過去、過去分詞

☐ **lame** 形①足が不自由な ②（議論、口実などが）説得力のない、貧弱な

☐ **lamp** 名ランプ、灯火

☐ **Lancet** 名ランセット《医学雑誌》

☐ **landholder** 名地主、借地人

☐ **landlady** 名女家主、女主人

☐ **landlord** 名①（男の）家主、地主 ②パブの主人

☐ **lane** 名車線、小道

☐ **Langmere** 名ラングメア《イギリスの村》

☐ **langur** 名ラングール、ヤセザル

☐ **lantern** 名手提げランプ、ランタン

☐ **last** 熟at last ついに、とうとう the last time この前～したとき

☐ **lat.** 略緯度（＝latitude）

☐ **late** 形亡くなった the late 故～ 熟be late for ～に遅れる of late 最近、近ごろ

☐ **lately** 副近ごろ、最近

☐ **later** 熟sooner or later 遅かれ早かれ

☐ **latest** 形最新の

☐ **latitude** 名緯度

☐ **latter** 形①後の、末の、後者の ②《the－》後者《代名詞的に用いる》

☐ **laugh at** ～を見て［聞いて］笑う

☐ **laughing** 熟burst out laughing 爆笑する

☐ **laughter** 名笑い（声）

☐ **law** 名法、法律

☐ **lawful** 形合法な

☐ **lawyer** 名弁護士、法律家

☐ **lay** 動①～を置く、～を横たえる、～を敷く ②～を整える ③卵を産む ④lie（横たわる、（ある状態に）ある）の過去 lay back 後ろに寄りかかる、のんびりする lay down ①下に置く、横たえる ②裏切る lay off レイオフする、一時解雇する lay oneself open 自分の正体を白日の下にさらす lay out ～をきちんと並べる、陳列する

☐ **Le Brun** 名ル・ブラン《人名》

☐ **lead** 名手がかり、きっかけ 熟lead into（ある場所）へ導く lead the way 先に立って導く、案内する、率先する lead the way to ～への道を開く lead to ～に至る、～に通じる、～を引き起こす

☐ **leading** 形有数の、主要な

☐ **league** 名同盟、連盟

☐ **lean** 動①もたれる、寄りかかる ②傾く、傾ける lean back 後ろにもたれる

☐ **learn of** ～のことを（聞いて）知る

☐ **leash** 名（動物をつなぐ）皮ひも、鎖

☐ **least** 名最小［少］ at least 少なくとも

☐ **leave** 動①去る、離れる ②あとに残す、置いていく leave ～ alone ～をそっとしておく leave behind あとにする、～を置き去りにする leave ～ for … …を～のために残しておく leave for ～に向かって出発する leave in ～をそのままにしておく leave over 残しておく make someone leave 退校［職］させる

☐ **led** 動lead（～を導く）の過去、過去分詞

☐ **Lee** 名リー《地名》

☐ **left** 動leave（去る、あとに残す）の過去、過去分詞

☐ **left-handed** 形左ききの、左きき用の

☐ **legal** 形法律（上）の、正当な

☐ **lemon** 名レモン

☐ **length** 名長さ、縦、たけ、距離 at full length 十分に、全身を伸ばして at length ついに、詳しく

☐ **lengthy** 形非常に長い、長ったらしい

☐ **Leon Sterndale** レオン・スターンデール《人名》

☐ **leper** 名ハンセン病患者

☐ **leprosy** 名ハンセン病

☐ **Leslie Oakshott** レズリー・オークショット《人名》

☐ **less** 形～より小さい［少ない］ 副～より少な

く，～ほどでなく **less and less** だんだん少なく，ますます～でなく **no less than** ～と同じだけの，～も同然 **not less than** ～以下ではなく，～にまさるとも劣らない

- [ ] **Lestrade** 图レストレード《人名》
- [ ] **Lesurier** 图ルスリエ《人名》
- [ ] **let** 熟 **let down** 期待を裏切る，失望させる **let go** 手を放す，行かせる **let go of** ～から手を離す **let in** ～を招き入れる **Let me see.** ええと。 **let out** (声を)出す，発する **let someone have his way** (人)の思う通りにやらせる **let us** どうか私たちに～させてください
- [ ] **letter-opening** 形手紙を開封するための
- [ ] **Leuk** 图ロイク《スイスの町》
- [ ] **Leverstoke** 图《Lord –》レヴァストーク卿《人名》
- [ ] **lie** 動①うそをつく ②横たわる，寝る ③(ある状態に)ある，存在する **lie down** 横たわる，横になる 图うそ，詐欺 **tell a lie** うそをつく
- [ ] **lieutenant** 图①中尉，少尉 ②代理，副官
- [ ] **life** 熟 **all one's life** ずっと，生まれてから **be given life in prison** 終身刑を言い渡される **for the rest of life** 死ぬまで **lead a ～ life** ～な生活を送る **matter of life and death** 重大問題，死活問題 **very life** 命
- [ ] **lifetime** 图①一生，生涯 ②寿命
- [ ] **lift** 動①～を持ち上げる，上がる ②～をとり除く
- [ ] **light** 熟 **bring the secret to light** 秘密を公表する **light sleeper** 眠りの浅い人 **throw some light upon** ～の解明にいくらか役立つ
- [ ] **light-colored** 形明るい色の，淡い色の
- [ ] **light-hearted** 形気楽な，快活な
- [ ] **lightly** 副①軽く，そっと ②軽率に
- [ ] **like** 熟 **feel like** ～がほしい，～したい気がする，～のような感じがする **look like** ～のように見える，～に似ている **rather like** ～に似ている，きらいではない **sound like** ～のように聞こえる **would like** ～がほしい **would like to** ～したいと思う **Would you like ～?** ～はいかがですか。
- [ ] **likeable** 形好感の持てる，魅力のある
- [ ] **likely** 形①ありそうな，(～)しそうな ②適当な **very likely** ～の可能性が非常に高い，十中八九 副たぶん，おそらく
- [ ] **likeness** 图(～に)よく似ていること，よく似たもの
- [ ] **limp** 動①足を引きずって歩く ②のろのろ進む 图足を引きずって歩くこと
- [ ] **line** 動①(～に)線を引く ②(～に)しわを寄

せる ③(～を)1列に並べる **be lined with** ～が立ち並ぶ 图専門，得手，(仕事の)方面 **line of** ～の系統，血筋 **take a high line** 高邁な方針[路線]をとる

- [ ] **lined** 形裏地のついた，裏打ちした，しわのある
- [ ] **lip** 图くちびる，《-s》口
- [ ] **list** 图名簿，目録，一覧表
- [ ] **listener** 图聞く人，ラジオ聴取者
- [ ] **lit** 動 light (火をつける，明るくする)の過去，過去分詞
- [ ] **live on** ～を糧として生きる
- [ ] **live out** 生き延びる，離れて暮らす
- [ ] **live upon** ～で生活を立てる
- [ ] **lively** 形①元気のよい，活発な ②鮮やかな，強烈な，真に迫った
- [ ] **liver** 图①肝臓 ②茶褐色
- [ ] **Liverpool** 图リヴァプール《イングランド北部の都市》
- [ ] **Liverpool Street** リヴァプール街《地名》
- [ ] **livestock** 图家畜
- [ ] **living** 熟 **make a living** 生計を立てる，暮らしていく
- [ ] **location** 图位置，場所
- [ ] **lock up** ～を閉じ込める
- [ ] **lodge** 图①番小屋 ②山小屋 動(～に)泊る[泊める]，下宿する[させる]
- [ ] **lodgekeeper** 图番小屋の管理人
- [ ] **lodger** 图下宿人，間借り人
- [ ] **London** 图ロンドン《イギリスの首都》
- [ ] **Londoner** 图ロンドン人，ロンドンっ子
- [ ] **lonely** 形①孤独な，心寂しい ②ひっそりした，人里離れた
- [ ] **long** 熟 **all day long** 一日中，終日 **as long as** ～する以上は，～である限りは **for long** 長い間 **long ago** ずっと前に，昔 **long way** はるかに **no longer** もはや～でない[～しない] **not ～ any longer** もはや～でない[～しない] **so long as** ～する限りは **take long** 時間がかかる **wait a long time** 長時間待つ
- [ ] **long.** 略経度(= longitude)
- [ ] **longitude** 图経度
- [ ] **look** 熟 **get a good look at** ～をよく見る **look about** あたりを見回す **look after** ～の世話をする，～に気をつける **look ahead** 先[将来]のことを考える **look along** ～に沿って見る **look around** まわりを見回す **look back** 後ろを振り返る **look back at** ～に視線を戻す，～を振り返って見る **look down** 見下ろす **look**

488

down upon 見下ろす，俯瞰する **look for** 〜を
探す **Look here.** ほら。ねえ。 **look in** 中を見る，
立ち寄る **look into** ①〜を検討する，〜を研究
する ②〜の中を見る，〜をのぞき込む **look
like** 〜のように見える，〜に似ている **look on**
傍観する，眺める **look onto** (建物が) 〜に向
いている，〜に面する **look out** ①外を見る ②
気をつける，注意する **look out of** (窓などから)
外を見る **look over** 〜越しに見る，〜を見渡す
look over at 〜の方を見る **look through** 〜を
のぞき込む **look to** 〜しようとする **look up**
見上げる，調べる **look upon** 〜を見る，見つめ
る **look upon 〜 as …** 〜を…とみなす，考え
る **take a look at** 〜をちょっと見る

- **looking-glass** 名拡大鏡
- **lookout** 名①見張り，警戒 ②見込み **keep a
lookout** 見張る，気をつける
- **loophole** 名小窓，抜け道，抜け穴
- **loose** 形自由な，ゆるんだ，あいまいな 動
〜をほどく，〜を解き放つ
- **lord** 名首長，主人，領主，貴族，上院議員
Good Lord! 《驚きを表して》ああ。おお。
- **Lord Balmoral** バルモラル卿《人名》
- **lose one's mind** 正気を失う
- **lose sight of** 〜を見失う
- **loser** 名敗者
- **loss** 名①損失(額・物)，損害 ②失敗，敗北 **at
a loss** 途方に暮れて
- **loudly** 副大声で，騒がしく
- **love** 名(特に女性の) 愛する[いとしい]人，愛
人，恋人 **be in love with** 〜に恋して，〜に心を
奪われて **fall in love with** 〜と恋におちる
love affair 恋愛(関係) **old love** かつて親しか
った人，昔の恋人
- **love-present** 名愛する人への贈り物
- **lovely** 形愛らしい，美しい，すばらしい
- **lover** 名愛人，恋人
- **lovingly** 副かわいがって，愛情を込めて
- **Lowenstein** 名ローゼンシュタイン《人名》
- **lower** 形もっと低い，下級の，劣った
- **Lower Brixton Road** 下ブリックストン
通り《通りの名》
- **Lower Gill Moor** 下ギル荒野《地名》
- **Lower Grove Road** 下グローブ通り《通り
の名》
- **Lowther Arcade** ローサー・アーケイド《ロ
ンドンの地名》
- **Lucerne** 名ルツェルン《スイスの都市》
- **luck** 熟 **bad luck** 災難，不運，悪運

- **luckily** 副運よく，幸いにも
- **Lucretia Venucci** ルクレチア・ヴェヌーチ
《人名》
- **lumbago** 名腰痛
- **Luxembourg** 名ルクセンブルク《大公国，
またはその首都》
- **lying** 動lie (うそをつく，横たわる)の現在分
詞 形①うそをつく，虚偽の ②横になっている
- **Lyons** 名リヨン《地名》

M

- **M.A.** 略文学修士 (=Master of Arts)
- **ma'am** 名奥さん，お嬢さん
- **Mackleton** 名マクルトン《地名》
- **Mackleton Station** マクルトン駅
- **Macphail** 名マクフェイル《人名》
- **mad** 形①気の狂った ②逆上した，理性をな
くした ③ばかげた ④(〜に)熱狂[熱中]して，
夢中の **go mad** 発狂する
- **madam** 名(丁寧な呼びかけ)奥様，お嬢様
- **Madame** 名〜夫人
- **made** 熟 **be made from** 〜から作られる **be
made of** 〜でできて[作られて]いる **be made
to** 〜させられる **be made up** 作り上げた，決
心した
- **madly** 副①気が狂って ②猛烈に，すごく
- **madman** 名①狂人 ②常軌を逸した人
- **madmen** 名madman(狂人，気違いじみた男)
の複数
- **madness** 名狂気，熱中
- **Mafia** 名マフィア
- **magic** 名①魔法，手品 ②魔力
- **magnifying glass** 名拡大鏡
- **maid** 名お手伝い，メイド
- **mailman** 名郵便配達人
- **main** 形①主な，主要な ②力いっぱいの
- **mainly** 副主に
- **majesty** 名①威厳，壮麗さ ②《M-》陛下
- **make** 熟 **I can make neither head nor tail
of it.** 何が何だかさっぱりわからない。 **make
a beginning** 糸口を開く，着手する **make a
guess** 見当をつけてみる，当て推量をする
make a living 生計を立てる，自活する **make
a mistake** 間違いをする **make away** 逃げる，
慌てて立ち去る **make for** 急いで進む，急行す
る，〜に突進する **make money** お金を儲ける

make noise 音を立てる make of 判断する, みなす make one's way 進む, 行く, 成功する make out 作り上げる, 認識する, 見分ける make sense 意味をなす, よくわかる make someone leave 退校[職]させる make sure 確かめる, 確認する make the most of ～を最大限利用する make up 作り出す, 考え出す, ～を構成[形成]する make up for 償う, ～の埋め合わせをする make up one's mind 決心する make use of ～を利用する, ～を生かす make way 道を譲る[あける], 前進する

- [ ] **maker** 名 製造業者, メーカー
- [ ] **makeup** 名 化粧(品)
- [ ] **man** 熟 changed man 別人 man and wife 夫婦 man of the world 世慣れた人 man to man 一対一で, 公明正大に
- [ ] **manage** 動 ①～を動かす, ～をうまく処理する, ～を経営[管理]する, ～を支配する ③どうにか～する
- [ ] **manager** 名 経営者, 支配人, 支店長, 部長
- [ ] **Manchester Street** マンチェスター街《地名》
- [ ] **manhood** 名 大人の男, 成年, 男らしさ
- [ ] **mankind** 名 人類, 人間
- [ ] **manner** 名 ①方法, やり方 ②態度, 様子 ③《-s》行儀, 作法, 生活様式
- [ ] **manor house** 領主の邸宅
- [ ] **mansion** 名 大邸宅
- [ ] **many** 熟 so many 非常に多くの
- [ ] **map-like** 形 地図のような
- [ ] **Mapleton** 名 メイプルトン《イギリスの地名》
- [ ] **march into** ～に行進する
- [ ] **mark** 名 ①印, 記号, 跡 ②点数 ③特色 動 ①印[記号]をつける ②採点する ③目立たせる mark you いいかい, 聞きなさい (=mind you)
- [ ] **marker** 名 標識, 指標
- [ ] **Marker** マーカー《人名》
- [ ] **marking** 名 印, 斑点
- [ ] **marriage** 名 結婚(生活[式])
- [ ] **marry** 動 (～と)結婚する
- [ ] **Martin** 名 マーティン《人名》
- [ ] **Marylebone Lane** メリルボーン横丁《ロンドンの地名》
- [ ] **mask** 名 面, マスク
- [ ] **Mason** 名 メイスン《人名》
- [ ] **master** 名 主人, 雇い主, 師 動 ①～を修得する ②～の主となる
- [ ] **masterful** 形 みごとな, 名人芸の

- [ ] **mat** 名 マット, 敷物
- [ ] **match** 名 マッチ(棒) 動 ～と調和する, ～とつり合う
- [ ] **matchbox** 名 マッチ箱
- [ ] **material** 名 材料, 原料
- [ ] **mathematical** 形 数学の, 数理的な, 正確な
- [ ] **matter** 名 ①状況, 事態 ②問題 a matter of ～の問題 as a matter of fact 実は, 実を言うと matter of life and death 重大問題, 死活問題 What is the matter? どうしたの？ 動《it－》重要[大]である no matter ～を問わず, どうでもいい no matter how どんなに～であろうとも no matter what たとえ何～でも not matter 問題にならない
- [ ] **Maupertuis** 名 モーペルテュイ《人名》
- [ ] **May I ～?** ～してもよいですか。
- [ ] **may well** ～するのももっともだ, 多分～だろう
- [ ] **Maynooth** 名 メイヌース《人名》
- [ ] **McCarthy** 名 マッカーシー《人名》
- [ ] **mean** 形 卑劣な 熟 I do not mean to ～するつもりはないのですが What do you mean by that? それ(を言ったの)はどういうつもりかね？
- [ ] **meaningless** 形 無意味な, つまらない
- [ ] **means** 名 ①手段, 方法 ②資力, 財産 by all means もちろん, ぜひとも by any means どうしても by no means 決して(～でない) means of ～する手段
- [ ] **meantime** 名 合間, その間 in the meantime その間(に), それまで(は) 副 その間に
- [ ] **meanwhile** 副 それまでの間, 一方では
- [ ] **measure** 動 ～を測る, ～の寸法がある
- [ ] **measurement** 名 ①測定 ②寸法
- [ ] **measuring** 形 測定用の
- [ ] **medical** 形 ①医学の ②内科の
- [ ] **Mediterranean** 形 地中海(沿岸)の 名《the－》地中海
- [ ] **meet** 動 ①～に直面する ②(費用, 負債など)を払う meet one's death [end] 最後を遂げる, 死ぬ meet with ～に出会う
- [ ] **Meiringen** 名 マイリンゲン《スイスの都市》
- [ ] **membership** 名 会員, 会員資格
- [ ] **memoir** 名 回顧録, 伝記
- [ ] **memory** 名 記憶(力)
- [ ] **mention** 動 ～について述べる, 言及する
- [ ] **Mercer** 名 マーサー《人名》

☐ **Meredith** 图メレディス《人名》

☐ **Merivale** 图メリヴェル《人名》

☐ **Merryweather** 图メリーウェザー《人名》

☐ **Merville** 图メルヴィル《人名》

☐ **metal** 图金属, 合金

☐ **metallic** 形金属の, 金属性の

☐ **meter** 图①メートル《長さの単位》②計量器, 計量する人

☐ **method** 图①方法, 手段 ②秩序, 体系

☐ **mew** 图《the -s；単数扱い》(中庭の)馬屋

☐ **microscope** 图顕微鏡

☐ **midday** 图正午, 真昼

☐ **middle** 图中間, 最中 **in the middle of** ～の真ん中[中ほど]に **right in the middle** ど真ん中 形中間の, 中央の **Middle Ages** 中世

☐ **middle-aged** 形中高年の

☐ **middle-sized** 形中型の, 中肉中背の

☐ **Middlesex** 图ミドルセックス《イングランド南東の州》

☐ **midnight** 图夜の12時, 真夜中 形真夜中の

☐ **might** 勔①～かもしれない ②～してもよい, ～できる

☐ **mile** 图①マイル《長さの単位。1,609m》②《-s》かなりの距離

☐ **millionaire** 图百万長者, 大金持ち

☐ **mind** 图①心, 精神, 考え ②知性 **change one's mind** 気[考え]が変わる **lose one's mind** 正気を失う, 頭[気]がおかしくなる **make up one's mind** 決心する **on one's mind** 念頭を去らないで, 気がかり[心配]で 勔①～を嫌だと思う ②～に気をつける, ～を用心する **Do you mind if ... ?** ～したらお邪魔ですか **mind you** よく聞いて, いいですか《念押し》, ひと言つけ加えるならば **Never mind.** 心配するな

☐ **mine** 图鉱山, 採掘場

☐ **Ming** 图明《中国の王朝。1368–1644年》

☐ **minister** 图①大臣, 閣僚, 公使 ②聖職者

☐ **minute** 熟 **in a minute** すぐに **Just a minute.** ちょっと待って。 **Wait a minute.** ちょっと待って。

☐ **misplace** 勔置く位置を間違える

☐ **missing** 形欠けている, 行方不明の **go missing** 行方不明になる

☐ **mistake** 熟 **make a mistake** 過ちを犯す, 失敗する

☐ **mistaken** 勔mistake(間違える)の過去分詞 形誤った

☐ **mister** 《男性に対して》～さん, ～氏

☐ **mix** 勔①混ざる[混ぜる] ②～を一緒にする **be mixed up with** ～とかかわりになる, ～と絡み合う

☐ **moment** 图①瞬間, ちょっとの間 ②(特定の)時, 時期 **at any moment** いつ何時, 今にも **at that moment** その時に, その瞬間に **at the moment** 今は **for a moment or two** 一瞬の間 **for the moment** 差し当たり, 当座は **in a moment** ただちに **one moment** ちょっとの間

☐ **money** 熟 **make money** 金をもうける

☐ **money-man** 图金融業者

☐ **Monica** 图モニカ《人名》

☐ **monkey** 图サル

☐ **Monsieur** 图《仏語》～氏(=Mr.)

☐ **Montague Street** モンタギュー街《ロンドンの地名》

☐ **Montmartre** 图モンマルトル《フランス, パリ北部にある丘, およびその周辺の地名》

☐ **mood** 图気分, 機嫌, 雰囲気, 憂鬱

☐ **moonlight** 图月明かり, 月光

☐ **moonshine** 图①月光, 月明かり ②ばかげた話

☐ **moor** 图原野, 沼地

☐ **Moore** 图ムーア《人名》

☐ **more** 熟 **more and more** ますます **more of** ～よりもっと **more than** ～以上 **no more than** もう～ない **no more than** ただの～にすぎない **once more** もう一度

☐ **Moriarty** 图《Professor – 》モリアーティ教授《人名》

☐ **morning** 熟 **one morning** ある朝

☐ **Morning Chronicle** 图《The – 》モーニング・クロニクル《新聞》

☐ **morphine** 图モルヒネ《麻酔薬》

☐ **Morphy** 图モーフィー《人名》

☐ **Morrison** 图モリソン《人名》

☐ **Morse Hudson** モース・ハドソン《人名》

☐ **mortgage** 图抵当(権)

☐ **Mortimer** 图モーティマー《人名》

☐ **Mortimer Tregennis** モーティマー・トリジェニス《人名》

☐ **Mortimer Street** 图モーティマー街《ロンドンの地名》

☐ **most** 熟 **make the most of** ～を最大限利用する **most surely** 確実に

☐ **mostly** 副主として, 多くは, ほとんど

□ **motive** 图動機, 目的, モチーフ

□ **mountain pass** 山道, 峠

□ **moustache** 图口ひげ

□ **mouthful** 图口いっぱい, ひと口分, 少量 (の)

□ **move** 熟move along ～に沿って動く move around あちこち移動する move away ①立ち去る ②移す, 動かす move away from ～から遠ざかる move in 引っ越す move on 先に進む move round ～を動き回る, あちこち移動する move to ～に引っ越す

□ **moveable** 形移動できる, 動かせる

□ **moved** 形《be –》感激する, 感銘する

□ **movement** 图①動き, 運動 ②《-s》行動 ③引っ越し ④変動

□ **Movement** 图政治的運動をする集団

□ **much** 熟as much as ～《数詞を伴って》～ほども (多く) be not much of a たいした～ではない too much 過度の

□ **mud** 图泥, ぬかるみ

□ **mud-covered** 形泥のついた, 泥だらけの

□ **muddy** 形泥だらけの, ぬかるみの

□ **muffler** 图マフラー, えり巻き

□ **murder** 图人殺し, 殺害, 殺人事件 動～を殺す

□ **murderer** 图殺人犯

□ **murderous** 形殺人を犯した, 殺人用の

□ **murmur** 動囁く, ブツブツ言う

□ **Murray** 图マレー《人名》

□ **muscle** 图筋肉, 腕力

□ **museum** 图博物館, 美術館

□ **Musgrave Ritual** 《the –》マスグレーヴ家の儀式 (書)

□ **musicland** 图音楽の国

□ **my** 熟my boy (親しい) 友達《呼びかけ》My God! おやまあ Oh my! おやまあ, まあ！

□ **Mycroft Holmes** マイクロフト・ホームズ《人名》

□ **mysterious** 形神秘的な, 謎めいた

□ **mystery** 图①神秘, 不可思議 ②推理小説, ミステリー

N

□ **nail** 图①爪 ②くぎ, びょう

□ **name** 熟by name 名前は, 名前で name one's price ～に値付けする, 値を示す to one's name 自分の所有物 [財産] として

□ **namely** 副すなわち, つまり

□ **Naples** 图ナポリ《地名》

□ **napoleon** 图ナポレオン金貨

□ **Napoleon** 图《– the First》ナポレオン (1世) (1769–1821)《フランス第一帝政の皇帝》

□ **Napoleonic** 形ナポレオンの

□ **Nara** 图奈良《地名》

□ **Narbonne** 图ナルボンヌ《フランスの都市》

□ **narrow** 形狭い

□ **nation** 图国, 国家,《the –》国民

□ **national** 形国家 [国民] の, 全国の

□ **nationality** 图①国籍 ②国民, 国家

□ **naturally** 副生まれつき, 自然に

□ **Naval Treaty** 《the –》海軍条約文書事件《ホームズが手がけた事件》

□ **nearby** 形近くの, 間近の 副近くで, 間近で

□ **nearly** 副①近くに, 親しく ②ほとんど, あやうく

□ **necessary** 形必要な, 必然の if necessary もし必要ならば

□ **neck-cloth** 图 (男性用) 首巻き, ネッカチーフ

□ **necklace** 图ネックレス, 首飾り

□ **Ned Hunter** ネッド・ハンター《人名》

□ **née** 形旧姓は

□ **Negro** 图黒馬《馬の名》

□ **neighborhood** 图近所 (の人々), 付近

□ **neighboring** 形隣接する, 近くの, 周辺の

□ **neither** 形どちらの～も…でない 代 (2者のうち) どちらも～でない 副《否定文に続いて》～も…しない I can make neither head nor tail of it. 何が何だかさっぱりわからない。 neither ～ nor … ～も…もない

□ **nerve** 图①神経 ②気力, 精力 ③《-s》神経過敏, 臆病, 憂うつ get on one's nerves かんにさわる, いらいらする have a nerve 図太い神経をしている have the nerve 勇気がある keep one's nerve 冷静でいる, ひるまずに自分を保つ

□ **nervous** 形①神経の ②神経質の, おどおどした

□ **nervously** 副神経質に, いらいらして

□ **nervousness** 图神経質, いらいら

□ **Netherland-Sumatra Company** オランダ領スマトラ会社

□ **never** 熟Never mind. 気にするな。 should never have done ～すべきではなかった (のにしてしまった)《仮定法》

- **Neville St. Clair** ネヴィル・セントクレア《人名》
- **New Jersey** 图ニュージャージー州《地名》
- **New York Police Office** ニューヨーク市警察署
- **New Zealand** ニュージーランド《国名》
- **newcomer** 图新しく来た人, 初心者
- **Newfoundland** 图ニューファンドランド《犬種》
- **Newhaven** 图ニューヘイブン《イギリスの町》
- **newly** 副再び, 最近, 新たに
- **Newmarket Heath** ニューマーケット・ヒース《地名》
- **newspaper** 图新聞（紙）
- **newspaperman** 图新聞記者
- **newsstand** 图新聞の売店
- **next to** ～のとなりに, ～の次に
- **nice-looking** 形美しい, ハンサムな
- **nicely** 副①うまく, よく ②上手に, 親切に, 几帳面に
- **night** 熟in the dead of the night 真夜中に night and day 昼も夜も, 休みなく night before last 一昨晩, おとといの夜 sit up all night 徹夜する the night before 前の晩
- **night-clothes** 图寝巻き
- **nightclothes** 图寝巻き
- **nightcoat** 图ガウン
- **nightdress** 图寝巻き
- **nightexpress** 图夜行特急
- **nightfall** 图夕暮れ
- **nightshirt** 图ナイトシャツ《主に男性用寝巻きとして用いるひざまでの長いシャツ》
- **Nimes** 图ニーム《フランスの都市》
- **no** 熟no less than ～と同じだけの, ～も同然 no longer もはや～でない［～しない］ no matter ～を問わず, どうでもいい no matter how どんなに～であろうとも no more もう～ない no more than ただの～にすぎない no one 誰も［一人も］～ない no one else 他の誰一人として～しない No problem. いいですよ。どういたしまして。問題ない。 no use 役に立たない, 用をなさない
- **nobody** 代誰も［1人も］～ない
- **noise** 图騒音, 騒ぎ, 物音 make noise 音を立てる
- **noiseless** 形静かな, 音を立てない
- **noiselessly** 副音を立てずに
- **noisily** 副音を立てて, 騒々しく

- **nominal** 形名目上の, 名称上の, 名詞の
- **none** 代～の何も［誰も, 少しも］…ない
- **nonsense** 图ばかげたこと, ナンセンス
- **nor** 熟I can make neither head nor tail of it. 何が何だかさっぱりわからない。 neither ～ nor … …も～もない Nor do I.《否定の文に続けて》私も（いや）です。
- **Norberton** 图ノーバートン《人名》
- **Norfolk** 图ノーフォーク《イギリスの州》
- **Norlett** 图ノーレット《人名》
- **normal** 形普通の, 平均の, 標準的な
- **Norman** 图ノルマン人 形ノルマン征服時代の
- **North Walsham** ノース・ウォルシャム《地名》
- **northern** 形北の, 北向きの, 北からの
- **northern Musgraves** 《the－》北マスグレーヴ家
- **Northumberland Avenue** ノーサンバーランド大通り《地名》
- **Norton** 图ノートン《人名》
- **Norwegian** 形ノルウェー（人・語）の 图①ノルウェー人 ②ノルウェー語
- **Norwich** 图ノリッジ《地名》
- **nose** 熟show one's nose 顔を出す, 現れる
- **not** 熟not ～ any longer もはや～でない［～しない］ not at all 少しも～でない not ～ at all 少しも［全然］～ない not ～ but … ～ではなくて… not fail to 必ず～する not in any way 少しも［全く］～ない not matter 問題にならない not only ～ but (also)… ～だけでなく…もまた not quite まったく～だというわけではない not … without ～ing ～せずには…しない, ～すれば必ず…する not yet まだ～してない
- **note** 图①メモ, 覚書 ②注釈 ③注意, 注目 ④手形, 紙幣 動①～を書き留める ②～に注意［注目］する
- **note-paper** 图メモ用紙, 便せん
- **notebook** 图ノート, 手帳
- **noteworthy** 形注目すべき, 著しい
- **nothing** 熟can do nothing どうしようもない have nothing to do with ～と何の関係もない know nothing of ～のことを知らない make nothing of ～を何とも思わない, ものともしない, ～を利用しそこなう nothing but ただ～だけ, ～にすぎない, ～のほかは何も…ない
- **notice** 图①注意 ②通知 ③公告 on short notice すぐさま, 急に take no notice 目もくれない 動①～に気づく, ～を認める ②～に通

告する

☐ **novel** 名 (長編) 小説

☐ **now** 熟 **by now** 今のところ，今ごろまでには **for now** 今のところ，ひとまず **from now on** 今後 **now that** 今や～だから，～からには **right now** 今すぐに，たった今

☐ **nowhere** 副 どこにも～ない

☐ **number of** 《a-》いくつかの～，多くの **a great number of** 非常に多くの

☐ **number one** ナンバーワンの，一流の，最高の

☐ **nurse** 名 乳母

O

☐ **oak** 名 オーク《ブナ科の樹木の総称》 形 オーク (材) の

☐ **object** 名 ①物，事物 ②目的物，(研究の) 対象 動 反対する，(～に) 異議を唱える

☐ **objection** 名 反対，異議，不服

☐ **objective** 名 目標，目的

☐ **observation** 名 観察 (力)，注目

☐ **observe** 動 ①～を観察 [観測] する，～を監視 [注視] する ②～に気づく

☐ **occasionally** 副 時折，ときたま

☐ **occur** 動 (事が) 起こる，生じる，(考えなどが) 浮かぶ

☐ **odd** 形 ①奇妙な ②奇数の ③(一対のうちの) 片方の

☐ **odds** 名 勝ち目，勝算，見込み

☐ **Odo** 名 オドー《人名》

☐ **of** 熟 **be of the opinion that** ～という意見である **of no use** 使われないで **of one's own** 自分自身の **of value** 貴重な，価値のある **of which** ～の中で

☐ **off** 熟 **be off to** ～へ出かける **carry off** 誘いする，さらって行く，運び去る **come off** 取れる，はずれる **cut off** 切断する，切り離す **day off work** 一日休み **fall off** 落ちる，落ち込む，下落する，減る，衰退する **far off** ずっと遠くに，はるかかなたに **get off** (～から) 降りる **go off** ①出かける，去る，出発する ②始める，突然～しだす ③(電気が) 消える **hurry off** 急いで立ち去る，急いで出掛ける **off with** (すばやく) ～を取り去る **pick off** ～をもぎとる **put off** ～から逃れる，延期する，要求をそらす，不快にさせる，やめさせる **see off** 見送る **set off** 出発する，発射する **take off** (衣服を) 脱ぐ，取り去る，～を取り除く，離陸する，出発する **take off work** 会社を休む **take one's eyes off**

～から目をそらす **throw off** 脱ぎ捨てる **turn off** ①興味を失う，～にうんざりする ②～を止める，(照明などを) 消す ③(道から) それる，(道が) ～から分かれる **walk off** 立ち去る

☐ **offer** 動 (～を) 申し出る，(～を) 申し込む，(～を) 提供する 名 提案，提供

☐ **officer** 名 役人，公務員，警察官 **police officer** 警察官

☐ **Oh my!** おやまあ，まあ！

☐ **oil** 名 油

☐ **old** 熟 **old love** 昔の恋人 **of old** 昔の，昔は

☐ **on** 熟 **on each side** それぞれの側に **on earth** ①いったい ②地球上で，この世で **on foot** 歩いて **on one's own** 自力で **on one's way** 途中で **on one's way to** ～に行く途中で **on the ground** 地面に **on the other hand** 一方，他方では **on the way** 途中で **on the whole** 全体として見ると **on time** 時間どおりに **on top of** ～の上 (部) に

☐ **once** 熟 **at once** すぐに，同時に **for once** 一度だけ **once and for all** これを最後にきっぱりと **once more** もう一度

☐ **one** 熟 **each one** 各自 **no one** 誰も [一人も] ～ない **no one else** 他の誰一人として～しない **one another** お互い **one by one** 1つずつ，1人ずつ **one day** (過去の) ある日，(未来の) いつか **one moment** ちょっとの間 **one morning** ある朝 **one on top of the other** 順に重ねて **this one** これ，こちら

☐ **one-off** 名 唯一無二のもの，比類ないもの

☐ **oneself** 熟 **by oneself** 一人で，自分だけで，独力で **for oneself** 独力で，自分のために **help oneself** 自分で取って食べる [飲む]

☐ **only** 熟 **if only** ～でありさえすれば **not only ～ but (also)** …～だけでなく…もまた

☐ **onto** 前 ～の上へ **look onto** (建物が) ～に向いている，～に面する **open out onto** ～に面して開け放す

☐ **opal** 名 オパール

☐ **open air** 野外，戸外

☐ **open carriage** 無蓋馬車

☐ **open out onto** ～に面して開け放す

☐ **open up** 熟 (可能性) を開く

☐ **opera** 名 歌劇，オペラ

☐ **operation** 名 手術

☐ **opinion** 熟 **be of the opinion that** ～という意見である **in my opinion** 私の考えでは

☐ **opium** 名 アヘン **opium den** アヘン吸引所

☐ **opposite** 前 ～の向こう側に

☐ **or so** ～かそこらで

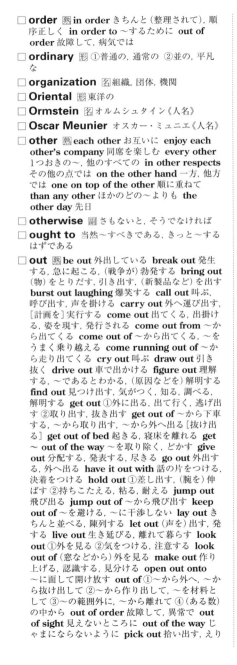

order 熟 in order きちんと（整理されて）, 順序正しく in order to ～するために out of order 故障して, 病気では

ordinary 形 ①普通の, 通常の ②並の, 平凡な

organization 名組織, 団体, 機関

Oriental 形東洋の

Ormstein 名オルムシュタイン《人名》

Oscar Meunier オスカー・ミュニエ《人名》

other 熟 each other お互いに enjoy each other's company 同席を楽しむ every other 1つおきの～, 他のすべての in other respects その他の点では on the other hand 一方, 他方では one on top of the other 順に重ねて than any other ほかのどの～よりも the other day 先日

otherwise 副 さもないと, そうでなければ

ought to 当然～すべきである, きっと～するはずである

out 熟 be out 外出している break out 発生する, 急に起こる,（戦争が）勃発する bring out（物）をとりだす, 引き出す,（新製品など）を出す burst out laughing 爆笑する call out 叫ぶ, 呼び掛ける carry out 外へ運び出す,［計画を］実行する come out 出てくる, 出掛ける, 姿を現す, 発行される come out from ～から出てくる come out of ～から出てくる, ～をうまく乗り越える come running out of ～から走り出てくる cry out 叫ぶ draw out 引き抜く drive out 車で出かける figure out 理解する, ～であるとわかる,（原因などを）解明する find out 見つけ出す, 気がつく, 知る, 調べる, 解明する get out ①外に出る, 出て行く, 逃げ出す ②取り出す, 抜き出す get out of ～から下車する, ～から取り出す, ～から外へ出る［抜け出る］get out of bed 起きる, 寝床を離れる get ～ out of the way ～を取り除く, どかす give out 分配する, 発表する, 尽きる go out 外出する, 外へ出る have it out with 話の片をつける, 決着をつける hold out ①差し出す,（腕を）伸ばす ②持ちこたえる, 粘る, 耐える jump out 飛び出る jump out of ～から飛び出す keep out of ～を避ける, ～に干渉しない let out（声を）出す, 発する live out 生き延びる, 離れて暮らす look out ①外を見る ②気をつける, 注意する look out of（窓などから）外を見る make out 作り上げる, 認識する, 見分ける open out onto ～に面して開け放す out of ①～から外へ, ～から抜け出して ②～から作り出して, ～を材料として ③～の範囲外に, ～から離れて ④（ある数）の中から out of order 故障して, 異常で out of sight 見えないところに out of the way じゃまにならないように pick out 拾い出す, えり抜く, 選び出す point out 指し示す, 指摘する, 目を向ける, 目を向けさせる pull out 引き抜く, 引き出す, 取り出す put out ①外に出す,（手など）を（差し）出す ②（明かり・火を）消す reach out 手を伸ばす read out 声を出して読む, 読み上げる run out of ～が不足する, ～を使い果たす rush out of 急いで～から出てくる smoke out いぶり出す, 明るみに出す speak out はっきり［遠慮なく］言う stand out 突き出る, 目立つ step out 外へ出る step out of ～から出る stick out 突き出す stretch out ①手足を伸ばす, 背伸びする ②広がる take out 取り出す, 取り出す, 連れ出す, 持って帰る take out of ～から出す, ～に連れ出す take out to ～に連れ出す throw out 放り出す try out 実際に試してみる turn out ①～と判明する,（結局～に）なる ②（照明などを）消す ③養成する ④出かける, 集まる ⑤外側に向く, ひっくり返す walk out into ～に出て行く walk out of ～から出る wash out 洗い落とす, 押し流す,（試合などを）中止させる, 落第させる way out 出口, 逃げ道, 脱出方法, 解決法 way out of ～から抜け出る道 work out うまくいく, 何とかなる,（問題を）解く, 考え出す, 答えが出る, ～の結果になる worn out 擦り切れた

out-going 形 外向性の, 社交的な

outer 形 外の, 外側の

outline 名 ①外形, 輪郭 ②概略

outsider 名 よそ者, 部外者, 門外漢

outward 形 ①外へ, 外へいく ②外側の ③外見の 名外部, 外界

over 熟 all over ～中で, 全体に亘って, ～の至る所で, 全て終わって, もうだめで be over 終わる bend over かがむ, 腰をかがめる, ～に身をかがめる come over やって来る, ～の身にふりかかる come running over 走ってやってくる cross over（領域・枠などを）越える fall over ～につまずく, ～の上に倒れかかる go over ～を越えて行く, ～へ渡る go over to ～の前に［へ］行く, ～に出向いて行く hand over 手渡す, 引き渡す, 譲渡する have control over ～を支配［コントロール］する hurry over ～を慌ててやる jump over ～の上を飛び越える leave over 残しておく look over ～越しに見る, ～を見渡す look over at ～の方を見る over and over 何度も繰り返して over here こっちへ［に］; ほら, さあ《人の注意を引く》over it all 全体にわたって over there そこに push over 押し倒す read over ～に目を通す run one's eyes over ～にザッと目を通す run over 一走りする, ～の上を走る, ひき［押し］倒す sing over 歌いながら take over 引き継ぐ, 支配する, 乗っ取る turn over ひっくり返る［返す］,（ページを）めくる, 思いめぐらす, 引き渡す walk over ～の方に歩いていく

- [ ] **overcame** 動 overcome (打ち勝つ, 負かす) の過去, 過去分詞
- [ ] **overcoat** 名 オーバー, 外套
- [ ] **overcome** 動 ①打ち勝つ, 克服する, 無力にする, 圧倒する ②overcomeの過去, 過去分詞
- [ ] **overjoyed** 形 大いに喜んで
- [ ] **overlook** 動 ①見落とす, (チャンスなどを) 逃す ②見渡す ③大目に見る 名 見晴らし
- [ ] **overtake** 動 ①追いつく ②上回る ③車を追い越す
- [ ] **overthrow** 動 ①ひっくり返す ②転覆する, 廃止する
- [ ] **overweight** 形 太り過ぎの, 重量超過の
- [ ] **owe** 動 (金) を借りている
- [ ] **Owen** 名 オーウェン《人名》
- [ ] **own** 熟 of one's own 自分自身の on one's own 自力で
- [ ] **owner** 名 持ち主, オーナー
- [ ] **Oxford** 名 オックスフォード《地名》, オックスフォード大学
- [ ] **Oxford Street** オックスフォード街《ロンドンの地名》

P

- [ ] **pace** 動 (人が歩いたり走ったりする速度を) 調整する
- [ ] **pack** 動 (～を) 荷造りする, 詰め込む
- [ ] **Paddington** 名 パディントン《ロンドンの地名》
- [ ] **paid** 動 pay (～を払う) の過去, 過去分詞 形 有給の, 支払いずみの
- [ ] **pain** 熟 take pains 気を配る [使う]
- [ ] **painful** 形 ①痛い, 苦しい, 痛ましい ②骨の折れる, 困難な
- [ ] **painless** 形 苦痛のない
- [ ] **painter** 名 画家, ペンキ屋
- [ ] **pair** 名 (2つから成る) 一対, 一組, ペア
- [ ] **pal** 友人, 友達, 相棒
- [ ] **palace** 名 宮殿, 大邸宅
- [ ] **pale** 形 ①(顔色・人が) 青ざめた, 青白い ②(色が) 薄い, (光が) 薄暗い
- [ ] **Pall Mall** ペルメル街《ロンドンの地名》
- [ ] **Palmer** 名 パーマー《タイヤの製造会社名》
- [ ] **Palmer-tired** 形 パーマー社製のタイヤをつけた

- [ ] **Pancras** 名 パンクラス《地名》
- [ ] **panel** 名 パネル, はめ板, 計器盤
- [ ] **paperweight** 名 文鎮, ペーパーウェイト
- [ ] **paperwork** 名 文書業務, 書類作成
- [ ] **parcel** 名 包み, 小包
- [ ] **Paris** 名 パリ《フランスの首都》
- [ ] **Park Lane** パーク・レーン《通りの名》
- [ ] **Park Lane Mystery** パーク・レーン事件《ホームズの手がける事件名》
- [ ] **Parker** 名 パーカー《人名》
- [ ] **part** 熟 for one's own part ～としては, ～の考えでは play a part 役割を果たす
- [ ] **particularly** 副 特に, とりわけ
- [ ] **partly** 副 一部分は, ある程度は
- [ ] **pass** 動 通り過ぎる pass away 過ぎ去る, 終わる, 死ぬ pass by ～のそばを通る [通り過ぎる] pass down (次の世代に) 伝える pass on ①通り過ぎる ②(情報などを他者に) 伝える pass out 気を失う, 意識をなくす pass through ～を通る, 通行する 名 ①通行証, 許可証 ②道, 山道 a pass to ～への通行証 mountain pass 山道, 峠
- [ ] **passage** 名 ①通過, 通行, 通路 ②一節, 経過
- [ ] **passage-way** 名 狭い通路
- [ ] **passerby** 名 通行人, 通りがかりの人
- [ ] **passersby** 名 passerby (通行人) の複数形
- [ ] **past** 形 過去の, この前の 名 過去 (の出来事) 前《時間・場所》～を過ぎて, ～を越して 副 通り越して, 過ぎて rush past ～を急いで通り過ぎていく walk past 通り過ぎる
- [ ] **pastime** 名 気晴らし, 娯楽
- [ ] **patched** 形 継ぎをして補強した
- [ ] **path** 名 (踏まれてできた) 小道, 歩道
- [ ] **pathway** 名 小道, 通路
- [ ] **patience** 名 我慢, 忍耐 (力), 根気
- [ ] **patient** 名 病人, 患者
- [ ] **Patric** 名《old－》老パトリック《人名》
- [ ] **Patterson** 名 パターソン《人名》
- [ ] **Paul** 名 ポール《人名》
- [ ] **pawnbroker** 名 質屋 (の主人)
- [ ] **pawnshop** 名 質屋
- [ ] **pay** 動 ～を払う, ～に報いる 名 給料, 報い
- [ ] **pay-list** 名 賃金支払簿
- [ ] **payday** 名 給料日, 決済日
- [ ] **payment** 名 支払い
- [ ] **peace** 熟 in peace 平和のうちに, 安心して

leave ～ in peace ～をそっとしておく　make a new peace with ～と仲直りする　take place （出来事などが）起こる, 行われる

- □ **peaceful** 形 平和な, 穏やかな
- □ **peacefully** 副 平和に, 穏やかに
- □ **Peak country** 山岳地方
- □ **pearl** 名 真珠
- □ **Peking** 名 北京《地名》
- □ **pen-knife** 名 懐中ナイフ
- □ **per** 前 ～につき, ～ごとに
- □ **perfection** 名 完全, 完成
- □ **perfectly** 副 完全に, 申し分なく
- □ **perhaps** 副 たぶん, ことによると
- □ **period** 名 期, 期間, 時代
- □ **person** 熟 in person （本人）自ら, 自身で
- □ **personal** 形 個人の
- □ **personally** 副 個人的には, 自分で
- □ **Peter Steiler** ペーター・シュタイラー《人名》
- □ **Petrarch** 名 ペトラルカ《イタリアの詩人》
- □ **Ph.D.** 略 哲学博士（=Pholosophiae Doctor）
- □ **photo** 名 写真
- □ **photograph** 名 写真
- □ **pick off** ～をもぎとる
- □ **pick out** 拾い出す, えり抜く, 選び出す
- □ **pick up** 拾い上げる, 車で迎えに行く, 習得する, 再開する, 回復する
- □ **picture** 熟 take a picture 写真を撮る
- □ **picture-maker** 名 額縁製造
- □ **piece-work** 名 請負仕事
- □ **pierced** 形 （耳たぶに）穴のあいた
- □ **Pietro Venucci** ピエトロ・ヴェヌチ《人名》
- □ **pike** 名 カワカマス《魚》
- □ **pillow** 名 まくら
- □ **pin** 名 ピン, 細い留め具
- □ **pipe** 名 管, 筒, パイプ
- □ **pit** 名 くぼみ, ピット
- □ **Pitt Street** ピット街《地名》
- □ **place** 熟 in the first place まず第一に　take place 行われる, 起こる
- □ **plain** 形 ①明白な, はっきりした ②簡素な ③平らな ④不細工な, 平凡な 名 高原, 草原, 平野
- □ **plain clothes** （警官の制服に対して）私服
- □ **plain-clothes** 形 （警官が）私服の
- □ **plainly** 副 はっきりと, 明らかに

- □ **plan** 名 計画
- □ **plant** 名 植物, 草木
- □ **plaster** 名 しっくい, 壁土, 石こう　plaster cast 石こう塑像（そぞう）, 石こう模型
- □ **play** 熟 act in plays 劇に出演する　play a part 役目を果たす　play with ～で遊ぶ, ～と一緒に遊ぶ
- □ **player** 名 競技者, 選手
- □ **pleasant** 形 ①（物事が）楽しい, 心地よい ②快活な, 愛想のよい
- □ **pleasantly** 副 楽しく, 心地よく
- □ **pleasantry** 名 冷やかし, からかい, 冗談
- □ **please oneself** 満足する
- □ **pleased to do** 《be－》～してうれしい
- □ **pleased with** 《be－》～が気に入る
- □ **pleasure** 名 喜び, 楽しみ, 満足, 娯楽 (It's) my pleasure. どういたしまして。
- □ **plenty** 名 十分, たくさん, 豊富　plenty of たくさんの～
- □ **Plymouth** 名 プリマス《イギリスの都市》
- □ **pocket book** 手帳
- □ **poetic** 形 詩の, 詩的な
- □ **point** 熟 at this point 現在のところ　point by point 逐一　point of view 考え方, 視点　point out 指し示す, 指摘する, 目を向ける, 目を向けさせる　That is the point. それが問題だ。そこなんだ。　to the point 要領を得た
- □ **pointed** 形 先のとがった
- □ **pointless** 形 ①先のない ②要領をえない ③無意味な
- □ **poison** 名 ①毒, 毒薬 ②害になるもの
- □ **Poldhu** 名 ポルドー《地名》
- □ **police officer** 警察官
- □ **police force** 警察, 警官隊
- □ **police-court** 名 治安判事裁判所
- □ **policeman** 名 警察官
- □ **policemen** 名 policeman（警察官）の複数
- □ **polo** 名 ポロ《馬に乗って行う球技》
- □ **poorly** 副 ①貧しく, 乏しく ②へたに
- □ **Pope** ①ローマ教皇 ②教祖
- □ **porky** 形 でぶの
- □ **port** 名 港, 港町
- □ **port wine** ポートワイン《甘口のワイン》
- □ **Porter** 名 ポーター《人名》
- □ **Portuguese** 形 ポルトガル（人, 語）の
- □ **position** 名 ①位置, 場所, 姿勢 ②地位, 身分,

職　③立場, 状況　**be in a position to** 〜できる立場にある

□ **possibility** 名可能性, 見込み, 将来性

□ **possible** 形①可能な　②ありうる, 起こりうる　**as 〜 as possible** できるだけ〜　**if possible** できるなら

□ **possibly** 副①あるいは, たぶん　②《否定文, 疑問文で》どうしても, できる限り, とても, なんとか

□ **postbag** 名郵便袋, 郵便物の束

□ **postmark** 名消印

□ **pot** 名つぼ　**flower pot** 植木鉢

□ **pottery** 名陶器

□ **pound** 名①ポンド《英国の通貨単位。記号£》　②ポンド《重量の単位。453.6g》

□ **powder** 名粉末, おしろい, 火薬

□ **powder-marking** 名火薬の跡

□ **powdered** 形粉末の

□ **powerful** 形力強い, 実力のある, 影響力のある

□ **powerless** 形力のない, 頼りない, 弱い

□ **practice** 名①実践, 実行　②(医者の)業務, 仕事

□ **Prague** 名プラハ《地名》

□ **prefer** 動〜のほうを好む, 〜のほうがよいと思う

□ **prepare for** 〜の準備をする

□ **prepared to** 〜する覚悟[用意]のできた

□ **Presbury** 名プレスベリー《人名》

□ **presence** 名①存在すること　②出席, 態度　**in the presence of** 〜　〜の面前で

□ **present** 形出席している, 居合わせる　**present oneself** 姿を現す[見せる] 名今, 現在　**at present** 今のところ, 現在は, 目下

□ **presently** 副①やがて, じき　②今, 目下

□ **preservation** 名保護, 保守

□ **press** 動圧する, 押す 名出版物[社], 新聞

□ **pressure** 名押すこと, 圧力, 圧縮, 圧搾, 電圧, 重荷 動圧力をかける

□ **pretend** 動①〜のふりをする, 〜を装う　②あえて〜しようとする

□ **Pretoria** 名プレトリア《地名》

□ **prevent** 動①〜を妨げる, 〜を邪魔する　②〜を予防する, 〜を守る

□ **previous** 形前の, 先の

□ **price** 名①値段, 代価, 代償, 犠牲　②《-s》物価, 相場 動値段をつける

□ **pride** 名誇り, 自慢, 自尊心

□ **priest** 名聖職者, 牧師, 僧侶

□ **prince** 名王子

□ **Prince** 名(ショスコム・)プリンス《馬の名》

□ **princess** 名王女

□ **Priory School** プライオリ学校《学校名》

□ **prison** 名①刑務所, 監獄　②監禁

□ **prisoner** 名囚人, 捕虜

□ **private** 形①私的な, 個人の　②民間の　③内密の, 人里離れた

□ **privately** 副内密に, 非公式に, 個人的に

□ **probable** 形ありそうな, 有望な

□ **probably** 副たぶん, あるいは

□ **problem** 熟 **No problem.** いいですよ。どういたしまして。問題ない。

□ **process** 名①過程, 経過, 進行　②手順, 方法, 製法, 加工

□ **produce** 動提示する, 示す, 見せる, 取り出す

□ **professor** 名教授, 師匠

□ **Professor Moriarty** モリアーティ教授《人名》

□ **promise** 熟 **be promised to** 〜と婚約している《古》 **keep one's promise** 約束を守る　**promise of spring** 春の兆し

□ **promising** 形前途有望な

□ **proof** 名証拠, (〜という)証明

□ **property** 名①財産, 所有物[地]　②性質, 属性

□ **propose** 動①申し込む, 提案する　②結婚を申し込む

□ **proud** 形①自慢の, 誇った, 自尊心のある　②高慢な, 尊大な　**be proud of** 〜を自慢に思う

□ **proudly** 副①誇らしげに　②うぬぼれて

□ **prove** 動①〜を証明する　②〜であることがわかる, 〜となる

□ **pshaw** 間ふん, ちぇっ《不快感を表す》

□ **public** 名《the－》世間, 国民　**in public** 人前で, 公然と

□ **public house** パブ, 居酒屋, 宿屋

□ **Pugilist** 名ピュージリスト《馬の名》

□ **pull away from** 〜から離れる

□ **pull on** 〜を引っ張る

□ **pull out** 〜を引き出す, 取り出す

□ **pull up** 引っ張り上げる

□ **punish** 動(人)を罰する

□ **pure** 形①純粋な, 混じりけのない　②罪のな

い, 清い

- □ **purely** 副 全くの, 単に, 純粋に
- □ **purple** 形 紫色の 名 紫色
- □ **purpose** 名 目的, 意図
- □ **purposeful** 形 目的のある, きっぱりした, 意味深長な
- □ **purposely** 副 わざと, 故意に
- □ **purse** 名 ①財布, 小銭入れ ②小物入れ
- □ **push** 熟 **push back** 押し返す, 押しのける **push down** 押し倒す **push forward** 前へ進む, 突き出す **push on** (困難をものともせず)前進する, (仕事などを)続行する **push one's way through** かき分けて前に出る **push over** 押し倒す **push through** (人ごみなどを)かき分ける **push up** 押し上げる
- □ **put** 熟 **put back** (もとの場所に)戻す, 返す **put down** 下に置く, 下ろす **put forward** 提出する, 提案する **put in** ～の中に入れる **put ～ in one's hands** ～に預ける **put into …** ～を…の状態にする, ～を…に突っ込む **put off** ～から逃れる, 延期する, 要求をそらす, 不快にさせる, やめさせる **put on** ①～を身につける, 着る ②～を…の上に置く **put out** ①外に出す, (手など)を(差し)出す ②(明かり・火)を消す **put together** ～をくっつける, 組み合わせる, 組み立てる, (考え)をまとめる **put up one's hand** 手を挙げる **put up with** ～を我慢する
- □ **puzzle** 動 ～を迷わせる, 当惑する[させる]

Q

- □ **quarrel** 名 けんか, 争論, 不和 動 けんかする, 口論する
- □ **quarter** 名 ①4分の1, 15分 ②25セント(銀貨) ②方面, 地域 ③部署 **Italian Quarter** イタリア人街 **quarter to ～** ～時15分前
- □ **quarter-past** 形 15分過ぎて
- □ **queen** 名 女王, 王妃
- □ **Queen Anne house** アン女王様式《18世紀初期の英国の建築様式》の家
- □ **Queen Anne Street** クイーン・アン街
- □ **question** 熟 **in question** 問題の, 論争中の
- □ **questionable** 形 疑わしい
- □ **questioning look** いぶかしそうな顔つき
- □ **quicken** 動 速める, 速くなる
- □ **quickly** 副 敏速に, 急いで
- □ **quiet** 熟 **in the quiet** 静けさ[静寂]の中で
- □ **quietly** 副 ①静かに ②平穏に, 控えめに

- □ **quietness** 名 静寂, 平穏
- □ **Quincey** 名 《Thomas de－》トマス・ド・クインシー《1785–1859, イギリスの評論家。著作：阿片吸引者の告白》
- □ **quit** 動 やめる, 中止する
- □ **quite** 熟 **not quite** まったく～だというわけではない **quite so**《相づち》まったくその通り **quite something** 大した物

R

- □ **race** 動 鼓動が早まる, はやる, 大急ぎでやる
- □ **Rachel Howells** レイチェル・ハウエルズ《人名》
- □ **Ragged Shaw** 野生林
- □ **railway** 名 鉄道
- □ **raincoat** 名 レインコート
- □ **raise** 動 ①～を上げる[高める] ②～を起こす ③～を育てる
- □ **Ralph** 名 ラルフ《人名》
- □ **Ralph Musgrave** ラルフ・マスグレーヴ《人名》
- □ **rang** 動 ring (鳴る)の過去
- □ **Rasper** 名 ラスパー《馬の名》
- □ **rat** 名 ①ネズミ ②裏切り者
- □ **rate** 名 ①割合, 率 ②相場, 料金 **at any rate** とにかく
- □ **rather** 副 ①むしろ, かえって ②かなり, いくぶん, やや ③それどころか逆に **rather like** ～に似ている, きらいはでない **rather than** ～よりむしろ **would rather** むしろ～したい[するほうがよい] **would rather ～ than …** …よりむしろ～したい
- □ **reach** 熟 **beyond reach of** ～の手の届かない **reach down** 手を下に伸ばす **reach for** ～に手を伸ばす, ～を取ろうとする **reach out** 手を伸ばす
- □ **reaction** 名 反応, 反動, 反抗, 影響
- □ **read out** 声を出して読む, 読み上げる
- □ **read over** ～に目を通す
- □ **read through** ～を読み通す
- □ **reader** 名 読者
- □ **readily** 副 ①すぐに, さっそく ②快く, 進んで
- □ **Reading** 名 レディング《イギリスの地名》
- □ **ready** 熟 **be ready for** 準備が整って, ～に期待する **get ready** 用意[支度]をする **ready oneself to** ～する準備をする **ready to go** す

っかり準備が整った
- □ **real** 熟 for real 本当に
- □ **realization** 名 ①理解, 認識 ②実現
- □ **realize** 動 ～を理解する, ～を実現する
- □ **really something** 大したものである, 半端ではない
- □ **reappearance** 名 再登場
- □ **reason** 熟 for some reason なんらかの理由で, どういうわけか reason for ～の理由
- □ **reasonable** 形 筋の通った, 分別のある
- □ **reasonably** 副 分別よく, 賢明に, 適当に
- □ **reasoning** 名 推理, 推論
- □ **recall** 動 思い出す, 思い出させる
- □ **recent** 形 近頃の, 近代の
- □ **recently** 副 ついこのあいだ, 近頃
- □ **recognize** 動 ～を認める, ～を認識[承認]する
- □ **record** 名 記録, 履歴 off the record 非公式で, オフレコで on record 記録されて, 公表されて 動 記録する
- □ **recover** 動 ①とり戻す, ばん回する ②回復する
- □ **red** 熟 go red 赤くなる turn red 赤くなる
- □ **Red Bull** レッド・ブル《宿屋の名》
- □ **red-faced** 形 赤ら顔の, 顔を赤くした
- □ **red-haired** 形 赤毛の
- □ **red-headed** 形 赤毛の
- □ **redden** 動 赤くなる[する]
- □ **reddish** 形 赤みがかった
- □ **reddish-brown** 形 赤茶色の
- □ **Redruth** 名 レッドルース《地名》
- □ **refer** 動 ～に言及する, 触れる, ～を参照する refer to ～を指す
- □ **reference** 名 言及, 参照, 照会 reference to ～への言及
- □ **refill** 動 詰め替える, 補充する
- □ **reformer** 名 改革(支持)者
- □ **refuse** 動 (～を)拒絶する, 断る
- □ **regain** 動 (～から)取り戻す, ～に戻る
- □ **regency** 名《the R-》摂政期
- □ **Regent Street** リージェント街《地名》
- □ **Reginald Musgrave** レジナルド・マスグレーヴ《人名》
- □ **Reichenbach** 名 ライヘンバッハ《地名, スイスの滝》
- □ **Reichenbach Fall** ライヘンバッハの滝《滝

の名前》
- □ **Reigate** 名 ライゲート《地名》
- □ **relation** 名 ①(利害)関係, 間柄 ②親戚
- □ **relationship** 名 関係, 関連, 血縁関係
- □ **relax** 動 くつろがせる, ゆるめる
- □ **release** 動 解き放す, ～を外す 名 解放, 釈放
- □ **religion** 名 宗教, ～教, 信条
- □ **religious** 形 ①宗教の ②信心深い ③(～について)熱心な
- □ **relock** 動 鍵を掛けなおす
- □ **rely** 動 頼る
- □ **remain** 動 残っている, 残る, ～のままである[いる]
- □ **remark** 名 ①注意, 注目, 観察 ②意見, 記事, 批評
- □ **remarkable** 形 ①異常な, 例外的な ②注目に値する
- □ **remarkably** 副 目立って, きわだって
- □ **remarry** 動 再婚する
- □ **remiss** 形 怠慢な, 不注意な
- □ **remove** 動 ①～を移す, ～を除去する ②引っ越す, 移動する ③(衣類)を脱ぐ
- □ **rent** 名 使用料, 賃貸料
- □ **rent-free** 形 地代なしの, 賃貸料なしの
- □ **reopen** 動 再び開く[かれる], 再び始まる, 再開する[される]
- □ **repair** 動 ～を修理する
- □ **repass** 動 再び通る, 引き返す
- □ **repay** 動 ①払い戻す, 返金する ②報いる, 恩返しする
- □ **repeat** 動 (～を)繰り返す
- □ **replace** 動 ①～を取り替える, 差し替える ②元に戻す
- □ **reply** 動 答える, 返事をする, 応答する 名 答え, 返事, 応答
- □ **report** 名 報告(書), レポート 動 報告する, 伝える
- □ **represent** 動 ①～を表現する ②～を意味する ③～を代表する
- □ **reproduce** 動 ①再生する, 再現する ②複写する, 模造する
- □ **reproduction** 名 複製品, 再生産, 再生, 復元
- □ **require** 動 ①～を必要とする, ～を要する ②～を命じる, ～を請求する
- □ **reread** 動 再び読む, 読み直す
- □ **rescue** 動 救う

□ **respect** 名①尊敬，尊重 ②《-s》観点 **in other respects** その他の点では 動 ～を尊敬［尊重］する

□ **respectable** 形①尊敬すべき，立派な ②（量など）相当な

□ **responsible** 形責任のある，信頼できる，確実な

□ **rest** 名①休息 ②残り **for the rest of life** 死ぬまで 動①休む，休ませる ②～を置く，そのままにしておく

□ **resting** 形休憩している **resting place** 休息場所

□ **restless** 形落ち着かない，不安な

□ **result** 名結果，成り行き，成績 **as a result** その結果（として） **as a result of** ～の結果（として）

□ **retold** 動retell（別な形式で語る）の過去・過去分詞

□ **return** 熟**in return for** ～に対する見返りとして，～の交換条件として **return to** ～に戻る，～に帰る

□ **Reuben Hayes** ルーベン・ヘイズ《人名》

□ **Reuter** 名①ロイター《人名》②《-s》ロイター《英国の通信社・新聞社》

□ **reward** 名報酬，償い，応報 動～に報いる，～に報酬を与える

□ **Rhone Valley** 《the – 》ローヌ渓谷《スイスの渓谷》

□ **Richard Brunton** リチャード・ブラントン《人名》

□ **Richards** 名リチャーズ《人名》

□ **richness** 名豊富であること，金持ちであること

□ **rid** 動～から（…を）取り除く **get rid of** ～を取り除く

□ **ride away** 馬に乗って去る

□ **rider** 名（自転車，オートバイ，馬などの）乗り手

□ **Riding Thorpe Manor** ライディング・ソープ荘園

□ **right** 熟**all right** 大丈夫で，よろしい，申し分ない，わかった，承知した **right away** すぐに **right in the middle** ど真ん中 **right now** 今すぐに，たった今 **That's all right.** いいんですよ。

□ **ring** 名①輪，円形，指輪 ②競技場，リング 動①輪で取り囲む ②鳴る，鳴らす ③電話をかける **ring for** （ベルを鳴らして）～を呼びつける

□ **rise** 動立ち上がる **rise above** ～を突破する

□ **risen** 動rise（立ち上がる）の過去分詞 形上が

った，起こった

□ **ritual** 名①儀式 ②行事 ③慣例

□ **rob** 動～を奪う，金品を盗む，～を襲う

□ **robber** 名泥棒，強盗

□ **robbery** 名泥棒，強盗

□ **Robert Norberton** ロバート・ノーバートン《人名》

□ **rocket** 形①岩の多い ②ぐらぐら揺れる，ぐらつく

□ **rode** 動ride（乗る）の過去

□ **roll** 動①ころがる［ころがす］，うねる ②（時が）たつ **roll one's eyes** （驚きや不快で）目をぎょろつかせる

□ **rolling** 形（ゆるやかに）起伏した，うねった

□ **Roman** ローマの，ローマ人の

□ **Ronald Adair** ロナルド・アデア《人名》

□ **room** 熟**dining room** 食堂 **take a room** （宿で）部屋を取る

□ **root** 名根

□ **rope** 名なわ［ロープ］（のようなもの）

□ **rose** 動rise（立ち上がる）の過去

□ **Rosenlaui** 名ローゼンラウイ《スイスの町》

□ **Ross** 名ロス《人名，地名》

□ **Rotterdam** 名ロッテルダム《地名》

□ **rough** 形①（手触りが）粗い ②荒々しい，未加工の ③乱暴な，粗暴な

□ **round** 名《しばしば-s》巡回，往復，往診 **all round** 全体において **go round** ～の周りを進む，歩き回る，回って行く **move round** ～を動き回る，あちこち移動する **turn round** 回す，向きを変える，振り返る **upon [on] one's rounds** 往診［巡回］中で

□ **rounded back** 猫背

□ **Roundhay** 名ラウンドヘイ《人名》

□ **routine** 名お決まりの手順，日課

□ **row** 名（横に並んだ）列 **a row of** 1列の～ **in a row** 1列に，連続して

□ **Roy** 名ロイ《犬の名前》

□ **royal** 形王の，女王の，国立の

□ **Roylott** 名ロイロット《人名》

□ **rubber** 名（トランプの）3番勝負

□ **ruler** 支配者

□ **ruling** 形①（人・階級などが）支配している ②有力な，優勢な

□ **rumor** 名うわさ

□ **run** 熟**come running** 飛んでくる，かけつける **come running out of** ～から走り出てくる

come running over 走ってやってくる make a run for it 必死で［急いで］逃げる run about 走り回る run across 走って渡る run after ～を追いかける run along おいとまする, 立ち去る run around 走り回る run away 走り去る, 逃げ出す run down （液体が）流れ落ちる, 駆け下りる,（車で人を）ひく run in 走って入る run into （思いがけず）～に出会う, ～に駆け込む, ～の中に走って入る run on ～を燃料とする, どんどん進む, 走り寄る run one's eyes over ～にザッと目を通す run out of ～が不足する, ～を使い果たす run over 一走りする, ～の上を走る, ひき［押し］倒す run through 走り抜ける run up ～に走り寄る run up and down かけずり回る run up to ～に達する

☐ **Ruritania** 图ルリタニア号《船名。伝説の王国の名前より》

☐ **rush** 動突進する, ～をせきたてる rush around 走り回る rush down 猛然と～に駆け寄る rush in ～に突入する, ～に駆けつける rush into ～に突入する, ～に駆けつける, ～に駆け込む rush out of 急いで～から出てくる rush past ～を急いで通り過ぎていく rush up to ～に駆け上がる 图突進, 突撃, 殺到

☐ **Russell Square** ラッセル・スクエア《地名》

☐ **Russia** 图ロシア

☐ **Russian** 形ロシア人の, ロシア語の 图ロシア人, ロシア語

S

☐ **sad-faced** 形悲しそうな顔をした

☐ **sadly** 副悲しそうに, 不幸にも

☐ **sadness** 图悲しみ, 悲哀

☐ **safe** 图金庫

☐ **safely** 副安全に, 間違いなく

☐ **safety** 图安全, 無事, 確実

☐ **safety-light** 图安全灯

☐ **sail** 图帆 動航海する, 出航する

☐ **sake** 图（～の）ため, 利益, 目的 for God's sake お願いだから work for the work's sake 仕事そのもののために仕事をする

☐ **sale** 图販売, 取引, 大売り出し

☐ **salt mine** 岩塩坑

☐ **Saltire** 图《Lord－》サルタイア卿《人名》

☐ **Sam** 图サム《人名》

☐ **same** 熟the same ～ as … …と同じ（ような）～

☐ **sample** 图見本, 標本

☐ **sand** 图①砂 ②《-s》砂漠, 砂浜

☐ **Sandeford** 图サンドフォード《人名》

☐ **Sandy Bain** 图サンディ・ベイン《人名》

☐ **sank** 動sink（沈む）の過去

☐ **sarcasm** 图皮肉, いやみ

☐ **satisfied with** 《be－》～に満足する

☐ **satisfy** 動①～を満足させる, ～を納得させる ②（義務）を果たす, 償う

☐ **save** 前～を除いて save for ～を除いては, ～を除けば 接《－that ～》～ということを除いては

☐ **Saxon** 图サクソン人《the－》サクソン族 形サクソン人の

☐ **scandal** 图スキャンダル, 醜聞

☐ **Scandinavia** 图スカンジナビア《ノルウェー, スウェーデン, デンマークの総称》

☐ **scar** 图傷跡

☐ **scarf** 图スカーフ

☐ **schemer** 图計画者

☐ **schoolboy** 图（小中学校の）男子生徒

☐ **schoolfriend** 图学友

☐ **schooling** 图学校教育

☐ **schoolmaster** 图①（男の）先生 ②校長

☐ **schoolteacher** 图学校の教師, 先生

☐ **Scotland** 图スコットランド

☐ **Scotland Yard** 图スコットランドヤード, ロンドン警視庁

☐ **scoundrel** 图悪漢, 悪党

☐ **scrape** 動こすり落とす, 削り取る, こする, すれる

☐ **scream** 图金切り声, 絶叫 動叫ぶ, 金切り声を出す

☐ **seal** 動印を押す, ふたをする, 密閉する

☐ **seaman** 图船乗り, 水夫

☐ **seamen** 图seaman（船乗り）の複数

☐ **search** 動（～を）捜し求める, 調べる 图捜査, 探索, 調査

☐ **Sebastian Moran** 《Colonel－》セバスチャン・モラン大佐《人名》

☐ **second only to** 《be－》～に次ぐのみである, ～を除けば1番である

☐ **secrecy** 图秘密であること

☐ **secret** 形秘密の, 隠れた 图秘密 bring the secret to light 秘密を公表する open secret 公然の秘密

- **secretary** 图秘書
- **secretive** 形秘密主義の, 隠し立てする
- **secretly** 副秘密に, 内緒で
- **see** 熟Let me see. ええと。 see 〜 as … 〜を…と考える see for yourself 自分で確かめる see if 〜かどうかを確かめる see off 見送る see that 〜 〜するように配慮する, 間違いなく〜する See you. ではまた。 you see あのね, いいですか
- **seek** 動捜し求める, 求める
- **seem** 動〜に見える, 〜のように思われる seem to be 〜であるように思われる
- **seemingly** 副見たところでは, 外見は
- **seldom** 副まれに, めったに〜ない
- **self** 图①自己, 〜そのもの ②私利, 私欲, 利己主義 ③自我
- **self-contained** 形無口な, 打ち解けない
- **self-control** 图自己抑制, セルフコントロール
- **selfless** 形私心のない, 無欲な
- **seller** 图売る人, 売れるもの
- **send away** 〜を追い払う, 〜に暇を出す send away for 手紙で〜を発注する
- **send for** 〜を呼びに[取りに]やる, 行かせる
- **send someone away** (人)をどこかに追い払う
- **sender** 图送り主, 荷主, 発信人
- **sense** 图①感覚, 感じ ②《-s》意識, 正気, 本性 ③常識, 分別, センス ④意味 in a sense ある意味では make sense 意味をなす, よくわかる make sense of 〜の意味を理解する 動感じる, 気づく
- **senseless** 形無感覚の, 無意識の, 無分別な, ばかげた
- **sensible** 形①分別のある ②理にかなっている ③気づいている
- **separate** 動①分ける, 分かれる, 隔てる ②別れる, 別れさせる 形分かれた, 別れた, 別々の
- **separation** 图分離(点), 離脱, 分類, 別離
- **Sergius** 图セルギウス《人名》
- **serious** 形①まじめな, 真剣な ②重大な, 深刻な, (病気などが)重い
- **seriously** 副①真剣に, まじめに ②重大に
- **servant** 图召使, 使用人, しもべ
- **servant-girl** 图女性の召使
- **serve** 動(〜に)仕える, 奉仕する
- **service** 图①勤務, 業務 ②奉仕, 貢献

- **set** 熟set down 〜を下に置く, 〜と見なす set free (人)を解放する, 釈放される, 自由の身になる set off 出発する, 発射する set oneself to 〜しようととりかかる[努める] set to 〜へ向かう, 〜に着手する, けんかを始める, 食べ始める, 本気で始める set to work 仕事に取り掛かる set up 配置する, セットする, 据え付ける, 設置する
- **settle** 動①安定する[させる], 落ち着く, 落ち着かせる ②《-in 〜》〜に移り住む, 定住する settle down 身を落ち着ける, 気分が落ち着く
- **shade** 图陰, 日陰
- **shaded** 形日陰になった
- **shake** 動①〜を振る, 揺れる[揺さぶる] ②〜を動揺させる
- **shaken** 動shake (〜を振る, 〜を動揺させる)の過去分詞 形動揺した, くじけた, 意気消沈した
- **shaky** 形震える, 揺れる
- **Shall I 〜?** 〜しましょうか?
- **Shall we 〜?** (一緒に) 〜しましょうか。
- **shame** 图①恥, 恥辱 ②恥ずべきこと, ひどいこと in shame 恥じて, 恥ずかしくて 動恥をかかせる, 侮辱する
- **shameful** 形恥ずべき, 下品な
- **shape** 图①形, 姿, 型 ②状態, 調子 動形づくる, 具体化する
- **share** 動共有する
- **sharp-eyed** 形目の[観察の]鋭い
- **shave** 動(ひげ・顔を)そる, 削る
- **sheep** 图羊
- **sheet** 图①シーツ ②(紙などの)1枚
- **Sherlock** 图シャーロック《人名》
- **Sherlock Holmes** シャーロック・ホームズ《人名》
- **shilling** 图シリング《英国の旧通貨単位。1/20ポンド》
- **shine** 動①光る, 輝く ②〜を光らせる, 〜をみがく shine in (光が)差し込む 图光, 輝き
- **Shinwell Johnson** シンウェル・ジョンソン《人名》
- **shiny** 形輝く, 光る
- **shiver** 動(寒さなどで)身震いする[させる]
- **shoe** 图靴, 蹄鉄(ていてつ)
- **shook** 動shake (〜を振る, 〜を動揺させる)の過去
- **shoot down** 撃ち殺す

□ **shopkeeper** 图小売り店主

□ **short cut** 近道

□ **short-sighted** 形近眼の

□ **shortly** 副まもなく,すぐに

□ **Shoscombe** 图ショスコム《地名》

□ **Shoscombe Old Place** ショスコム荘

□ **Shoscombe Park** ショスコム猟園

□ **Shoscombe Prince** ショスコム・プリンス《馬の名》

□ **Shoscombe Spaniel** ショスコム・スパニエル《犬種》

□ **Shoso-in** 图正倉院

□ **shot** 图①射撃手 ②発砲(音)

□ **should have done** 〜すべきだった(のにしなかった)《仮定法》

□ **should never have done** 〜すべきではなかった(のにしてしまった)《仮定法》

□ **shoulder** 图肩

□ **show ～ around** 〜を案内して回る

□ **show someone in** [人を]中に案内する,招き入れる

□ **show up** 顔を出す,現れる

□ **shown** 動show(〜を見せる)の過去分詞

□ **shrug** 動图(肩を)すくめる(こと)

□ **shut** 動①閉まる,閉める,閉じる ②たたむ ③閉じ込める ④shutの過去,過去分詞

□ **sick of** 〜の病気にかかって,〜にうんざりして

□ **sick-room** 图病室

□ **sickness** 图病気

□ **side** 图側,横,そば,斜面 **by the side of** 〜のそばに,横 **either side of** 〜の両側に **far side** 向こう側,反対側 **from side to side** 左右に **on each side** それぞれの側に **side by side** 並んで 形側面の,横の

□ **side-table** 图サイドテーブル

□ **sidelight** 图側灯

□ **Sigerson** 图ジーゲルソン《人名》

□ **sight** 熟**at first sight** 一目見て **catch sight of** 〜を見つける,〜を見かける **lose sight of** 〜を見失う **on sight** 見るとすぐに **out of sight** 見えないところに

□ **sightseer** 图観光[見物]客

□ **Sigismond** 图ジギスモンド《人名》

□ **signal** 图信号,合図

□ **Silas Brown** サイラス・ブラウン《人名》

□ **silence** 图沈黙,無言,静寂 **in silence** 黙って,沈黙のうちに

□ **silent** 形①無言の,黙っている ②静かな,音を立てない ③活動しない

□ **silently** 副静かに,黙って

□ **silk** 图絹(布),生糸

□ **sill** 图敷居,(窓の)下枠

□ **silver** 图銀,銀貨,銀色 形銀製の

□ **Silver Blaze** シルバー・ブレーズ《馬の名》

□ **similar** 形〜に類似した

□ **simple-minded** 形お人好しの,単純な,愚かな

□ **simply** 副①簡単に ②単に,ただ ③まったく,完全に

□ **Simpson's** 图シンプソンズ《料理店の名》

□ **sin** 動罪を犯す

□ **since** 接①〜なので,〜だから ②〜して以来 **ever since** それ以来ずっと

□ **sincerely** 副真心をこめて

□ **sing over** 歌いながら

□ **singer** 图歌手,詩人

□ **single** 形たった一つの,独身の

□ **Singleford** 图シングルフォード《人名》

□ **sink** 動沈む[沈める],落ち込む

□ **Sir** 图〜卿

□ **sit** 熟**sit at the table** 食卓につく **sit back** 椅子に深く腰掛ける,くつろぐ **sit on** 〜の上に乗る,〜の上に乗って動けないようにする **sit still** じっとしている,じっと座っている **sit up** 起き上がる,寝ずに起きている,上半身を起こす **sit up all night** 徹夜する **sit up straight** 背筋を伸ばして座る

□ **sitting room** 图《主に英》居間,リビングルーム

□ **sitting-room** 图居間,リビングルーム

□ **situation** 图①場所,位置 ②状況,境遇,立場

□ **slave** 图奴隷

□ **Slavic** 形スラブの,スラブ語の

□ **sleep** 熟**go to sleep** 寝る **sleep in** 寝床に入る,朝寝坊する,住み込む **sleep off** 眠って〜を取り除く

□ **sleeper** 图眠っている人[動物,植物] **light sleeper** 眠りの浅い人

□ **sleepless** 形眠れない,不眠の

□ **sleepy** 形①眠い,眠そうな ②活気のない

□ **sleeve** 图そで

□ **sleuth-hound** 图警察犬

□ **slightly** 副わずかに, いささか

□ **slip** 動滑る[らせる], 滑ってころぶ **slip away** すり抜ける, こっそり去る, 静かに立ち去る

□ **slow down** 速度を落とす

□ **slowly** 副遅く, ゆっくり

□ **smart** 形利口な, 洗練された

□ **smelly** 形いやなにおいのする

□ **smelt** 動 smell ((～の)においがする) の過去, 過去分詞

□ **smile at** ～に微笑みかける

□ **Smith** 名スミス《人名》

□ **smoke** 動喫煙する, 煙を出す **smoke out** いぶり出す, 明るみに出す 名①煙, 煙状のもの ②《-ing》喫煙

□ **smoke-rocket** 名発煙筒

□ **smoker** 名喫煙家, 煙草を吸う人

□ **smoking-room** 名喫煙室

□ **smoky** 形くすんだ

□ **snake** 名蛇

□ **so** 熟 **and so** そこで, それだから, それで **and so on** ～など, その他もろもろ **or so** ～かそこらで **so as to** ～するように, ～するために **so far** 今までのところ, これまでは **so far as** ～に関しては, ～する限り **So far so good.** これまでは順調だ。(今後の問題を暗示) **so long as** ～する限りは **so many** 非常に多くの **so that** ～するために, それで, ～できるように **so ～ that** … 非常に～なので…

□ **soap** 名石けん

□ **sofa** 名ソファ

□ **soft-nosed** 形 (弾丸が) 当たった衝撃で膨張[拡散]した

□ **soften** 動柔らかくなる, ～を柔らかくする, 和らぐ

□ **softly** 副柔らかに, 優しく, そっと

□ **softness** 名柔らかさ, 柔軟, 優しさ

□ **soil** 名土, 土地

□ **soldier** 名兵士, 兵卒

□ **solid** 形固体[固形]の

□ **solution** 名解決(策), 解明, 回答

□ **solve** 動～を解く, ～を解決する

□ **some** 熟 **for some reason** なんらかの理由で, どういうわけか **for some time** しばらくの間 **in some way** 何とかして, 何らかの方法で **some time** いつか, そのうち

□ **somebody** 代誰か, ある人

□ **somehow** 副①どうにかこうにか, ともかく, 何とかして ②どういうわけか

□ **someone** 代ある人, 誰か

□ **something** 代①ある物, 何か ②いくぶん, 多少 **quite something** 大した物 **really something** 大したものである, 半端ではない

□ **sometimes** 副ときどき

□ **somewhat** 副いくらか, やや, 多少

□ **somewhere** 副①どこかへ[に] ②ある時, いつか, およそ

□ **Somomy** 名ソモミー《馬飼育場の名》

□ **soon** 熟 **as soon as** ～するとすぐ, ～するや否や **as soon as possible** できるだけ早く **sooner or later** 遅かれ早かれ

□ **sorrow** 名悲しみ, 後悔

□ **sorry** 熟 **be sorry for doing** ～して申し訳なく思う **feel sorry for** ～をかわいそうに思う

□ **sort** 名種類, 品質 **a sort of** ～のようなもの, 一種の～ **what sort of** どういう 動～を分類する

□ **Sotheby** 名サザビー《人名, オークション会社名》

□ **soul** 名①魂 ②精神, 心

□ **sound like** ～のように聞こえる

□ **source** 名源, 原因, もと

□ **South African** 南アフリカの

□ **Southampton** 名サウサンプトン《地名》

□ **spaniel** 名スパニエル《犬種》

□ **spare** 動容赦する, 救う, (苦労など) をかけないように気を配る

□ **Spaulding** 名スポルディング《人名》

□ **speak about** ～について話す

□ **speak of** ～を口にする

□ **speak out** はっきり[遠慮なく]言う

□ **speak up** 率直に話す, はっきりしゃべる

□ **specialist** 名専門家, スペシャリスト

□ **specialty** 名専門, 専攻, 本職, 得意

□ **speckle** 名斑点, ぽつぽつ, しみ

□ **speckled** 形たくさんの小さな斑点のついた

□ **Spectator** 名《the－》スペクテイター《新聞》

□ **speed** 名速力, 速度

□ **spite of** 《in－》～にもかかわらず

□ **splash** 名シュプリューゲン峠《地名》

□ **spoon-jack** 名スプーンジャック《釣りの疑似餌》

□ **sportsman** 名スポーツマン, 運動家

□ **spot** 名①地点, 場所 ②斑点, しみ **on the**

spot その場で, ただちに 動 ～に点を打つ, ～にしみをつける

- □ **sprang** 動 spring (跳ねる, 跳ぶ) の過去
- □ **springtime** 名 春季, 春時間
- □ **spy** 名 スパイ
- □ **squadron** 名 騎兵中 [大] 隊
- □ **square** 名 正方形, 四角い広場, (市外の) 一区画 形 正方形の, 四角な
- □ **St.** 略 ①saint の略《名前の前につけて》聖 ～ ②Street (～通り) の略
- □ **St. Clair** 名 セントクレア《人名》
- □ **stab** 動 刺す, 突き刺す
- □ **stable** 名 馬小屋, 厩舎
- □ **stable-boy** 名 馬小屋の世話をする少年, 馬丁
- □ **stable-yard** 名 馬屋 [厩舎] の敷地
- □ **stablemen** 名 馬屋番, 馬屋の世話人
- □ **stair** 名 ① (階段の) 1段 ② (-s) 階段, はしご
- □ **stand by** そばに立つ, 傍観する, 待機する
- □ **stand for** ～を表す, ～を我慢する, ～をこらえる
- □ **stand on end** 直立して
- □ **stand out** (血管などが) 浮き出る
- □ **stand still** じっと立っている
- □ **stand up** 立ち上がる **stand up to** ～に耐える
- □ **Stanley Hopkins** 名 スタンレー・ホプキンス《人名》
- □ **stare** 動 ～をじっと [じろじろ] 見る
- □ **start** 熟 get started 始める give ～ a start ～をぎょっ [はっ] とさせる let's get started on さあ～を始めよう, さあ～にとりかかろう start upon ～を始める
- □ **starter** 名 ①始める人 ②スタート合図係, スターター, 起動装置
- □ **starting point** 起点, 出発点
- □ **state** 名 ①有様, 状態 ②《the -》国家, (アメリカなどの) 州 動 ～を述べる
- □ **stately** 形 堂々とした, 威厳のある
- □ **statement** 名 声明, 述べること
- □ **statesman** 名 政治家
- □ **stationmaster** 名 駅長
- □ **stay** 熟 stay at (場所) に泊まる stay back 後に下がっている, 離れている stay behind 後ろにつく, 後に残る, 留守番をする stay in 家にいる, (場所) に泊まる, 滞在する stay on 居残る, とどまる, (電灯などが) ついたままである stay

up 起きている, 夜更かしする **stay with** ～の所に泊まる

- □ **stay-at-home** 形 出不精の
- □ **steadily** 副 しっかりと
- □ **steam** 名 蒸気, 湯気
- □ **step** 熟 be stepped on ひどい目にあう step back 後ずさりする, 後に下がる step by step 一歩一歩, 着実に step on ～を踏みつける step out 外へ出る step out of ～から出る step up (低いところから) 上がる take steps to ～するための処置を取る, 方策を講じる
- □ **stepfather** 名 継父
- □ **Stephens** 名 スティーブンズ《人名》
- □ **Stepney** 名 ステップニー《ロンドンの旧区》
- □ **Sterndale** 名 スターンデール《人名》
- □ **stethoscope** 名 聴診器
- □ **Stewart** 名《Mrs. -》スチュアート夫人《人名》
- □ **stick** 名 棒, つえ 動 ① (突き) 刺さる [刺す] ②くっつく [くっつける] stick out 突き出す stick to ～にくっつく, 張り付く, ～に固執する, ～をやり通す stick up 上に突き出る
- □ **stile** 名 (人は越せるが家畜は通れないように, へいなどに設けた) 踏み段
- □ **still** 熟 sit still じっとしている, じっと座っている stand still じっと立っている
- □ **Stoke Moran** 名 ストーク・モーラン《地名》
- □ **stolen** 動 steal (～を盗む, こっそりと手に入れる) の過去分詞
- □ **stone** 名 石, 小石 形 石 (製) の
- □ **stone-floored** 形 石床の
- □ **Stoner** 名 ストーナー《人名》
- □ **stonework** 名 石造物
- □ **stonily** 副 冷酷に, 冷ややかに
- □ **stop at** ～の所に (短期間) 泊まる, 滞在する
- □ **stop at nothing** 何があってもやめたりしない
- □ **stop by** 途中で立ち寄る, ちょっと訪ねる
- □ **stop dead** ぴたりと止まる
- □ **store** 熟 in store 蓄えて, 用意されて
- □ **storm** 名 ①嵐, 暴風雨 ②強襲
- □ **stormy** 形 ①嵐の, 暴風の ②激しい
- □ **story of the old Russian woman** 《the -》ロシアの老婆事件《ホームズが手がけた事件》
- □ **storyteller** 名 ①物語をする人, 物語作家 ②うそつき
- □ **stout** 形 頑丈な, 丈夫な, 太った

- [ ] **straight** 形率直な, 包み隠しをしない, 遠慮のない **sit up straight** 背筋を伸ばして座る
- [ ] **straighten** 動 ①まっすぐにする[なる] ②整頓[整理]する
- [ ] **Strand** 名ストランド《ロンドンの地名》
- [ ] **strange-looking** 形変な様子の, 奇妙な顔つきの
- [ ] **strangely** 副奇妙に, 変に, 不思議なことに, 不慣れに
- [ ] **strangeness** 名未知, 奇妙, 不思議
- [ ] **stranger** 名 ①見知らぬ人, 他人 ②不案内[不慣れ]な人
- [ ] **Strasbourg** 名ストラスブール《フランスの都市》
- [ ] **strawberry** 名イチゴ
- [ ] **stream** 名 ①小川, 流れ ②(出来事などの)連続, 流れ
- [ ] **strength** 名 ①力, 体力 ②長所, 強み ③強度, 濃度
- [ ] **strength-giving** 形力を与える
- [ ] **stretch** 動 (〜を)引き伸ばす, 広がる[広げる] 名伸ばす[伸びる]こと, 広がり **stretch out** 手足を伸ばす, 背伸びする
- [ ] **strike** 動 ①打つ, ぶつかる ②(災害などが)急に襲う ③(考えなどが)(人)に突然思い浮かぶ **it struck me that** 突然〜ということに思いついた **strike a blow** 一撃を加える **strike against** 〜にぶつかる **strike back** 打ち返す, 仕返しする **strike off** 削除する, 除名する **strike on** 〜を思いつく
- [ ] **striking** 形印象的な, 目立った
- [ ] **string** 名ひも, 糸
- [ ] **strip** 動 (人)を裸にする, 脱衣する, 〜をはぐ, 〜をとり去る
- [ ] **stripe** 名筋, 縞, ストライプ
- [ ] **strode** 動stride (大またで歩く)の過去
- [ ] **strong room** 名金庫室
- [ ] **strongly** 副強く, がんじょうに, 猛烈に, 熱心に
- [ ] **struck** 動strike ((〜を)打つ, 急に襲う)の過去, 過去分詞
- [ ] **Stuart** 形スチュアート王家の
- [ ] **stuck** 動stick (刺さる)の過去, 過去分詞 **be [get] stuck** いきづまる
- [ ] **study** 名書斎, 研究 動調査する, 研究する
- [ ] **Study in Scarlet** 緋色の研究《ホームズが手がけた事件》
- [ ] **study-table** 名書き物机

- [ ] **stupid** 形馬鹿な
- [ ] **subject** 名主題, 論題, 対象, 実験材料, 被験者
- [ ] **subtle** 形微妙な, かすかな, 繊細な, 敏感な, 器用な
- [ ] **subway** 名地下鉄, 地下道
- [ ] **succeed** 動 ①成功する ②(〜の)跡を継ぐ
- [ ] **success** 名成功, 幸運, 上首尾
- [ ] **successful** 形成功した, うまくいった
- [ ] **successfully** 副首尾よく, うまく
- [ ] **such** 熟 **as such** 〜など **such a** そのような **such as** たとえば〜, 〜のような **such 〜 as** ……のような〜 **such 〜 that …** 非常に〜なので…
- [ ] **sudden** 形突然の, 急な
- [ ] **suffer** 動損害を受ける, (病気に)なる, 苦しむ, 悩む
- [ ] **suggest** 動 ①〜を暗示する ②〜を提案する
- [ ] **suicide** 名自殺
- [ ] **suit** 名スーツ, 背広 動 ①適合する[させる] ②似合う
- [ ] **suitable** 形適当な, 似合う, ふさわしい
- [ ] **suitably** 副ふさわしく
- [ ] **sum** 名 ①総計 ②金額
- [ ] **sunburn** 名 (炎症を起こした)日焼け
- [ ] **sunclock** 名日時計
- [ ] **Sung** 名宋《中国の王朝。960–1279年》
- [ ] **sunset** 名日没, 夕焼け
- [ ] **supplier** 名供給者, 供給業者, 納入業者
- [ ] **supply** 動 〜を供給[配給]する, 〜を補充する 名供給(品), 給与, 補充
- [ ] **support** 動 〜を支える
- [ ] **suppose** 動 〜と仮定する, 〜と推測する
- [ ] **supposed to** 《be –》〜することになっている, 〜するはずである
- [ ] **sure** 熟 **be sure to do** 必ず〜する **for sure** 確かに **make sure** 確かめる, 確認する **sure enough** 思ったとおり, 確かに **to be sure** 確かに, なるほど
- [ ] **surely** 副確かに, きっと **most surely** 確実に
- [ ] **surprise** 熟 **in surprise** 驚いて **to one's surprise** 驚いたことに
- [ ] **surprised** 熟 **be surprised at** 〜に驚く **be surprised to do** 〜して驚く
- [ ] **surprising** 形驚くべき, 意外な
- [ ] **Surrey** 名サリー州《地名》

☐ **surround** 動 〜を囲む，〜を包囲する

☐ **Susan Tarlton** スーザン・タールトン《人名》

☐ **Sussex** 名 サセックス《イギリスの旧州名》

☐ **swamp** 名 沼地，(低) 湿地 **swamp adder** 沼マムシ《架空のヘビ種》

☐ **Swandam Lane** 名 スワンダム小路

☐ **Sweden** 名 スウェーデン《国名》

☐ **sweetness** 名 ①甘さ ②優しさ，美しさ

☐ **swiftly** 副 速く，迅速に

☐ **Swiss** 形 スイス (人) の 名 スイス人

☐ **Switzerland** 名 スイス《国名》

☐ **Sydney** 名 シドニー《オーストラリアの都市》

☐ **sympathy** 名 ①同情，思いやり，お悔やみ ②共鳴，同感

☐ **syringe** 名 注射器，注入器

T

☐ **table** 熟 **sit at the table** 食卓につく

☐ **tail** 名 ①尾，しっぽ ②後部，末尾 **I can make neither head nor tail of it.** 何が何だかさっぱりわからない。

☐ **take** 熟 **take a chance** 一か八かやってみる **take a look at** 〜をちょっと見る **take a note back** 報告に戻る **take a picture** 写真を撮る **take a room** (宿で) 部屋を取る **take a short cut** 近道をする **take a walk** 散歩をする **take an interest in** 〜に興味を持つ **take away** ①連れ去る ②取り上げる，奪い去る ③取り除く **take back** ①取り戻す ②(言葉，約束を) 取り消す，撤回する **take care** 気をつける，注意する **take care of** 〜の世話をする，〜の面倒を見る，〜を管理する **take control of** 〜を制御 [管理] する，支配する **take down** 下げる，降ろす **take from** 〜から引く，選ぶ **take in** 取り入れる，取り込む，(作物・金などを) 集める **take into** 手につかむ，中に取り入れる **take long** 時間がかかる **take no notice** 目もくれない **take off** (衣服を) 脱ぐ，取り去る，〜を取り除く，離陸する，出発する **take off work** 会社を休む **take on** 雇う，(仕事などを) 引き受ける **take one's eyes off** 〜から目をそらす **take out** 取り出す，取り外す，連れ出す，持って帰る **take out of** 〜から出す，〜に連れ出す **take out to** 〜に連れ出す **take over** 引き継ぐ，支配する，乗っ取る **take place** 行われる，起こる **take someone away** (人) を連れ出す **take someone by the hand** (人) の手を取る **take someone home** (人) を家まで送る **take 〜 to …** 〜を…に連れて行く **take to court** 裁判沙汰になる **take up** 取り上げる，拾い上げる，やり始める，(時間・場所を) とる

☐ **talk at** 〜に一方的に話す

☐ **talk of** 〜のことを話す

☐ **talking** 名 話題，おしゃべり **town talking** 街中の話題

☐ **Tang** 名 唐《中国の王朝。618–907年》

☐ **Tang-ying** 名 唐英《清朝の陶工》

☐ **Tarleton murders** 《the –》タールトン殺人事件《ホームズが手がけた事件》

☐ **taste** 名 味

☐ **Tavistock** 名 タヴィストック《イギリスの町》

☐ **taxi** 名 タクシー

☐ **tear off** はぎ取る

☐ **tear up** ズタズタに引き裂く

☐ **telegram** 名 電報

☐ **telegraph** 名 ①電報，電信 ②《the T-》テレグラフ紙《新聞名》動 電報を打つ

☐ **tell** 熟 **I tell you.** 確かに。本当に。 **tell a lie** うそをつく **tell of** 〜について話す [説明する] **tell 〜 how to** 〜に…のやり方を教える **tell 〜 to** 〜に…するように言う

☐ **ten-mile** 名 10マイル

☐ **ten-pound** 形 10ポンドの

☐ **tenderhearted** 形 心の優しい，思いやりのある

☐ **tent** 名 テント，天幕

☐ **terribly** 副 ひどく

☐ **terror** 名 (たいへんな) 恐怖，恐ろしい人 [物]

☐ **Thames** 名 テムズ川

☐ **than** 熟 **more than** 〜以上 **no less than** 〜と同じだけの，〜も同然 **no more than** ただの〜にすぎない **rather than** 〜よりむしろ **than any other** ほかのどの〜よりも **than usual** いつもより **would rather 〜 than …** …よりむしろ〜したい

☐ **thank 〜 for** 〜に対して礼を言う

☐ **Thank God.** ありがたい，助かった。 **Thank God for that.** それはありがたい。

☐ **thank-you** 形 感謝の，お礼の

☐ **thankful** 形 ありがたく思う

☐ **thanks to** 〜のおかげで

☐ **that** 熟 **after that** その後 **at that moment** その時に，その瞬間に **at that time** その時 **in that case** もしそうなら **now that** 今や〜だから，〜からには **so that** 〜するために，それで，〜できるように **so 〜 that …** 非常に〜なので… **such 〜 that …** 非常に〜なので… **That is that.** それだけの話です。 **That's about it.** ま

あそんなところだ。**That's all right.** いいんですよ。**those that** それらの物

☐ **theft** 名 盗み, 窃盗, 泥棒

☐ **them** 熟 both of them 彼ら[それら]両方とも

☐ **then** 熟 even then その時でさえ from then on それ以来 just then そのとたんに

☐ **theorem** 名 定理

☐ **theory** 名 理論, 学説, ～論[説]

☐ **there** 熟 down there 下の方で[に] get there そこに到着する, 目的を達成する, 成功する here and there あちこちで over there あそこに there is no way ～する見込みはない

☐ **thereby** 副 それによって, それに関して

☐ **therefore** 副 したがって, それゆえ, その結果

☐ **these days** このごろ

☐ **thick** 形 厚い, 密集した, 濃厚な

☐ **thick-set** 形 ずんぐりした

☐ **thick-soled** 形 底の厚い

☐ **thief** 名 どろぼう, 強盗

☐ **thieves** 名 thief（どろぼう, 強盗）の複数

☐ **thin** 形 薄い, 細い, やせた, まばらな

☐ **thin-faced** 形 貧弱な顔の

☐ **think of** ～の心当たりがある, 思いつく, ～のことを考える come to think of it 考えてみると

☐ **think out loud** 考えごとを口に出す

☐ **think up** ～を考え出す, 考案する

☐ **thinker** 名 思想家, 考える人

☐ **thinking** 熟 fall to thinking 考え始める

☐ **this** 熟 at this これを見て, そこで（すぐに） at this point 現在のところ at this time 現時点では, このとき in this way このようにして this one これ, こちら this way このように

☐ **Thorneycroft Huxtable** ソーニークロフト・ハクスタブル《人名》

☐ **those** 熟 in those days あのころは, 当時は those that それらの物 those who ～する人々

☐ **though** 接 ①～にもかかわらず, ～だが ②たとえ～でも even though ～であるけれども, ～にもかかわらず 副 しかし as though あたかも～であるかのように

☐ **thought** 名 考え, 思考, 見解, 考えること be lost in one's unhappy thoughts ひとり縁起の悪い物思いにふける deep in thought しきりに考えて, 思索にふけって 動 think（考える）の過去, 過去分詞

☐ **thoughtful** 形 思慮深い, 考え込んだ

☐ **thoughtfully** 副 考え[思いやり]深く

☐ **thousands of** 何千という

☐ **three-roomed** 形 3部屋の, 部屋が3つある

☐ **Throgmorton Street** 名 スログモートン街

☐ **through** 熟 break through ～を打ち破る come through 通り抜ける, 成功する, 期待に沿う get through 乗り切る, ～を通り抜ける go through 通り抜ける, 一つずつ順番に検討する look through ～をのぞき込む pass through ～を通る, 通行する push one's way through かき分けて前に出る push through（人ごみなどを）かき分ける read through ～を読み通す run through 走り抜ける walk through the dangers 危険を乗り越える

☐ **throughout** 前 ①～中, ～を通じて ②～のいたるところに 副 初めから終わりまで, ずっと

☐ **throw** 熟 throw aside わきに投げ捨てる throw away ～を捨てる；～を無駄に費やす, 浪費する throw back（記憶など）を後戻りさせる throw back one's head 頭をのけぞらせる throw down 投げ出す throw ～ into ～ ～を …の状態に陥れる throw off 脱ぎ捨てる throw out ～を解雇する, 追い出す, 放り出す throw up 跳ね上げる throw up one's hands 降参する

☐ **thrown** 動 throw（（～を）投げる）の過去分詞

☐ **thumb** 名 親指

☐ **Thurston** 名 サーストン《人名》

☐ **thus** 副 ①このように ②これだけ ③かくて, だから

☐ **thy** 代《英古語》《形容詞的に》なんじの, そなたの

☐ **tidy** 形 整然とした, こぎれいな

☐ **tie** 名 ネクタイ 熟 tie up ひもで縛る, 縛り上げる, つなぐ, 拘束する, 提携させる tie up with ～と契約を結ぶ, ～と提携する

☐ **tight** 副 堅く, しっかりと

☐ **tightly** 副 きつく, かたく

☐ **till** 前 ～まで（ずっと）

☐ **time** 熟 all the time ずっと, いつも, その間ずっと at a time 一度に, 続けざまに at that time その時 at the same time 同時に, 一緒に at the time そのころ, 当時 at this time 現時点では, このとき at times 時には by the time ～する時までに each time ～するたびに for a time しばらく, 一時の間 for some time しばらくの間 for the first time 初めて from time to time ときどき have no time to do ～する時間がない in no time すぐに, 一瞬で in time 間に合って, やがて in time for ～に間に合うように on time 時間どおりに some

time いつか, そのうち the last time この前
〜したとき wait a long time 長時間待つ
□ **timetable** 名時刻表, 時間割
□ **tired from** 《be − 》〜で疲れる
□ **tired-looking** 形疲労した様子の, 疲れたよ
うな
□ **tiredness** 名疲労, 倦怠
□ **title** 名題名, タイトル
□ **to** 熟to be sure 確かに, なるほど to begin
with はじめに, まず第一に to death 死ぬまで,
死ぬほど to one's feet 両足で立っている状態
に to one's surprise 〜が驚いたことに to
the point 要領を得た
□ **tobacco** 名たばこ
□ **too** 熟far too あまりにも〜過ぎる too much
過度の too well 十二分に
□ **tool** 名道具, 用具, 工具
□ **toothbrush** 名歯ブラシ
□ **top** 熟on top of 〜の上(部)に one on top
of the other 順に重ねて
□ **top-hat** 名シルクハット
□ **topic** 名話題, 見出し the topic of 〜につい
て
□ **tore** 動tear (〜を裂く, 〜を引き離す)の過去
□ **torn** 動tear (〜を裂く, 〜を引き離す)の過去
分詞
□ **total** 形総計の, 全体の
□ **touch** 熟in touch with (〜と) 連絡を取って
keep in touch 連絡を取り合う
□ **towel** 名タオル
□ **town talking** 街中の話題
□ **trace** 名①跡 ②(事件などの)こん跡
□ **track** 名①通った跡 ②競走路, 軌道, トラッ
ク on one's track (人を) 追跡して, (人の) 後
を追って throw 〜 off the track 〜をまく,
〜に手がかりを失わせる 動追跡する
□ **tracker** 名追跡者
□ **trade** 名取引, 貿易, 商業 動取引する, 貿易す
る, 商売する
□ **tragedy** 名悲劇, 惨劇
□ **trail** 名(通った)跡
□ **trainer** 名①トレーナー, 指導者 ②調教師,
調馬師
□ **training-stable** 名調教用厩舎
□ **traveler** 名旅行者
□ **treat** 動〜を取り扱う
□ **treatment** 名取り扱い, 待遇

□ **Tredannick Wartha** トレダニック・ウォ
ーサ《屋敷の名前》
□ **Tredannick Wollas** トレダニック・ウォラ
ス《地名》
□ **tree-lined** 形木の立ち並んだ, tree-lined
street 並木道
□ **Tregennis** 名トリジェニス《人名》
□ **Trevor Bennett** トレヴァー・ベネット《人
名》
□ **trial** 名裁判
□ **trick** 名①策略 ②いたずら, 冗談 ③手品, 錯
覚 動〜をだます
□ **tricky** 形油断のならない, 扱いにくい, ずるい
□ **tried** 動try (〜しようと試みる)の過去, 過去
分詞
□ **trigonometry** 名三角法
□ **trip** 熟go on a trip 旅行する
□ **trouble** 熟get into trouble 面倒を起こす,
困った事になる, トラブルに巻き込まれる in
trouble 面倒な状況で, 困って
□ **trousers** 名ズボン
□ **trout** 名《魚》マス
□ **truly** 副本当に, 心から
□ **trust** 動信用 [信頼] する, 委託する 名信用,
信頼, 委託
□ **trustworthy** 形信用できる, あてになる
□ **truth** 名①真理, 事実, 本当 ②誠実, 忠実さ
tell the truth 真実を述べる, 本当のことを言う
to tell the truth 実は, 実を言えば
□ **truthful** 形正直な, 真実の
□ **truthfully** 副正直に
□ **try on** 試着してみる
□ **try out** 実際に試してみる
□ **tunnel** 名トンネル
□ **Turkey** 名トルコ共和国
□ **Turkish bath** 名トルコ風呂 (の浴場) 《スチ
ームバスの一種》
□ **turn** 熟in turn 順番に, 立ち代わって turn
around 振り向く, 向きを変える, 方向転換する
turn away 向こうへ行く, 追い払う, (顔を) そ
むける, 横を向く turn away from 〜から顔を
そむける turn back 元に戻る turn down (音
量などを) 小さくする, 弱くする, 拒絶する turn
in 向きを変える, (向きを変えてわき道などに) 入る, 床につく turn into 〜に変わる turn
off ①興味を失う, 〜にうんざりする ②〜を止
める, (照明などを) 消す ③(道から) それる, (道
が) 〜から分かれる turn on ①〜の方を向く
②(スイッチなどを) ひねってつける, 出す turn

one's head (人)をのぼせ上がらせる **turn out**
①〜と判明する, (結局〜に)なる ②(照明など
を)消す ③養成する ④出かける, 集まる ⑤外
側に向く, ひっくり返す **turn over** ひっくり返
る[返す], (ページを)めくる, 思いめぐらす [返
す], 引き渡す, 熟考する **turn red** 赤くなる **turn
round** 回す, 向きを変える, 振り返る **turn to**
〜の方を向く, 〜に頼る, 〜に変わる **turn up**
(音量などを)上げる, 大きくする **turn white**
青ざめる, 血の気が引く

- [ ] **Turner** 图ターナー《人名》
- [ ] **Tut-tut** 間チェッ(舌うち)
- [ ] **Tuxbury Old Hall** タックスベリー古館《屋
敷の名前》
- [ ] **Tuxbury Old Park** タックスベリー・オー
ルド・パーク《地名》
- [ ] **twin** 图双子の一方, 双生児, よく似た1対の
人の一方
- [ ] **twisted** 形ねじれた, ひん曲がった
- [ ] **two** 熟a 〜 or two 1〜か2〜, 2, 3の **for a
moment or two** ほんの少しの間
- [ ] **two-horse** 形(馬車が)2頭立ての
- [ ] **two-year** 形2年にわたる, 2年越しの

U

- [ ] **ugly** 形①醜い, ぶかっこうな ②いやな, 不快
な, 険悪な
- [ ] **uh** 間(文のつなぎや考えをまとめている時に)
あー, えー
- [ ] **unable to** 《be –》(人が) 〜することができ
ない
- [ ] **unarmed** 形武器を用いない
- [ ] **unbelievable** 形信じられない(ほどの), 度
のはずれた
- [ ] **unbelievably** 副信じられないほど
- [ ] **unbelieving** 形疑い深い, 信じようとしない
- [ ] **unbroken** 形壊されていない
- [ ] **uncared for** 世話をされていない, ほったら
かしの
- [ ] **unchanged** 形変化していない
- [ ] **unclean** 形汚れた
- [ ] **unclear** 形明確でない, はっきりしない
- [ ] **uncover** 動ふたを取る, 覆いを取る, 暴露す
る
- [ ] **undecided** 形未解決の
- [ ] **under one's own name of** 〜という実
名で

- [ ] **underground** 形①地下の[にある] ②地下
組織の
- [ ] **underneath** 副真下に(の, を)
- [ ] **underside** 图下側, 底(裏)面
- [ ] **understandable** 形理解できる, わかる
- [ ] **undertake** 動①引き受ける ②始める, 企て
る
- [ ] **undertaken** 動undertake (引き受ける)の
過去分詞
- [ ] **underworld** 图地下社会, 暗黒街
- [ ] **undiscovered** 形未発見の, 未知の
- [ ] **undone** 形解かれた, ほどけた
- [ ] **undoubtedly** 副疑う余地のない
- [ ] **uneasily** 副落ち着きなく, 不安そうに
- [ ] **uneasiness** 图不安, 心配
- [ ] **uneasy** 形不安な, 焦って
- [ ] **uneven** 形平らでない, でこぼこの, むらのあ
る
- [ ] **unexpected** 形思いがけない, 予期しない
- [ ] **unexplained** 形説明されていない, 明らか
にされていない
- [ ] **unfair** 形不公平な, 不当な
- [ ] **unfairly** 副不正に, 不当に
- [ ] **unfinished** 形終わっていない, 不完全な
- [ ] **unfortunately** 副不幸にも, 運悪く
- [ ] **unfriendly** 形友情のない, 不親切な
- [ ] **unfriendly-looking** 形不親切そうな, 敵意
を抱いたような
- [ ] **unhappily** 副不幸に, 運悪く, 不愉快そうに
- [ ] **unhappiness** 图不運, 不幸
- [ ] **unhappy** 形不運な, 不幸な
- [ ] **unimportant** 形重要でない, ささいな, と
るにたらない
- [ ] **unique** 形唯一の, ユニークな, 独自の
- [ ] **university** 图(総合)大学
- [ ] **unkind** 形不親切な, 意地の悪い
- [ ] **unkindly** 副不親切に, 思いやりなく
- [ ] **unknown** 形知られていない, 不明の
- [ ] **unless** 接もし〜でなければ, 〜しなければ
- [ ] **unlike** 形似ていない, 違った
- [ ] **unlikely** 形ありそうもない, 考えられない
- [ ] **unlock** 動(錠)を開ける
- [ ] **unlucky** 形①不運な ②不吉な, 縁起の悪い
- [ ] **unmarried** 形未婚の, 独身の
- [ ] **unmoved** 形心を動かされない, 冷静な, 決

心を変えない

- □ **unnatural** 形不自然な, 異常な
- □ **unnecessarily** 副むだに, 不必要に
- □ **unnecessary** 形不必要な, 余分な, 必要以上の
- □ **unpleasant** 形不愉快な, 気にさわる, いやな, 不快な
- □ **unseen** 形目に見えない, 人目につかない, 見られない
- □ **unsolved** 形解決されていない
- □ **unsuccessful** 形失敗の, 不成功の
- □ **unsure** 形確かでない, 自信がない
- □ **unthinkable** 形考えられない
- □ **untidy** 形きちんとしていない, だらしない
- □ **untie** 動ほどく, 解放する
- □ **untrue** 形真実でない, 事実に反する
- □ **unusual** 形普通でない, 珍しい, 見[聞き]慣れない
- □ **unusually** 形異常に, 珍しく
- □ **unwelcome** 形歓迎されない, 気に食わない, 嫌な
- □ **unworthy** 形値しない, ふさわしくない
- □ **up** 熟 be made up 作り上げた, 決心した be mixed up with ～と絡み合う blow up 破裂する[させる] break up ばらばらになる, 解散させる bring up ①育てる, 連れて行く ②(問題を)持ち出す clear up きれいにする, 片付ける, (疑問, 問題を)解決する come up 近づいてくる, 階上に行く, 浮上する, 水面へ上ってくる, 発生する, 芽を出す come up with ～に追いつく, ～を思いつく, 考え出す, 見つけ出す cover up 身をくるむ, すっかり覆う draw up (車を)止める drive up 車でやって来る end up 結局～になる follow up (人) の跡を追う get up 起き上がる, 立ち上がる give up あきらめる, やめる, 引き渡す go up ①～に上がる, 登る ②～に近づく, 出かける ③(建物などが) 建つ, 立つ go up to ～まで行く, 近づく grow up 成長する, 大人になる hold up ①維持する, 支える ②～を持ち上げる ③(指を)立てる jump up 素早く立ち上がる keep up 続ける, 続く, 維持する, (遅れないで)ついていく, 上げたままにしておく lock up ～を閉じ込める look up 見上げる, 調べる make up 作り出す, 考え出す, ～を構成[形成]する make up for 償う, ～の埋め合わせをする make up one's mind 決心する open up 広がる, 広げる, 開く, 開ける pick up 拾い上げる, 車で迎えに行く, 習得する, 再開する, 回復する pull up 引っ張り上げる push up 押し上げる put up one's hand 手を挙げる put up with ～を我慢する run up

～に走り寄る run up and down かけずり回る set up 配置する, セットする, 据え付ける, 設置する show up 顔を出す, 現れる sit up 起き上がる, 上半身を起こす sit up all night 徹夜する sit up straight 背筋を伸ばして座る speak up 率直に話す, はっきりしゃべる stand up 立ち上がる stand up to ～に耐える stay up 起きている, 夜更かしする step up (低いところから)上がる stick up に突き出る take up 取り上げる, 拾い上げる, やり始める, (時間・場所を)とる throw up 跳ね上げる tie up ひもで縛る, 縛り上げる, つなぐ, 拘束する, 提携させる turn up (音量などを)上げる, 大きくする up and down 上がったり下がったり, 行ったり来たり, あちこちと up in the air 空中に up to ～まで, ～に至るまで, ～に匹敵して use up ～を使い果たす wake up 起きる, 目を覚ます walk up 歩み寄る, 歩いて上る walk up and down 行ったり来たりする walk up to ～に歩み寄る
- □ **upcoming** 形やがて来る, 来たる
- □ **upon** 副①《場所・接触》～(の上)に ②《日・時》～に ③《関係・従事》～に関して, ～について, ～して 副前へ, 続けて call upon 求める, 頼む, 訪問する come upon (人) に偶然出合う fall back upon 当てにする fall upon ～の上にかかる hit upon ～を思いつく jump upon 飛び乗る look down upon 見下ろす, 俯瞰する look upon ～を見る, 見つめる start upon ～を始める upon entering 入った途端 walk upon ～の上を歩く
- □ **upper** 形上の, 上位の, 北方の
- □ **upper-class** 形上流階級の
- □ **upright** 形まっすぐ立った, 直立した
- □ **upset** 形①憤慨して ②動揺して 動気を悪くさせる
- □ **upstairs** 副2階へ[に] 形2階の, 階上の 名2階, 階上
- □ **upward** 副上の方へ, 上向きに
- □ **urge** 動せき立てる, 強力に押し進める
- □ **us** 熟 let us どうか私たちに～させてください
- □ **use** 熟 be of no use 役に立たない be of use 役に立つ have no use for ～には用がない, ～に我慢できない have other uses for ～にとって役に立つことがある in use 使用されて make use of ～を利用する, 使用する no use 役に立たない, 用をなさない of no use 使われないで use up ～を使い果たす
- □ **used to** 助(以前は)よく～したものだった 形《be～》～に慣れている get used to ～になじむ, ～に慣れる
- □ **useless** 形役に立たない, 無益な

- **usual** 形 通常の, いつもの, 平常の, ふつうの as usual いつものように, 相変わらず than usual いつもより

V

- **vacancy** 名 ①空虚, 空間 ②あいた所, 空き室, 空き地
- **valley** 名 谷, 谷間
- **valuable** 形 貴重な, 価値のある, 役に立つ 名 《-s》貴重品
- **value** 名 価値, 値打ち, 価格 of value 貴重な, 価値のある 動 ～を評価する, ～に値をつける
- **van** 名 (小型)トラック, バン, (ほろのついた)荷車
- **various** 形 変化に富んだ, さまざまの, たくさんの
- **vase** 名 花瓶, つぼ
- **veil** 名 ベール, 覆い隠す物
- **vein** 名 静脈, (一般に)血管
- **Vere Street** ビア街《ロンドンの地名》
- **Vernon Lodge** ヴァーノン・ロッジ《地名》
- **very life** 命
- **very likely** たぶん
- **very well** 結構, よろしい
- **vicar** 名 代理牧師, 副牧師
- **victim** 名 犠牲者, 被害者
- **Victor Trevor** ヴィクター・トレヴァー《人名》
- **Victoria Station** ビクトリア駅《ロンドンの駅》
- **Victorian** 形 ビクトリア朝(時代)の
- **view** 熟 point of view 考え方, 視点
- **Vincent Spaulding** 名 ヴィンセント・スポルディング《人名》
- **violence** 名 ①暴力, 乱暴 ②激しさ
- **violent** 形 暴力的な, 激しい
- **violet** 名 スミレ色, スミレ
- **Violet de Merville** ヴァイオレット・ド・メルヴィル《人名》
- **violin** 名 バイオリン
- **visitor** 名 訪問客
- **von** 前 ～の, ～からの(ドイツ人, オーストリア人の貴族の家名の前につける)
- **Von Herder** フォン・ヘルデル《人名》

W

- **wage** 名 賃金, 給料
- **wagon** 名 荷馬車, ワゴン(車)
- **Wainwright** ウェインライト《人名》
- **wait** 熟 lie in wait 待ち伏せする wait a long time 長時間待つ Wait a minute. ちょっと待って. wait for ～を待つ
- **waiter** 名 ウエイター, 給仕
- **wake up** 起きる, 目を覚ます
- **waken** 動 目覚めさせる
- **Wales** 名 ウェールズ《イギリス南西部の地方》
- **walk** 熟 go for a walk 散歩に行く take a walk 散歩をする walk about 歩き回る walk across ～を歩いて渡る walk along (前へ)歩く, ～に沿って歩く walk around 歩き回る, ぶらぶら歩く walk away 立ち去る, 遠ざかる walk off 立ち去る walk on 歩き続ける walk out into ～に出て行く walk out of ～から出る walk over ～の方に歩いていく walk past 通り過ぎる walk through the dangers 危険を乗り越える walk up 歩み寄る, 歩いて上る walk up and down 行ったり来たりする walk up to ～に歩み寄る walk upon ～の上を歩く
- **walking-stick** 名 ステッキ
- **walkway** 名 歩道, 通路
- **wall** 熟 against the wall 壁を背にして
- **wander** 動 ①さまよう, 放浪する, 横道へそれる ②放心する
- **Wardlaw** 名 ウォードロー《人名》
- **warmly** 副 温かく, 親切に
- **warmth** 名 暖かさ, 思いやり
- **warn** 動 警告する, 用心させる
- **Warsaw** 名 ワルシャワ《地名》
- **wash away** 押し流す
- **wash out** 洗い落とす, 押し流す
- **watch** 熟 keep a watch upon ～を厳重に監視する
- **watch-pocket** 時計用のポケット
- **watcher** 名 見張る人, 監視者
- **watchful** 形 用心深い, 油断のない
- **water** 熟 deep waters 危険, 困難
- **watercourse** 名 水の流れ, 水流
- **waterfall** 名 滝
- **watering can** じょうろ
- **watering place** (主に英)湯治場, (飲み屋など)社交場
- **Waterloo** 名 ワーテルロー, ウォータールー

《地名》

☐ **Watson** 图ワトソン《人名》

☐ **wave** 動①揺れる［揺らす］,波立つ ②（手など）を振って合図する

☐ **way** 熟 along the way 途中で,これまでに,この先 by the way ところで,ついでに,途中で come one's way〈事が人に〉起こる,うまく運ぶ,〈物が人の〉手に入る get one's way 自分の思いどおりにする,勝手なまねをする get ～ out of the way ～を取り除く,どかす give way 道を譲る,譲歩する,負ける in a way ある意味では in any way 決して,多少なりとも in no way 決して～でない in some way 何とかして,何らかの方法で in the way 邪魔になって in this way このようにして lead the way 先に立って導く,案内する,率先する lead the way to ～への道を開く long way はるかに make one's way 進む,行く,成功する make way 道を譲る［あける］,前進する not in any way 少しも［全く］～ない on one's way 途中で on one's way to ～に行く途中で on the way 途中で one's way（to ～）（～への）途中で push one's way through かき分けて前に出る there is no way ～する見込みはない this way このように way out 出口,逃げ道,脱出方法,解決法 way out of 出口,打開［解決］策 way to ～する方法

☐ **weakly** 副弱々しく

☐ **weakness** 图弱さ,もろさ ②欠点,弱点

☐ **weapon** 图武器,兵器

☐ **wear away** 消耗する,憔悴（しょうすい）する

☐ **wear out** 疲れきる

☐ **wearer** 图着用者,利用者

☐ **wedding** 图結婚式,婚礼

☐ **weekly** 形週に1度の,毎週の 图週刊誌

☐ **Wei** 图魏《国名》

☐ **weigh** 動①（重さ）をはかる,比較検討する ②圧迫する,重荷である

☐ **weight** 图重さ

☐ **Weiss & Co.** ワイス社《会社の名》

☐ **Welbeck Street** ウェルベック街《ロンドンの地名》

☐ **welcome** 熟 You're welcome. どういたしまして。

☐ **well** 熟 as well その上に,おまけに,同様に as well as ～だけでなく,～と同様に,同じく,～に加えて,その上に be well -ed よく［十分に］～された do well 成績が良い,成功する do well to ～するのは結構［賢明］である may well ～するのももっともだ,たぶん～だ too well 十二分に very well よろしい,結構,確実に,明白に well done うまくやった Well, well. やれやれ,まあ,これは驚いた。

☐ **well house** 井戸小屋

☐ **well-chosen** 形よりすぐりの,適切な

☐ **well-dressed** 形身なりのよい

☐ **well-known** 形よく知られた,有名な

☐ **well-liked** 形好かれた

☐ **well-paid** 形いい給料を取っている,待遇のいい

☐ **well-picked** 形選び抜かれた

☐ **well-qualified** 形十分に資格のある

☐ **well-remembered** 形よく覚えている

☐ **well-to-do** 形裕福（そう）な

☐ **Welsh** 形ウェールズ的な,ウェールズ人の

☐ **Wessex Cup**《the－》ウェセックス・カップ《競馬のレース》

☐ **western** 形西の,西側の

☐ **wet** 形ぬれた,湿った,雨の get wet ぬれる

☐ **what** 熟 at what cost! なんという代償を払ったことでしょうか。 Guess what. あのね。何だと思う？ 知ってるかい？ What about ～? ～についてあなたはどう思いますか。～はどうですか。 What do you mean by that? それ（を言ったの）はどういうつもりかね？ what … for どんな目的で What（～）for? 何のために,なぜ what sort of どういう

☐ **whatever** 代①～するものは何でも ②どんなこと［もの］が～とも 形①どんな～でも ②《否定文,疑問文で》少しの～も,何らかの

☐ **whatsoever** 形《否定・疑問構文で（代）名詞の後に用いて》少しの［何らの］～も

☐ **wheel** 图輪,車輪

☐ **where to** どこで～すべきか

☐ **whereas** 援～であるのに対して［反して］,～である一方

☐ **wherever** 援どこでも,どこへ［で］～するとも

☐ **whether** 援～かどうか,～かまたは…,～であろうとなかろうと whether or not ～かどうか

☐ **which** 熟 of which ～の中で

☐ **while** 熟 for a while しばらくの間,少しの間 while way（時）をのんびり過ごす

☐ **whilst** 援①～の間に,～する間（に）②いっぽう,～なのに

☐ **whip** 图むち

☐ **whiskey** 图ウイスキー

□ **whisper** 動 ささやく, 小声で話す

□ **whistle** 動 口笛 [笛] を吹く 名 ①口笛 ②汽笛

□ **white** 熟 turn white 青ざめる, 血の気が引く white with anger 怒りで白くなる

□ **white-haired** 形 白髪の

□ **Whitney** 名 ホイットニー《人名》

□ **who** 熟 those who ～する人々 Who cares for ～. ～はいらない, どうでもよい。 Who knows? 誰にわかるだろうか。誰にもわからない。

□ **whoever** 代 ～する人は誰でも, 誰が～しようとも

□ **whole** 形 全体の, すべての, 完全な, 満～, 丸～ 名《the-》全体, 全部 as a whole 全体として on the whole 全体として見ると

□ **wholesale** 形 卸の

□ **whom** 代 ①誰を [に] ②～するところの人, その人を [に]

□ **why** 間《簡単すぎる質問に対して》もちろん, むろん,《意外・驚きを表して》いやはや, おや, まあ 熟 Why don't you ～? ～したらどうか Why not? どうしてだめなのですか。いいですとも。ぜひそうしよう!

□ **wide** 形 幅の広い, 広範囲の 副 広く, 大きく開いて

□ **wig** 名 かつら

□ **wild-looking** 形 乱暴そうな, 野蛮そうな

□ **wildly** 副 荒々しく, 乱暴に, むやみに

□ **Wilhelm Gottsreich Sigismond von Ormstein** ヴィルヘルム・ゴッツライヒ・ジギスモンド・フォン・オルムスタイン《人名》

□ **will** 名 ①意志 ②遺言状 against one's will 意に反して free will 自由意志 of one's own free will 自ら進んで, 自らの意志で 動 will have done ～してしまっているだろう《未来完了形》

□ **William** 名 ウイリアム《人名》

□ **William Derbyshire** ウィリアム・ダービシャー《人名》

□ **willing** 形 ①喜んで～する, ～しても構わない, いとわない ②自分から進んで行う

□ **Willoughby Smith** ウィロビー・スミス《人名》

□ **Wilson** 名 ウィルソン《人名》

□ **Wilson Hargreave** ウィルソン・ハーグリーヴ《人名》

□ **Winchester** 名 ウィンチェスター《イギリスの都市》

□ **winding** 形 曲がりくねった

□ **wine** 名 ワイン, ぶどう酒

□ **winner** 名 勝利者, 成功者

□ **Winter** 名 ウィンター《人名》

□ **wire** 名 ①針金, 電線 ②電信 動 ～に電報を打つ, ～に配線をする

□ **wise** 形 賢明な, 聡明な, 博学の

□ **wisely** 副 賢明に

□ **wish** 熟 as you wish 望み通りに good wishes 好意, 厚情

□ **with** 熟 agree with (人) に同意する along with ～と一緒に be busy with ～で忙しい be covered with ～でおおわれている be familiar with ～をよく知っている, ～と親しい be filled with ～でいっぱいになる be in love with ～に恋して, ～に心を奪われて be lined with ～が立ち並ぶ be mixed up with ～と絡み合う be pleased with ～が気に入る be satisfied with ～に満足する begin with ～で始まる change with ～とともに変化する come up with ～に追いつく, ～を思いつく, 考え出す, 見つけ出す do with ～を処理する fall in love with 恋におちる fight with ～と戦う get away with うまく逃れる, やり過ごす go with ～と一緒に行く, ～と調和する, ～にとても似合う have it out with 話の片をつける, 決着をつける have nothing to do with ～と何の関係もない have to do with ～と関係がある help ～ with …… …を～の面で手伝う in touch with (～と) 連絡を取って meet with ～に出会う off with (すばやく) ～を取り去る play with ～で遊ぶ, ～と一緒に遊ぶ put up with ～を我慢する stay with ～の所に泊まる to begin with はじめに, まず第一に white with anger 怒りで白くなる with all ～がありながら with all one's heart 心から

□ **withdraw** 動 引っ込める, 取り下げる, (預金を) 引き出す

□ **within** 前 ①～の中 [内] に, ～の内部に ②～以内で, ～を越えないで 副 中 [内] へ [に], 内部に

□ **without** 熟 go without ～なしですませる not … without ～ing ～せずには…しない, ～すれば必ず…する

□ **witness** 名 ①証拠, 証言 ②目撃者

□ **woke** 動 wake (目がさめる) の過去

□ **wolfhound** 名 ウルフハウンド, 大型猟犬

□ **won't** ～しようとしない

□ **wonder** 動 ①不思議に思う, (～に) 驚く ②～かしら (と思う) wonder if ～ではないかと思う 名 驚き (の念), 不思議なもの in wonder 驚いて

□ **wonder-woman** 名すばらしい女性

□ **wondrous** 形不思議な, 驚くべき

□ **wooden** 形木製の, 木でできた

□ **word** 熟 be as good as one's word 約束を守る, 信頼できる　give someone one's word (人) に約束する　in a word 一言で言うと

□ **work** 熟 day off work 一日休み　set to work 仕事に取り掛かる　take off work 会社を休む　work against ～に反する働きをする, ～に反対する　work in ～の分野で働く, ～に入り込む　work of ～の仕業　work on ～で働く, ～に取り組む, ～を説得する, ～に効く　work out うまくいく, 何とかなる, (問題を) 解く, 考え出す, 答えが出る, ～の結果になる　works of art 芸術作品

□ **worker** 名働く人, 労働者

□ **workman** 名労働者, 職人

□ **workmanlike** 形職人らしい, 職人かたぎの, 腕の立つ

□ **workmen** 名 workman (労働者, 職人) の複数

□ **workpeople** 名工具, 労働者

□ **workshop** 名作業場, 講習会, 勉強会

□ **world** 熟 in the world 世界で, 《疑問詞を強めて》いったい (全体)　It takes all sorts to make a world. 世の中にはあらゆる種類の人やものがいる。《ことわざ》 man of the world 世慣れた人　world of 大量の, 無数の

□ **worldly** 形現世の, 世俗的な

□ **worn out** 擦り切れた

□ **worried about** 《be –》(～のことで) 心配している, ～が気になる [かかる]

□ **worry about** ～のことを心配する

□ **worse** 形いっそう悪い, より劣った, よりひどい

□ **worst** 形《the –》最も悪い, いちばんひどい

□ **worth** 形 (～の) 価値がある, (～) しがいがある

□ **worthless** 形価値のない, 役立たずの

□ **worthy** 形価値のある, 立派な

□ **would** 熟 would have … if ～ もし～だったとしたら…しただろう　would like ～がほしい　would like to ～したいと思う　would rather ～する方がよい　would rather ～ than …… …よりむしろ～したい　Would you like ～? ～はいかがですか。Would you ～? ～してくださいませんか。

□ **wound** 名傷　動①～を負傷させる, (感情) を害する　②wind (～を巻く, からみつく) の過去, 過去分詞

□ **write** 熟 write down 書き留める　write … into … を～に書き加える

□ **writer** 名書き手, 作家

□ **writing** 熟 in writing 書面で

□ **writing-table** 名書きもの机

□ **wrong** 熟 go wrong うまくいかない, 調子が狂う, 身を持ちくずす, 堕落する

□ **wrong-headed** 形判断を誤った, 誤っても改めようとしない

Y

□ **yard** 名ヤード《長さの単位。91.44cm》

□ **yawn** 名あくび

□ **year** 熟 for ～ years ～年間, ～年にわたって

□ **yell** 動 (～に向かって) 大声をあげる

□ **Yeomanry** 名義勇農騎兵団

□ **yet** 接けれども, それなのに, それにもかかわらず　and yet それなのに, それにもかかわらず　not yet まだ～してない　副けれども, それなのに, それにもかかわらず　yet another さらにもう一つの

□ **York** 名ヨーク《地名》

□ **you** 熟 as you know ご存知のとおり　as you wish 望み通りに　See you. ではまた。you know ご存知のとおり, そうでしょう　you see あのね, いいですか　You're welcome. どういたしまして。

□ **yourself** 熟 see for yourself 自分で確かめる

□ **yourselves** 代 yourself (あなた自身) の複数

□ **Yoxley Old Place** ヨックスリー古館《屋敷の名前》

□ **Yuan** 名元《中国の王朝。1279–1368年》

□ **Yung-lo** 名永楽帝《中国明の第3代皇帝。在位1402–1424年》

E-CATとは…
英語が話せるようになるための
テストです。インターネット
ベースで、30分であなたの発
話力をチェックします。

www.ecatexam.com

● iTEP®とは…
世界各国の企業、政府機関、アメリカの大学
300校以上が、英語能力判定テストとして採用。
オンラインによる90分のテストで文法、リー
ディング、リスニング、ライティング、スピーキ
ングの5技能をスコア化。iTEP®は、留学、就職、
海外赴任などに必要な、世界に通用する英語力
を総合的に評価する画期的なテストです。

www.itepexamjapan.com

英語で読む
シャーロック・ホームズ傑作短編20選

2023年8月4日　第1刷発行
2023年11月4日　第2刷発行

原著者　　コナン・ドイル

発行者　　浦　晋亮

発行所　　IBCパブリッシング株式会社
　　　　　〒162-0804 東京都新宿区中里町29番3号 菱秀神楽坂ビル
　　　　　Tel. 03-3513-4511　Fax. 03-3513-4512
　　　　　www.ibcpub.co.jp

印刷所　　株式会社シナノパブリッシングプレス

ISBN978-4-7946-0768-3